ALSO BY DAVID A. BELL

The West: A New History (with Anthony Grafton)

*Shadows of Revolution: Reflections on France,
Past and Present*

Napoleon: A Concise Biography

*The First Total War: Napoleon's Europe
and the Birth of Warfare as We Know It*

*The Cult of the Nation in France:
Inventing Nationalism, 1680–1800*

*Lawyers and Citizens: The Making of a Political Elite
in Old Regime France*

MEN ON
HORSEBACK

MEN ON HORSEBACK

THE POWER *of* CHARISMA
IN THE AGE *of* REVOLUTION

DAVID A. BELL

FARRAR, STRAUS AND GIROUX
NEW YORK

Farrar, Straus and Giroux
120 Broadway, New York 10271

Portions of chapter 1 were previously published, in slightly different form,
in the May 11, 2016, issue of *Princeton Alumni Weekly*.

Owing to limitations of space, illustration credits can be found on page 337.

Library of Congress Cataloging-in-Publication Data
Names: Bell, David A. (David Avrom), author.
Title: Men on horseback : the power of charisma in the Age of Revolution / David A. Bell.
Other titles: Power of charisma in the Age of Revolution
Description: First edition | New York : Farrar, Straus and Giroux, 2020. | Includes
    bibliographical references and index.
Identifiers: LCCN 2019056126 | ISBN 9780374207922 (hardcover)
Subjects: LCSH: Biography—18th century. | Charisma (Personality trait) | Political leadership. |
    Statesmen—Biography. | Generals—Biography.
Classification: LCC CT118 .B45 2020 | DDC 909.7—dc23
LC record available at https://lccn.loc.gov/2019056126

Designed by Gretchen Achilles

To John Merriman, Richard Kagan,
and Gabrielle Spiegel

The great problem in politics, which I compare to that of the squaring of the circle in geometry . . . is to find a form of government that sets the law above man. If this form of government is attainable, then let us seek it out and try to establish it . . . But if, unfortunately, this form of government is not attainable, and I frankly confess I do not think it is, then it is my opinion that we should go to the other extreme and at once put man as high above the law as possible and therefore establish an arbitrary despotism, indeed the most arbitrary despotism possible. I would wish that the despot could be God.

—JEAN-JACQUES ROUSSEAU,
letter to Victor de Riqueti, marquis de Mirabeau, July 26, 1767

CONTENTS

MEN ON HORSEBACK

CHARISMA

Why, man, he doth bestride the narrow world
Like a Colossus, and we petty men
Walk under his huge legs and peep about
To find ourselves dishonorable graves.

—Julius Caesar, *act 1, scene 2*

When Shakespeare's character Cassius used these words to describe Julius Caesar, he evoked one of the most durable myths in human culture: there are giants among us titans, heroes, *Übermenschen*. They may be mortal, but something about them nonetheless seems miraculous and supernatural. They have extraordinary genius, vision, courage, strength, virtue, sheer magnetism. They seem to burn with a flame that leaves the rest of the human race looking cold and gray. In a word—and it is a word that literally means "a gift of divine grace"—they have charisma.

But read the rest of Cassius's speech, which this febrile, anxious conspirator, he of the "lean and hungry look," makes to an audience of one: his fellow Roman senator Marcus Junius Brutus. Cassius has not come to praise Caesar, and his description of Caesar as a colossus comes slathered in thick, pungent irony. For Cassius, Caesar is a man like any other, despite his oversize reputation. The idea that Caesar is a superman both alarms and disgusts him. He recalls episodes in which Caesar (already aging in the play) showed himself weak and helpless, like a "sick girl," and concludes, in a tone of heavy sarcasm, "And this man is now become a god." To call Caesar a god is blasphemy; to call him a king, treason. If Caesar lives, and the Romans raise him to royal or divine dignity, then the Republic, in Cassius's view, will die. Caesar's charisma is something both false and dangerous, and Cassius's intention is to enlist the wavering Brutus, Caesar's protégé, into the conspiracy against him.

And yet, as is so often true with Shakespeare, the words have a power that goes beyond the characters' intentions. Cassius wants to ridicule Caesar, to bring the false god down to earth, to smash the idol. But his description of Caesar as a colossus bestriding the narrow world is magnificent, and when his barbed condemnations of Caesar have faded from memory, these words remain, a glimmering reminder of the myth that Cassius wants so desperately to expose as a lie.

Both the lure and the dangers of charisma pointed to by Cassius remain with us today. Around the world, in both democratic and autocratic states, there is a perennial longing for leaders with magnetic appeal and extraordinary abilities who can unite viciously divided communities, overcome apparently intractable problems, and by sheer force of personality give whole nations a new start. But charisma also generates anxieties—especially in democracies. Modern democracies pride themselves on being governments of laws. What will happen if we treat ordinary, limited, and perhaps even corrupt and criminal individuals as superhuman, making them into idols? What if the intensity of attraction leads whole countries to follow such leaders blindly, unquestioningly, even as constitutions are flouted, human rights trampled, minorities oppressed and killed, and nations marched off to war?

Democracies are particularly suspicious of charismatic leaders. Yet, paradoxically, the longing for such leaders acquired new importance, and a distinct new shape, during the very same period that witnessed the first stirrings of modern democracy: the eighteenth and early nineteenth centuries. It was during the moment of extraordinary intellectual fermentation that we now call the Enlightenment, and then in the great revolutions that washed across much of the Western world between 1775 and the 1820s, that the powerful forms of political charisma we are familiar with today took shape. These forms of charisma posed challenges to democracy but were also symbiotically linked to it. Indeed, from this period onward the stories of charisma and democracy have wound tightly around one another in their own political version of the double helix. They have done so thanks to a revolutionary transformation in the relationship between ordinary people and their political leaders that began in the eighteenth century but that has never been fully understood. That transformation is the subject of this book.

What, exactly, is charisma, and what does it mean to write its history? In popular usage, the word serves as a rough synonym for personal magnetism. A famous photograph of John F. Kennedy greeting enthusiastic admirers on the beach in Santa Monica in 1962 perfectly illustrates this notion—he seems to be drawing people to him as if by invisible threads (figure 1). Kennedy remains, even many decades after his death, the paradigmatic example of a charismatic politician, in the United States and well beyond.

But this popular notion is vague and elusive. As the magazine *Psychology Today* puts it, "charisma is often said to be a mysterious ineffable quality—you either have it or don't have it." The magazine goes on to propose that charisma in fact inheres in qualities such as "confidence, exuberance, optimism, a ready smile, expressive body language, and a friendly, passionate voice."[1] This definition may seem more useful, but it quickly breaks down as well. Not only are these qualities impossible to measure in any meaningful way, but a moment's reflection suggests that certain combinations of them could easily strike observers as overbearing and obnoxious, rather than as charismatic.

A better approach starts from precisely this last point, and from the recognition that charisma is not just an individual quality but a relationship.[2] People deserve to be called charismatic only if they are recognized

as such—if others *believe* they possess extraordinary qualities and feel
an intense emotional attraction to them, even (as the photograph of
Kennedy hints) erotic desire.[3] The ability to appear charismatic depends
not only on the individual in question but on which traits are likely to
elicit such beliefs and feelings within a particular community. In other
words, it is a question not just of psychology but of culture. Some things
may remain forever mysterious about the appeal of particular individuals: a Kennedy, a Garibaldi, even a Hitler. But we can analyze how they
interacted with admirers, how admirers discussed and represented them,
and which of their specific qualities, traits, and actions appeared most
attractive and emotionally resonant.

Historians have mostly discussed charisma in the course of writing
biographies of figures like Kennedy—or Hitler.[4] But the subject deserves broader historical attention. If we want to understand why certain democratic regimes have given way to the rule of charismatic
authoritarians, we cannot simply ask why the regimes failed. It is also a
question of the positive appeal of charismatic leadership itself within a
particular culture. By creating a direct, intense, emotional bond between a political leader and followers, charisma can enable the circum-
vention or even destruction of existing political rules and traditions. It
can also create new rules and traditions. To quote the great German
social theorist Max Weber—who first developed the modern concept of
charisma more than a century ago—it is a "revolutionary force."[5]

This book tells the story of how the revolutionary force of charisma
developed during the Enlightenment and then helped shape four of the
greatest revolutions in history: in the United States, France, Haiti, and
Venezuela (whose break with Spain led to the independence of what
eventually became six separate nations). The book does not offer a general history of these revolutions or full biographies of the principal
figures it examines: George Washington, Napoleon Bonaparte, Toussaint Louverture, and Simón Bolívar. It does not look at charisma in
nonpolitical contexts. And it is not a theoretical inquiry into the nature
of charisma, although readers interested in learning more about the

concept are invited to turn to the short excursus at the end of the book entitled "Writing Charisma into History." My focus is on the way charismatic political leaders came to dominate each of the four revolutions and the consequences for the societies in question.

What historians have often called "the age of democratic revolutions" appears in a somewhat somber light when examined from this angle.[6] But then, despite the hopes of many participants, democratic constitutional rule did not actually fare very well in these revolutions. None of them fully delivered on the promise of the U.S. Declaration of Independence to secure the equal rights of "all men," to say nothing of women. Very few of the original constitutions survived more than a few years. Very few of the new states avoided calamitous bouts of civil war, and in all of them, dictatorship had a compelling appeal. The revolutionary states did experience what could be called democratization, as millions of men and women began to participate in politics in a newly active, conscious manner. But this participation could take many forms and did not necessarily contribute to the foundation of stable democratic regimes. Indeed, it could include actively supporting authoritarian rulers.[7]

Perhaps it is only at this moment in the early twenty-first century, when the forward trajectory of democracy has come to seem anything but inexorable, that we can clearly glimpse this other side of the age of revolution. It is at moments like the present that we are forced to confront the reality that charismatic authoritarianism in no sense represents a backsliding, an atavistic and presumably temporary return to the days of warlords and kings, before the onward march of liberal democracy continues. A potentially authoritarian charisma is as modern a phenomenon as any of the liberal ideas and practices that arose in the age of revolution, including human rights and democratic republicanism and constitutional government. And it had many of the same cultural and intellectual sources. As the epigraph to the book reminds us, even for thinkers considered to be architects of modern democratic theory, the line between democracy and authoritarian one-man rule could be vanishingly thin.[8] The study of charisma reveals this darker potential of the age of revolution and of the Enlightenment culture out of which it emerged.

The book argues that while political charisma has existed throughout history, its modern forms started to develop only in the mid-1700s. In previous centuries, in Europe and the European overseas empires, political power had a very different visage from what we know today. It was intensely personal but largely concentrated in monarchs whose legitimacy derived from royal inheritance and from the blessing of established churches. While some rulers—Elizabeth I of England, Louis XIV of France—certainly had a strong charismatic appeal, their rule did not depend on it. Even Oliver Cromwell, the parliamentarian and military commander who rose to supreme power during the British Civil Wars of the 1640s, attracted a large and passionate following above all because his supporters saw him as the chosen instrument of divine Providence, not because they believed he had innate talents that set him high above other men.[9] Nor did Cromwell manage to establish a lasting regime. For literate men and women in the early eighteenth-century West, the most prominent examples of leaders who had come to power thanks to their charismatic appeal were not their own contemporaries but ancient Romans and Greeks, who belonged to a seemingly closed chapter of history. The most prominent of these ancient figures was Julius Caesar.

But in the later eighteenth century, the tectonic plates of Western political culture shuddered and broke apart. Even before minutemen and redcoats opened fire on one another at Lexington in 1775, an intellectual and cultural revolution of sorts had already created the conditions under which figures without royal pedigrees or religious sanction could rise to supreme power on the basis of their charisma. On the one hand, powerful new ideas of human equality were circulating, according to which even the most ordinary of men—although not yet women—might well possess greater talent, leadership ability, and moral worth than nobles and princes. The century's most audacious writers argued that it was the worthiest, most talented men who should rule. Meanwhile, a media revolution was under way. Striking changes in the world of print were making it possible for men and women from the most ordinary backgrounds to achieve unprecedented fame. They could become, to use a word invented in the period, celebrities.[10] Periodicals reported on them on a daily basis—and not only on their public actions but on their private lives as well. Engraving technology made their faces (or, at least, what artists imagined they looked like) familiar to a broad public. And new literary styles associated with that dizzily developing genre, the novel, helped authors to present them as familiar, approachable characters with whom readers could imagine a close, even intimate connection.

Media revolutions tend to have powerful political consequences, because they so fundamentally alter the way ordinary people and their rulers perceive and relate to one another. The invention of the printing press in pre-Reformation Europe, and the invention of radio and television in the twentieth century, had such consequences. We are living today through yet another media revolution with enormous political consequences. In the age of revolution, similarly profound effects followed from new forms of print media, new genres and styles, and an exponential increase in the sheer amount of print in circulation. The changes played out unevenly across the different revolutionary states. But even charismatic leaders in largely illiterate countries were still creatures of print. They wrote constantly for publication and knew the importance of doing so. They paid close attention to the way newspapers, books, pamphlets, and engravings portrayed them. Their written correspondence bore the mark of prevailing literary styles. It was in large part through these engagements with print that they forged their bonds with their followers.

And these bonds, the book goes on to argue, deeply shaped the course of political events. In revolutionary regimes that were still fragile, untested, and forbiddingly strange to men and women raised in monarchies and empires, the ability to feel a bond of trust with leaders counted heavily indeed. Charisma mattered. It came to matter even more as the revolutions continued and frail new constitutional structures wavered and sometimes collapsed. In such moments of turmoil, the lure of charismatic leadership came to loom over all political life. No leader enjoyed as enthusiastic a degree of support as his admirers liked to boast, but each could still count on a base of genuinely fervent, indeed sometimes fanatical, followers.

It was in fact widely believed that the survival of the new states *required* powerful, charismatic leaders linked to citizens by strong emotional bonds that knit the entire body politic together into an indivisible whole, the way monarchs had done in earlier states. Was the mere "consent of the governed" enough to hold together fractious states, most of them new creations, riven by regional, ideological, and in some cases racial divisions? Such states needed to be "governed more by sentiments and affections than by orders and laws," as an acolyte of Napoleon Bonaparte put it. They needed what Simón Bolívar called "acclamation," a collective enthusiasm that served, in his view, as "the sole legitimate source of human power." They needed what a well-known British writer called, in reference to an earlier charismatic hero, a "despotism founded . . . on the affection of love."[11] European monarchs certainly boasted of their subjects' love, but they never relied on it as the basis of their legitimacy. The intense emphasis now placed on the emotional bond between rulers and ruled was something new, and it meant that the revolutionary leaders were in no sense simply substitute kings. Their political authority was of a fundamentally different sort.

Contemporaries acknowledged this difference. They did not, however, treat the new form of charismatic leadership as something wholly novel. Instead, most often they sought to legitimize the break with the recent past by appealing to a different, more distant past and depicting the new leaders as figures out of classical antiquity. Just as classically republican and democratic forms of government appeared to be reawakening in the Atlantic revolutions after a sleep of centuries, it now also seemed possible that new versions of Greek and Roman heroes could rise to power.[12] In country after country, revolutionaries looked at one another and asked: Which one of us is Caesar? Which one Brutus? (In the same way, Russian revolutionaries in a later century would ask, Which one of us is Robespierre? Which one Bonaparte?) The revolutionary states revived Roman titles such as "consul," "senator," even "dictator" (an official granted temporary extraordinary powers). They crowned leaders with Roman-style laurel leaves and paraded them through Roman-style triumphal arches. Such language and practices came easily to cultures where formal education still consisted in large part of immersion in the Greek and Roman classics. Early modern European societies had always invoked the authority of antiquity, but the revolutionaries did so far more intensely and with far more literal intent, almost as if they could actually re-create ancient republics. During one debate in the French revolutionary assembly, a deputy extolled the progress that the human race had made since antiquity. Another immediately shot back, "If we have not been either Spartans, or Athenians, we should become them."[13]

In reality, the world had changed far too greatly for the revolutionaries to revive anything close to genuine ancient political forms. True, the unanimous "acclamation" described by Bolívar recalled ancient Greek practices of collective decision-making that relied on "shouts and murmurs" rather than actual vote-counting, but the context of Greek city-states was far removed from that of large territorial states in the age of gunpowder and print.[14] The classical idiom did, though, have important consequences for how the new forms of charismatic authority took shape—not least because, as Shakespeare's play suggested, the name of Caesar could arouse such deep currents of suspicion and fear. The tradition of classical republican thought revived in the Renaissance warned sharply of the dangers of personal political ambition, what Shakespeare's Mark Antony called that "grievous fault" for which Caesar had so grievously answered. No story out of Roman history had greater political purchase than that of the ambitious Caesar leading his legions across the Rubicon toward Rome and destroying the Republic. Classical republicanism taught that "government . . . is an empire of laws, not of men" (James Harrington, 1656), and throughout the revolutionary period, writers and politicians influenced by it warned sternly against treating fallible mortals as demigods.[15] Some even accused their fellow citizens of projecting outsize hopes and desires onto mere "idols." A dialectical tension played out between the lure of charismatic leaders and suspicions of the same. The classical idiom shaped both sides of it.

The period's charismatic leaders, needless to say, were not all alike. Most came from the upper levels of their societies, but Toussaint Louverture was born into bondage, the son of Africans violently transported across the Atlantic to the hell of a Caribbean slave colony. Napoleon Bonaparte was a ceaseless self-promoter who sometimes seemed to spend almost as much energy celebrating his victories as he did winning them. George Washington, although scrupulously concerned about his reputation, received overly effusive praise with distinct unease and loathed familiarity. While all the men engaged with the great intellectual currents of the day, to an extent that would put virtually any twenty-first-century politician to shame, only Simón Bolívar qualifies as a genuinely original political thinker.

Still, many qualities remained largely the same from country to country and from decade to decade. Indeed, each figure in turn provided a model for the others. Bonaparte explicitly compared himself to Washington on many occasions. Louverture was called both the Bonaparte and the Washington of the Antilles. Bonaparte's coronation made a lasting impression on the young Bolívar, who would later sometimes revel in the sobriquet "the Washington of South America."[16] These connections, and this modeling, which have attracted surprisingly little attention from previous historians, will serve as a major thread through the chapters that follow. Indeed, I will argue that images of charismatic leadership played just as important a role as formal political doctrines in helping revolutionary movements spread across the Atlantic world. In this sense, this book is very much a transnational history, although one that sets transnational relations and exchanges within the context of shared cultural and political developments.[17]

Three qualities common to all the leaders stand out in particularly high relief. They reflect a shared experience of revolutionary civil strife, large-scale war, and the founding or refounding of states. In the age of revolution, only figures who possessed these qualities were in a position to receive the sort of charismatic "acclamation" Bolívar described.

First, and crucially, these leaders were all, like Caesar, military heroes, renowned for their victories, their military talent, their stamina, and their sheer physical courage. Washington, Bonaparte, Louverture, and Bolívar all came to prominence as army officers who led men in battle personally, risking their lives and winning notable engagements. Each had a reputation for military expertise, with Bonaparte in particular considered, quite accurately, a true military genius, one of the greatest commanders in history. Although some currents of Enlightenment thought condemned war as destructive and futile, other, equally powerful currents defended it as a positive good and indeed exalted it in a way that even the most bellicose of traditional monarchs had not dared do. The revolutionary leaders all embodied this vision of war as potentially regenerative and sublime.

War and military leadership played into the second common quality as well. Each of these men was widely hailed as a redeemer who had arisen in the midst of frightful crisis and supposedly saved his people from otherwise certain destruction. Washington, in this view, single-handedly saved the newborn United States from defeat at the hands of the British. Bonaparte saved France from the chaos and strife unleashed in the French Revolution. Toussaint Louverture saved his fellow former slaves, who had carried out the largest and most successful slave revolt in history, from defeat and re-enslavement. Simón Bolívar saved South America from reconquest by the Spanish and from civil war. In each case, salvation was credited both to the men's supposedly extraordinary military skill and also to their ability to inspire and unify entire populations behind them.

Finally, each of the figures was seen as a founder, a person who either brought a new nation into being or, in Bonaparte's case, so thoroughly "regenerated" it as to amount to the same thing. Admirers referred to each as the "father of his country," by which they did not just mean that he governed with a father's tender care (the traditional sense of the term) but that he had effectively given it life. Each man had a close connection

with his country's written constitution—in Washington's case from pre-
siding over the American Constitutional Convention, in the three
others' as the effective author of the document. This position as founder
also gave each of them a way of appearing to stand above his country's
divisions and partisan politics. Doing so could help foster the emergence
of a political culture in which all parties had a commitment to a common good, but it could also encourage followers to consider the leader
himself above the law.

As the importance of military heroism and the role of the father
should make clear, these forms of political charisma also came deeply
bound up with prevailing ideals of masculinity. Women can of course
possess political charisma. Elizabeth I of England offers one of the greatest historical examples. In the eighteenth century, Catherine the Great
of Russia made strenuous attempts to pose as a redemptive figure who
elicited deep love from her subjects.[18] But in the eighteenth century it
was becoming more difficult, not less, for women to be perceived as
charismatic saviors. Women were widely seen as lacking the sheer vital
strength and energy necessary to accomplish great deeds—especially
sublime military ones. Nor could women become the object of passionate, intimate connections with ordinary supporters—even purely imagined connections—without seeming to sacrifice their modesty and
decency.[19] Significantly, Western European accounts of Catherine II
tended to oscillate between praise of her unusually "masculine" characteristics and voyeuristic condemnations of her sexual indecencies.[20]

In short, the paradigmatic charismatic leaders of the period were, as
the title of this book has it, "men on horseback"—masculine military
heroes riding in to save their states from destruction and, indeed, to give
these states a new birth. The phrase "the man on horseback" itself has
long served as a metaphor for a military leader seeking political power.[21]
But in the case of these leaders, it also had a quite literal meaning, for
equestrian skills contributed powerfully to their charismatic appeal. Today, with cavalry long vanished from the battlefield and horseback riding largely associated with racing and the sports of a privileged elite, we
easily forget just how impressive the spectacle could be of a commander

in a brightly colored uniform wielding a heavy, sharpened sword from atop a warhorse that could weigh as much as twelve hundred pounds and cost many times a skilled artisan's annual salary. It is no coincidence that Thomas Jefferson remembered Washington as "the best horseman of his age, and the most graceful figure that could be seen on horseback."[22] Louverture gained a reputation before the Haitian Revolution for breaking wild horses by leaping fearlessly onto their backs.[23] Bolívar could reputedly stay in the saddle longer than any of his soldiers.[24] Bonaparte was actually a mediocre rider but did everything he could to disguise the fact. It is no coincidence that the most famous image ever produced of him, by the painter Jacques-Louis David, shows him on a magnificent, rearing cavalry horse during his crossing of the Alps in 1800 (he actually undertook the journey on a mule, wrapped in a heavy blanket). When the British engraver Samuel William Reynolds sought to honor Simón Bolívar in 1824, he copied David's image down to the smallest details (figures 2 and 3).[25]

As much as possible, the book will look not only at such representations but also at the way the followers and admirers of these charismatic leaders received and understood them. And this raises a tricky question. How can we know what these men and women really thought and felt? People may have cheered, voted for, or even fought for a charismatic leader, but they could have been coerced. Even diaries and private correspondence, which I have drawn on wherever possible, do not provide unmediated glimpses of inner thoughts and desires. Even in the most intimate forms of writing, people still followed established conventions and wrote what they felt was expected of them. They could lie to their friends and family, even to themselves. Much of the evidence in this book comes not from such private sources but from the much more copious public ones: newspaper articles, political pamphlets, printed biographies (many heavily fictionalized), printed memoirs, poetry, speeches, and visual sources (mainly engravings). Much of it was produced for what we would now call propaganda purposes.

We cannot know for certain what the people of the age of revolution thought and felt, but these sources, taken together, can still give us important clues. If we cannot know for sure how people understood what they read, we can determine, at least in part, what they liked to read best. We cannot know for sure how people reacted to propaganda, but we can trace, from the evolution of the material, what the propagandists themselves thought worked best. And while we may never know what emotions people experienced, the sources do give a sense of what people were expected to feel and what they tried to make one another feel. It is out of such shards and fragments that all histories of this sort are constructed.

It is important to emphasize here that emotions, like everything else, have a history. They obviously have a physiological basis as well, but culture shapes the way people understand, process, and control their emotional reactions, including how they come to consider some reactions natural and legitimate and others shameful or harmful. Historians and psychologists even speak of different "emotional regimes," which can succeed one another in historical time.[26] Historians of France have recently led the way in exploring the role of emotions in the age of revolution.[27] In this book, I will use the sources as best I can to show how the emotion of love, and claims about it, powerfully contributed to the development of modern charismatic leadership.

Emotional regimes crossed the boundaries of literacy, but because of the nature of the source material, this book still deals, not entirely but to an unavoidably large extent, with people who could read and had access to printed matter. In the case of Toussaint Louverture, for instance, we have more direct evidence about how literate white colonists and soldiers reacted to him than we do about the reactions of the former slaves, a majority of them African born, and most illiterate, who fought under his command. To the extent that we have reliable information about this latter group—which vastly outnumbered the former—I will provide it. But the form of charisma about which we know the most in this period took shape and operated through print media, which aimed in the first instance at the literate segments of society. And as noted, the charismatic leaders, very much including Louverture, were themselves shaped by engagements with the written word.

It would also be wrong to equate the literate segments of society simply with "elites." By the end of the eighteenth century, most adult men in Britain's American colonies, and also in many French and British cities, were literate, as well as were a majority of women. All but the poorest of them had access to some printed material, whether by purchase or by frequenting coffeehouses and libraries that made it available to visitors. Everywhere, including in Haiti and South America, the circulation of printed matter exploded during the revolutionary period itself. Furthermore, illiterate people could hear speeches. They could hear literate relatives, friends, and neighbors read printed material out loud and follow campaigns on maps, as in Louis-Léopold Boilly's painting of a French family following the bulletins of Napoleon's Grande Armée (figure 4). They could view the printed images that circulated in large numbers. An extraordinary engraving from the 1820s shows a black or mixed-race couple in Venezuela holding up a picture of Simón Bolívar to their young children (figure 5). The caption reads: "Here is your liberator."[28] In short, ordinary people, including illiterate ones, could follow, and actively participate in, the extraordinary intellectual ferment of the Enlightenment and the age of revolution. They could conceive of overturning ancient customs and arrangements and rebuilding their society on new principles. And even before the revolutions began, they could look to a small number of apparently extraordinary men—charismatic men—as saviors.

ONE

MR. BOSWELL GOES
TO CORSICA

Paoli sways the hearts of his countrymen . . . [His] power . . .
knows no bounds. It is high treason so much as to speak against him . . .
a species of despotism founded, contrary to the principles of
Montesquieu, on the affection of love.

—James Boswell, An Account of Corsica, *1768*

On October 11, 1765, James Boswell boarded a small boat in the Italian port of Livorno, bound for the island of Corsica. The future author of *The Life of Samuel Johnson* was then just twenty-five years old and entirely unknown. Expensively dressed, with a wide face, thick, well-groomed hair, and a ruddy drinker's complexion, he would have struck casual observers as just another well-off, dissipated young Briton guzzling his way across Europe on the Grand Tour. Certainly, since leaving London two years before, Boswell had denied himself few pleasures of the flesh. Despite his tender age, he had already endured several bouts with the lifetime sparring partner he privately nicknamed "Signor Gonorrhea."[1]

But in fact, Boswell was anything but a stereotypical Grand Tourist. During his time on the Continent, he applied himself to serious study of languages and the law and read voraciously. More striking, in addition to the usual paintings, palaces, and ruins, he sought out a different, uncommon sort of tourist attraction: great men. He set himself the challenge of meeting Frederick the Great, Voltaire, and Rousseau, and while the Prussian monarch did not receive him, the other two did. To find Rousseau, Boswell made his way to the remote Swiss village of Môtiers, and there he practically besieged the *philosophe's* modest cottage until he won admittance. He would later repay Rousseau very badly for the favor by seducing his mistress, Thérèse Levasseur, but at the time he impressed Rousseau with his wit and enthusiasm. Boswell, although prone to spells of dark melancholy, otherwise had an effervescent temperament that made him highly entertaining company. As he himself confided to his journal, "I am one of the most engaging men that ever lived."[2]

It was, in fact, because of Rousseau that Boswell now found himself en route to Corsica. For several decades, the island had been fighting a slow-burning war of independence against its longtime overlord, the Italian Republic of Genoa. The Corsicans had won Europe-wide attention for their supposed attachment to republican liberty. British radicals, who wanted to expand the franchise and limit the powers of the royal ministry, held them up as an inspiration.[3] Rousseau himself praised them, in his *Social Contract*, as the "one country in Europe which is fit to receive laws . . . I have a presentiment that this little island will one day astonish Europe."[4] Corsican leaders had subsequently asked Rousseau to help draw up a new constitution. Rousseau not only talked to Boswell about the island but told him in glowing terms about the heroic leader of the rebel forces, Pasquale Paoli. Here was another great man for Boswell to add to his collection.

Paoli quite deserved the attention. His father, Giacinto, had dominated the early stages of the Corsican independence struggle but fled to Naples in 1739 after the failure of an ill-fated project to install a German adventurer as the island's king. Pasquale, then aged just fourteen, left as well, enrolling in a Neapolitan military school and then serving as a junior officer in the Neapolitan army. He also developed a taste for history and for philosophical musings. "The world is a stage play," he once wrote to his father in a Shakespearean vein, "and we must deliver our lines well on stage."[5] But as the turmoil in Corsica continued, with the Genoese arranging the assassination of another independence leader, Pasquale saw an opportunity to take command of the revolt. He returned home in 1755 and convinced a portion of the island's leading families to name him the supreme "General" of Corsica, with almost unlimited executive powers. He was just thirty. He defeated a rival backed by other families and won a series of victories over the Genoese. He issued a written constitution—one of the first in Europe—that gave all adult men, and also widows, a role in choosing representatives. He settled conflicts among the perennially fractious Corsican clans, reorganized the government and the military, and even founded a press and a university, despite conditions of such poverty that he routinely scraped the ink off letters he received so as to reuse the paper. He impressed visitors with his asceticism, his work ethic, his learning, and his friendly manner.[6] He was, in short, an irresistible attraction for Boswell, despite the not-inconsiderable risk the young Scot ran of falling prey to pirates on the journey to Corsica or being taken by the Corsicans for a spy.

In any event, no pirates materialized, and Boswell suffered nothing worse on the two-day journey than fleas, vermin, and the dark warnings of the crew to stay away from their women (they clearly knew their man). He landed safely at the northern tip of Corsica and then undertook a grueling, 120-mile trek southward, arriving more than a week later in the town of Sollacaro, where he met Paoli. Paoli himself initially reacted with suspicion, thinking that Boswell—who kept scribbling down detailed notes of everything he saw—had indeed come to spy.[7] But soon enough, a letter of introduction from Rousseau, plus the usual Boswellian charm, had the desired effect. As Paoli later remembered, Boswell was "so cheerful! So gay! So pleasant!"[8] Paoli also realized that Boswell might prove useful in mobilizing British support for the rebellion, so he treated his visitor sumptuously, feasting him, introducing him to Corsican clan leaders, allowing him to ride his own finely outfitted horse, and spending long hours in conversation with him. Paoli spoke excellent French and some English in addition to Italian, and the talk ranged over literature, history, religion, philosophy, and politics. When, after nearly two weeks, Boswell began the long trip back to the mainland, Paoli gave him a series of rich gifts, including an elegant scarlet suit embroidered with the Corsican crest, a brace of pistols, and a dog. Boswell asked Paoli to write him letters, and to do so as a philosopher and man of letters. "He took me by the hand," Boswell later wrote, "and said, as a friend." Boswell nearly collapsed with pleasure.[9]

Almost from the moment he landed back in Italy, Boswell started writing about Corsica and Pasquale Paoli.[10] Over the next several years he sent at least eighty articles on the subject to *The London Chronicle*, urging British support for the rebels.[11] He told everyone that his experiences on the island had left him a changed man. "Paoli," he wrote to Rousseau, "has infused my soul with a firmness that it will never lose."[12] Arriving back in Britain in early 1766, Boswell talked of nothing but Corsica and Paoli to his literary acquaintances, and they in turn urged him to write a book. "Give us as many anecdotes as you can," Samuel Johnson told him.[13] Boswell set to work, and in February 1768 there appeared *An Account of Corsica, The Journal of a Tour to That Island, and Memoirs of Pascal Paoli*.

As the triple title suggests, the book, which ran to 380 pages, was something of a patchwork. It combined a detailed account of Corsican geography, flora, and fauna with a brief history of the island and thorough, if heavily stereotyped, accounts of local customs.[14] To this material Boswell joined a much more personal narrative of his own trip and, within it, gave pride of place to a portrait of Paoli. He described Paoli's physical appearance at length and provided numerous vignettes of the man in informal, intimate settings, emphasizing his interactions with ordinary Corsicans and their devotion to him. He said that Paoli had become "the father of a nation."[15] Boswell also highlighted his own role as the privileged observer. "One morning I remember," he wrote, "I came in upon him without ceremony, while he was dressing. I was glad to have an opportunity of seeing him in those teasing moments, when, according to the Duke de la Rochefoucault, no man is a hero to his valet de chambre."[16] (The line was less of a cliché in 1768.) While revising his first draft for publication, Boswell cut out stories that might reflect

badly on Paoli, but he left in what he called "small peculiarities of character," including Paoli's inability to keep still for more than ten minutes
and his astonishing memory. But Boswell also added numerous passages
of pure, sweaty, breathless adulation. He endorsed Paoli's comparison of
himself to Judah Maccabee and added comparisons of his own to heroes
of Roman and Greek antiquity, calling the Corsican a man who "just
lives in the times of antiquity." He concluded that in Paoli, "I saw my
highest ideal realized."[17]

The book had an immediate and spectacular success. It sold at least
seven thousand copies in Britain, to say nothing of four pirated Irish
editions—possibly some Irish readers warmed to the tale of an island
nation fighting for its liberty against a longtime foreign occupier?[18] It
was translated into French, German, Dutch, and Italian. The reviewers
gushed. The poet Thomas Gray wrote to Horace Walpole that the book's
sections on Paoli "pleased and moved me strangely," although Gray
added acidly, "Any fool may write a most valuable book by chance, if he
will only tell us what he heard and said with veracity." King George III
himself remarked that "I have read Boswell's book which is well written."[19] Paoli, who had waited eagerly for the book to appear, excitedly
predicted that it would help his cause.[20] The book was Boswell's big
break, establishing him as a man of letters and allowing him to avoid the
full-time legal career for which his demanding father had destined him.
In 1769, he appeared at the Shakespeare Jubilee in Stratford-upon-Avon
carrying a pistol, musket, and stiletto and wearing the scarlet suit Paoli
had given him, plus a cap embroidered with the phrase "Viva la Libertà"
in gold letters. In an engraving, an artist changed it to "Corsica Boswell." As Boswell himself later put it, "I had got upon a rock in Corsica,
and jumped into the middle of life."[21]

Boswell was not the only British writer to visit Corsica during these
years of its quasi-independence, but he was by far the most important.
Following the publication of his *Account*, references to Paoli and the
rebels multiplied manyfold in the British press. Engraved portraits of
Paoli appeared, as did a profusion of mostly mediocre poems, including
one entitled *The Paoliad*. The well-known poet Anna Barbauld praised

"the godlike man who saved his country." Another spoke of "the savior of the land" whose "drawn sword flames in his uplifted hand." A certain Timothy Scribble burbled that "brave PAOLI strove to free mankind!" Much of the poetry mentioned Boswell by name. Meanwhile, a lady's magazine published a recipe for "Chicken Paoli," and the sporting press tracked at least four racehorses named Pascal Paoli. In some novels from the late 1760s, characters speak of "going a volunteer under the brave Paoli" much as Britons of the 1930s spoke of going to fight in Spain.[22]

Although no radical, Boswell gladly allied himself with radical members of the Whig party who were urging the British government to support Paoli. In his book, he quoted at length a poem called "Pride," which its anonymous author had dedicated to the radical hero John Wilkes and which proposed Corsica as a model that a degenerate Britain should emulate:

On CORSICA reflect and see
Not what you are, but what you ought to be; [. . .]
In this vile age [. . .] No godlike Patriot Prodigy appeared [. . .]
'Till one small spot [. . .] Produc'd the man, and—PAOLI his
    name.[23]

These political efforts turned even more urgent in 1768. Four years earlier the Genoese, unable to defeat Paoli, had secretly agreed to sell the rights over Corsica to France. Now France moved in to secure its new possession. Paoli's ragtag forces had sufficed to hold off the corrupt and incompetent Genoese military, but they had no chance against the modern, professional French army. In Britain, radical Whigs excoriated the government for not intervening to save the Corsicans from French despotism. Paoli himself published open letters in the British papers, pressing his cause.[24] Boswell edited a book of essays in favor of the "brave Corsicans" and raised seven hundred pounds to buy weapons for them. Wealthy peers and merchants contributed at least fourteen thousand pounds more—a vast sum at the time.[25] But the agitation and fundraising had little effect. Lord Holland, Paymaster General of the

Forces, commented: "Foolish as we are, we cannot be so foolish as to go to war because Mr. Boswell has been in Corsica."[26] In May 1769, the French crushed Pasquale Paoli at the Battle of Ponte Novu. Four months later, after an adulatory tour through the Low Countries, he arrived in exile in London, where Boswell gave him a warm welcome.[27]

With these events, the "Corsican moment" in Britain rapidly faded. After settling in London, Paoli declined to associate himself with the radical Whigs, and they soon abandoned him as a symbol. Dr. Johnson told Boswell, "I wish you would empty your head of Corsica, which I think has filled it rather too long."[28] Boswell protested, but as time passed, he took up a different great man as the subject of his literary ambitions: Samuel Johnson himself. Boswell did remain close to the exiled Paoli, who often provided him with a bed in his spacious London town house. Paoli in turn became a member of Johnson's circle and makes frequent appearances in Boswell's *Life of Samuel Johnson*. That book, which did so much to create the modern art of biography, follows directly from Boswell's *Account of Corsica*, employing the same mixture of intimate observation, humorous anecdote, and myth-making to sketch an unforgettable portrait of its subject.[29]

Yet even as the vogue for Paoli faded in Britain, it remained strong elsewhere in the world, most notably in Britain's North American colonies. There, the climax of the Corsican drama coincided with the Stamp Act crisis and the first great wave of pre-revolutionary colonial agitation. Pasquale Paoli, as a symbol of resistance against despotic overseas rule, served an even more obvious political purpose in America than in Britain. Boswell's book sold well in America, and a popular almanac reprinted extracts.[30] Paoli's name regularly appeared in American newspapers, which reprinted, at least six times, the selections Boswell had quoted from the poem called "Pride," and at least seven times Paoli's own most important public letter.[31] As late as 1775, *The Newport Mercury* commented on this letter: "The noble ardor and sentiments it breathes, I could wish to see infused into the breast of every American."[32] The editor of *The New York Journal* called Paoli "the greatest man on earth."[33] Pre-revolutionary societies such as the Sons of Liberty in Philadelphia and Boston routinely included "the truly heroic Pascal Paoli" in their toasts. John Hancock named one of his ships the *Paoli*, and a number of unfortunate Americans grew up with names such as Pascal Paoli Macintosh and Pascal Paoli Leavens. A tavern called the Paoli outside Philadelphia eventually gave its name to Paoli, Pennsylvania, the first of at least six communities called Paoli in the United States.[34]

Paoli himself did have one more moment of fame, decades later. In 1790, after the start of the French Revolution, the French government allowed him to return to Corsica, where he quickly became president of the island's departmental council. But as the Revolution turned increasingly radical and violent, Paoli quarreled both with the government in Paris and its local supporters—notably several hot-tempered young members of the Bonaparte family. In 1793, after driving the Bonapartes into exile on the mainland and forcing the young Napoleon to pursue his career there (an event with truly world-historical consequences), Paoli led a short-lived British protectorate on the island, but in 1796 the British abandoned it, and the French returned, this time for good. Paoli died in London in 1807.

Today, few people remember Pasquale Paoli outside Corsica, whose people still revere him as the island's greatest native son (Bonaparte may have won more battles, but he also committed the unforgivable sin of leaving for France). Paoli's defeat may have been a glorious one, but it was still a defeat, on a small, remote island, and exile to a comfortable London town house, with Johnson and Boswell for company, was not exactly the sort of heroic martyrdom on which undying legends are built. Paoli soon faded in Western memory.

Yet for a brief moment in the 1760s and 1770s, Paoli stood out as one of the most revered and well-known figures in the Western world, and the most important exemplar, before George Washington, of a new and potent form of political charisma. I am not speaking here of the charismatic bond that linked him to his followers in Corsica itself. There, political life remained more traditional than Paoli's foreign devotees usually recognized. These devotees may have burbled in amazement over the liberal constitution of 1755, but in practice Paoli still depended for support on long-standing clan loyalties. And while he published an impressive newspaper on his new printing press, it had a circulation of only five hundred—not to mention the fact that most Corsicans were still illiterate.[35] Paoli's charismatic reputation in Corsica depended above all on personal contacts and family loyalties. But the charismatic reputation Paoli developed elsewhere in the Western world, thanks above all to Boswell, was a different matter. This broader reputation, even if short-lived, demonstrated the power of print fervently to attach a far-flung set of admirers to a previously unknown, charismatic figure. Outside Corsica, Paoli could serve only as a model of charismatic rule, not as an actual ruler. But such models are important. They shape how societies envision political leadership. And in this case the model was particularly important, because in just a few more years, revolutionary upheavals would give the societies that had read about Paoli with such fervor the chance to experiment with new political forms of their own.

Was Paoli's charismatic appeal actually so new? His classically educated admirers tended to portray him not as quintessentially modern but rather as quintessentially ancient. In descriptions of Paoli, Boswell and others drew liberally from descriptions given by ancient Greek and Roman historians of steadfastly virtuous and brave figures such as Pericles, Horatius, or Cato the Younger. Particularly influential were Plutarch's parallel lives of the most famous Greeks and Romans, which remained enormously popular and a staple of school curricula, thanks to their combination of humorous and titillating anecdotes and thrilling accounts of heroic deeds. No less a figure than the British prime minister William Pitt the Elder called Paoli "one of those men who are no longer to be found but in the *Lives* of Plutarch."[36] Meanwhile, the tender paternal care Paoli supposedly showed to his people echoed familiar narratives of praise for European monarchs. When Boswell called Paoli the "father of a nation," he seemed to be recalling the common description of kings as "fathers of their country."[37] Finally, if Boswell and others frequently resorted to hyperbole in praising Paoli's extraordinary courage, virtue,

and vision, they had many predecessors in the large stables of propagandists European monarchs had long employed to glorify themselves.[38]

Paoli did indeed have admirable personal qualities that recalled
Plutarch's heroes, but his charismatic appeal depended not just on these
qualities but on the cultural context in which his admirers perceived him.
This cultural context, as we will see more fully in a moment, was very
distinctly modern. The relationship between Paoli and his non-Corsican
admirers, established largely through print, did not resemble anything
ever seen in the ancient world. These admirers might have explicitly imi-
tated Plutarch and other classical authors. But unlike Plutarch, they were
not writing as historians. It was one thing to provide intimate, humorous,
titillating portraits of figures who were safely dead and buried, quite another to present a living leader in this informal and irreverent manner in
newspapers and pamphlets.

The differences from the cults of Christian absolute monarchs, even
relatively recent ones, were just as important, and as revealing. The artists and writers who had worked full-time to promote the image of
kings like France's Louis XIV (1638–1715) always took pains to emphasize the distance separating these monarchs from their subjects. They
never would have depicted the imperious "Sun King" half-dressed, in
what Boswell called "teasing moments," or commented on his personal
quirks. Their purpose, and more generally the purpose of royal propagandists before the Enlightenment, was not to depict a ruler as a distinct individual but to show how well he fit a general model of glorious
kingship.

By the same token, the panegyrists of these monarchs would never
have portrayed them interacting, on a familiar, equal basis, with ordinary people, in the way Boswell described Paoli meeting ordinary Corsicans and visitors such as himself. The panegyrists might gush over the
people's "love" for the king, but in their works the "people" generally
remained a passive, indistinguishable mass. Louis XIV presided over
what was probably the largest propaganda operation ever seen in Europe
before the modern age, wholly dedicated to the celebration of himself.
But of the thousands of images produced for his undying glory, not a

single one showed him being applauded by ordinary French people. Nor in any sense did the propaganda ever suggest that the people had a choice about whether to love their king. It was their duty, as his subjects.

Today, politicians in most of the world—and not just in democratic societies—routinely stage spectacles of their personal interactions with ordinary supporters. Campaign videos show them in physical contact with enthusiastic crowds, hugging or shaking hands and engaging in conversation. The camera pans to the supporters' rapt, smiling faces. In large countries, only a tiny percentage of the population may ever actually have the chance to interact with leading politicians in this way, but the spectacles allow everyone else to imagine having a personal, human connection. This imagined connection is an essential fiction of modern politics. It allows ordinary people to feel that their participation in political life is not limited to the formal act of voting—that their leaders know them, understand them, and take their concerns seriously. Charisma crucially amplifies and intensifies this sense of connection.

We take these aspects of political life so much for granted that we easily forget that political systems in the West used to operate on very different principles. In the heyday of absolute monarchy, as the philosopher Immanuel Kant recognized in 1793, rulers most often saw their subjects as "minor children" who relied on their metaphorical "fathers" to tell them what they should want and even what they should feel. The monarchs expected their subjects' love but might have seen applause as impertinent. Applause had by then become a practice associated with the theater and, unlike deferential bowing or saluting, implied a freely made decision to register approval.[39]

When Boswell called Paoli "the father of a nation," he actually meant something different by the phrase than did the royal panegyrists.[40] Their point was that kings ruled with a father's tender care—and with his unquestioned authority (which Kant called "the greatest despotism thinkable"). Boswell saw Paoli, by contrast, as the metaphorical progenitor of the nation, the man who actually brought the nation into being through his heroic efforts. In one sense, his usage might imply an even greater degree of subordination on the part of the "children" to the father figure. Yet these offspring were not presented as minors, incapable of independent action. Like Athena, they supposedly sprang from their father fully grown.

Furthermore, in the eyes of his admirers, at least, Paoli owed his office to the people's will. It had not come to him as an inheritance or because prophet or priest had proclaimed him the Lord's anointed. Even as he metaphorically brought the people into being, they chose him freely as leader, in recognition of his extraordinary personal, natural qualities. In turn, these qualities constituted the basis of his legitimacy in a way that could never be true for a monarch. History amply demonstrated that monarchs could be exceptionally cowardly, corrupt, stupid, and lacking in popular appeal without thereby ceasing to be regarded as legitimate sovereigns.

One might think that Paoli's reliance upon the people would have been seen as a restraint on his power, compared to that of absolute monarchs. In fact—and this is another, crucial way in which he represented an innovation—the opposite was true. However great the authority claimed by some European kings in the so-called age of absolutism, they still operated, in practice, under numerous constraints. They had to maintain the Christian religion and respect the laws of royal succession. They had to exercise their rule through a host of intermediary bodies. They had to cooperate with powerful social elites. It was their readiness to respect these arrangements that distinguished them, in contemporary eyes, from despots. Montesquieu, perhaps the most influential political philosopher of the eighteenth century, argued that the governing principle of monarchy was honor, by which he meant in large part a respect for the status and office of powerful subjects. By contrast, he identified the governing principle of despotism as naked fear. But Paoli's direct, personal connection with the people, as well as their fervent, unquestioning emotional attachment to him, seemed to override the sort of restraints that monarchs operated under and that distinguished them from despots. Boswell noted that Paoli's constitution did establish theoretical limits on his authority. He praised Corsica as "a complete and well-ordered democracy" and insisted that "the power of the general is properly limited," even if he held office for life. Yet in practice, Boswell continued, "the power of Paoli knows no bounds. It is high treason so much as to speak against, or calumniate him; a species of despotism founded, contrary to the principles of Montesquieu, on the affection of love."[41]

In all these ways, the vogue for Paoli gave educated elites in the Western world a new way to envision political leadership. It provided a model for a new form of political charisma, grounded not in a hierarchical relationship between a remote, anointed ruler and passive, obedient subjects but in an imagined personal, intimate, and intense relationship between active followers, on the one hand, and a leader whose extraordinary qualities did not stop him from relating to these followers as equals and friends, on the other. It was, in one sense, a democratic charisma, because the leader's position seemed to depend on the followers' active support. But it always contained within it the threat to override constitutional restraints and turn authoritarian. Boswell himself recognized the danger of a single man possessing such extraordinary personal authority. The Corsicans, he wrote, "submit to one for whom they have a personal regard." But he continued, "They cannot be said to be perfectly civilized until they submit to the determinations of their magistrates as officers of the state."[42]

It may seem strange that before the American Revolution, it was a Corsican who offered the most striking, and most important, example of this new form of charisma. Corsica was, after all, a small, poor island far removed from the Western world's centers of power and advanced thought. But where else did a leader like Pasquale Paoli have a chance to emerge? In the 1760s, the West remained almost entirely a world of hereditary monarchies. In Peru, for five months in the early 1780s, the charismatic José Gabriel Condorcanqui led a multi-ethnic rebellion against the Spanish authorities before they captured and publicly executed him. But he based his claim to power on his supposed descent from the Incas, taking the Inca name Túpac Amaru. And while he received considerable attention in Europe and North America, Paoli received far more.[43] Before 1776, it was Paoli, the Corsican, who offered the most prominent example of a charismatic revolutionary leader in the new mold. And perhaps it is not actually so surprising that innovative political forms were first seen to emerge in a place like Corsica. As the great historian Franco Venturi once wrote, "The first links in the long chain of reforms and revolutions, projects and delusions, rebellions and repressions that led in the eighteenth century to the collapse of the old regime, are to be sought not in the great capitals of the West . . . but on the margins of the continent, in unexpected and peripheral places."[44]

Even so, Paoli was not wholly alone in this corner of the Western imagination. Such was the longing for figures like him that some observers in Western Europe and North America could, in their works, transform even absolute monarchs into heroic, self-made revolutionary legislators who brought their nations into being, playing down these men's royal lineages almost entirely. One striking example was Peter the Great of Russia, who ruled from 1682 to 1725. Peter was, in reality, an autocrat who brutally repressed a military uprising in 1698, had his own son killed as a traitor, and governed a society where millions lived in the virtual slavery of serfdom. Yet he also attempted to modernize Russia and open it to the West, and these aspects of his life encouraged Western admirers to cast him as a charismatic hero. For decades after his death in 1725, Peter received extraordinary attention and adulation in Western Europe. Scores of eulogistic poems appeared there, as well as at least ten major biographies in French, English, and German, by authors as prominent as Daniel Defoe and Voltaire, along with flattering paintings and engravings.[45] Largely ignoring the realities of Russian autocracy, the admirers stressed Peter's virtuous devotion to the public good. In his hands, wrote the French poet Antoine-Léonard Thomas (who devoted much of his career to a never-finished epic poem about the tsar), despotism promoted human happiness.[46] The admirers also rhapsodized about Peter's natural gifts, rarely failing to mention his enormous height—six feet, eight inches—and physical strength. To the English poet Aaron Hill, Peter was a "giant-genius . . . divinely sized—to suit his crown's extent!"[47] It mattered as well that Peter personally led troops in battle, especially in his epic victory over invading Swedes at Poltava in 1709.

All these factors fed into the contention that Peter, through sheer talent and willpower, had single-handedly transformed Russia into a new country. The prolific English moralist W. H. Dilworth called his biography of Peter *The Father of His Country*, saying that when the tsar came to the throne, the Russians "had nothing of Humanity but their Form" and were "Fierce and Savage as the Bears."[48] Such ideas found their way into one of the most popular English poems of the century, James Thomson's *The Seasons*:

> What cannot active government perform,
> New-moulding man? . . .
> Immortal Peter! First of monarchs! He
> His stubborn country tamed, her rocks, her fens,
> Her floods, her seas, her ill-submitting sons;
> And while the fierce barbarian he subdued,
> To more exalted soul he raised the man.[49]

Peter's admirers also insisted that what Aaron Hill called his "more than mortal sway" had allowed him to forge a personal connection with his subjects very much like Paoli's—one that allowed him to rule with far fewer checks on his authority than mere "common kings."[50]

Peter, unlike Paoli, had no Boswell to catch him in "teasing moments" of undress. Still, his biographers found ways to portray him in a way that allowed ordinary readers to imagine a personal connection to the great man. All of them, without exception, stressed that he had traveled through Western Europe from March 1697 to late August 1698 incognito, disguised as "Pyotr Mikhailov," an ordinary *desyatnik*, or junior officer. His British biographer John Mottley carefully noted that "he commonly went about in the Jacket of a Dutch Skipper, that he might the more easily mix with the Seafaring People, and get among the Shipping, without being taken notice of."[51] Dilworth even included an engraving of him working as an ordinary ship's carpenter.[52]

An equally impressive process of reinvention took place later in the century in regard to Frederick the Great, who transformed his small northern German kingdom of Prussia into a major European power. Although a repressive monarch addicted to military conquest, Frederick also had a distinctly literary cast of mind, wrote prolifically (in French), and cultivated relations with Voltaire and other *philosophes*.[53] Much of the material published about him, in Prussia and elsewhere, hailed his "godlike" qualities, including his extraordinary mental abilities and personal courage. After he dealt the hated French a stinging defeat during the Seven Years' War of 1756–63, he became especially popular with his British allies, who cheered him in hymns, songs, poems, newspaper articles, and full-length biographies (including one by W. H. Dilworth), and who put his face—and distinctive hat—on everything from prints to handkerchiefs to crockery.[54] Recall that during his Grand Tour the young James Boswell singled out Frederick as the one European monarch he hoped to meet, alongside Voltaire and Rousseau.

Frederick's admirers paid particularly great attention to the love he showed his subjects. Books of "anecdotes" portrayed him giving alms to poor families, protecting peasants against greedy landlords, sharing the privations of the lowest-ranking of his soldiers, and shunning the luxuries that other kings indulged in. In one story, he came across a soldier who wore a lead musket ball on a watch chain. When Frederick asked him why, the soldier replied that he could not afford a watch but wore the musket ball to remind him that at any moment he might have to die for king and country. Frederick, overcome by emotion, gave the man his own watch.[55] Frederick himself wrote in 1739 that ruling by fear meant ruling "over cowards and slaves," but that a king "who has the gift of making himself loved will reign over his subjects' hearts, since they will find that having him as master is in their own interest."[56] One of his ministers, preparing a royal visit to Königsberg a year later, loyally reported that "Your Majesty reigns more sovereignly over all his subjects' hearts . . . than any monarch has ever done."[57]

Very much like Boswell, Frederick and his admirers were coming to understand the "love" between a ruler and his subjects in a new way.

They did not see subjects as playing the role of minor children who loved their king-father out of duty, but as adults who loved him because he deserved their love and, indeed, actively strove to elicit it. Tellingly, one of the places where Frederick enjoyed his greatest popularity outside Prussia was in far-off New England. Newspapers there eagerly reported his exploits, and for decades after his death, engravings and books of anecdotes about him circulated widely. John Quincy Adams (who had served as U.S. minister to Prussia) burbled over with enthusiasm for "immortal Frederic! . . . the father of thy country—the benefactor of mankind!"[58] One historian has written that New Englanders—without any particular difficulty—"reinvented him as a republican hero."[59] As in the case of Peter the Great, this reinvention said much less about the monarch himself than about the intense longing of audiences around the Western world for charismatic heroes in the new mold whom they could hold up as models.

Why did this new sort of political charisma develop? One obvious explanation involves the advent of democratic ideas and practices. True, the word "democracy" itself had little currency in the eighteenth and early nineteenth centuries. It usually denoted direct rule by the people without representatives, as in ancient Greek city-states, and many political writers considered it barely distinguishable from mob rule (Boswell was one of the rare writers to use the word in a positive sense).[60] But the broadly democratic principle of popular sovereignty, while in no sense new to the period, was starting to become widely accepted as the basis of political legitimacy well before the American Revolution.[61] Even in France, where kings continued to claim that their authority derived solely from God, the most influential of the *philosophes* were insisting, in the words of Denis Diderot, that "the prince holds from his subjects themselves the authority he has over them."[62] It was no accident that Pasquale Paoli, in the 1760s, enjoyed particular popularity among the most prominent Western advocates of popular sovereignty at the time: radical Whigs in Britain and proto-revolutionaries in North

America. Among such groups, it made sense that a figure like Paoli, whose authority they saw as stemming directly from the Corsican people, would emerge as a model of charismatic leadership. The revolutions that brought charismatic leaders to power after 1776 all enshrined popular sovereignty as a bedrock principle, even if they restricted the actual right to vote.

But the advent of democracy and popular sovereignty, while a crucial part of the story, is still only one part of it. Charisma is a matter not just of consent but of enthusiasm. At an extreme, the followers of a charismatic leader can look less like prudent, rational voters than like members of a frenzied religious cult. Charisma also operates by encouraging followers to see the object of their adoration as virtually superhuman. In modern times, as Paoli's case suggests, they do not link these superhuman qualities to the leader's ancestry or to any religious blessing, but see them as a pure product of nature. Finally, modern forms of charisma, as Paoli's case also demonstrates, produce enthusiasm for the leader by encouraging followers to feel a personal bond with him—to feel as if they know him intimately, "like a friend."

This new type of charisma involved not just the advent of democracy but also a series of cultural developments that we now associate with the Enlightenment. These developments include the weakening of orthodox religious beliefs, new artistic and literary genres and styles, new practices of reading, new venues for political and literary discussion, new forms of fame, and new visions of warfare. Scholars of the eighteenth century have often associated these phenomena with the origins of modern liberal political phenomena such as human rights, secularism, egalitarianism, and democracy itself.[63] But there is a clear connection as well to the rise of modern charismatic politics, even to charismatic authoritarianism. In this regard, as in many others, the age of Enlightenment has a far more ambivalent legacy than we would like to think. Its advanced thinkers may have announced that humanity was finally throwing off its self-imposed subjugation to gods and kings, and their admirers have echoed this claim ever since. But this revolution of the mind did not in fact mean throwing off all forms of subjugation. Indeed, the rejection of gods and kings made it easier, not harder, for peoples around the Atlantic world to subjugate themselves willingly to apparently extraordinary men who offered themselves as saviors.

The story of these cultural developments begins in the realm of religion. Before the mid-eighteenth century, if ordinary people in the Western world felt an intense, intimate emotional bond with a person they knew only through books or images, that person was most likely a saint, preacher, or other religious figure. In the Catholic world, the cult of saints remained powerful in the eighteenth century, reinforced by the production and display of sacred art, by ritual processions, and by books that often recounted intimate personal details about the saint in question.[64] The most striking example of what we now call charisma in an early eighteenth-century Catholic society was to be found not in a royal court but in a graveyard. In 1727, a now largely forgotten French cleric named François de Pâris was interred in the cemetery of Saint-Médard on the Left Bank of Paris. While noble-born, he had devoted his life to ministering to the urban poor. A follower of the austere current of Catholic thought known as Jansenism, he also deprived himself of every comfort and rigorously scourged himself for sin, sleeping on a bare plank and wearing sharp, rusty wires under his clothing to score his flesh. He attracted a passionate following among the poor of his district, and after his death they flooded to his graveside. Soon, it was claimed, miracles were taking place there: blind men recovered their sight; lame women walked without their crutches; men and women alike felt a holy spirit take possession of them, and they shook with convulsions or had visions. Popular newssheets attested to the spectacle, closely describing the crowds who streamed to pay homage to the man they called a saint.[65]

While this sort of religious enthusiasm waned in much of Catholic Europe over the course of the eighteenth century, in Britain and America it continued straight through the age of revolution. The charismatic Methodist preachers George Whitefield and John Wesley (who died in 1770 and 1791, respectively) attracted huge crowds and passionate interest in their life stories. Whitefield was a consummate actor who acted out the part of biblical saints before his audiences, inviting them to feel the same intense passions he did. His preaching had a decisive role in launching the Great Awakening and the turn toward evangelical-ism in American Protestantism.[66]

Secular historians once told a comforting story about how, even as these waves of wild religious fervor were sweeping over much of the West, educated elites were rejecting faith for reason and embracing a secular Enlightenment whose adherents would soon come to power in the great eighteenth-century revolutions. More recent scholarship has discarded this narrative, demonstrating that supposed rationalists often thought and wrote for the greater glory of the Christian God, while the defenders of faith often engaged in daring heterodox speculation. What we now call the Enlightenment arose within Christianity as much as it did in reaction to it.[67]

Yet the structures of belief did change. Even within the established churches, speculation spread about God's withdrawal or absence from the world. Some thinkers suggested that perhaps God had never taken an active role in the affairs of humanity at all, that he had created the world, set it in motion, and then left it to whirl about on its own. A handful of provocateurs even dared to profess full-fledged atheism. To many who embraced these new ideas, traditional forms of religious observance looked like intolerant obscurantism and superstition.

But had the world really been, as historians once thought, disen-chanted, desacralized? In fact, a longing for the sacred and the supernat-ural did not disappear so easily. Even as the philosophers of the age pondered a world from which God had withdrawn, they looked for something that could take God's place as a source of ultimate meaning and perhaps as a standard of goodness. Most often they found it in what the atheist *philosophe* Baron d'Holbach called the sovereign divinity of nature. Humans, he wrote, should submit themselves utterly to nature's laws, dissolve themselves into nature as thoroughly as some Christian mystics had once sought to dissolve themselves into God.[68]

Subjecting all people to nature's law might seem a radically demo-cratic move that would place all people on the same level. But it was one thing to say that all men were created equal in the sense of having the same natural rights, and quite another to say that all men had essentially the same powers and faculties. No Enlightenment thinker would have agreed to this second proposition. To the contrary, these thinkers often had a fascination, verging on obsession, with figures to whom nature had apparently given disproportionately great abilities. For these exceptional individuals, they had an attitude that could be called reverent—perhaps even worshipful.

They fixated particularly on the figure of the genius—indeed, they helped invent it. Before the eighteenth century, as the historian Darrin M. McMahon has written, genius was most often seen as something that a person *had*. During the eighteenth century, it increasingly became something that a person *was*, from birth.[69] The thinkers of the Enlightenment described geniuses as mysterious, terrifying titans in human form whose minds managed to reach beyond the visible world and who infused otherworldly truths and passions into their creations. Printed accounts proliferated of both artistic and scientific geniuses: Homer, Shakespeare, Mozart, and of course that towering figure Isaac Newton. The astronomer Edmond Halley took to verse to hail "Newton, that reach'd the insuperable line / The nice barrier 'twixt human and divine."[70] God might have withdrawn from the world, but geniuses still managed to reach out and grasp his outstretched hand.

Both Peter the Great and Frederick the Great were frequently hailed as geniuses. Pasquale Paoli's admirers used the word less often, but they believed that, like a genius, Paoli had a mysterious, direct connection to nature that endowed him with powers denied to others. They repeatedly resorted to religious language to signify this utter exceptionality: "godlike man," "godlike prodigy," "immortal man," "savior of the land," "fir'd from heaven with energy divine."[71] Boswell used every rhetorical device he could muster to underline Paoli's extraordinary qualities. He claimed he had no more believed a man like Paoli could exist in the world than "seas of milk" or "ships of amber."[72] In short, the absence of God did not prevent the thinkers of the Enlightenment from treating certain human beings as virtually divine. And in a world where God no longer designated those who ruled, such idolization could descend on people from all walks of life.

But it was not only these changes in religious beliefs and practices that made possible the sort of charismatic authority attributed to Paoli. Other, more material developments had an important effect as well. In large states whose populations numbered in the millions, charismatic authority could not be established through personal contact alone. It depended on media—above all, the printing press.

The printing press dated back to the mid-fifteenth century, but even in the late seventeenth century, most men and women around the Atlantic world engaged with the printed word, if at all, in limited ways. Literacy rates remained low, especially for women, and everywhere government censors did their best to police the presses. Devotional religious works tended to predominate in book markets, along with large, heavy volumes of jurisprudence and theology, Roman and Greek classics, and other tomes meant to be consulted as reference works or studied slowly, intensively, and repetitively. Before 1700, itinerant booksellers did hawk cheaply bound volumes of stories and fables, and some early newspapers circulated. The volume of novels published expanded greatly toward the end of the seventeenth century, along with travel literature. Illegal, seditious pamphlets could circulate widely, especially in moments of political turmoil. But the world of print remained circumscribed.[73]

The years around 1700 marked the start of what can only be called a media revolution, although it affected the Atlantic world unevenly. In 1695, the English parliament allowed the Licensing Act, which mandated censorship of printed works, to lapse. An explosion of print quickly followed, with a particularly dramatic rise in the periodical press.[74] By the mid-eighteenth century, Great Britain had thirty-nine daily newspapers and hundreds of other papers and magazines published at regular intervals. Books appeared in vertiginously increasing numbers and at the same time took on a more secular cast. They also appeared in smaller, cheaper editions that could be easily carried in a pocket.[75] The novel established itself as the century's dominant literary genre. Literacy rates rose dramatically, especially in cities. Other areas of the Atlantic world saw less dramatic progress but still followed the powerful British example. The British American colonies had thirty-eight newspapers by 1775, as well as a rapidly expanding book market.[76] In France, Spain, and their colonial possessions, harsh censorship regimes remained in place. Yet even there, and especially in metropolitan France, the world of print still expanded and evolved dramatically—in part thanks to a thriving illicit book trade.[77] What all the changing forms of print had in common was less their multifarious content than the sort of reading they encouraged: not slow and intensive but rapid and casual. New venues arose where people could read a wide range of material without paying to own it, including coffeehouses and the first lending libraries. And some venues, including coffeehouses, learned societies, and the gatherings of high society that the French later called "salons," also encouraged discussion and debate about what was being read.

Historians long liked to imagine that this new world of print and conversation was a serious, egalitarian, proto-democratic place where rational discussion and debate generated a rigorous critique of existing power structures.[78] But this is too earnest and idealistic an interpretation of a print world that was in fact raucous, freewheeling, and frequently crude, driven as much by readers' quest for entertainment, and publishers' quest for profit, as by anyone's quest for edification and improvement. It is no coincidence that the word "pornography" was coined in the eighteenth century (one learned French literary study of the period has the title *These Books That One Reads with One Hand*).[79] The critique of existing power structures relied on obscene satire as much as it did on rational argument, and throughout the century cultural Cassandras stridently warned that the reading of novels was inducing moral weakness and decay.

This particular accusation, while absurd, did point to the fact that novels could exert a peculiarly powerful hold on their readers. The most popular novels of the century, such as Samuel Richardson's *Pamela* and Jean-Jacques Rousseau's *Julie; or, The New Eloise*, were epistolary, couched in the form of letters that the author most often claimed merely to have "discovered." As such, readers could approach them as voyeuristic glimpses into the private thoughts, experiences, and emotions of real people leading emotionally intense lives. New literary conventions encouraged readers to develop close emotional relationships to these characters through their emphasis on the quality that geniuses supposedly possessed in an especially high degree, namely, "sensibility"—a quivering sensitivity, in their very nerve endings, to the world about them. These conventions also highly valued sentimentalism, by which was meant the ability to feel and express sympathy and compassion for others.[80]

Denis Diderot, one of the leading exponents of these conventions, explained in an essay on Richardson how he thought the experience of novel-reading could change lives. Novels could create so perfect an illusion, he wrote, that readers could feel like children taken to the theater for the first time, unable to distinguish between literary artifice and reality.[81] Some readers, dutifully absorbing these lessons, seem to have formed a more intense attachment to the characters of their most beloved novels than to their own flesh and blood, reporting that the books drove them to fits of hysterical weeping or sent them into a dead faint.[82]

These new literary conventions and styles, however, did not just help readers form passionate attachments to fictional characters but to real people as well, and especially to imposing political leaders. Boswell's *Account of Corsica* provided a perfect example, for while he presented his story as faithful to actual events, he wrote much of it in the style of a melodramatic, sentimental novel. A passage describing Paoli preparing to return to Corsica from youthful exile in Naples was just one of many that gave Boswell the chance to describe an effusion of tender sentiment:

> There was something particularly affecting, in his parting from his father; the old man, hoary and gray with years, fell on his neck, and kissed him, gave him his blessing, and with a broken feeble voice, encouraged him in the undertaking, on which he was entering; "my son," said he, "I may, possibly, never see you more; but in my mind, I shall be ever present with you."[83]

Boswell described Paoli comforting ordinary Corsicans in ways that "touched my heart in the most sensible manner," and he presented the Corsicans themselves as a people possessing "an exquisite degree of sensibility." He cast Paoli himself as a perfect eighteenth-century man of feeling, quoting him saying, "I act from sentiment, not from reasonings."[84] The emphasis placed by Frederick the Great's admirers on the love that bound him to his subjects reflected the same literary emphasis on sentiment and sensibility.

There was another literary genre whose remarkable transformation in the eighteenth century even more directly helped readers imagine connections with real people they did not personally know: biography. This genre itself of course dated back to antiquity (Plutarch being the most prominent ancient practitioner). Lives of kings, commanders, and saints had all long functioned as *exempla* for readers to learn from and emulate. They provided moral instruction, testimony to the glories of the kingdom and the faith, and occasionally (think Suetonius on Caligula) a catalogue of entertaining horrors to be avoided. In France, the Académie Française actively promoted the essay-length biographical eulogy as an instrument of patriotic edification, with the result that moralizing, and often horrifically dull, *éloges* proliferated, along with scores of volumes recounting the lives of the "great men of the fatherland."[85]

In the eighteenth century, the number of biographies in print exploded, as illustrated by the number devoted to Peter the Great. In addition, the genre changed in important ways.[86] While kings remained popular subjects, biographers became more egalitarian in their choice of subjects, opting also to write about lawyers, doctors, artists and writers, scientists, even master criminals. Second, they turned more present-minded, increasingly choosing their subjects from among the living or the very recently deceased. It was in this period that autobiography, with its emphasis on providing a full self-portrait, separated itself from the arts of memoir-writing and religious apologia—notably thanks to those two remarkable practitioners of the genre, Benjamin Franklin and Jean-Jacques Rousseau.

Finally, and most importantly, the goal of the exercise shifted. Earlier

biographies, especially those that presented their subjects as noble examples to be emulated, emphasized public behavior and the way the
biographical subjects approximated an ideal type: the wise king, the
gallant warrior, the holy bishop. The French *éloges* largely continued in
this vein through the eighteenth century. The "great men" they celebrated conformed in most cases to a single recognizable type: the
selfless—indeed often self-abnegating—benefactor of humanity in general and the French kingdom in particular. But increasingly, biographers tried to stress their subjects' individuality, to paint them as unique
characters whose public actions grew out of their unique personalities,
and they did so by putting new emphasis on private, intimate scenes.
"The business of a biographer," wrote Samuel Johnson, is "to lead the
thoughts into domestic privacies, and display the minute details of daily
life."[87] Johnson's friend Boswell put this lesson into practice in his portrait
of Paoli, then perfected it with his biography of Johnson himself. Like
the sentimental novels, biographies offered readers a new and strikingly
powerful way of creating an imagined but emotionally intense relationship with a character they knew only on the printed page—in this case, a
real one.

The media revolution of the eighteenth century not only gave ordinary people many new ways of reading about public figures but also
changed the process of reading itself, and this shift had political implications as well. The new volume of printed matter available, in the form
of periodicals, pamphlets, and small, cheaply bound books, meant that
readers were less likely to read single texts intensively, over and over
again, than many different texts.[88] This made a difference in how they
would form a bond with people they knew only on the page. After first
coming across Paoli in Boswell's book, for instance, they might then
follow his exploits, and read verse dedicated to him, in newspapers and
magazines. The British newspapers printed Paoli's own public letters
and even reported on his victories and defeats within a few weeks of
the events themselves. Between 1750 and 1770, the name Paoli appeared
in British newspapers more than three thousand times and in North

American ones nearly two thousand times.[89] Paoli became, in other words, a living, changing presence in readers' lives.

But it was not only through printed words that figures like Pasquale Paoli came to the public's attention. During the eighteenth century, innovations took place in the technology of engraving that allowed the printing of many copies of an image from a single plate. New engravings appeared in profusion: in Paris, between 1764 and 1782, at the rate of seventy-two a year. A high proportion were portraits, and most of the portraits depicted contemporaries. They sold for as little as one French pound or, in Britain, a single shilling, a sum well within the reach of moderately well-off artisans and shopkeepers. Of eighteenth-century Parisians wealthy enough to have an inventory of their property compiled at their death—a majority of the city's population—more than half appear to have owned engravings.[90] Monarchs like Frederick the Great appeared in scores of eighteenth-century engravings. Paoli, whose period of fame lasted only a few years, still appeared in at least sixteen, including at least eleven produced for the British market. The artists likely indulged their imaginations when it came to Paoli's appearance, for they mostly had no idea what he actually looked like. But all presented a man with distinct, pleasant features and a heroic, determined expression (for examples, see figure 6).[91]

This proliferation of images, along with the intensive coverage in the periodical press, and the curiosity about leaders' private lives, bring us to a quintessentially modern phenomenon born out of the eighteenth-century media revolution: leaders were becoming celebrities. We generally associate "celebrity culture" with the twentieth century, but it goes back much further. The historian Antoine Lilti has noted that the word "celebrity" took on its modern meaning precisely in the middle of the eighteenth century. What he calls the "mechanisms of celebrity," while nowhere near as powerful as in our own day, already operated in recognizable form. Ordinary members of the reading public were coming to treat famous actors, musicians, writers, soldiers, and political figures as personal acquaintances, boasting familiarity with intimate details of their private lives. Voltaire and Rousseau attracted huge followings, with thousands of admirers bombarding them and their publishers with correspondence, while the details of their highly irregular private lives (including Voltaire's sexual relationship with his niece, as well as Rousseau's abandonment of five children to orphanages) became grist for hundreds of publications.

Modern charismatic leadership could not have arisen without these mechanisms of celebrity. The intensity of the bond that a charismatic leader's followers felt was nourished by the same proliferation of details and images present in celebrity culture. And along with the sort of passionate, intimate attachment that sentimental novels taught readers to feel for characters they knew only on the page, the mechanisms of celebrity made it possible for followers to play a very different role than had their predecessors in earlier periods. A modern charismatic leader's followers may see him as superhuman, but even so, they do not follow him passively, obediently, like the faceless "people" who were imagined to have professed their subservient love for a monarch like Louis XIV. These modern followers cheer their heroes on, applaud, and hope above all for some individual mark of recognition that the leader might bestow upon them. As Boswell wrote, breathlessly, about Paoli: "He took me by the hand, and said, as a friend."[92] For the follower of a charismatic leader, as for the devoted fan of a celebrity, there can be no more ecstatic a moment. And for the leader himself, there can be no more important a moment than the moment of freely given applause. His appeal, his charisma, and ultimately his power depend on it.

Political celebrity first emerged in the country that led the century's media revolution and that did the most to turn Pasquale Paoli into an international icon: Great Britain. As early as 1710, the Tory clergyman Henry Sacheverell had attracted widespread attention and fanatical support after the House of Commons condemned him for his attacks against dissident Protestants.[93] In the early 1740s, it was the turn of Admiral Edward Vernon, who, after winning a major victory, became the subject of thousands of articles, verses, and printed ballads.[94] George Washington's half brother, who served under the admiral, named the family estate Mount Vernon in his honor. By the mid-century, the French had joined the British in generating masses of printed material celebrating military heroes.[95]

Then, in the 1760s, the extraordinary radical politician John Wilkes demonstrated the full political potential of celebrity culture. A poor public speaker, with jagged teeth, crossed eyes, and terrible personal hygiene, Wilkes was not an obvious candidate for public adoration, although he had a passion for expanding the restricted British suffrage and for freedom of speech. But he was a born showman with a genius for provocation, for publicity, and for inserting his own outrageous personality into political conflict. Repeatedly jailed for his attacks on the government, repeatedly refused membership in the House of Commons despite winning elections, he became a popular hero. He called on his followers to show their support, and they in turn not only adored him but treated him as a personal friend in their letters and conversation. These supporters also became a commercial market for savvy entrepreneurs who sold them images of Wilkes and the slogan "Wilkes and Liberty" on everything from handbills to handkerchiefs to medals and crockery.[96] Admirers named children for him—including, many decades later, a British-born American actor who christened his son John Wilkes Booth. It was radical "Wilkite" Whigs who first seized on Paoli as an incarnation of liberty and often compared the two men (who in fact heartily disliked each other).[97] But if the vogue for Paoli owed much to Wilkes's example, in some crucial respects it went further.[98] Wilkes's supporters did not celebrate him for any supposedly superhuman gifts, still less call him a man who might have stepped out of the pages of Plutarch. They did not hail Wilkes as the incarnation of the British nation or think of him as a potential national leader. While Wilkes's celebrity exceeded Paoli's, his charisma was decidedly more limited.

Changing attitudes toward warfare, and military heroism, also put a stamp on the new charisma. For a time, it seemed that the allure of war might fade away entirely during the Enlightenment. The greatest writers of the age, their hope trumping their experience, frequently disparaged war as a relic of humanity's primitive, violent past, a relic that would surely disappear in modern times. No less an icon of the Enlightenment than Voltaire insisted that mere "despoilers of provinces" could not be truly great men.[99] Even George Washington could muse, after the American Revolutionary War, that it was time for peaceful pursuits to "supersede the waste of war and the rage of conquest."[100] The growing market for laudatory biographies of nonmilitary figures reflected this shift.

Yet the allure of military glory did not evaporate so easily. European states still devoted the lion's share of their budgets to war, and sovereigns still made military success central to their public images. European monarchs continued to appear personally on battlefields, while male members of the nobility gravitated to the military more frequently than to any other career. Meanwhile, elite European men still spent much of their educations reading Greek and Roman classics that celebrated military valor and that closely associated the health and virtue of a society with its ability to conquer.

During the Enlightenment, even as some thinkers hopefully predicted the end of war, many of them simultaneously lamented the prospect. Jean-Jacques Rousseau wrote longingly about the martial glories of Sparta, while even Immanuel Kant, who famously composed a plan for perpetual peace among nations, also asserted that "war has something sublime in it . . . By contrast, a long peace generally brings about . . . low selfishness, cowardice, and effeminacy."[101] The German author Wilhelm von Humboldt presented combat as the ultimate experience, one that revealed the deepest truths about humanity and one in which human actions could achieve the highest degree of beauty.[102] For these authors, in short, war had a transcendent—indeed, almost a sacred—character that contributed to the charismatic aura of its practitioners. Soldiers also, of course, remained exemplars of discipline and selflessness and powerful symbols of sheer human strength and vitality. Nothing could be better calculated to elicit passionate, quasi-erotic responses to a charismatic leader than the courage and physical skill he displayed on the battlefield. It was hardly surprising, then, that if any word in the

eighteenth century conveyed something of the meaning we today associate with "charisma," it was "glory" (although it most often referred to
a person's deeds rather than to innate qualities).[103]

Put together, the cultural transformations I have surveyed, taking
place in tandem with the spread of belief in popular sovereignty,
created the possibility for ordinary people to see political figures in a
radically new way. They could now imagine that they knew these figures
personally and intimately and could feel a powerful emotional connection to them—a connection heightened by their sense of the figures'
sublime, transcendent, extraordinary qualities. In keeping with prevailing theories of sensibility, the contemplation of an adored figure was
even seen as capable of eliciting a strong physical reaction. "When you
see a portrait of our most famous Hero," a French author wrote about
George Washington in 1789, "do you feel your chest tremble under
your hand? Does your eye grow wet with sweet and precious tears? Do
your cheeks flush with the fire of admiration?"[104] Boswell claimed to
have reacted so powerfully to Paoli's professions of friendship that he
hinted coyly at a forbidden passion: "I dare not transcribe from my
private notes the feelings which I had at this interview. I should perhaps
appear too enthusiastic."[105] Paoli was an object of desire.

I do not mean to suggest that Paoli's male admirers had what would
now be called a homosexual attraction to him.[106] The category "homosexual" makes little sense for this period, and men could feel intense attraction to other men without the intention to consummate it sexually. It is
absurd, here as elsewhere, to reduce the mysteries and complexities of
longing and desire, shaped by both innate drives and complex social
norms, to nothing but sex. Indeed, the fierce strictures against "sodomy"
that prevailed in the eighteenth century, and the assumption of its "unnat-
ural" character, paradoxically allowed men publicly to express an attraction to other men in erotically charged language without raising what we
would now call questions about their sexual orientation.[107] The sentimental novels of the period overflow with men declaring passionate love for

one another—as friends, comrades, or "brothers"—in language that reads as far more sexually suggestive today than it did at the time.

We cannot know how many readers actually experienced such erotically charged reactions to charismatic leaders, but everywhere these readers looked, cultural signposts instructed them that it was normal and natural to have these reactions. As a result, it came to seem normal and natural that especially dynamic, transformative political figures should have the ability to elicit powerful emotional reactions from their supporters. In earlier periods, to the extent that political power was linked to extreme emotion, it was above all through a ruler's ability to paralyze enemies with fear.[108] Now, for their charismatic successors, the emotion in question had changed. Domination, as Boswell and the admirers of Frederick the Great implied, was to be achieved through love.

This love was one that specifically had powerful masculine figures as its object. Some of the changes I have discussed in this chapter did, arguably, work, in the long run, to promote sexual equality. Sentimental novels, for instance, through their sympathetic treatment of female characters, helped instill the belief that women as well as men possessed certain basic rights.[109] But women could not command men in battle, and they could not pose as the potent progenitors of their nations. Nor could women appear so easily in the private, intimate moments that were so important to the new charismatic bond, or provoke erotic desire, without appearing indecent. The eighteenth century had its share of female celebrities, including Catherine the Great of Russia and Marie-Antoinette, but the conditions of celebrity culture made it almost impossible for them to appear sublimely heroic and virtuous in the way that men like Paoli did.[110] Paoli, with what Boswell called his "manly and noble carriage," exemplified the eighteenth-century ideal of strong, courageous, confident, and self-controlled masculinity.[111]

Until 1775, when the first of the great Atlantic revolutions began in Lexington, the new forms of charismatic leadership illustrated by the vogue for Pasquale Paoli still existed only as visions. While readers throughout the Western world might sigh over Paoli's fate, no one seen as comparable to him had yet come to power in a major Western state. Paoli's moment of fame mattered mostly for what it revealed about how the political culture of the Western world was changing, and about the forms of leadership that could now excite widespread public enthusiasm.

Yet this episode did have a few tantalizing, direct consequences for the age of revolution. One set of these played out in Corsica itself and, more particularly, in the family of a prominent lawyer named Carlo Buonaparte, who, unlike Paoli, decided to stay in Corsica and make his peace with his new French overlords. His second son, although dispatched to France at an early age to train for a military career, grew up a passionate believer both in Corsican independence and in Paoli. When just fifteen, he wrote his father from his military school in France, asking for a copy of Boswell's *Account of Corsica*, and he seems to have read it closely (in his adolescent writings, he referred to many of the incidents Boswell recounted and gave the same mistaken date for Paoli's birth found in the Italian translation of Boswell).[112] Just before the French Revolution, he even wrote to Paoli himself. "General," began the young man who would soon style himself Napoleon Bonaparte, "I was born when the fatherland perished."[113] He would soon meet Paoli in the flesh, and there followed, in 1793, their spectacular break. But as Stendhal later wrote: "Paoli was the model and image for all the future life of Napoleon."[114]

Nor did Paoli entirely fade away on the other side of the Atlantic. At the start of the American Revolution, several newspapers reprinted his most-cited public letter from a decade earlier, calling its "noble ardor and sentiment" an inspiration for every American.[115] In 1778, a Maryland paper reprinted without attribution a long selection from Anna Barbauld's well-known British poem about Corsica but slyly substituted the name Washington for that of the Corsican leader.[116] And as late as 1780, newspapers in New Jersey and Connecticut again reprinted the verse praising Paoli in Boswell's *Account of Corsica*, with the editors adding the following note of explanation: "The character of the above General [Paoli], and that of our illustrious Commander in Chief, are so similar, that the following selected lines made on the former are well adapted and very applicable to the latter—only for the words CORSICA and PAOLI, substitute AMERICA and WASHINGTON."[117]

TWO

AMERICAN IDOL

I have been distressed to see some of our members disposed to idolize an image which their own hands have molten. I speak here of the superstitious veneration which is paid to General Washington.

—John Adams to the Continental Congress, 1777

General Washington entered Philadelphia on his way to Congress . . . Children, men and women expressed as much happiness and satisfaction as if the Savior had entered Jerusalem!

—Diary of Francisco de Miranda, 1784

I n the fall of 1776, it looked as if the United States of America would not survive to its first birthday. Just a few months before, during the intoxicating, independence-declaring days of early July, the military situation had seemed favorable. The recently formed Continental Army had forced the British to withdraw from Boston, leaving nearly all the new nation free of enemy occupation. But then, in August, the inexperienced Continentals faced seasoned British regulars for the first time in a large-scale battle, in Brooklyn. The American commanders first mistook the British attack there for a feint and failed to commit sufficient troops. They then let the British outflank them, and a large number of the American soldiers panicked and ran as soon as the first shots rang out. The result was a calamitous defeat. The Americans retreated across the East River to Manhattan and then, over the next weeks and months, retreated farther: across the Hudson to New Jersey, then across the Delaware to Pennsylvania. The British occupied New York, the strategically located second-largest American city, taking thousands of American prisoners as they did so. As other soldiers reached the end of their enlistments or simply gave up and left for home, the American forces dwindled to just 10 percent of their summertime strength.[1] Already in late September the American commander in chief told a cousin, "I never was in such an unhappy, divided state since I was born."[2] By late November, a British lieutenant was boasting to a Boston loyalist, "Their army is broken all to pieces . . . I think one may venture to pronounce that it is well nigh over with them."[3] In December, Thomas Paine put out the first issue of *The American Crisis*, which opened with the famous words "These are the times that try men's souls."[4] Devotees of Shakespeare—a category that included most of the American leadership at the time—might well have thought back to Henry V's description of his army on the eve of Agincourt: "Even as men wrecked upon a sand, that look to be washed off the next tide."[5]

In these desperate circumstances, some on the American side were quick to blame the men in charge of military operations. John Adams, who chaired the committee of the Continental Congress overseeing the army, bitterly quipped to his wife in October that "in general, our generals were out-generalled."[6] From within the top ranks of the armed forces, the sharpest criticisms landed on the carefully powdered head of one man in particular. Five days after the last American troops fled across the Hudson to Fort Lee in November, Adjutant General Joseph Reed wrote to General Charles Lee, portraying their commander in chief in scathing terms: "Oh! [. . .]—an indecisive mind is one of the greatest misfortunes that can befall an army."[7] Lee replied that he shared this opinion and then in December put an even harsher appraisal into a letter to General Horatio Gates: "*Entre nous*," he wrote, "a certain great man is most damnably deficient . . . Unless something which I do not expect turns up we are lost."[8]

One might assume that these accusatory sentiments were widely shared. Few societies have much tolerance for military failure, and just within the previous twenty years a British admiral and a French general had both earned death sentences for the unpardonable crimes of losing major engagements.[9] General Lee might reasonably have expected himself to float upward on a tide of public anger that would simultaneously engulf the man apparently responsible for the American reverses: George Washington.

Instead, something remarkable took place. Despite the scale and severity of the reverses, Washington's reputation in the general public suffered no harm—to the contrary, it flourished. From the moment he had taken command of the American forces in July 1775, he had been greeted with a torrent of adulation. Ships were named for him and his wife—at least fifteen by the end of 1776—and so were six towns, starting with Washington, Massachusetts. Children were given his name, while thousands of copies of printed portraits circulated. His face even appeared on handkerchiefs widely advertised in the newspapers.[10] Harvard gave Washington an honorary degree, and when he arrived in New York in the spring of 1776, more people turned out to see him than had ever gathered together in the city.[11] Poets and songwriters competed to sound his praises. Already in 1775 Jonathan Mitchell Sewall had composed verses, to be sung to the tune of "The British Grenadiers," whose chorus ended with praise for "glorious Washington," "conquering Washington," "great Washington," even "God-like Washington."[12] Phillis Wheatley, the enslaved African-American poet, hailed Washington with words that would make him distinctly uneasy, by seeming to promise him a monarchy:

> Proceed, great chief, with virtue on thy side,
> Thy ev'ry action let the goddess guide.
> A crown, a mansion, and a throne that shine,
> With gold unfading, WASHINGTON! be thine.[13]

In mid-1776, a New Jersey family rewrote the anthem "God Save the King" with the words "God Save great Washington . . . God damn the King!"[14]

The works praising Washington enjoyed great popularity, and the calamities of 1776 did nothing to stem the flood. The desperate autumn of that year saw the publication of yet more adoring poetry, expressions of support, portraits, and a play called *The Fall of British Tyranny*, which featured Washington as a lead character. Written by a well-to-do Philadelphian named John Leacock and performed at various times during the next decade, the play contrasted heroic, masculine Americans to effete and ineffectual British officers and ended with Washington solemnly proclaiming, "I have drawn my sword, and never will I sheathe it, till America is free, or I'm no more."[15] Even as the defeated and depleted Continental Army withdrew across New Jersey, American newspapers do not seem to have published a single line of serious criticism of Washington—certainly nothing to compare with the complaints privately voiced by Adams, Reed, and Lee. No other general in the army received anything like this degree of attention and praise.

Then American fortunes recovered, and the waves of praise became a tsunami. At the start of the winter, Washington carried out his famous crossing of the Delaware River, and in a surprise Christmas Day attack the Continental Army overcame a garrison of Hessian mercenaries in Trenton. Nine days later he defeated a divided British force at Princeton. Within days, newspapers across the country were hailing the glorious victories and delivering hyperbolic paeans to (as one anonymous Philadelphia poet put it) "the immortal Washington" who could "rise a hero, and . . . tower a God."[16] A Virginian author proudly compared Washington favorably to the greatest heroes of the Roman Republic and named him the "deliverer and guardian genius" of America.[17] A member of Congress, in a private letter, called him "the greatest man on earth."[18] By mid-February, the delegate and poet Francis Hopkinson could write: "The title of Excellency is applied [to Washington] with the greatest propriety . . . If there are spots in his character they are like the spots in the sun; only discernable by the magnifying powers of a telescope. Had he lived in the days of idolatry, he had been worshipped as a god. One age cannot do justice to his merit."[19]

At first glance, much of this praise seems to belong to an earlier, religious era of charisma. Continuities from this earlier era certainly existed—not surprisingly, given the strength of Protestant belief in colonies initially settled in many cases by fervent religious refugees, and following the first Great Awakening. But the language itself suggests the limits to these continuities. When authors described Washington as a "god" or "savior," they, of course, were not speaking literally. It would have been blasphemous to do so. They saw his status as analogous to, rather than actually, divine. Acolytes of Oliver Cromwell in mid-seventeenth-century England rarely described their idol in such terms, although they had believed quite literally in his divine mission. And praise for Washington as a classical hero reborn was just as common.

Washington would not always remain on top of Olympus, venerated like an idol. During the years of his presidency and the birth of a party politics that could rival or even exceed that of our own day in its viciousness, squawks of criticism threatened to drown out the hallelujahs, despite Washington's extraordinary reputation. But for many years after 1776, the chorus of praise would continue to swell. After Washington's retirement from the presidency in 1797 and his death in 1799, it would become deafening. But the basic pattern was already set in 1776—and this fact is somewhat puzzling.

Even 240 years later, it is easy to take this initial surge of idolatry for granted—to see it as an obvious recognition of Washington's actual greatness. After all, since his death Washington has remained very much a demigod for most Americans, with the capital city, a state, and hundreds of institutions named for him, his image appearing on coins and bills, not to mention monuments and statues scattered through major cities. Unlike in the case of Thomas Jefferson, his ownership of slaves has not badly tarnished his halo—even after revelations that his famous dentures were made not from wood but from human (almost certainly slaves') teeth and that he implacably hunted down his own fugitive slaves.[20] He does, admittedly, seem a rather stiff and formal demigod. "Did anyone ever see Washington naked?" Nathaniel Hawthorne once wrote. "It is inconceivable. He had no nakedness, but, I imagine, was born with his clothes on and his hair powdered, and made a stately bow on his first appearance in the world."[21] Even so, Washington leaves even many of those who study him professionally in awe. The historian Gordon Wood calls him "an extraordinary heroic man" who towered above "more ordinary mortals."[22] The biographer Richard Brookhiser insists that "we are not willing enough" to "be awed" by Washington.[23]

Certainly, Washington often dazzled those who met him in person—especially in northern states unaccustomed to the sight of elegant Virginian aristocrats. He was tall (six feet, three inches) and physically strong, with handsome features and graceful movements. He dressed in an impeccably elegant style and, of course, rode horses superbly. He spoke plainly and with an appealing modesty and reserve. His first encounter with a starstruck Abigail Adams left her misquoting Dryden to her husband: "He's a temple / Sacred by birth, and built by hands divine" (the words were actually written about a woman).[24] A young physician from Cape Cod, James Thacher, who met him in 1775, found it "not difficult to distinguish him from all others; his personal appearance is truly noble and majestic, being tall and well proportioned."[25] Thacher later described Washington in professional detail, noting "the strength and proportion of his joints and muscles . . . the serenity of his countenance . . . [the] majestic gracefulness of his deportment . . . the fine symmetry in the features of his face."[26] The Philadelphia physician and congressional delegate Benjamin Rush likewise discerned "so much martial dignity in his deportment, that . . . there is not a king in Europe but would look like a valet de chambre by his side."[27] In November 1776, a Long Island woman named Lydia Post anxiously wrote her army officer husband about the poor military outlook. But she immediately added, "I confess a womanly admiration of a noble exterior. Washington's influence and authority must be enhanced by his gallant bearing and commanding figure."[28] In other words, Washington certainly looked the part of a heroic savior.

We have to remember, though, that until the last days of 1776 the American commander had, as yet, done relatively little to justify the enormous confidence and the even more enormous hope that Americans were investing in him. He had been born, in 1732, into a moderately wealthy family of slave-owning Virginia gentry. Ambition and a taste for adventure led him to work as a surveyor in wilderness areas of the colony and then to take a commission as a British militia officer. His first experience of war, though, was anything but glorious. In 1754 a small detachment under his command opened fire on French troops in the Ohio Valley, unintentionally sparking hostilities that would soon explode into the worldwide conflict between the French and British empires known as the Seven Years' War. Two months later, the French defeated and captured Washington and his men and forced him to sign a statement admitting he had "assassinated" a peaceful French envoy. A concerted French propaganda campaign excoriated him as a monster and a villain (when France became Washington's ally twenty-four years later, the incident was tactfully forgotten).[29] Washington made up for this potentially career-ending disaster only by courageously leading the retreat after the ambush of British forces and the death of General Braddock in the Battle of the Monongahela in 1755.

By 1775, he had ascended into the highest ranks of Virginian society. Soon after the end of the Seven Years' War he retired from the militia, acquired vast wealth through his marriage to Martha Custis, and settled into the life of a gentleman squire. A diligent, sober, and serious man who consciously modeled himself after the stern Roman republicans portrayed in Joseph Addison's play *Cato*, he gained respect from leaders of the colony. But he lacked the fiery oratorical skills of a Patrick Henry or the mercurial brilliance of a Thomas Jefferson. After taking command of the Continental Army in 1775, he had his victory at Boston to his credit. Still, as his subordinates recognized, he also deserved much of the blame for the catastrophic defeat in Brooklyn. He subsequently did his best to keep the army together. He brought strong organizational skills, derived from his experience as a plantation owner, to the task.[30] The results, by the late fall of 1776, were nonetheless anything but inspiring.

The simple fact, though, is that Americans were desperate for a

"great man" and convinced themselves—for the moment without much
evidence—that they had found him in the physically dazzling Washington. The burgeoning cult of the commander in chief derived less from
his own achievements, then, than from the longings of his fellow citizens. Looking back thirty-six years later, John Adams reflected on this
process with unusual insight:

> The great Character, was a *Character of Convention* . . . There was a
> time when . . . Statesmen, and . . . Officers of The Army, expressly
> agreed to blow the Trumpets of Panegyrick in concert; to cover and
> dissemble all Faults and Errors; to represent every defeat as a Vic-
> tory, and every Retreat as an Advancement; to make that Character
> popular and fashionable, with all Parties in all places and with all
> Persons, as a Centre of Union, as the Central Stone in the Geomet-
> rical Arch. There you have the Revelation of the whole Mystery.
> Something of the same kind has occurred in France and has pro-
> duced a Napoleon and his Empire.[31]

The short, tubby, balding Adams certainly felt twinges of jealousy
toward Washington (which could not have been helped by his wife's
gushing reaction to the Virginian). As late as 1807 he was writing, with
barbed humor, that Washington's principal talents were "a handsome
face," "tall stature," "an elegant form," and "graceful attitudes and move-
ments."[32] He also called Washington "too illiterate, unlearned, unread
for his Station and reputation."[33] But the jealousy helped him to see
something that most of his countrymen missed.

The longings for a savior figure were entirely understandable. Just
consider the enormous anxieties felt by most white Americans at this
moment in their history. They were taking up arms against a country
that they had, until very recently, considered their own—against a king
whom they had, until very recently, revered as a father figure.[34] They
knew that if they lost the war, they would face harsh penalties, up to and
including execution as traitors for the leaders. They were fighting the
most powerful empire in the world and as yet had no foreign allies.

Their new nation consisted of thirteen colonies that differed markedly in social systems, cultural practices, religion, and even forms of speech—indeed, that sometimes seemed to have little other than the independence struggle itself in common. The promise that a man endowed with extraordinary abilities could come to their rescue was irresistible.

Just as important, the cultural changes discussed in the previous chapter had given them alluring new ways of imagining heroic political leadership. The groundswell of adulation for Washington that began as soon as he took command of the Continental Army in 1775 followed closely on the patterns already established in previous decades around earlier popular idols—especially Pasquale Paoli. Engraved images of the sternly determined hero in elegant military dress circulated in much the same fashion. There was the same proliferation of these images in every available medium, including handkerchiefs and crockery. There was the same naming of objects, and even children, for the hero. Eighteenth-century Americans delighted in making elaborate toasts, and the same people who had toasted Paoli in the 1760s now toasted Washington.[35] Most important, the voluminous articles, poems, and songs of praise employed much the same language (in some cases, as we have seen, quite literally). The hero was presented as impossibly virtuous and impossibly talented (a "genius"). He was credited with powerful masculine strength and impressively masculine self-command. He was compared to the great foundational figures of the Roman Republic and also, in this devout and largely Protestant country, to biblical heroes (Washington frequently received the sobriquet of the American Moses or the American Joshua).[36] Indeed, his devotees did not shrink from calling him "godlike," sacralizing him even as they were founding a firmly secular republic. In short, the Americans eagerly slotted Washington into a preexisting role born out of eighteenth-century cultural change.

This role was, crucially, not that of a substitute king. Of course, the emerging cult of Washington had some monarchical overtones, whether in the case of Phillis Wheatley promising a crown or in the rewriting of the song "God Save the King." Recent scholarship has emphasized the breadth and depth of popular royalism in America before the Revolution.[37] But the very essence of revolutionary moments such as the one America lived through in 1776 is that reverence—for a monarchy, for a social order, for a church—can turn to revulsion with frightening speed. Many American revolutionaries still hoped, even after the outbreak of hostilities, that their heretofore beloved King George might still side with them against Parliament, or at least restore peace. When he spurned their entreaties, they turned against him with a blind fury, destroying royal coats of arms, defacing paintings and engravings, and tearing down the massive equestrian gilded-lead statue of the king that stood on Bowling Green in Manhattan, impaling its head on a fence pole and melting down the rest for some 42,000 bullets.[38] The Declaration of Independence, of course, consists in large part of a bill of indictment against the king.

Indeed, so radical was this moment that the revolutionaries turned not just against a specific king but against the institution of monarchy itself.[39] Thomas Paine's *Common Sense*, by far the most popular of all the tracts published in the American Revolution, put the case blisteringly: "But where says some is the King of America? I'll tell you Friend, he reigns above." Paine also asserted that it was "sinful to acknowledge any being under that title but the Lord of Hosts."[40] Many others repeated the sentiment, such as the prominent Boston lawyer Benjamin Hichborn, who declaimed in a public oration that God alone "is fit to be a MONARCH."[41] John Adams hoped that Americans would "renounce some of our Monarchical Corruptions, and become Republicans in Principle, in Sentiment, in feeling and in Practice."[42] These were the dominant American sentiments toward monarchy at precisely the moment the cult of Washington was taking shape and floating upward like an untethered balloon. Washington's admirers saw in him what Europeans and Americans alike had previously seen in Pasquale Paoli: not a monarch, anointed by God to rule, but a revolutionary hero endowed by nature with extraordinary qualities. Benjamin Rush's comment that any king would look like a servant next to Washington perfectly illustrates this shift.

How far did the cult of Washington extend? Given its dependence on print media, its scope was at least partly circumscribed by the limits of literacy and by the circulation of printed matter. Since American printing presses were heavily concentrated in northern urban areas with close to universal white adult male literacy (these areas had, at the time, the highest literacy rates in the world), this cult of a rural southerner ironically looked strongest in northern cities (well over 80 percent of revolutionary newspapers appeared in the northern states).[43] Evidence as to the cult's impact on ordinary people also comes largely from literate men and women whose letters and diaries have survived. This material, too, is largely white, northern, and urban. Printed matter of course circulated outside these areas and could reach the illiterate and partially literate through oral transmission, notably in church sermons. But for the period of the Revolution, we have little evidence for how Washington's image made its way outside northern, urban, literate circuits (there is dramatically more documentation for the 1790s).

Still, the circulation of the image in these circuits mattered enormously, and the printed texts could have a compelling impact, especially when they drew on arguments and imagery that were already well established in the culture. The often-quoted sales figure of 500,000 copies for *Common Sense* is a wild exaggeration, but copious evidence still points to the pamphlet's crucial effect in persuading Americans to complete the break with Great Britain.[44] "If you know the author of COMMON SENSE," an anonymous Marylander wrote to *The Pennsylvania Evening Post* in the language of scripture, "tell him he has done wonders and worked miracles, [and] . . . made a great number of converts here."[45] As for the impact of the newspapers, consider what a British staff officer reported to the Secretary of State for the Colonies in 1776: "Among other engines, which have raised the present commotions none has had a more extensive or stronger influence than the Newspapers . . . One is astonished to see with what Avidity they are sought after, and how implicitly they are believed by the great Bulk of the People."[46] Overall, the American press played a role comparable to that of its European counterparts.

The early American cult of Washington did differ from European precedents in one important respect. Despite the burgeoning periodical press, America still had a much less developed celebrity culture than Western Europe. There were as yet no American actors whose fame could compete with that of London's much-lionized David Garrick, no American writers with reputations comparable to Voltaire's or Rousseau's, and of course America entirely lacked the gleaming spectacle of a court society, with aristocrats on permanent preening display. In America's relatively subdued public sphere, ordinary people did not yet peer with anything like the intensity of Western Europeans into the private lives of public figures.[47] Before 1776, only one American regularly received the sort of glaring media attention that European-style celebrities did: Benjamin Franklin. Americans lavished him with praise for his writings, his inventions, and his defense of American rights. But Franklin's pioneering *Autobiography*, with its intimate glimpses of his own private life, was not published in his lifetime, and relatively little of the American press coverage pried into his private affairs.[48]

For these reasons, the attention paid to Washington in the early years of the Revolution included very few Boswell-like glimpses of the private man. Nearly all the printed accounts of his life and character from before 1780 were in fact published in Britain, not America.[49] The first lengthy biographical sketch, by John Bell, appeared only in 1780, in London.[50] The closest thing to sensational revelations about Washington at the time came in the British, and American loyalist, press—for instance, the false news that Washington's wife had left him because of her loyalty to the British crown, or that his (nonexistent) daughter had fled to Britain after the death of her loyalist lover. A series of forged letters was published in which Washington seemed to condemn the American cause.[51]

Washington himself, throughout his public life, consciously resisted the early stirrings of American celebrity culture. He did understand the importance of a public image. During the French and Indian War he had been enormously impressed by splendidly attired French and British officers who considered all of public life a kind of aristocratic performance.[52] A keen devotee of the theater, he well understood the power of consummate acting and a well-delivered speech. But both his reserved temperament and his sense of what sober republican leadership demanded led him to shun familiarity or, indeed, any attention to his private life. He willingly sat for many hours for portrait painters he trusted to convey a sense of dignity and self-command (first Charles Willson Peale and then Gilbert Stuart). He let Joseph Wright oil his face and then cover it with plaster to make a lifelike mask, shocking Martha when she walked in on the proceedings.[53] But he disliked the often crude images that circulated in other media.[54] The result of this attitude was the stiff public image that Hawthorne mocked and that differs considerably from the much warmer private person who figures in the memoirs of his friends and close associates.

The mechanisms of celebrity would catch Washington in their gears soon enough, despite his objections. But even without this element of modern charisma yet in place, the extent and intensity of Washington's charismatic appeal still amounted to something new in the Western world. Paoli's charismatic reputation had taken shape largely outside his own country. British objects of adulation like Admiral Vernon and John Wilkes were not potential leaders of their nation. Washington, of course, did not hold supreme political office during the Revolutionary War. But already in 1776 he had become, along with Franklin, one of the two most famous, most admired, and most celebrated Americans who had ever lived. And of the two, only Washington was treated as a godlike savior (the tubby, bespectacled, seventy-year-old Franklin hardly fit this particular part).

Washington's extraordinary and unprecedented charismatic status posed a serious challenge for the newborn American republic. Just how far would Americans follow their savior? Would their love for him override their commitment to republican government? Throughout 1776, American orators warned against the rise of, as a New Jersey doctor named Ebenezer Elmer put it, "some factious and aspiring demagogue, possessed of popular talents and shining qualities, a Julius Caesar or an Oliver Cromwell."[55] At the end of the year, after the Continental

Congress voted Washington extraordinary powers for six months to raise money, supplies, and men, rumors quickly spread that it had abdicated all its power to him. "It's further said that Gen. Washington is appointed sole dictator," the Philadelphia pharmacist Christopher Marshall recorded in his diary.[56] Speakers in the British House of Commons started referring to Washington as the "Dictator of America," while loyalist newspapers in New York began to call him by the title of "Lord Protector," which had been adopted by Cromwell some years after the fall of England's King Charles I.[57] In February 1777, following the victories at Trenton and Princeton, Congress debated whether to increase Washington's powers by granting him the right to name other generals on his own authority. They decided not to, but the idea itself was enough to prompt John Adams's anxious warning about the growing cult of the commander in chief, which anticipated the more developed reflections he would compose in 1812. "I have been distressed to see some of our members disposed to idolize an image which their own hands have molten," he told the delegates. "I speak here of the superstitious veneration which is paid to General Washington."[58]

Adams's words were remarkable for two reasons. First, he already grasped, more clearly than anyone else at the time, the way that charisma does not just radiate outward from charismatic figures but is projected onto them by admirers. And second, he saw that the "idolization" of Washington was potentially dangerous. Adams was, as his remarks on monarchy suggested, by background and temperament a classical republican. He believed in a moderate government, balanced between its different branches and sustained by the virtue of its citizens. In 1780 he would insert James Harrington's phrase "a government of laws and not of men" into the constitution of Massachusetts.[59] He feared popular passions, tyranny, and praetorian armed forces devoted more to their commander than to their country (the example of Julius Caesar weighed especially heavily on his classically educated mind). Although Adams had warmly supported Washington's appointment in 1775, the spectacle of a professional army commander who evoked boundless popular enthusiasm and had already acquired unprecedented authority could not have been better calculated to inflame his political anxieties.

In retrospect, Adams's concerns look unfounded. Washington himself genuinely had no desire for dictatorial power, and throughout the Revolutionary War he would scrupulously respect the authority of the civilian Congress. He insisted on his own "inadequacy" for the position he occupied and expressed visible unease at the hyperbolic praise he received—declining, for instance, requests to sponsor a printing of Phillis Wheatley's poem promising him a "throne."[60] When congratulated on his achievements, he invariably replied by giving the credit to Providence.[61] If he had a Roman model, it was not Caesar but the earlier Roman general Cincinnatus, who reluctantly accepted the emergency powers necessary to save the Republic and then at the first opportunity surrendered them and returned to his farm.[62] At two crucial points in his career, Washington would consciously reenact this gesture—when he resigned his commission at the end of the Revolutionary War and when he left the presidency after two terms in 1797. As the American writer Garry Wills has quipped, Washington was "a virtuoso of resignations."[63]

Given Washington's own conduct and intentions, the adulation he enjoyed now looks like something that strengthened the infant republic rather than threatened it. In their enthusiasm for Washington, the disparate states found a crucial source of unity. In this alluring man, whose very features seemed to invite confidence, citizens discovered a human symbol of their new country, one that put warm flesh on the cold abstractions of republican political principle. Even better, in his modesty, his unquestioned rectitude, and even in his calm, taciturn reserve, Washington seemed to exemplify qualities that Americans hoped to find in themselves. In these ways, Washington's charisma did indeed strengthen the American experiment.

But hindsight can be misleading. If Washington could successfully play the role of Cincinnatus, it was only because of a set of exceedingly fortunate circumstances. Throughout the War of Independence, the

American civilian government remained fundamentally united, and it largely commanded the obedience—if not always the approval—of the majority of the population that backed the revolutionary cause (loyalists were of course another matter). Despite further defeats and reversals, the army would never again come as close to disaster as it had done in the fall of 1776. This unity and success did not come without a high price in blood. It was achieved through the ruthless, violent suppression of loyalists, as well as through the reinforcement of slavery and the repression of nonwhite minorities.[64] But it came, and it allowed for the survival into peacetime of an unquestionably legitimate and undivided civilian government to which Washington remained willingly subordinate. None of the other great revolutions of this period enjoyed this kind of good fortune. In nearly all of them, revolutionary forces fell out among themselves, faced what seemed at moments like virtually certain destruction at the hands of foreign or domestic enemies, and failed to achieve their objectives. In these circumstances, the charismatic appeal of a powerful general became the single most potent and volatile factor in political life.

During the remainder of the Revolutionary War, Washington's military record remained distinctly mixed. In 1777 he lost the Battles of Brandywine and Germantown in Pennsylvania, allowing the British to occupy the capital city of Philadelphia through the following spring. Much of the blame, especially for the first defeat, belonged squarely to Washington, who again allowed the British to outflank him. It was not this losing campaign of Washington's but the near-simultaneous American triumph at Saratoga, under Horatio Gates and Philip Schuyler, that marked a major turning point in the Revolutionary War and persuaded France to sign its alliance with the United States. Even so, the American cause remained at risk for several years more, as Continental Army soldiers came close to starvation in frigid winter quarters (most famously, at Valley Forge) and the British nearly seized control of the southern states. Finally, in 1780–81, the American generals Nathanael Greene and Daniel Morgan scored critical victories in the southern campaign, while the French fleet routed the Royal Navy at the Battle of the Chesapeake, cutting off supplies and reinforcements for the British army under Lord Cornwallis. These events set up Washington and the French general Rochambeau's defeat of Cornwallis at Yorktown in 1781, which finally brought the war to a successful conclusion and ensured American independence.

While the first of these events was unspooling, Washington again received some scathing criticism. After Brandywine, Adjutant General Timothy Pickering called him more "a passive spectator than the commanding general."[65] Benjamin Rush, who had so admired the commander in chief's "martial dignity" at the start of the war, called him "outgeneraled" and "outwitted" in a letter to Adams after Brandywine and Germantown, and he cited officers who had "compared Washington's imitation of an army to an unformed mob" (like Adams, Rush was a committed republican who had begun to worry about Washington as a new Caesar).[66] The attorney general of Pennsylvania complained that Washington had committed "blunders as might have disgraced a soldier of three months standing."[67] An anonymous missive that circulated among members of the Congress called Washington's army "disordered" and used the same language as did John Adams in assigning blame: "The people of America have been guilty of Idolatry by making a man their god . . . The God of Heaven and Earth will convince them by woeful experience that he is only a man."[68] Some officers and members of Congress even bruited about the possibility of replacing Washington, although nothing came of the so-called Conway Cabal (named for a particularly critical general), which hardly deserves the sinister title historians have given it. Rush, who had taken part, had to resign his position as an army surgeon general when his role became known.

But once again, virtually none of the criticism appeared in public. When American newspapers reported on Brandywine and Germantown, they tended to place the blame on faulty intelligence or insufficient troop strength, not on Washington's mistakes.[69] A few months after the battles, a Boston orator again described Washington in sacralized terms, saying he had been "raised up by Heaven, to show to what an height Humanity may soar."[70] An army officer quoted the phrase in a letter soon afterward, showing how such imagery could circulate among a broader public.[71] A "Song of Washington" appeared, telling Americans that "when he commands we will obey."[72] And at the end of the year, a German-language Pennsylvania almanac included a woodcut of an angel holding a portrait of Washington crowned with laurel leaves and proclaiming him "the father of the country" (figure 7).[73] It was the first time Washington had received this particular accolade, which recalled the earlier treatment of Paoli and Peter the Great as founding fathers of their nations. The anthem "God Save Great Washington" remained popular through the late 1770s.[74]

Throughout 1777 and 1778 both Benjamin Rush and John Adams continued to lament the political "idolatry" that seemed to have bewitched their fellow Americans. In the same letter in which he complained to Adams of Washington's leadership, Rush warned that "if our Congress can witness these things with composure . . . I shall think we have not Shook off monarchical prejudices, and that like the Israelites of old we worship the work of our hands."[75] Adams, after hearing of the American victory at Saratoga, confessed himself relieved that Washington had not been the man to win it. "If it had been," he wrote to his wife, "Idolatry, and Adulation would have been unbounded, so excessive as to endanger our Liberties . . . Now, we can allow a certain Citizen to be wise, virtuous, and good, without thinking him a Deity or a savior."[76] Rush, bitter at Washington because of the loss of his army position, was still complaining to Adams a year later that "we have substituted an idol" for George III. And in a Philadelphia newspaper article in the summer of 1779, he described "fears within me that I am afraid to utter . . . Are you sure we have no Caesars nor Cromwells in this country?"[77] Significantly, Rush still did not dare use Washington's name in this rare public expression of concern for where the cult might lead.

But if Adams and Rush were hoping that Americans would heed their warnings and turn away from idol worship, they would be sorely disappointed. And after Yorktown and the end of the war, the mania for Washington dwarfed anything seen before. By mid-1783 General Nathanael Greene could write to him, "You were admired before, you are little less than adored now."[78] *The Connecticut Journal* agreed, burbling that "all panegyric is vain and language too feeble to express our ideas of his greatness" (see figure 8).[79] Songs and poetry appeared in profusion, echoing the now-familiar themes about "great godlike Washington."[80] As early as 1782, communities across the country began to celebrate Washington's birthday with dinners, balls, fireworks, and cannon fire.[81] And churches held services of thanksgiving, in which Washington's name featured almost as prominently as that of the country itself.[82] Not surprisingly, given the religious setting, most of these orators, echoing earlier ages of charisma, praised Washington as the chosen instrument of divine Providence, "sent . . . to perform wonders, under God . . . a second Matthias."[83] Ezra Stiles, the president of Yale, compared Washington to the biblical Joshua and called him "the great ornament of humankind," whose fame was "of sweeter perfume than Arabian spices in the gardens of Persia."[84] As before, virtually no public criticism of this idolization appeared, although one "Mary Meanwell" did write to a newspaper after Yorktown, saying that "I respect our great general, but let us not make a GOD of him."[85]

One of the most interesting sermons, delivered by the Presbyterian pastor John Murray in Newburyport, Massachusetts, consisted of a lengthy parallel between the American Revolution and the biblical Book of Judges, with Washington cast as the "American Gideon . . . divinely raised, and singularly qualified to tread in the steps of his renowned predecessor." More explicitly than earlier authors (and with a nod to Shakespeare), Murray used the parallel to cast Washington not only as the savior of the American Republic but as its founder, despite his lack of a civil office: "Under his auspices, the people of the most distant provinces—hitherto separated by diversity of local prejudices, interests, and manners—were wonderfully consolidated into one body, and became a united band of brothers."[86] Murray also echoed the republican rhetoric that distinguished Washington from a king: "Thoroughly does the heart of our GIDEON feel the wide differences between the title of HIS COUNTRY'S DELIVERER, and that of his country's LORD AND MASTER . . . *The LORD alone shall be king of AMERICA.*"[87]

With independence secured, several writers tried their hand at composing epic poetry to celebrate the new nation and to give it a worthy literature. Both Timothy Dwight's *The Conquest of Canaan* and Joel Barlow's *The Vision of Columbus* gave a starring role to Washington, in each case using scriptural language (not surprising, given their clerical backgrounds). Dwight, who would succeed Stiles at Yale, repeated his comparison to Joshua in an allegory that praised the "Chief divine," and, in painfully stilted verse, paid particular attention to Washington's natural gifts: "His form majestic, seem'd by God design'd / The glorious mansion of so vast a mind."[88] Barlow dwelled at length on Washington's early years, most likely drawing on John Bell's early biography, which by now had appeared in an American edition.[89] It was becoming harder for Washington to resist the mechanisms of celebrity and the curiosity they sparked about every aspect of his life.

The extent to which all these paeans to Washington resonated with ordinary Americans was also becoming clear, to judge from the delirious crowds that gathered wherever he appeared. Foreign visitors, starting with Frenchmen who served in the Revolutionary War, were particularly quick to comment on this popular enthusiasm. Mathieu Dumas, a French officer who traveled with the general in 1780, described the scene when he arrived in Providence after nightfall: "The whole of the population had assembled from the suburbs, we were surrounded by a crowd of children carrying torches, reiterating the acclamations of the citizens; all were eager to approach the person of him whom they called their father, and pressed so closely around us that they hindered us from proceeding."[90]

The French chaplain Charles-César Robin recounted similar scenes in a memoir, claiming that Americans considered Washington "in the light of a beneficent God . . . and think themselves happy, once in their lives to have seen him . . . [they] are roused, animated and inflated at the very mention of his name."[91] In December 1783, when the general arrived in Philadelphia to resign his army commission, the city put on a concert at which crowds sang "See, the Conquering Hero Comes."[92] A visiting South American, the future revolutionary leader Francisco de Miranda, wrote in his diary: "Children, men and women expressed as much happiness and satisfaction as if the Savior had entered Jerusalem!"[93] Miranda added the caustic note that Americans had unfairly given Washington alone the praise they should have shared among the revolutionary leadership in general. But another foreigner present, a Dutch commercial traveler named Gerard Vogels, who also noted the popular "ecstasy," had no doubt that the praise was deserved. "I saw," he wrote to friends in the Netherlands, "the greatest man who has ever appeared on the surface of this earth."[94]

Many other foreign visitors to America in these years came away with worshipful feelings toward Washington, and through their reports the cult of the great man spread beyond America. European poets and essayists competed to sing Washington's praises, travelers published lengthy, gushing accounts of their meetings with him, and playwrights put him on the stage as a heroic lead character. The most popular of the plays presented "Vashington" as a figure of almost inhuman virtue and as the "fortunate founder" of the American nation.[95] European newspapers compared Washington to the "great men of antiquity," engravers eagerly turned out printed portraits, and no less a figure than Voltaire sponsored a medallic one (figures 9 and 10).[96]

More material appeared in France than anywhere else, because of the wartime alliance, but the cult did not stop there. A German magazine called Washington the most worthy military commander to have appeared in two thousand years and recounted an anecdote, similar to ones being told about Frederick the Great, in which the general supposedly insisted on sharing a table with "very common people" when taking shelter from the rain in an inn.[97] Dutch poets composed odes in both Dutch and French.[98] Even in Great Britain, where Washington quite literally had the status of a rebel in arms, guilty of high treason,

coverage of him skewed highly favorable—and not just among opponents of the war. "He is a man of sense and great integrity," *The Scots
Magazine* proclaimed.[99] A Welsh clergyman burbled in a private letter
that "immortal Washington . . . has outshined and Eclipsed all Asiatic,
African, and European Generals, and Commanders from the Creation
of the World to this Day."[100]

The testimony of French officers who served in the Revolutionary
War, and who often came to know Washington personally, had the
greatest impact. The most famous of these officers was, of course, the
marquis de Lafayette, who came to fight at Washington's side in 1777
and quickly became something of a surrogate son. "I admire him more
each day for the beauty of his character and his spirit," Lafayette soon
told a French correspondent.[101] Recalling Washington's inspiring presence at the Battle of Monmouth in 1778, he later wrote: "I thought
then as now that I had never beheld so superb a man."[102] Even more
influential in France was the now largely forgotten *philosophe* the marquis de Chastellux, who served in America from 1780 to the end of the
war, corresponded extensively with Washington thereafter, and in 1786
published a hugely popular account of his American experiences.
Chastellux noted Washington's popularity, poetically describing the
United States as "a great book in which every page rings with his praise."
He rhapsodized over Washington's "exterior form," even comparing him
to ancient statues of Apollo. But above all Chastellux adored Washington's "republican" virtues. Very much the French nobleman, he found
much of the United States rude and vulgar, but he had no doubt that in
time Washington could transform it into a republic worthy of the
name.[103]

Americans took note of Washington's fame in Europe. In 1785 another future French revolutionary, the comte de Mirabeau, published a
pamphlet on American affairs that suggested that American children
should "stammer the name of WASHINGTON as their first word," to
ensure a properly patriotic start in life.[104] Thanks to a quick, inaccurate
American translation, "children lisping the name" of Washington
quickly became an American catchphrase, including in Noah Webster's

influential pamphlet on education.[105] Meanwhile, the poet Philip Freneau, who had been chanting Washington's praises since 1775, claimed for Washington an exaggerated global reputation:

> Throughout the world thy growing fame has spread,
> In every country are thy virtues read;
> Remotest India hears thy deeds of fame,
> The hardy Scythian stammers at thy name;
> The haughty Turk, now longing to be free,
> Neglects his Sultan to enquire of thee.[106]

A Connecticut journalist quite correctly promised that as the United States expanded westward, all the way to the "western ocean," the name of Washington would accompany it.[107] The apparent worldwide admiration for Washington helped Americans believe that their country had fulfilled the promise of the Declaration of Independence, assuming "among the powers of the earth, the separate and equal station to which the laws of nature and of nature's God entitle them."

Ever since the eighteenth century, observers have debated the ways in which the American Revolution influenced the upheavals that soon followed in Europe—most importantly, the French Revolution. Did American ideas of liberty spread outward, like irresistible inkblots, by the sheer force of their intellectual logic? Or did the American example in fact have relatively little appeal for Europeans seeking not just to found new governments but violently to uproot centuries of established practices, policies, and prejudices?[108] While translations of American political documents (including state constitutions) circulated in Europe, there is relatively little evidence of their direct influence. Astonishingly, not once in the early years of the French Revolution does a single political figure seem to have quoted the American Declaration of Independence.[109] What impressed Europeans was not specific American political arrangements so much as exemplary American men, above all Benjamin Franklin and George Washington. The first of these, who represented the United States in France during the Revolution, became an enormously popular French celebrity, a symbol of homespun American simplicity and ingenuity.[110] But it was Washington who was the great political model. He struck many of the French who met him in much the way that Paoli had struck Boswell: they could not believe that a man like him actually existed in modern times. Heroic, masculine, virtuous, and modest, he seemed to have stepped directly out of a history of republican Rome, and he seemed proof that a regime like republican Rome could again come to exist. His very existence offered an implicit rebuke to the royal court that dominated French society and that was widely seen as corrupt, effeminate, ineffective, and inclined toward despotism.

Given Washington's ever-more-exalted status, it is not surprising that some Americans continued to think of him as a potential benevolent dictator. In 1780, with the British advancing rapidly in the south, and with the main French force seemingly bogged down in New England, members of Congress began to discuss granting Washington sweeping new powers. A member from Rhode Island wrote to his governor, "The necessity of appointing General Washington sole dictator of America, is again talked of, as the only means, under God, by which we can be saved from destruction."[111] The French minister to the United States reported to Versailles that Washington, thanks to his popularity, had "Congress and the thirteen states at his mercy," adding with aristocratic circumspection, "it would not be wise to expose even the most virtuous man to the delicate temptations of ambition."[112]

Again, nothing came of the discussions, and the victories of 1781 dispelled the threats that had given rise to them. But over the next eight years, the United States experienced more dangerous political instability than at any other time before the Civil War. In 1782–83, discontent rumbled through the army, which had not received promised pay and pensions. A group of officers discussed the idea of threatening Congress with force unless it satisfied their demands; some of them may even have plotted a coup. In 1786–87, desperate ex-soldiers in Massachusetts started trying to shut down debtors' courts, and the actions soon blew up into a series of violent confrontations known as Shays' Rebellion. And through the decade, attempts to carry out the ordinary business of the new republic, to say nothing of these crises, were hobbled by the weakness of the central government established by the Articles of Confederation.

If the United States managed to overcome these crises and design and ratify a new constitution, much of the credit goes to Washington and the charismatic authority he had acquired. If at any point in his career he deserved the hyperbolic accolades he received, it was now. In March 1783 he defused the army crisis by promising to secure the desired pay, giving a brilliant address to his assembled officers in Newburgh, New York. In a moment of well-scripted pathos that quickly became a key part of his legend, after seeming to stumble over his first sentences, Washington put on a pair of spectacles, saying, "Gentlemen, you must pardon me. I have grown gray in your service and now find myself growing blind." His concluding peroration, promising to oppose any man who might try to "open the floodgates of civil discord and deluge our rising empire in blood," testified to the gravity of the crisis.[113]

Nine months later, in Philadelphia, Washington ceremonially surrendered his military commission to Congress and retired to Mount Vernon. The act astonished many observers, especially in Europe, and confirmed Washington's reputation as a dedicated republican, the modern Cincinnatus who wanted nothing more than to slough off the cares of leadership and return to his plow. King George III himself supposedly remarked that if Washington voluntarily gave up his position, then "he will be the greatest man in the world."[114] Before the resignation, no American could have competed with Washington for a position of political power. After it, no American could have dared violate the precedent he had set for respecting civil government.

Then, in 1787, Washington reluctantly came out of retirement to serve in the Constitutional Convention in Philadelphia and was quickly chosen as its president. Already in 1783 he had made his constitutional views known in an open letter to the states insisting on the need for "an indissoluble union of the states under one federal head"—i.e., something stronger than the Articles of Confederation.[115] In Philadelphia, where he attracted the usual adoring crowds, his presence inspired confidence in the proceedings, which had attracted some angry criticism because the delegates had chosen to deliberate behind closed doors. *The Pennsylvania Gazette* intoned: "In 1775, we beheld him at the head of the armies of America, arresting the progress of British tyranny. In the year 1787, we behold him at the head of a chosen band of patriots and heroes, arresting the progress of American anarchy."[116]

Washington did not play a major role in writing the new constitution, but he supported it. More important, his backing played a crucial role in assuring ratification, especially in his wavering home state of Virginia.[117] James Monroe, then a young member of the Virginia Ratifying Convention, wrote to Thomas Jefferson: "Be assured [Washington's] influence carried this government."[118] And it was not just Washington's active support that counted. The federal constitution of course created a powerful new executive office in the presidency. Could fallible, ambitious men be trusted not to abuse presidential power? Would the checks and balances written into the constitution suffice to keep a wayward president in check? In the same letter to Jefferson, Monroe confided his fears about "those qualities which we have *too much reason* to believe are almost inseparable from the frail nature of our being."[119] If a person partaking of these qualities were to come to power, "the people of America will perhaps be lost."

But already during the ratification process Americans generally assumed that Washington would become the first president, and the belief played a decisive role in relieving their anxieties. If anyone could be trusted with the presidency, it was Washington, the American Cincinnatus, the virtuous demigod, the "great ornament of human kind." A poem, originally written in Britain in 1786, appeared in the American press during the ratification debates lamenting the "barbarous" and "perverted" age in which "ambition . . . deluges the Globe with blood." But it identified one great exception to the rule: Washington, "whom boundless trust ne'er tempted to betray / Nor power impelled to arbitrary sway."[120] James Monroe, after confessing his anxieties to Jefferson, likewise expressed his "boundless confidence" in Washington. Jefferson himself claimed that his own concerns were "only put to sleep by the unlimited confidence we all repose" in Washington, even as he fretted that "after him, inferior characters may perhaps succeed and awaken us to the danger which his merit has led us into."[121] Numerous poems commemorating the constitution gave Washington the credit—once again—for saving his country.[122] It is fair to say that had Washington died before the Convention met, the federal constitution might never have been ratified.[123]

Washington deserves credit for helping steer the country through the political shoals of the 1780s, but he could not have done so without the extraordinary charismatic reputation that his admirers had been constructing around him since 1776. Most Americans did not know Washington personally, the way Jefferson and Monroe knew him. They knew the charismatic image, as transmitted through the poetry, the sermons, the orations, the newspaper accounts, the engravings—which is to say that they knew the impossibly virtuous "godlike man," the Moses who had led them out of British slavery toward the promised land of independence. It was the powerful emotional response evoked by this Washington of the imagination that persuaded Americans—or, rather, the literate white American men who dominated the country—to put their trust in a man who would now wield the sort of personal power that they had previously associated with a king and had violently rejected.

In 1789, George Washington was duly elected president, and the beginning of his presidency saw—hard as it may be to believe—the levels of popular adulation rise even higher. On his way to his inauguration in the temporary capital of New York, and then in the first years of his presidency, he undertook a series of trips through the country designed to strengthen the new government.[124] Everywhere, record crowds turned out to see him, in ceremonies designed to show that the great days of classical antiquity had returned. In Trenton, the women of the city put up a Roman-style triumphal arch on a bridge and covered it with laurel leaves, flowers, and a banner reading "December 26, 1776"— the day of his victory at Trenton over the Hessians. Women and girls dressed in white strewed flower petals along his path as he passed.[125] In Philadelphia, the painter Charles Willson Peale, who had done the first great portraits of Washington, directed the construction of several more laurel-covered arches. Foreshadowing the much more elaborate political theater masterminded for Robespierre and Napoleon by the French painter Jacques-Louis David, Peale served as impresario for a ceremony, witnessed by twenty thousand spectators, in which his daughter, perched atop one of the arches, lowered a laurel wreath onto Washington's head as he passed underneath (an embarrassed Washington quickly brushed it off).[126] In New York, a flotilla of vessels greeted him in the harbor. In Charleston, South Carolina, he made his way to shore on a gaudily decorated barge.[127] The historian T. H. Breen has noted that the only figure capable of assembling such large and enthusiastic crowds in America before Washington's journey was the Great Awakening preacher George Whitefield.[128] The comparison demonstrates how a form of personal charisma previously present only in the religious sphere was now passing into a transformed secular political one.

As usual, during these events the newspapers tripped over one another to see who could praise Washington most fervently. The prize probably went to a Philadelphia newspaper that—again demonstrating how religious language and practices shaped political charisma— described him with verses that echoed the Book of Revelation: "And behold a white horse: and he that sat on him had a bow; and a crown was given unto him: and he went forth conquering, and to conquer."[129] The dyspeptic Benjamin Rush was again driven to muse despairingly about his fellow countrymen's inability to distinguish one particular human being from God: "We have not instituted divine honors to certain virtues in imitation of the inhabitants of Paris, but we ascribe all the attributes of the Deity to the name of General Washington."[130] Again, no one listened.

The newspapers paid close attention not only to Washington but also to the popular reactions he inspired. A writer for *The Pennsylvania Packet* noted the way the entire population of Philadelphia displayed "the most undisguised attachment and unbounded zeal for their dear Chief, and I may add, under God, the Savior of their Country—Not all the pomp of majesty, not even Imperial dignity itself, surrounded with its usual splendor and magnificence, could equal this interesting scene."[131] A newspaper in Salem, Massachusetts, carefully described the reception that Washington had received at each of his stops in New England, praised him as the instrument chosen by heaven for America's salvation, and claimed that all the spectators had "but one uniform sentiment" of admiration, molding them into a "Great Family" over which Washington presided, as father.[132] Such accounts had their own, critical role in the development of Washington's charismatic reputation. Like Boswell's descriptions of Pasquale Paoli's interactions with worshipful Corsicans, they demonstrated the charismatic hero's ability to elicit freely given applause and admiration—to form a bond with people who were in a crucial sense his equals. At the same time, the accounts instructed readers, most of whom would never actually see Washington in the flesh, how they should feel toward him.

The beginning of Washington's presidency also marked a new stage in his transformation into a celebrity. In 1790 the geographer Jedidiah Morse published the first relatively extensive biography of Washington. Like Boswell writing about Paoli and Johnson, Morse insisted that "the private life of General Washington" offered just as important an example as his public actions.[133] Morse then provided a close description of Washington's virtuous daily routine, including his breakfast of "three small Indian hoe-cakes and as many dishes of tea," plus his half-pint or more of Madeira in the afternoon, followed by "a small glass of punch, a draught of beer, and two dishes of tea" with dinner (in this pre-temperance America, teetotaling was not yet counted a virtue).[134] An "Ode on General Washington's Birth-Day" published with the book even offered up an image of angels carrying Washington to heaven—but hopefully, the author added, not for many years.[135]

The effects that Washington's charisma could have on ordinary Americans was demonstrated by an extraordinary letter written by a woman—probably the sister of the prominent Massachusetts physician Joshua Fisher—to her brother after Washington's visit to Salem.[136] "You must know," she wrote, "that I have had the happiness . . . of seeing this incomparable President. You may laugh but he has a most beautiful face. Did you ever see a countenance a thousandth part so expressive of that goodness, benevolence, sensibility, and modesty which characterize him?" Washington was only a man, not an angel, Fisher admitted, but "that is the cream of it in my opinion, for if he were an angel, what would he be to us? Besides if that were the case, there would be nothing extraordinary in the matter, for I imagine there are many such [angels]. But he is a man and we feel proud of it." She noted that Washington himself "looked oppressed at the attention that was paid him" and re-peatedly lowered his head or wiped his face with a handkerchief. She concluded by joking that her brother should take a note he had received from Washington and cut it up "into Washington rings and lockets; one letter each will do, or at most one syllable." It would be "worth a mil-lion." Here was the intense emotional reaction—prompted in part by a clear physical attraction but also by an appreciation of the moral quali-ties described in print—and an appreciation of Washington, however angelic he might seem, as a human being distinguished by his natural qualities, not royal descent or anointment by a church. And, while joc-ular, her remark about rings and lockets suggests something of the thirst of Americans for relics of this secular saint. Incidentally, such lockets did exist, and as recently as 2001, one from 1789 sold for $1.2 million, showing that the thirst has not yet abated (see figure 11).[137]

In this crucial period for the newborn American republic, Washing-ton's charismatic reputation did a great deal to determine the character of the presidency. In the uncertain and turbulent years before the new constitution, more than a few Americans who had supported the Revo-lution wondered if, after all, the country needed a monarch to keep it together. A 1784 poem that praised Washington after his retirement from the army nonetheless concluded with the words "Behold the shrine! Prepare the crown, / To deck the brow of WASHINGTON!"[138] The same year, a luckless Irish-born officer named Lewis Nicola incurred Washington's wrath for suggesting he might become king of a new state, settled by former soldiers, west of the Appalachians.[139] Even John Adams, despite his republicanism, thought that some sort of constitutional monarchy might in the end prove necessary for the United States: "Our Ship must ultimately land on that shore or be cast away."[140] After Washington's election, Adams argued that the president should be addressed as "Your Highness."

But even as the crowds scrambled for a glimpse of the president, and the versifiers competed to devise ever-more-extravagant adjectives for him, most observers insisted on distinguishing Washington from gods, angels, and kings. He was a man, an American, and, despite his extraordinary qualities, the equal of his fellow citizens. *The Pennsylvania Packet* made the point with particular acuity: "The first magistrates of Europe assume the title of Gods, and treat their subjects like an inferior race of animals. Our beloved Magistrate delights to show, upon all occasions, that he is a man—and instead of assuming the pomp of master, acts as if he considered himself the father—the friend—and the servant of the people."[141] Washington was a charismatic if sober hero for the new, revolutionary age. Washington's own conduct reinforced this impression. And in the same spirit, the new Congress decisively rejected the title "Your Highness" for "President Washington." He would not be a king by another name.

George Washington's two terms as president marked another striking change in the history of his charismatic authority. Many years after first being hailed as the savior, founder, and father of his country, he had finally ascended to a position of formal, preeminent political power: both head of state and head of government of the American republic, the country's symbolic embodiment and also its actual chief executive. Yet, paradoxically, rather than rising even higher, his charismatic stature diminished during his nearly eight years in office.

The reason was quite simple: politics. Washington's instinct was to stay above the political fray, but it became evident very quickly that he could not. The country, and his own government, soon divided, and divided bitterly, over a host of questions. In foreign policy, should the United States retain its friendship with France, even as the French Revolution turned more radical, or seek a rapprochement with its old enemy, Great Britain? In domestic policy, should the administration pursue Treasury Secretary Alexander Hamilton's vision of a powerful federal government and national bank helping to develop the country as a commercial and industrial powerhouse, or reject it in favor of Secretary of State Thomas Jefferson's vision of a much looser union of primarily agrarian states? During Washington's administration, political parties began to form: the pro-British, Hamiltonian Federalists against Jefferson's Democratic-Republicans. Washington could not remain above the fray and ended up siding with the Federalists.

As he did so, he encountered something that was, for him, very new: sustained, intense, and often unfair public criticism. And opponents did not stop at criticizing his policies. Although Washington had no desire for a royal title, and though his modest residence in Philadelphia looked nothing like a European palace, he did insist on strict etiquette and ceremony, giving opponents the chance to pillory him as stiff and monarchical. They denounced Hamilton's policies as destructive and the rapprochement with Britain as treasonous. After the United States signed a treaty with Britain in 1794, the Democratic-Republican newspaper *Aurora*, edited by Benjamin Franklin's grandson Benjamin Franklin Bache, even claimed that Washington had accepted bribes from Britain during the war.[142] Thomas Paine broke angrily with Washington and in a vitriolic public letter claimed that the great man's reputation was fraudulent. He added, "The world will be puzzled to decide whether you are an apostate or an imposter; whether you have abandoned good principles, or whether you ever had any."[143] Some of the strongest, most sustained criticism came from the poet Philip Freneau, who had previously celebrated Washington in adoring verse but in 1791 became editor of the fiercely Democratic-Republican *National Gazette*.

Now in late middle age and declining health, Washington himself was badly stung by the criticism and frequently lashed out in private at his critics, including "that rascal Freneau."[144] Even as his administration accomplished a considerable amount—effectively inventing much of the American government machinery, negotiating treaties, moving aggressively to expand settlement into the Ohio Valley at the expense of Native Americans, and defeating the Whiskey Rebellion (Washington personally led troops on this occasion, the only time a sitting American president has done so)—the rawness of the political fray steadily wore him down. In a draft passage of his farewell address that he eventually edited out, he berated the newspapers for publishing "all the Invective that disappointment, ignorance of facts, and malicious falsehoods could invent, to misrepresent my politics and affections, to wound my reputation and feelings, and to weaken, if not entirely destroy, the confidence that you have been pleased to repose in me."[145]

Washington did not grasp that the United States had changed deeply since the mid-1770s. It had become a much more freewheeling, raucous society, where gentlemanly figures like him could no longer expect deference.[146] The press continued to expand (the number of newspapers more than doubled between 1790 and 1800) and increasingly reported on the private lives of its subjects as well as their public actions, bringing America's celebrity culture more into line with that of Europe.[147] The development of party politics meant that organized networks of clubs and newspapers would mount sustained efforts to glorify their own leaders but also sustained efforts to vilify their opponents. Frustrated and exhausted from trying to deal with these changes, in 1797 Washington was all too happy to retire for a second time and to return to his beloved Mount Vernon. This second retirement soon quelled the worst criticism. It reinforced the Cincinnatus legend, and historians rightly credit it with establishing the crucial republican precedent that American presidents would not hold office for life.

Despite the frustrations he expressed during his terms in office, Washington deserves just as much praise for the political restraint he showed while president as for his voluntary departure from the office.

Not only did he respect the new constitution and the rule of law during his two terms, but he steadfastly refused to exploit the charismatic legend that had grown so enormously powerful by the time of his inaugural tour of the states. Unlike some of his successors, Washington did not boast of the size of his crowds, still less attempt to silence or threaten his opponents by reference to his level of popular support. Nor did he let his Federalist partisans exploit his popularity in this way. His charismatic reputation in 1789 constituted a potential political weapon of enormous power. A Bonaparte would not have hesitated to use it. Washington never did.

On December 14, 1799, George Washington died, and immediately his charismatic image underwent one last dramatic transformation. The event came as an emotional blow to most of those Americans who could participate in the country's fledgling and very imperfect democracy. Especially given Washington's passing in the closing days of the century, they saw it as marking the end of the founding era for the United States. With party politics growing more vituperative (some feared the election of 1800 might trigger a civil war), these Americans also mostly seized on Washington as a figure of national unity. His own partisan politics now became a thing of the past, and Democratic-Republicans rushed to praise him as fervently as the Federalists did.[148]

The outpouring was astonishing. "This event has cast a gloom over the whole continent," one Bostonian claimed.[149] In virtually every town of any size in the country, people gathered to hear orations and eulogies, of which at least 340 found their way into print.[150] All the familiar themes from the well-established earlier cult of Washington—his virtue, moderation, courage, strength, paternal care, and genius—sounded out once again. Newspapers published special editions framed in black, while businesses shut down as the news spread. Meanwhile, with the Protestant revival of the Second Great Awakening now in full swing, evangelical preachers rushed to present the religiously reticent Washington as a fervent model Christian. The engraver David Edwin, working from a painting by Rembrandt Peale, quickly produced an image of Washington ascending to heaven. Another such image, painted in 1865, now decorates the eye of the rotunda of the United States Capitol (see figure 12).

At the same time, with Washington himself no longer on the scene to protect his image, and with a boisterous press culture continuing to develop, the mechanisms of celebrity seized on Washington more firmly than ever. Now, everything about the great man became meat for writers and entrepreneurs of all stripes hungrily competing to profit from his disappearance. Even as a flood of new biographical writings came on the market, merchants announced special sales of black crepe and produced commemorative plates, pitchers, quilts, clocks, necklaces, and rings bearing Washington's image.[151]

Exemplifying all these trends at once was a thirty-year-old itinerant bookseller, huckster, and evangelical preacher named Mason Locke Weems. Just weeks after Washington's death, he wrote to a Philadelphia publisher: "I've got something to whisper in your lug. Washington, you know is gone! Millions are gaping to read something about him. I am very nearly primed and cocked for them."[152] Within months, Weems had published his *Life of George Washington*, which would appear in dozens of bestselling editions throughout the nineteenth century.[153] It did more than any other single work to fix the image of Washington in the American mind—to present him as the measure of charisma against which all subsequent American political figures have had to live up.

The book often seems to read like the work of a less talented, fervently evangelical, and occasionally hallucinating Boswell.[154] Weems gleefully made up story after story to illustrate Washington's virtue—most famously, that of the boy Washington tearfully confessing to his father that he had chopped down a cherry tree, because "I can't tell a lie, Pa."[155] To draw in readers, Weems produced horrifying, gory descriptions of Indian atrocities during the French and Indian War ("the raw and bloody skeletons, fed on by the hogs . . .").[156] He also spared no effort in fitting Washington's life story into an evangelical Christian framework. In his account, Washington has a dream similar to Daniel's, hears Jehovah telling him, "Fear not, for I am with thee," and spends an excruciating number of pages dying and rising up into heaven, where he rejoices at the sight of old comrades ("swift on angel's wings the brightening saint ascended").[157] Most important, like Boswell and Johnson before him, Weems promised to reveal the true Washington by pulling back the curtain: "It is not in the glare of public, but in the shade of private life, that we are to look for the man. Private life is always real life."[158]

Weems's *Life* also depicted a Washington well suited to the more egalitarian American ethos of the nineteenth century. Although still, of course, an absolutely exceptional human being, this Washington was also a man of the people. Weems described the plantation society of his birth as little more than a backwoods settlement, and he presented his hero—despite his hugely advantageous marriage to Martha Custis—as that most American of figures, an entirely self-made man. Weems also emphasized Washington's easy manner with people from all walks of life, and he cast his virtues as expressions of the American democratic character. But in one respect the book did harken back to an older period in decrying faction and presenting its hero as a man who utterly rejected party politics, seeking nothing but national unity.

This most American of books said very little about the larger world. Yet oddly, in the final version, published in 1809, Weems did not begin his story in America but in the French city of Toulon, in the year 1798. There, he recounted, a group of young Americans had supposedly come in search of a different great man, who was embarking for Egypt. They succeeded in wangling an introduction, and to their surprise, once past the initial pleasantries, the man's first question was "How fares your countryman, the great Washington?" They reassured him as to Washington's health, at which point Napoleon Bonaparte then continued, rhapsodically, "Ah, gentlemen! Washington can never be otherwise than well . . . Posterity shall talk of him with reverence . . . when my name shall be lost in the vortex of Revolutions."[159]

Weems made up this scene, too, and obviously designed it to impress readers with the unmatched breadth and depth of his subject's fame. But at the same time, it betrayed at least a hint of anxiety on Weems's part. Could it be the case that in another, older part of the world, far away from the new American nation, there might be another heroic leader whose charismatic appeal exceeded even that of George Washington? In 1809, most observers outside the United States would have responded that there was indeed.

THREE

WAITING FOR CAESAR
IN FRANCE

Until now, our revolution has given rise to great events, not great men.

—Lucien Bonaparte, 1800

If I had been in America, I would have willingly been a Washington,
and I would have deserved little praise for it, since I don't see how it would have
been possible to do otherwise. But if he had been in France, with the divisions
within and the invasion from without, I would have defied him to be himself;
and if he had been, he would have been nothing but a fool. As for me,
I could only be a crowned Washington.

—Napoleon Bonaparte, 1815

A t the end of January 1800, ships landed in France bringing reports of George Washington's death. The news did not spur anything like the grief that had erupted in the United States a month before. Not only had Washington, as president, signed a friendship treaty with France's enemy Great Britain, but after his retirement the United States had fallen into the undeclared conflict with France called the Quasi-War, marked by violent naval skirmishes and venomous diplomatic hostility. When, on February 2, the moderate republican French legislator Félix Faulcon asked his colleagues to hold a ceremony in honor of Washington, they balked. Some of them even denounced the American as an "aristocrat" and a foe of French liberty.[1]

But where these politicians saw Washington through the prism of ongoing events, Napoleon Bonaparte remembered how the French had once worshipped the American president and spied an opportunity. Less than three months before, the thirty-year-old general had seized power in a coup d'état, claiming that he wanted to save the republic born out of the French Revolution from chaos and corruption. But his authority was still fragile and untested. What better way to demonstrate his commitment to republican government, while also underscoring his own leadership qualities, than to stage a celebration that implicitly compared him to America's republican savior figure? Even before Bonaparte's rise to power, a friendly author had praised him as "France's Washington."[2] Now he quickly ordered a ten-day period of national mourning. Newspapers he controlled published gushing obituaries of Washington. Bonaparte also quickly planned an elaborate memorial service at the Invalides, featuring the display of the French sculptor Houdon's bust of Washington and an hour-long oration by the journalist Louis de Fontanes.[3] The service took place on February 9.

Bonaparte chose Fontanes wisely. A well-known conservative noble, indebted to the new leader for ending his banishment from France, he knew how to make praise for the republican Washington serve the purposes of a nascent authoritarian regime. "Ordinarily, after great political crises," he declaimed in a line obviously designed to fit Bonaparte as much as the oration's ostensible subject, "an extraordinary personality comes to the fore, who, thanks to his glory alone . . . imposes order in the midst of confusion."[4] Fontanes argued that in the early history of republics, customs and morals mattered more than the letter of the law— which Bonaparte's coup had rather spectacularly violated—and suggested that Washington had "governed more by sentiments and affections than by orders and laws."[5] In other words, Fontanes was holding up Washington as a model of charismatic, as opposed to constitutional, rule. In the doubtful case that anyone had missed the point of the oration, he concluded by praising "the man who, while still young, has surpassed Washington in battles, and will, like him, bind up the wounds of his country with his triumphant hands."[6]

The memorial service served its purpose for Bonaparte, but the new leader's "Washingtonian" moment did not last long. In June 1800, his spectacular military victory over Austria at the Battle of Marengo did more than any oration to solidify his rule. Soon he began openly to contemplate staying in power permanently, at which point a punctiliously republican "virtuoso of resignations" like Washington no longer made an appropriate model. In early 1801, Bonaparte used a failed assassination attempt as an excuse to purge the remnants of the left-wing republican opposition (the attack had actually been carried out by right-wing royalists, but no matter). A year and a half later, he made himself consul for life. Much later, in his final exile from France, he insisted that if he had been born in America, he would willingly have played a Washingtonian role. But in a country like France, torn apart from within and assaulted from without, "I would have defied [Washington] to be himself; and if he had been, he would have been nothing but a fool. As for me, I could only be a crowned Washington."[7] Indeed, in December 1804, Bonaparte quite literally put a crown on his own head, accepting the monarchical role that Washington had so steadfastly refused and taking the title of emperor.

In subsequent years, some of the greatest writers of the nineteenth century compared Washington and Bonaparte in print. That number included Lord Byron, Samuel Coleridge, Madame de Staël, Benjamin Constant, Chateaubriand, and the great Cuban poet José María Heredia.[8] Invariably, the point of the exercise was to excoriate the Frenchman for not following the American's virtuous, self-denying example. Yet the very possibility the authors insisted on and that Bonaparte denied— that he *could* have been a French Washington—underscores fundamental similarities between the men as charismatic revolutionary leaders. Like Washington, Bonaparte was a professional soldier who, in the midst of his country's revolution, came to be seen as a heroic, almost superhuman savior and the father of his country. As was the case with Washington, his ability to play this role was attributed to his extraordinary natural gifts—in his instance, above all his genius. Like Washington's, his charismatic reputation depended both on the new political ideas in circulation and also on the media in which ordinary people came to know him as a celebrity and to imagine a relationship with him. And as with Washington, his ascent took place during a moment of national crisis.

But Napoleon's emergence as a charismatic leader poses more of a historical puzzle than Washington's. In revolutionary France, fear of a Caesar ran far deeper than in revolutionary America. In revolutionary America, the king was figuratively decapitated when the crowd in New York wrenched the head off the lead statue of George III. In revolutionary France, King Louis XVI was very literally decapitated, in a blood sacrifice designed to choke off and cauterize the very possibility of a single individual ever again wielding absolute power in the country. Throughout the Revolution, political figures frenetically accused one another of plotting to seize personal power—of becoming a dictator, a Caesar, a Cromwell. In many cases, the accusations led directly to death sentences. Personal ambition, as in Shakespeare's works—and much of the Christian tradition—was considered a "grievous fault" indeed. Bonaparte himself, while still an obscure, twenty-two-year-old army officer in 1791, wrote that "ambition, like all disordered passions, is a violent and unthinking delirium . . . Like a fire fed by a pitiless wind, it only burns out after having consumed everything in its path."[9] According to an idea that became particularly powerful in the most radical phase of the Revolution, between 1792 and 1794, any form of personal power whatsoever was illegitimate. "We must," declared the Jacobin Louis-Antoine de Saint-Just, "substitute the strength and the inflexible justice of the law for personal influence."[10] The German radical Anacharsis Cloots, drawn like a moth to the French revolutionary flame, went so far as to declare at the end of 1793, "France . . . you will only be happy when you are cured of individuals."[11]

Just six years later, Napoleon Bonaparte, with a significant base of support in the French population, seized dictatorial personal power. To understand this wrenching shift, we have to start with the French Revolution itself.

I n the beginning was the king. Until the Revolution of 1789, far more than in North America, everything in political life revolved around this one figure. Indeed, in theory, politics itself did not exist outside the king's head. France before 1789 was a theoretically absolute monarchy in which the king served as chief executive, sole legislator, and supreme judge. Politics therefore, in a sense, consisted of him making up his mind. "All the state is in him," declared one of the period's most influential political treatises, "and the will of the entire people is contained within his own." In 1766, King Louis XV reaffirmed that "sovereign power resides in my person only . . . public order in its entirety emanates from me."[12] The king's authority depended less on the monarch's own personality and deeds than on the mystique and tradition of the office itself, and on a line of ancestors stretching back well over a thousand years. In this sense, it was actually less personal and individualized than the authority of most modern political leaders.[13] But this symbolic weight only reinforced the centrality of the office for most of the French, who could not imagine their country without a king at its head. They dated their history from the foundation of the monarchy in the late fifth century and measured it in dynasties.

In practice things didn't always work the way "absolutist" theory dictated. "If I were the Paris Lieutenant-General of Police," the same Louis XV is supposed to have remarked, "I would ban two-wheeled carriages."[14] Kings ruled only with the cooperation of powerful officials and social elites, whom they could not easily challenge. They were expected to respect certain established legal precedents—especially in matters of taxation—and often retreated in the face of concerted public opposition to their more unpopular policies. Over the course of the eighteenth century, despite the existence of a vast and cumbersome system of censorship and a large police force dedicated to rooting out dissent, a raucous public sphere of political debate and discussion arose. While the French universe of print did not have the dimensions of its British counterpart, it still disseminated a very large range of works, including those we now think of as the core of the French Enlightenment. Many of these advocated popular sovereignty. Many more questioned the religious basis for the claim that the king received his authority directly from God—that his very person was sacred. And even as these ideas and other forms of cultural change eroded the monarchy's sacred aura, royal attempts to stifle protest led critics to charge that the kings were acting less like Christian monarchs than like "oriental despots." In short, despite the symbolic place of the monarchy in national life, France's kings were much less popular than Britain's had been in America until just before the American Revolution.

Louis XVI, who, at the age of twenty, succeeded his grandfather Louis XV in 1774, was no one's idea of a charismatic leader, and he did little to improve the monarchy's battered image.[15] Naturally intelligent and kind, he was also painfully shy, indecisive, overweight, and desperate to please. "I wish to be loved," he reportedly remarked soon after his accession, but the people's love did not come easily to him.[16] Worse, the inexperienced young man and his even younger and equally inexperienced queen, Marie-Antoinette, failed to consummate their marriage for several years, making Louis the object of more mockery than adulation (it did not help that his hobby was lockmaking, leading to all manner of ribald jokes about locks and keys). Mindful of the precedent set by Frederick the Great in Germany, Louis's advisors diligently tried to increase his popularity by publicizing stories about his kindness to the poor and by commissioning paintings of him giving out alms.[17] But these efforts had little effect amid continuing political strife and also, in the late 1780s, a massive fiscal crisis coupled with a severe economic downturn.

The French Revolution born out of this crisis did not immediately overthrow the king. In 1788, a desperate Louis called for the election of a representative body that had not met in nearly 175 years: the Estates

General. In May 1789, 561 deputies from the clergy and nobility (the First and Second Estates) assembled in Versailles along with 578 from the Third Estate (everyone else; its deputies came mostly from the professional middle classes). The body immediately fell into a stalemate over the question of whether all the deputies would meet together—with the Third Estate in the majority—or in separate chambers. After several weeks, the leaders of the Third Estate took matters into their own hands by inviting noble and clerical deputies to join them in a single National Assembly that would provide a written constitution for the country. A large number of clerics responded enthusiastically, along with some liberal nobles, and after initial resistance, the king reluctantly recognized the Assembly's existence. At this point, it was universally assumed that the forthcoming constitution would establish a constitutional monarchy, with the king as a powerful chief executive.

But in the dramatically turbulent summer and fall of 1789, what started as constitutional reform turned into a revolution. When the king appeared to be reversing course and on the point of dissolving the new Assembly by force, the ordinary people of Paris took matters into their own hands, storming the fortress and prison of the Bastille—long the country's premier symbol of royal "despotism." Royal troops defected to their side, and within days, leaders of the Third Estate had seized control of major municipalities across the country. In late August, the Assembly issued a Declaration of the Rights of Man and Citizen. "The principle of all sovereignty," the document proclaimed, "lies essentially in the Nation. No body or individual may exercise any authority that does not emanate expressly from it."[18] It failed entirely to mention the king.

In this radically transformed political atmosphere, the question of personal political authority quickly came to the fore. What role would the king play under the new constitution? And if a weak king were restrained in his powers, might other individuals rise up to entrance the public? Already in the summer of 1789, several members of the National Assembly were becoming genuine political celebrities. Most prominent was Honoré-Gabriel Riqueti, comte de Mirabeau, who before the Revolution had acquired a reputation for scandalous love affairs but also for eloquent writings against royal despotism. In June 1789, he quickly emerged as a leader of the Assembly thanks to the thunderous oratory with which he defended it against the king. Although badly scarred by smallpox, he knew, like John Wilkes, how to make his unsightly appearance work in his favor. "No one knows the full power of my ugliness," he boasted.[19] At Mirabeau's side was the marquis de Lafayette, who owed his prominence to his service in the American war and his closeness to George Washington. Tall and handsome, he looked particularly good on horseback and commanded the newly formed National Guard.

The Assembly also included a man who made for a far less obvious political idol but who would have much greater importance in the Revolution and play one of the strangest roles in the history of modern political charisma. In 1789, Maximilien Robespierre was only thirty-one years old. A lawyer from the northern French town of Arras, he had a modest reputation for fighting "enlightened" legal cases, but nothing to compare with the fame of Mirabeau or Lafayette. He was short, humorless, and fussy, always appearing in public with a carefully powdered wig and reading his speeches word for word in a weak voice from prepared scripts. *The Times* of London would later offer this cruel but not inaccurate description: "Robespierre is of a weak, puny constitution; his complexion is dark and livid, his eye-sight short and delicate, and his voice very faint and low. He possesses, of course, none of those physical advantages which captivate and seduce the multitude."[20]

But in 1789, Robespierre discovered his mission. He espoused the idea that society should be governed not by individuals but by the impersonal, abstract, just, and rational principles laid out in the Declaration of Rights. The program fit in well with his reserved—indeed, repressed— personality, and also with the political philosophy of his intellectual idol, Jean-Jacques Rousseau, whose *Social Contract* advocated the collective sovereignty of a body of wholly equal citizens. Many other people in France had a similar revelation in 1789, but Robespierre stood out immediately for his utter force and conviction. From this moment on, he would deliberately seek to efface his own already colorless self, living a spartan, celibate existence in a modest set of rented rooms and dedicating every waking moment to politics. Supporters soon started calling him "the Incorruptible."[21] He was embracing what can only be called an anti-charismatic ethos. According to Max Weber, he perfectly expressed the Revolution's "charismatic glorification of 'Reason'" as opposed to the charismatic glorification of particular individuals.[22]

In September 1789, when Robespierre broke out of obscurity, it was precisely over the issue of personal political power. The Assembly was debating whether the king should have any right at all to veto legislation, and Robespierre put the case for limiting his role to the absolute minimum. Kings, he explained, should properly do nothing but execute the will of the people. "Why should the sovereign will of the nation cede for any time at all to the will of a man?" he asked. Allowing this to happen would mean claiming that "the nation is nothing and that a single man is everything."[23] Power should remain as abstract and impersonal as possible. Robespierre did not prevail on the issue of the veto, but he had made a name for himself.

The National Assembly took two long, laborious years to draft a constitution, during which time it enacted many sweeping reforms, including the end of France's oppressive system of "feudal" land tenure, a massive reorganization of local government, and the abolition of the nobility. But in the process, momentous political divisions opened up in the country. In the Assembly itself, a set of progressive deputies sitting on the left side of the meeting hall (including Robespierre) faced off against conservatives on the right, incidentally giving birth to this key element of modern political terminology. Outside the Assembly, the end of what the French were already calling the "old regime" had brought with it the collapse of censorship. Hundreds of new newspapers were appearing, many of them violently partisan and devoted to apocalyptic conspiracy theories about their enemies' evil intentions. In addition, political "clubs" (referred to by the English word) were multiplying throughout the country, exerting pressure over local governments and the Assembly itself. And the popular movement that had taken shape spontaneously in the summer of 1789 was gaining strength. In October, as the people of Paris suffered from dire food shortages and rumors spread of a royal coup, crowds led by market women and accompanied by National Guard detachments marched on the palace of Versailles, twelve miles from Paris. After a brief standoff, they forced the royal family to return with them to the capital. The Assembly took up residence there as well, in a hastily converted indoor riding arena, under the gaze of boisterous spectators and journalists. In Paris and other major cities, popular militants going by the name of *sans-culottes* (i.e., those who wore trousers rather than the "culotte" breeches of the upper classes) set up power bases in neighborhood assemblies meeting in permanent session.

Under these conditions, the most prominent political figures became celebrities, developing fervent followings. Printers rushed to publish their biographies, and engravers competed to sell their portraits. These portraits emphasized each deputy's individual features and often depicted them in casual dress so as to increase a sense of intimacy with the viewer. Mirabeau was by far the favorite subject, with more than two hundred separate images produced.[24] Lafayette featured prominently as well, profiting from his prominence as head of the National Guard. On July 15, 1790, when he appeared in public in Paris alongside Mayor Jean-Sylvain Bailly, a famous astronomer, the city's official orator hailed them with the words, "France too has its Franklin and its Washington."[25] Robespierre developed a large following as well, thanks to his stern speeches, both in the Assembly and in the most prominent left-wing political club, the Jacobins.

A very different sort of hero emerged on the Revolution's far left. Jean-Paul Marat, a Swiss doctor born in 1743, had spent formative years in London, where he fell under the spell of John Wilkes. In Paris, in 1789, he began publishing his own newspaper, *L'ami du peuple* ("the people's friend"), which adapted Wilkes's knack for pushing the limits of acceptable speech to the increasingly paranoid political atmosphere of revolutionary Paris. In every issue of his paper, Marat warned of counterrevolutionary plots and insisted that they could be stopped only with merciless violence. Never hesitate, he repeatedly exclaimed, to cut off a few hundred heads to save thousands more.[26] He made himself into the central character of his story, promising to uncover corruption, to root out evil, and to defy "the idols of favor" and "the idols of power."[27] In the process, he himself quickly became the idol of the left-wing clubs and the *sans-culottes*.

King Louis XVI himself briefly became a popular idol of sorts as well. Although he accepted the early revolutionary reforms grudgingly, his acceptance of them did calm widespread fears of imminent civil war. Relieved commentators quickly hailed him as the "restorer of French liberty" and portrayed him in engravings as a new Augustus.[28] Even the suspicions of the Parisian crowds could transmute into enthusiasm for the king with stunning speed, notably after he gave in to their demands during the popular march on Versailles in October.[29] The many odes, addresses, and pamphlets that appeared in praise of Louis during the first years of the Revolution had more in common with paeans to Paoli and Washington than with anything prepared on behalf of earlier French monarchs. They presented Louis as a second founder of his country and as a servant of public liberty.[30]

The popularity enjoyed by these various figures shows just how enthusiastically the French were seeking living, human leaders with whom they could feel a bond of trust in the midst of rapid, swirling, threatening change. However beautiful and inspiring the Declaration of Rights, its words remained abstractions. The constitution was as yet unfinished, and citizens knew that when it came into effect, it might place them under the rule of men they had voted against and whose principles they abhorred. The very idea of political representation was still strange and unfamiliar in France.[31] John Adams's description of the way Americans had chosen a "character of convention" to serve as the living symbol of their Revolution, and a source of unity, applies very well to the early idolization of Mirabeau, Lafayette, Marat, Robespierre, and Louis XVI.

But the deepening political polarization quickly turned every hero for one side into an enemy for the other, above all in the case of Louis XVI himself. In 1790 the Assembly, which had already nationalized the vast landholdings of the French clergy, voted for a radical subordination of the Catholic Church to the French state, with priests and bishops to be chosen by election. The reform left the king all the more troubled over the Revolution's course, and in June 1791 he attempted to flee the country and rendezvous with a counterrevolutionary army across the border. Instead, he was caught in the small town of Varennes and brought back to the capital, where moderate figures in the Assembly—including Lafayette—desperately pretended that he had been rescued from kidnappers. But no one was fooled, and the event seemed to confirm the most outlandish of Marat's conspiracy theories. The new constitution took effect in September 1791, confirming Louis as chief executive, but it struck many observers as dead on arrival.

In this atmosphere of febrile suspicion, nearly every prominent political figure found himself accused of coveting absolute power. Lafayette, commanding the significant military force of the National Guard, made one obvious target. Marat denounced him repeatedly and darkly warned his readers of the example of Julius Caesar.[32] Writing to George Washington in August 1790, Lafayette jokingly referred to himself as "this so much blackened Cromwell, this ambitious dictator."[33] But the king himself received the most accusations. When crowds cheered him in public, left-wing newspapers complained that "the people . . . are not yet cured of their penchant for idolatry."[34] A popular book called *The Crimes of the Kings of France* dilated at length on the charge, in language that recalled Robespierre's strictures against personal power in general: "The people of France . . . are sensitive to the point of idolatry. People, change your character with your government, or you will have broken your chains in vain! The freer the government the less idolatrous the people; idolatry is a vice of despotic states. Austere republicans never had this kind of enthusiasm for their equals."[35] In the wake of the king's attempted flight, these claims about idolization not only served to discredit Louis XVI in particular but helped convince many on the left of the need to abolish the monarchy altogether.

By early 1792, nearly all the idols of the early Revolution had disappeared or lost their luster. The king's flight had discredited him among a wide swath of the population, and the discredit extended to his more prominent supporters, notably Lafayette. Mirabeau had died in April 1791. Marat remained, but while his venomous tirades made him a hero to radical militants, they repelled most of the rest of the political spectrum. But then there was the great opponent of political idolatry in all its forms, and of the very idea of an emotional bond between the people and their leaders that might trump constitutional principle: Robespierre.

Throughout 1791, Robespierre's reputation on the left continued to grow. Thanks to a measure that he himself had proposed, members of the National Assembly barred themselves from serving in the new constitution's Legislative Assembly. But Robespierre found an equally effective rostrum at the Jacobin Club. There, the major division pitted him against a faction led by the prominent writer and deputy Jacques-Pierre Brissot, who wanted France to declare war on Austria and Prussia and to extend the Revolution beyond France's borders. Robespierre insisted, to the contrary, that the Revolution needed above all to root out its enemies in France itself.

In his debates with Brissot, Robespierre continued his long-standing denunciations of personal power and the very idea of a leader deliberately cultivating popular support. "I do not know how to flatter the people so as to destroy it," he stated. "I do not know the art of leading it towards a precipice along a path strewn with flowers."[36] In the first months of 1792, the Jacobin Club became the scene of howling, chaotic debates in which the "Brissotins" and Robespierre accused one another of coveting personal power. Brissot's ally Marguerite-Élie Guadet called Robespierre "a man who, whether by ambition or misfortune, has become the idol of the people" and charged him with aspiring to dictatorship. Robespierre responded angrily: "You dare accuse me of wanting to mislead and flatter the people! How could I? I am neither the courtier, nor the moderator, nor the tribune, nor the defender of the people. I am people myself."[37]

As these debates continued, a certain irony became obvious. The man who claimed to be the passive, transparent instrument of the people's will, the "Incorruptible" who insisted on keeping all political power abstract and impersonal, nonetheless kept drawing attention to his own person. "I have never spoken of myself except when forced to refute calumnies and to defend my principles," he protested.[38] But his conduct made even some of his supporters uneasy. "We invite Monsieur Robespierre . . . to persuade himself that, since he is not a god, he can sometimes make mistakes," one of them wrote in a friendly newspaper. "Robespierre," another declared, "the patriots do not like you making a spectacle of yourself."[39]

Meanwhile, the already frantic pace of events accelerated. Brissot convinced the Legislative Assembly to declare war, but the first months of hostilities saw a series of French defeats, which led to an intensification of conspiracy theories and weakened the king even further. In August 1792, armed *sans-culottes*, reinforced by militants from around the country, stormed the royal palace of the Tuileries and massacred the king's guard. The king placed himself under the protection of the Legislative Assembly, which quickly voted to hold elections for a National Convention that would write a new republican constitution. They also declared Lafayette a traitor, forcing him to flee across the lines to the Austrians. In early September, as enemy forces broke through French defenses in the east, *sans-culottes* attacked prisons holding suspected counterrevolutionaries and killed well over a thousand, leaving Parisian streets awash in blood.

Until the summer of 1791, the idea of France without a king had been largely unthinkable. Robespierre himself had mocked the idea, arguing that monarchy was the only suitable form of government for the country.[40] But in September 1792, the new National Convention, elected by universal manhood suffrage and again including Robespierre as a deputy, formally abolished the monarchy and proclaimed France a republic. Three months later, it put Louis XVI on trial and, upon the urging of Robespierre and other radicals, found him guilty and condemned him to death. On January 21, 1793, the king went to the guillotine before a vast crowd in what is now the Place de la Concorde in Paris. The blood sacrifice was complete.

Now, it seemed to many, for the first time in the age of revolution, an opportunity had arisen to create a government of pure principles, abstract and impersonal, without the slightest trace of charismatic political authority. In December 1792, as the Convention discussed the new constitution, Robespierre's ally Edmond-Louis-Alexis Dubois-Crancé made the point directly: "The Jacobins want a true and singular republic, founded on the purity of the principles of the declaration of rights, where the law alone dominates, never an individual."[41] Over the next months, a remarkable egalitarian spirit made itself felt in France, reinforcing this ambition. Robespierre even proposed a plan, never implemented, by which the state would remove all children over the age of five from their families, to be raised in public boarding schools.[42] The power of the *sans-culottes* was at its zenith, and they pushed for the Convention to adopt an unprecedented range of social reforms, including maximum prices on staple goods. One of their popular songs, adapting a biblical verse, ran: "Giants must be shortened / And the small made taller, / All the same height / That is true happiness" (the implied reference to literal "shortening" by the guillotine gave the words an added sting).[43] It was the atmosphere in which Anacharsis Cloots could express his wish for France to be cured of individuals.

Whether the revolutionaries could have achieved such a goal even under ideal circumstances is debatable. But the circumstances were far from ideal, and in the first half of 1793 the Revolution came close to violent collapse. First the war expanded, pitting France against a coalition that now included Britain and Spain. Attempts at drafting peasants into the army spurred revolts, especially in the western region of the Vendée, where a Catholic and Royal Army briefly threatened to overwhelm revolutionary forces. In Paris itself, factional rivalry grew more and more intense between the Brissotins on one side and the group around Robespierre, supported by the *sans-culottes*, on the other. At the end of May 1793, armed *sans-culottes* staged another insurrection, surrounding the Convention's meeting hall and forcing the expulsion and arrest of the Brissotin deputies. In reaction, another wave of revolts flared, this time in provincial cities where the Brissotins had dominated. In Paris, a young woman stabbed the idol of the radical left, Jean-Paul Marat, to death as he sat in his bathtub nursing a painful skin condition.

In response to these events, the Convention undertook a series of extraordinary, improvised emergency measures, many of them carried out by deputies acting as autocratic "Representatives on Mission" in the provinces. These included an unprecedented conscription effort, a draconian centralization of French government, and the creation of "revolutionary armies" to maintain domestic order. In September 1793 there also began the policies of severe repression that would come to be known as the Reign of Terror. Even as the armed forces finally crushed the revolt in the Vendée and then carried out horrific large-scale massacres in the region, thousands more went to their deaths across the country for alleged counterrevolutionary activity, after mostly perfunctory trials. The Convention approved a new, egalitarian constitution but voted to suspend its implementation for the duration of the war. Effective power increasingly passed to two of the Convention's committees: the Committee of General Security and, especially, the notorious twelve-man Committee of Public Safety. Robespierre joined the latter in late July 1793 and soon became its most visible member.[44]

This revolutionary government saved the French Revolution with its harsh and forceful measures, but the Terror eventually tore the government itself apart. The group of deputies around Robespierre—known as "the Mountain," because they occupied the highest seats in the meeting hall—remained engaged in deadly conflict with factional rivals, even after vanquishing the Brissotins (whose leaders were executed in the fall of 1793). In the winter and spring of 1794, they succeeded in purging and executing other groups of deputies, including one around the great orator Georges Danton—also accused of plotting to seize absolute power—but at the cost of driving the levels of fear and suspicion in the Convention to an unbearable pitch. As they did so, the Terror intensified. Between March 1793 and June 1794 the Revolutionary Tribunal had passed some 1,251 death sentences—roughly three per day. After June 10, the pace shot up tenfold, with 1,376 people condemned over the next six weeks.[45] Robespierre denounced conspiracy after conspiracy, most of which existed only in his own fevered imagination.

Ironically, the one conspiracy Robespierre failed to see was the very real one that formed against him in the Convention itself, leading to his overthrow. On July 26, he gave a rambling, disjointed speech, again defending himself against accusations of dictatorship ("this word has magic effects . . . it destroys the Republic") but drawing more attention to himself than ever—he used the word "I" (*je*) some 136 times.[46] The next day—the Ninth of Thermidor, Year II, according to the new calendar the Revolution had adopted—a group of deputies, fearful for their own lives, won over the mass of their colleagues and succeeded in declaring Robespierre and his allies outlaws. After a day of confused maneuvering in which the man who had sworn so often to sacrifice himself for the Revolution tried to commit suicide but succeeded only in shooting himself in the jaw, the group was taken prisoner. The next day they met the same fate to which they had condemned so many opponents: they died on the guillotine.

The mesmerizing figure of Robespierre continues to loom very large in the historical imagination. Even today, popular works of history and fiction routinely present him as an unhinged demagogue and dictator who personally masterminded the Reign of Terror in order to serve his megalomaniacal ambition.[47] The truth is different. The only dictatorship in France in 1793–94, and then only at certain moments, was the collective one of the Committee of Public Safety, over which Robespierre had influence, not control. Robespierre genuinely had no interest in seizing personal power for himself, while his intense, obsessive devotion to political work left him in a state of severe exhaustion, absent from the Convention for weeks on end during the crucial spring of 1794 and prey to delusions and paranoia. As the historian Colin Jones nicely puts it, he was "less . . . the man who ruined the Revolution than . . . a man the Revolution ruined."[48] His moment of greatest visibility came on June 8, 1794, during the so-called Festival of the Supreme Being: his inauguration of a new, deist cult he hoped would, over time, eclipse the Catholic Church. Wearing a brilliant sky-blue coat, Robespierre presided over the elaborate festivities, which included children dressed in white carrying baskets of flowers, and the incineration of effigies representing Atheism and Ambition, among other vices. But the event did not mark the start of personal rule. One of Robespierre's enemies, the philosopher Condorcet (a Brissotin who committed suicide at the end of March), better captured the essence of the role Robespierre saw himself playing: "Robespierre preaches, Robespierre censors . . . He creates disciples . . . he has acquired a reputation for austerity that aims at saintliness . . . he speaks of God and Providence and calls himself the friend of the poor and the weak . . . Robespierre is a priest and will never be anything else. The accusation of dictatorship was thus misplaced."[49] Robespierre's enemies certainly repeated the accusation of dictatorship with numbing frequency. As Bertrand Barère, an ally on the Committee of Public Safety, expostulated in April 1793, "We never stop talking about dictatorship!"[50] But the repetition simply shows that Robespierre's own warnings against charismatic authority had won general acceptance. Before 1794 only one leading political figure—Marat—openly advocated a "supreme dictator" as a means of saving the Revolution, and Marat's extreme reputation ensured that few outside his own circle of admirers listened to him.[51] All the other leading revolutionaries agreed that "idolatry," as the Brissotin interior minister put it in late 1792, should "never be substituted for the cult of the law."[52] When Robespierre's enemies accused him of dictatorship, they did so in his own language. For instance, in a particularly thorough attack launched in the fall of 1792, the Brissotin deputy Jean-Baptiste Louvet declaimed:

> [Robespierre has] declared most impudently that he is the only virtuous man in France, the only one to whom the task of saving the country can be confided . . . [He] showered the lowest kind of flattery on a few hundred citizens whom he called the people of Paris, and then the people full stop, and then the sovereign . . . [He] presented himself as an idol to supposedly free men . . . an overweening usurper, whom his faction treated almost as a god.[53]

Louvet also (of course) compared Robespierre to Caesar and Cromwell, but the speech is notable above all for its emphasis on the idea of the "idol"—for seeing the greatest danger to the Republic in the charismatic bond that a figure like Robespierre could forge with his most fervent followers. In response, Robespierre's ally Barère agreed that a man with "Caesar's genius or Cromwell's daring" indeed had to be feared—but that Robespierre did not fit the bill. Barère added that anyone who had "great popularity" qualified as a potential enemy of the Revolution.[54]

But as these accusations flew, even more than before, a tremendous irony made itself felt. Despite all these denunciations of personal power, throughout France a significant section of the population had in fact come to think of Robespierre as a supreme ruler and clamored for him to accept the title. Nothing like this had been seen in France since the start of the Revolution. The only comparable degree of enthusiasm for an individual had come after the assassination of Marat, whose most fervent supporters staged genuinely idolatrous mourning ceremonies in the summer of 1793 (among other things, they compared the dead hero to Jesus and his death to the Crucifixion). But as with Washington in the United States in 1799, less was at stake in directing such reverence to the dead.

Robespierre, on the other hand, was still very much alive, and the adulation directed toward him from the fall of 1793 onward compared in intensity, if not in volume, to the adulation of George Washington during the American Revolution. One indication comes from the breathlessly hyperbolic letters that Robespierre received in this period.[55] They must be read with care, since many of the authors clearly wanted something from him, but they show how easily the authors could imagine him as a charismatic hero, with the same superhuman qualities previously attributed to Paoli or Washington. For one woman, he was "an eagle soaring in the skies, with a seductive heart." Others claimed that "you enlighten the universe by your writings, you regenerate the human race"; "you fill the world with your renown"; "you are our savior"; "you are the founder of the Republic."[56] A widow from Nantes even proposed marriage, saying she had been in love with him since the start of the Revolution: "You are my supreme divinity, my guardian angel."[57]

Nor was this all. Formal declarations from clubs and municipalities across the country reported on a wave of popular enthusiasm for Robespierre. Children were learning his writings by heart. Babies were being named after him. At public festivals, crowds were shouting "Vive Robespierre" along with "Vive la République." A young Englishman who visited Paris in early 1794 reported Robespierre's apparent annoyance at the attention. "Why come to me?" Robespierre asked him. "Everyone applies to me, as if I had an omnipotent power."[58]

In the spring of 1794, with France's military situation still perilous and the political situation enormously unstable, a dictatorship even became thinkable for some in the Convention. Louis-Antoine de Saint-Just had worshipped the "Incorruptible" since the start of the Revolution (when he was only twenty-one) and after 1792 became a crucial political ally.[59] A year later, in a never-completed work on republican institutions, he mused that "in every revolution, there is a need for a dictator to save the State by force, or censors to save it by virtue."[60] And in 1794, according to Bertrand Barère's admittedly untrustworthy memoirs, Saint-Just told the Committee of Public Safety: "I see only one means of salvation: this means, it is the concentration of power . . . we need a dictatorial power . . . we need a man who has enough genius, strength, patriotism and generosity . . . This man, I declare that it is Robespierre. He alone can save the state."[61] On July 28, Saint-Just went to the guillotine along with his idol.

In short, no matter how powerful the suspicion of personal power, no matter how deep the belief in a "cult of the law" and a government of pure principle, the longing for a charismatic leader made itself felt in revolutionary France as well and fastened on to one of the men apparently least suitable for the role. But as I have noted, charismatic appeal emerges out of the hopes and expectations of the followers as much as it does out of the personality and actions of the leader. In the moment of crisis and exaltation in which revolutionary France fought for survival, the need for a flesh-and-blood figure with whom ordinary people could feel a bond of trust and confidence came close to overwhelming the fear of a new Caesar that had impregnated revolutionary culture since 1789.

And while the name Washington—associated with a far less radical revolution—went largely unmentioned in France in 1793 and 1794, the memory of the earlier adulation he had enjoyed there may still have played a role, in the background, in feeding the abortive cult of Robespierre.

Precisely because of this abortive cult, Robespierre's fall only seemed to further strengthen French suspicions of charismatic leadership. He was overthrown not by counterrevolutionaries but by men who had largely supported him and who had helped implement the Terror. After the Ninth of Thermidor they stopped the spiral of executions, but to dissociate themselves from the bloodshed of the previous year, they needed to do more. Their solution was to place nearly all the blame for the Terror squarely on Robespierre's severed head, creating one of the most fearful black legends in all of history around it. In innumerable speeches, pamphlets, and newspaper reports, they did not merely paint Robespierre as a dictator but as a bloodthirsty monster who had single-handedly masterminded the Terror in pursuit of his own overweening ambition. According to one fanciful report he had even planned to marry the surviving daughter of Louis XVI and claim the crown of France for himself. A popular engraving depicted him guillotining an executioner who had just finished guillotining everyone else in France.[62] He was the center of every plot, the true picture of the counterrevolu-tion, the example to be avoided at every cost.

One revolutionary writer, a Jacobin naval official named Étienne Barry, even used Robespierre as the principal illustration for a speech on "the dangers of individual idolatry in a republic," delivered just six weeks after the Ninth of Thermidor. Barry admitted that even in the most egalitarian republic, certain "superior men" would nonetheless come to the fore—he cited the examples of Washington and Franklin in the United States and Marat in France. The trouble came, he argued, when ordinary citizens began to treat a man of great virtue, talent, and accom-plishments as "a living idol, a tutelary divinity, a worthy object of the respect, homage, and finally the obedience of mere mortals." This was "individual idolatry," and it all too easily corrupted men who already had a desire for domination.[63] Barry's analysis was a striking one, because of the emphasis it put on "idolatry" rather than malevolent intent as the most potent source of harm. It was the popular adulation, the exaggerated response to perceived charisma, as illustrated in this case by the cult of Robespierre, that had the most corrosive effect on republican institutions.

This same sense of the dangerous power of charisma still prevailed a year later, when the "Thermidorians" finally drew up a new constitution for the battered French republic. Determined to rein in what they saw as the unruly forces of popular democracy, they again restricted the suffrage to well-off property holders and also decided to restrain the popularly elected legislature with the reinstitution of a strong executive power. But to avoid putting any single man in a position again to subject the state to personal rule, they divided that power among no fewer than five executive "directors."

The First French Republic survived for another five years after the fall of Robespierre and even, in some ways, flourished. Although the government crushed attempts at insurrection by the remnants of the *sans-culottes* movement, and while it restricted full political rights to the well-off, it also made a renewed commitment to projects of public education and welfare. The principal reforms of the early Revolution, from the end of "feudal" landholding to the confiscation of Church property, from the establishment of press and religious freedom to the holding of regular elections, remained secure.

But the government was also prey to flagrant corruption and massive instability. Moderate royalists and neo-Jacobins both emerged as serious political forces and struggled, sometimes violently, for political power. A brutal "white Terror" in the provinces targeted those blamed for the repression of 1792–94, and revolts again flared in the west. Increasingly, the executive Directory resorted to authoritarian practices to maintain order, such as the widespread substitution of military commissions for the civilian justice system.[64] In the late summer of 1797, left-wing politicians used the army to nullify elections and expel royalists from the government, in the so-called Coup of Fructidor. Over the next two years, two more coups followed, without putting an end to the turmoil.

Strikingly, even amid what most observers perceived as a permanent crisis, none of the period's civilian politicians developed any sort of charismatic reputation—certainly nothing to compare with that of Robespierre or, before him, of Marat, Mirabeau, or Lafayette. Of the thirteen men who served as executive "Directors" between 1795 and 1799, most remained little-known even at the time. The most famous of them, Emmanuel Sieyès, owed his public reputation mostly to his role at the start of the Revolution, as a leader of the Third Estate.[65] Official portraits of the "Directors" in their elaborate and much-mocked tricolor costumes were deliberately impersonal, as if to forestall any popular identification with the actual individuals (see figure 13). It might seem, then, that the Revolution was finally triumphing over "individual idolatry."

In fact, something of the reverse was taking place. No civilian leaders under the Directory attracted a powerful personal following. But men in uniform did. In the American Revolution, the hour of the general came at the very beginning. In France, it took until 1796, seven years after the start of the French Revolution and four years after the start of a continent-wide war.

It had taken so long for several reasons. In the first years of the Revolution, virtually the entire officer corps of the old royal army—almost wholly staffed by nobles—resigned or were dismissed because of their opposition to the Revolution.[66] Their replacements were largely unknown and untested. In the first years of the war, the French mostly fought on or close to their own soil, under the strict and sometimes deadly supervision of the revolutionary authorities. In 1793–94 alone, 84 generals received death sentences, and 352 others were dismissed.[67] Moreover, at a moment when charismatic leadership of all sorts aroused great suspicion, the memory of Julius Caesar and Oliver Cromwell directed particular mistrust toward military leaders, starting with Lafayette. General Charles-François Dumouriez enjoyed a moment of acclaim after an important victory over the Austrians in November 1792, but it did not last long. After quarrels with radicals in the Convention put him in danger, he tried to rally his troops to march on Paris. They refused to obey him, and he fled across the lines to the Austrians. The episode of course only further increased mistrust of generals.

Toward the end of the Terror, the recognition that political interference had hurt the army and thereby threatened the Revolution finally began to overcome this mistrust. By the spring of 1794, the revolutionary government was giving greater latitude to professional commanders to run the army as they saw fit. These commanders themselves were learning how best to employ the masses of new recruits the Convention had drafted, and they began to win important victories. As they did so, the theaters of operations moved farther from France's 1789 borders, allowing the generals to operate even more independently. Their successes made a striking contrast to the political chaos and violence back home, and between 1795 and 1799 many of them became popular heroes. Their campaigns were followed in detail in the newspapers, engraved portraits circulated widely, and odes and speeches were delivered in their honor. Jean-Victor-Marie Moreau, Jean-Baptiste Jourdan, Lazare Hoche, and others became household names.

Very quickly, one name came to gleam more brightly than any other. Napoleon Bonaparte was still in his mid-twenties in 1796 and at first glance did not seem an obvious charismatic hero. Of slightly less than average height (although not the dwarf portrayed in British propaganda), skinny and sallow, with long, unkempt hair, he entirely lacked the physical grace that George Washington possessed in such abundance. He had an intense manner, speaking quickly and assertively in a noticeable Italian accent.[68] He came, of course, from Corsica, which had belonged to France only since 1768. His father, a lawyer and a member of the island's gentry, had supported Pasquale Paoli but declined to follow the fabled leader into exile. Instead, he took advantage of his (just barely) noble status to send Napoleon, his second son, to one of the military schools newly founded to train young French nobles for the officer corps. There, far from home, mocked for his ungainly accent and name, the young man nursed a fierce loyalty to Corsica and dreamed of helping lead it back to independence. He developed a particular fixation on Paoli, whom he most likely read about in the pages of Boswell. After his graduation, as a young officer in a series of boring provincial posts, knowing that he could never rise very high in the socially exclusive army of the Old Regime, he also fantasized about becoming a famous writer. He read obsessively in classic French literature and the works of the Enlightenment and tried his hand at writing philosophical essays and (very poor) stories in the then-fashionable gothic style.[69] His denunciation of ambition as a form of madness came in a submission to an academic essay contest on the theme of happiness.

When the French Revolution began, Bonaparte returned to Corsica on leave and plunged into the island's tumultuous politics. At first he attached himself to Paoli, whom the revolutionary authorities had finally allowed home. But soon he came to resent the now-aging leader, who in turn disparaged the impatient Napoleon and his brothers as "*ragazzoni inesperti*"—inexperienced boys—and tried to bar them from positions of influence. Matters came to a head in 1793, as Napoleon and his fervently revolutionary younger brother Lucien supported the policies of the Mountain, while the more conservative Paoli moved toward a break with the Parisian government. In June 1793 the Convention condemned Paoli as a traitor, leading him to stage a successful revolt on the island, with the support of the British fleet. The Bonaparte family fled to the mainland while Paoli's supporters sacked their family home.

It was a decisive turning point. On the mainland, Bonaparte committed himself fully to the French revolutionary cause and quickly distinguished himself. In the siege of a port city that had rebelled against the Convention and welcomed in the British fleet, he displayed both military acumen and considerable bravery. Robespierre's younger brother, on the scene as a "Representative on Mission," praised him as "an officer of transcendent merit."[70] Although this connection led to his brief imprisonment after the Ninth of Thermidor, Bonaparte soon proved his worth to the "Thermidorian" government by helping it suppress violent royalist riots in Paris in the autumn of 1795. Less than six months later, he took command of the Army of Italy.

There followed one of the most astonishing military campaigns in European history. Bonaparte turned out to be a genuine military genius, with a preternatural ability to envisage battlefields, keep the positions of different units in his head even in the midst of enormous confusion, and quickly bring decisive strength to bear upon the enemy's weak points. In barely nine months, in a series of brilliant battles and maneuvers, he and his subordinates won victory after victory, occupied most of northern Italy, and forced the Austrian empire to the negotiating table. The final peace treaty, signed in October 1797, acknowledged French gains—including the creation of a new, revolutionary Cisalpine Republic allied with France—as well as France's annexation of present-day Belgium, formerly an Austrian territory. French strategists had dreamed of such gains for centuries without ever achieving them. Now, thanks to Napoleon Bonaparte, they were a reality.

The French public greeted the victories ecstatically and with an apparently unquenchable thirst to learn as much as possible about their latest unlikely hero. The Directorial regime encouraged this enthusiasm, even as it attempted to tamp down displays of collective emotion in the domestic political sphere.[71] In Paris, government agents filed regular reports on public opinion (in point of fact, mostly the opinion of literate men who frequented the capital's cafés), and in 1797 they testified overwhelmingly to the "public admiration" and "flood of praise" for Bonaparte. His "military and diplomatic talents are being praised to the highest degree."[72] Between 1795 and 1799 at least 150 separate engraved portraits appeared of Bonaparte—far more than of any other figure of the period.[73] Poets rushed to celebrate him. "In the path you are taking as a giant," wrote one, "[you are] stronger than Jupiter, as bold as lightning."[74] Another praised "this hero, child of Italy, / Who, having become French, saved his *patrie*."[75] Joseph Charron, president of the department of the Marne, told his fellow citizens in a public address that Napoleon ranked with the great generals of antiquity: "nothing in modern times can be compared to him."[76] An ex-monk turned Parisian bookseller named Jean-Louis Dubroca delivered an overexcited speech to a congregation of deists, insisting that for many years "men will not have a hero to praise equal to he who has conquered the continent of Europe."[77] Between 1796 and 1799, French theaters put on at least thirty plays that either mentioned Bonaparte or featured him as a character.[78] The first short biography of Napoleon, full of anecdotes about his childhood, appeared in England in 1797 and was translated into French within months.[79]

Like Washington's followers, the early admirers of Bonaparte extolled his virtue and his masculine restraint almost as fervently as they praised his victories. The poet who compared him to Jupiter claimed that "your noble works / Have as a goal the happiness of a people of heroes."[80] Dubroca pointedly told Napoleon that "in the euphoria of victory you have not been tempted, like Caesar, to cross the Rubicon so as to enslave your country. You conquered for the interest of liberty alone."[81] A newssheet appeared in Paris entitled *Journal of Bonaparte and Virtuous Men*.[82] It seemed as if Napoleon was being cast in the Washingtonian mode: as a virtuous republican.

And yet, even among these same authors, different tendencies were at work as well. Charron, for instance, contemptuously contrasted the brilliance of Napoleon's victories to the "imbecilic chatter of the skeptics and the bland speechmakers who obsess us . . . the pygmies of all the parties."[83] It was precisely the sort of language that would justify Napoleon's coup d'état two years later. As for Jean-Louis Dubroca, he would soon lose his inhibitions about the crossing of Rubicons and become an enthusiastic propagandist for Bonaparte. He would write a lengthy, adulatory biography, as well as a long eulogy for George Washington at Bonaparte's behest, and a hostile biography of Bonaparte's Caribbean nemesis Toussaint Louverture. We might almost call him the period's leading specialist in charismatic authority, had he not been such a mercenary hack.

The frequently made comparison between Napoleon Bonaparte and

Julius Caesar offers a particularly sharp illustration of how opinions about charismatic leadership were changing. Both Charron and the anonymous poet favorably invoked Caesar's name when praising Napoleon's military genius.[84] In July 1798, when the paper *Le conservateur* called Bonaparte "the French Caesar," another paper angrily responded that Bonaparte was "the hero of French liberty" and not its oppressor. *Le conservateur* backpedaled, saying that "in calling Bonaparte the French Caesar, we were thinking of nothing but the military glory of one of the greatest commanders of antiquity; a glory, in truth, that our hero has so greatly eclipsed, that he can only be compared to himself."[85] Several weeks later, another journalist wrote with tongue in cheek that the French people were not going to fall in love with a charismatic leader: "They are ripe for liberty, as it is said, because they no longer worship anyone, even God the father." But he also quipped that "if we are irrevocably destined to bow our heads under the yoke of a new despotism, I confess that, despot for despot, I would prefer the one who has taken for a model Caesar, who pardoned his enemies."[86]

The most important figure crafting Bonaparte's image was Bonaparte himself. From early on in the Italian campaign—in his own recollections, after the victory at Lodi on May 10, 1796—he became convinced of his destiny as "a superior man." "The ambition came to me," he said, "of executing the great things which so far had been occupying my thoughts only as a fantastic dream."[87] These "great things" were political as much as military and made nonsense of Bonaparte's youthful, pro forma denunciations of personal ambition. As early as 1792 his brother Lucien had written to another brother, Joseph: "I have always detected in Napoleon an ambition that is not altogether selfish, but which overcomes his love for the common good . . . He seems inclined to be a tyrant, and I think that he would be one if he were king."[88] Napoleon had no more respect than Charron for the political squabblers of the Directory, and as his victories accumulated, he set his sights on supreme power. "Do you imagine that I triumph in Italy in order to aggrandize the lawyers of the Directory?" he asked an associate in 1797. "The nation needs a leader, a leader decked in glory, and not in theories of government, phrases, speeches."[89] In the late summer of

1797, when left-wing politicians purged the Directory and assemblies of royalists, Bonaparte sent troops to ensure that the Coup of Fructidor succeeded. At the same time, he frequently ignored the Directory's instructions and, as a British newspaper put it, "reign[ed] in Italy with more uncontrolled sway than the Dictator and Emperor Julius Caesar."[90]

In short, Bonaparte most emphatically did not see himself as a modest, self-effacing Washington, called only reluctantly to political office and a scrupulous respecter of republican institutions. His model, despite the recent quarrels, was more the Pasquale Paoli he had read and dreamed about as a boy, who ruled with absolute, unmediated, and unquestioned authority over an adoring people thanks to the sheer force of his personality. And Bonaparte understood that to acquire that sort of authority—to bond the French people to him in a despotism of love—he needed to develop a powerful propaganda apparatus.

Bonaparte approached this task with a particularly brilliant instinct. He knew how deeply the very idea of personal political power had been mistrusted in revolutionary France, with charismatic generals coming in for special suspicion. After he aided the 1797 Coup of Fructidor, the right-wing press fulminated against "military despotism" in general and Bonaparte in particular. "Is the Rubicon already crossed?" asked one paper. "Will we avoid a military republic by going to prostrate ourselves at the feet of the dictator?"[91] Bonaparte also knew very well that Robespierre had tried to deflect such attacks by presenting himself as an individual stripped of all individuality—the pure vessel of the Revolution. But rather than adopt a similar strategy, Bonaparte did the precise opposite and engaged in what the French call a *surenchère*: overbidding. In his propaganda, he presented himself not merely as superior but as an individual whose unique qualities were so extraordinary that a single human body could barely contain them. He presented himself as so massively superior to and different from other humans that the ordinary rules did not apply to him. The French might not trust ordinary humans, even talented ones, with excessive personal power, he implied, but they could trust him. I cannot say whether Bonaparte pursued this strategy consciously. But his superb political instincts led him directly to it.

The propaganda came in many different forms.[92] The Army of Italy published two newspapers, one primarily for the soldiers, one for the French public. Allies back in France, including his brothers, published the *Journal of Bonaparte and Virtuous Men*. Bonaparte's own boastful, bombastic military dispatches and his addresses to his soldiers were designed for public consumption and appeared in publications across Europe. The visual arts played an important role as well. The great French artist Antoine-Jean Gros painted a particularly stunning canvas depicting Bonaparte in the act of seizing a flag and leading his men to victory at the Battle of Arcole (figure 14). It mattered little that Bonaparte's charge had not actually succeeded and that another general had behaved more heroically. Gros highlighted Bonaparte's shining face and brilliant costume as he strode forward, turning back to urge his men on to victory: the embodiment of confident, masculine, charismatic appeal. Supposedly, Bonaparte had trouble standing still for Gros, and his wife Joséphine had to grasp him around the knees to keep him in one place.[93] Engravings of this painting and others, as well as the 150 original engraved portraits, circulated widely. Finally, Bonaparte staged impressive spectacles around his own person—which his own newspapers and others, of course, reported on. He established a virtual court for himself in Italy and dined there before spectators, as French kings had done at Versailles.[94] On Bastille Day 1797, during a military parade honoring the dead of the campaign, he gave a speech deploring the political turmoil back in France. On cue, a soldier stepped out of the ranks and shouted, "General, you have saved France. Your children, who glory in belonging to this invincible army, will shield you with their own bodies. Now, save the Republic!"[95]

In his propaganda, Bonaparte cultivated two distinct audiences: the public back in France but also the army. He knew well that he could never reach his goal without the passionate backing of his own troops, and he did as much as possible to ensure they would provide it. He made their material comfort—food, drink, boots, tents—a top priority, even if the supplies had to be stolen from the surrounding country, and he boasted with considerable exaggeration about how greatly conditions had improved under his command. He liberally distributed honors as well, such as a hundred specially engraved sabers given to soldiers—including privates and drummer boys—who had demonstrated exemplary courage. He treated his soldiers as equals, addressing them in deliberately familiar, emotional language: "I can't express the feelings I have for you any better than by saying that I bear along in my heart the love that you show me every day."[96] At the Battle of Lodi, he stepped in to help ordinary soldiers load a cannon, leading them to joke that they would elect him their new corporal. The nickname of "the little corporal" stuck.[97]

This deliberately orchestrated propaganda campaign obviously differed hugely from the largely spontaneous, undirected outpourings of adulation for George Washington during and after the American Revolution. And yet the essential attributes of Bonaparte's image as a charismatic leader did not differ enormously from that earlier case—or, for that matter, from Paoli's. Like Washington, Bonaparte was portrayed as a man of high virtue, meaning, above all, devotion to the common good. Both men were compared incessantly to figures from classical antiquity—one engraving depicted Bonaparte on a medal atop medals of Alexander and Hannibal (figure 15). Both men were hailed as the embodiment of military glory and as the saviors of their countries. And both were described as utterly exceptional, superior human beings. Bonaparte's admirers obviously did not boast of his height or physical strength, but they fastened with delight upon a different innate quality of his: his genius. A famous passage from the newspaper of the Army of Italy illustrates just how deeply into the pool of hyperbole Bonaparte's propagandists were willing to plunge on this score:

> Today, glory has written a new name on its immortal tablets, with no fear of it ever being erased. The divinations which predicted a brilliant destiny for the young islander have come true. The time is past in which he locked himself up in his tent, a voluntary prisoner, a new Archimedes always at work . . . He knows that he is of those men who have no limit to their power but that conferred by

their own will, and whose sublime virtues complement their over-whelming genius . . . He promised victory, and brought it. He flies like lightning, and strikes like thunder. The speed of his move-ments is matched only by their accuracy and prudence. He is every-where. He sees everything. Like a comet cleaving the clouds, he appears at the same moment on the astonished banks of two sepa-rate rivers.

The article—written by a former acolyte of Robespierre, no less—praised Bonaparte's exquisite dignity, the touching clemency he showed to his enemies, and his firm resolution in all matters. Clearly such a man was born to rule.[98]

Despite such boasts, Bonaparte did not immediately attempt to seize power. Returning to Paris in triumph from Italy, he did not judge the moment ripe or see an obvious path forward. Instead, at the behest of the Directorial regime he embarked on an astonishing new venture: conquering Egypt. Landing there in the summer of 1798, he quickly defeated the country's Mameluke rulers and founded what he envisaged as an enlightened French colony. Back in France, news of the victories only added to his legend. His hopes quickly foundered, however, as the destruction of a French fleet by the British in the Mediterranean cut off the possibility of resupply, the city of Cairo revolted against French rule, and the Turkish Ottoman Empire assembled its own invasion force. Although Bonaparte suppressed the revolt and held off the Ottomans, it was obvious that the colony could not survive for long.[99]

Meanwhile, in France, both the military and political situations were deteriorating. The peace Bonaparte had negotiated with Austria did not hold, and soon the French Republic found itself at war with a new European coalition that also included Russia. Massive revolts broke out in areas the French had conquered, wiping away many of their ear-lier gains—including Bonaparte's. France itself was again threatened. And at the same time, the political turmoil grew worse, with deputies and then Directors illegally removed from office amid threats of military force. It was becoming painfully obvious that the regime of the Directory could not survive. Emmanuel Sieyès, now the most powerful of the five Directors, famously remarked, "I need a sword."[100]

It was against this background that Bonaparte and his top commanders quietly left Egypt and slipped past the British fleet, landing on the French coast in early October 1799. Most of the French public still, mistakenly, believed the Egyptian campaign another brilliant success and treated his return as providential. His triumphant trip to Paris and his arrival in the capital matched George Washington's inaugural trip through the United States for the sheer volume and intensity of praise that drenched the charismatic hero. In Lyon, as he passed through, townspeople placed lanterns in their windows, and the theater staged a hastily written play entitled *The Return of the Hero; or, Bonaparte at Lyon*, inviting him to attend.[101] When the news of his landing reached Paris, theater audiences stood up and cheered, while police spies reported that he was being hailed in popular songs as the exiled hero and "our father, our savior."[102] The government newspaper the *Gazette nationale* reported that "nothing equals the joy that has greeted Bonaparte's return. Along with our recent victories, it is the only event in a long time to have sparked popular enthusiasm. They are drinking to his return in the cabarets, they are singing about him in the streets; everywhere there are the most brilliant hopes."[103] Crowds gathered in front of his house in the aptly named rue de la Victoire, hoping for a sight of the great man.[104]

The coup itself quickly followed. Bonaparte met with Sieyès and devised a plan to replace the government of the Directory with a new regime headed by three "consuls": Bonaparte and Sieyès and another Director, Roger Ducos. It was all supposed to take place peacefully, and legally, with the parliament, under the "protection" of Bonaparte's troops, removing itself to the suburban town of Saint-Cloud and then voting to dissolve. In the event, as in most such cases, the plan went awry. Although the first vote took place as planned on November 9—18 Brumaire under the Republican calendar still in force—the next day a large number of deputies refused to dissolve the regime and cried out the familiar names of Caesar and Cromwell. Bonaparte himself was reduced to angry, stumbling threats. He was saved by his brother Lucien, who brandished a

dagger and promised to commit fratricide if Napoleon betrayed the republic, and by his deputy and future brother-in-law Joachim Murat, who
marched troops into the meeting hall with the words "Citizens! You are
dissolved." After Murat had expelled most of the deputies, the remainder
meekly voted as ordered.[105] The charismatic hero had come to power.

N apoleon Bonaparte would rule France for fifteen of the most eventful years in European history (and for an additional, especially
eventful "Hundred Days" a year later). It was a period of almost constant
war, in which the extent of his conquests rivaled anything seen in Europe
since the days of Charlemagne, Julius Caesar, or even Alexander the Great.
But while he subdued nearly all his enemies on the European continent
and enormously expanded the frontiers of France itself, he could not defeat his great maritime rival, Great Britain, on the seas or wreck its economy by cutting off its European trade. Worse, his overconfident attempts
to dictate policy to the Continent led him into disastrous conflicts in
Iberia and Russia that weakened him sufficiently for his enemies to reverse
his conquests and overthrow his regime in 1814 (and then for a second
time, after the "Hundred Days," in 1815). The wars cost millions of lives,
involved the brutal repression of occupied populations, and devastated
the French economy.

In France itself, despite the initial "Washingtonian" gestures, Bonaparte's rule was thoroughly authoritarian from the start, with heavy
press censorship and a tame parliament that largely followed his orders.
As we have seen, within three years of taking power he modified his own
constitution to become consul for life and then, just two years after that,
took the title of emperor. Still, in some ways the authoritarianism was a
moderate one. In France, the numbers of those imprisoned or executed
for political offenses did not come close to those of the Terror, to say nothing of twentieth-century dictatorships. And Bonaparte left a lasting
domestic legacy, including especially a reformed civil administration and
law code.

The writer Germaine de Staël, after Bonaparte's final defeat, memorably described how the Eighteenth Brumaire had changed the way the French spoke about political power:

> It was the first time, since the Revolution, that a proper name was heard in every mouth. Until then, it was said: "The Constituent Assembly did so and so, the people, the Convention." Now, no one spoke of anything except this man who needed to take the place of all, and to leave the human race anonymous by monopolizing all celebrity for himself alone, and preventing all other existing beings from ever being able to acquire any.[106]

Obviously, she was exaggerating. The name Robespierre had attracted more than its share of attention. But the remark testifies not just to how thoroughly Bonaparte now dominated the country but also to the collapse of the anti-charismatic ethos that had done so much to shape French political life in the previous ten years. A new Caesar had arisen, and no one now doubted that political power in France would henceforth take an intensely personal form, completely and entirely bound up with the fate of a single man. Dissidents might attack Bonaparte as a tyrant plundering France out of selfish ambition and long for a system that would do without such overproud "individuals," but Bonaparte's firm control of the press and the police ensured that their voices would remain thin and plaintive, drowned out by the thundering chorus of praise for the consul turned emperor. Needless to say, after the coup of the Eighteenth Brumaire, Bonaparte's already expert propaganda operation could continue with the full backing of the French state.

Throughout the years from 1799 to 1815, this propaganda operation disseminated an image of Bonaparte that fit the model of the charismatic leader that had developed in regard to Pasquale Paoli and then George Washington. It rarely failed to apply the word "genius" to him and rarely failed to praise the superhuman natural abilities that lifted him to the level of a "demi-god."[107] The visual works commissioned by the government carried the same message, none more eloquently than

Jacques-Louis David's most famous painting, of Napoleon crossing the Alps in 1799 (figure 3). It has deservedly become one of the best-known historical images of military glory, showing an utterly confident, masterful Bonaparte who, astride a rearing horse, seems to blend into the sublime natural landscape that the painting depicts and to command the very wind.

And there was more. To his propagandists, Bonaparte was of course the "savior" of France who had rescued it from political turmoil and military disaster.[108] Indeed, he had so fundamentally "regenerated" the country that he deserved to be seen as its "second founder." Some of the more exaggerated literary works suggested that he had literally brought a child back to life during the Egyptian campaign and that he would restore fertility to French fields.[109] Meanwhile, newspaper reports and biographical writings continued to offer plentiful details about his childhood and his private life (Dubroca's voluminous *Life* appeared as early as 1802 and did well enough to be translated into English).[110] Much in the manner of Weems's *Life of Washington*, the authors of these accounts happily invented stories that purported to show the determined character and military genius of Bonaparte already present in the boy: notably one in which he led his small comrades in military school to victory in an epic snowball fight. And as was done in the adulatory material about Paoli and Washington, Bonaparte's admirers constantly stressed the strength of his connection with ordinary French people. His authority, in their view, did not come solely from his own superhuman qualities but also from the emotional attachments he stimulated. Napoleon's triumphant return to France in 1799 offered them a particularly powerful example. "How to describe the enthusiasm, the euphoria which his return produced?" asked the author of one typical pamphlet. "All the citizens hurrying, rushing in tumultuous floods to see him as he passed, their eyes looking everywhere for him, gazing avidly at him; his name flying from mouth to mouth . . . public joy . . . is the most constant expression of national gratitude."[111] Such perceived "joy" (*allégresse*) comprised a key element of his charismatic authority.

At the start of his rule, Bonaparte still denied that he was profiting from his charisma to overturn constitutional restraints. As in his early tribute to Washington, at that point he still presented himself as a charismatic *republican* hero: a genius, a savior, a founding father, but one who was using his powers to put the French Republic on a sound footing. Dubroca's early biography argued that Bonaparte carried out his coup only so as to rescue the Republic, and the French Revolution, from the chaos and corruption into which it had fallen. He highlighted Bonaparte's claim that "liberty is dearer to me than life" and concluded that in Bonaparte, "France may justly boast that she also has her Washington."[112] The Bonaparte described in his pages in fact bore more than a little similarity to the Washington whom Dubroca praised in a lengthy eulogy the same year.[113] The moderate jurist Charles-Antoine Saladin likewise insisted, in a widely circulated pamphlet, that Bonaparte had much more in common with Washington than with Caesar or Cromwell and that a "democratic God" had brought him back to France in 1799.[114]

But already, toward the end of 1800, a curious publication signaled a change in course. Entitled *A Parallel Between Caesar, Cromwell, Monck and Bonaparte*, it appeared at the instigation of Bonaparte himself, who gave the writing assignment to his interior minister: none other than his brother Lucien. Lucien in turn enlisted the help of Louis de Fontanes, the orator at Washington's memorial service.[115] The *Parallel* started with the claim, reminiscent of Germaine de Staël's, that "until now, our revolution has given rise to great events, not great men."[116] Lucien rejected the idea that Bonaparte had anything in common with Cromwell, or with George Monk, the general who helped engineer the British Restoration of 1660. Both, he said, were inferior generals and morally flawed. He then continued, "We must go back two thousand years to find a man at all similar to Bonaparte. This man was Caesar." Lucien admitted that Caesar was a demagogue, while Bonaparte properly refused to cater to the whims of the "deranged multitude."[117] Even so, "it cannot be denied that their character and their destiny have striking analogies . . . dominant characters, to whom all obstacles and all wills bow," and with apparently "supernatural inspirations."[118] Caesar, who had for so long symbolized the danger of personal political power, had now been transformed, at least partially, into a model leader.

Even in his 1800 oration about Washington, Louis de Fontanes had already grasped how Bonaparte truly hoped to rule. Founders of states, he had said, governed "more by sentiments and affections than by orders and laws."[119] Indeed, to an extent remarkable in Western history, Bonaparte tried to ground his regime in the emotional relationship between himself and the French people—the charismatic relationship. In doing so, however, he did not simply rely on the French adoring him for his character. What mattered especially was to provoke an amazed admiration for the great deeds that his superhuman genius had accomplished or, as he himself repeatedly put it, for his "glory."[120] He had won glory in Italy, glory in Egypt, and glory again when he crossed the Alps and won his brilliant victory at Marengo in 1800. The next few years would bring further chapters of glory: Ulm, Jena, Friedland, and above all the Battle of Austerlitz, over the combined forces of Austria and Russia, in 1805. Bonaparte's example would stimulate the passion for glory in the population at large, leading them to do their own great deeds for the country—especially in war. And his own glory would forever unshakably attach the French to him through the emotion of love. "Napoleon," the head of his highest court of law declared in 1807, "is beyond all human history. He belongs to the time of heroes. He is above admiration. Only love can rise to his level."[121] As with Paoli, his rule would be a true despotism of love.

There is no doubt that many of the French professed an intense love for Bonaparte throughout his rule, and not just in flowery speeches made for his own ears. Measuring its actual extent is difficult, but historians generally agree that Bonaparte enjoyed genuine popularity, especially at the beginning of his rule. Admittedly his administration tampered with the results of the plebiscite on his first constitution, in 1800, to create the appearance of a crushing victory. But he did in fact receive a majority.[122] Even after the horrific sacrifices of his failed Russian campaign, and his subsequent defeat in 1814, a year later he could still count on sufficient popular support to stage his spectacular return to power during the "Hundred Days." Letters sent to him spontaneously on the occasion of his coronation, often with irregular grammar and spelling, overflow with awkward hyperbolic praise (one called him "more a divinity than a man").[123] Later memoirs and literature testify abundantly to the devotion his admirers claimed to feel, as does the survival of a powerful cult of the emperor for decades after his fall (in 1848 it propelled his far less talented nephew Louis-Napoleon to power).[124] Most famous among the literary accounts are the stories by the soldier and novelist Alfred de Vigny called *Military Servitude and Grandeur*, based in part on his own early memories of the empire. One of his characters recalled of Bonaparte: "His approach intoxicated me. His presence magnetized me. The glory of being attached to this man seemed to me the greatest thing in the world, and never did a lover feel the presence of his mistress with more lively and crushing emotions than the sight of him produced in me every day."[125] This was not the passive and dutiful love for a father felt by the subjects of Old Regime kings. It was something far more active, intense, and erotic, and far more tied to the emperor's cult of military glory.

The cult of Bonaparte, like the cult of Washington, quickly extended across the Western world. Liberal Russian aristocrats and radical American artisans alike applauded his victories, in most cases seeing them as triumphs for the French Revolution. The initial enthusiasm of Pierre Bezukhov, Tolstoy's hero in *War and Peace*, reflects the actual history quite accurately.[126] Even in Britain, which was at war with France for all but a few months of Bonaparte's rule, a surprisingly strong current of admiration for the man made itself felt, especially among political radicals, notably during the brief peace of 1802–1803, and then again after his fall.[127] The English radical Henry Redhead Yorke recalled witnessing a military parade in Paris in 1802. "Several English gentlemen," he wrote, "who were not very distant from me, made themselves conspicuous by their ecstatic exclamations of adulation towards Bonaparte, one of them, a person of rank and fortune, bawling out loud enough to be heard by fifty people, 'By God! This man deserves to govern the world!'"[128]

Bonaparte himself, however, knew how fragile and transient political authority could be when it depended on popular adulation, which in turn required a constant succession of glorious deeds. However devoted his hard core of supporters, especially among his soldiers, it was another matter to maintain the enthusiasm of the population as a whole. In the first years of his rule he confessed to an aide: "You have to remember that a First Consul is not like those divinely-anointed kings who regard their states as an inheritance. Their power is supported by long-standing customs. With us, by contrast, long-standing customs are obstacles . . . A government like ours needs brilliant actions, and therefore war . . . I repeat, a new-born government like ours needs to amaze and astonish people, in order to consolidate itself, or it will go under."[129] Many years later, in his final exile, he repeated the point: "The destiny of France depended entirely on the character, the actions and the conscience of the man on whom it had conferred this accidental dictatorship; from that day on . . . *the State was me* [*l'État ce fut moi*] . . . I was, myself, the keystone of a new edifice built on such fragile foundations! Its survival depended on each one of my battles."[130]

In fact, precisely because he knew the fragility of these foundations, Bonaparte soon tried to reinforce them by providing himself with a different, far more venerable form of political legitimacy—indeed, the most venerable form he knew: divinely anointed monarchy. Already in 1800, Lucien Bonaparte concluded his *Parallel* with a warning of the disasters that might befall France if Napoleon died without a clear successor (the passage infuriated Napoleon, because it clearly hinted at Lucien's own eagerness for the position).[131] Making himself consul for life in 1802 was a decisive step toward monarchy, and two years later the consul became emperor. In speeches supporting this last step, members of his tame Senate spoke of Bonaparte's extraordinary qualities but also stressed the stability and permanence that would come with a return to hereditary monarchy.[132]

In creating the empire, Bonaparte—or Napoleon I, as he now styled himself—did not restore France's Old Regime. He had the change approved by stage-managed plebiscite and took the title "Emperor of the French," to emphasize that the principle of popular sovereignty re-

mained operative. Although he welcomed back members of the old nobility from exile and created a new nobility of his own, he did not give
them legal privileges. While he had already made his peace with the
Catholic Church and acknowledged its role in French society, he did
not restore Church property.

Yet at the same time, he tried his utmost to associate himself symbol-
ically with the royal past. His formal coronation painting by Ingres ren-
dered him as a medieval icon buried under ermine and bearing almost
every possible symbol of monarchy: scepter, hand, orb, sword, chain,
crown of laurels (figure 16). The trusty propagandist Dubroca, his earlier republicanism now forgotten, published a lengthy history of the
"four French dynasties" (including the Bonapartes) and their founders,
from the early Middle Ages to the reign of "Napoleon the Great."[133]
Bonaparte invited Pope Pius VII to preside at his coronation in Notre
Dame—echoing the coronation of Charlemagne a millennium earlier—
and tried to present his reign as blessed by God himself. An *Imperial
Catechism* instructed his subjects that "God has made the Emperor the
minister of his power and image on earth," and a French cardinal did not
hesitate to call Bonaparte "God's chosen."[134] Bonaparte even cajoled the
pope into "discovering" an obscure Christian martyr named Neapolis
and renaming him "Saint Napoleon." His saint's day—not coincidentally Bonaparte's birthday—became France's new national holiday.[135]

Bonaparte was attempting what Max Weber called the "routinization of charisma"—to take the authority inherent in the bond between
a charismatic individual and his followers and transfer it to a stable
institution—in this case the newborn French Empire.[136] A similar process of routinization arguably worked in the case of the American presidency, which to this day bears traces of Washington's republican
charisma. But in Bonaparte's case the process failed. The legitimacy of
his regime depended too intimately on his personal appeal and his
victories. His charisma could not easily be transferred to what many of
his subjects saw as cheap, ersatz copies of France's ancient monarchical
institutions, blessed by a church that the emperor himself visibly despised (French troops occupied Rome in 1808, leading Pius VII to

excommunicate Bonaparte, who in turn imprisoned him). It was Napoleon Bonaparte the individual, not the office of emperor, that attracted ecstatic devotion. When, in 1812, conspirators spread the false rumor that he had died in the Russian snows, deceived officials debated what sort of provisional government to establish in his place. Not for a moment did any of them consider proclaiming his infant son the new emperor.[137] Such are the weak points of regimes founded on a single person's charisma.

Although his career ended in defeat, exile, and humiliation, and although it took a terrible toll in blood and suffering, Napoleon Bonaparte had nonetheless amazed and astounded. His legend continued to obsess the Western world throughout the nineteenth century and remains potent today, with new biographies appearing at almost an annual pace. Yet astonishing as his career was, it was not perhaps the most astonishing of the age of revolution. That honor belongs to another charismatic leader, one whom Bonaparte himself despised and ultimately destroyed, and one who established his reputation in a very different part of the world.

FOUR

THE SPARTACUS OF
THE CARIBBEAN

Whatever high opinion I had formed of his heart and mind
before meeting him was far from the reality. He is a philosopher,
a legislator, a general and a good citizen. Toussaint Louverture's
merit is . . . transcendent.

—Philippe-Rose Roume de Saint-Laurent, 1799

A year after the Battle of Waterloo, Napoleon Bonaparte admitted a terrible error. He was now, in 1816, a British prisoner on the small, isolated island of Saint Helena in the South Atlantic, accompanied by a tiny entourage of loyal followers who spent much of each day in his moldy, drafty house, listening to his long, rambling monologues, occasionally dashing to a corner to scribble down notes for posterity. On this occasion, the emperor's thoughts had turned to his failure, back at the start of his rule, to reestablish France's control over its most important overseas colony: Saint-Domingue, or, as we call it today, Haiti. "It was a great mistake to try to subdue it by force," Bonaparte mused. "I should have been content to govern it through the intermediary of Toussaint Louverture . . . He was not a man without merit, although he wasn't what he was painted as at the time."[1]

It was one of the few occasions in his life when Bonaparte acknowledged Louverture's existence. Back in 1801–1802, when this former slave turned French general had proclaimed himself Saint-Domingue's governor-general for life, Bonaparte had ignored most of his letters.[2] Two years later, Bonaparte likewise ignored a long, plaintive, self-justifying memoir that Louverture addressed to him after being brought to France as a prisoner. Bonaparte's later remark suggests he knew of the widespread praise Louverture had received from around the Western world. Some had even compared him favorably to the French leader. The English poet Samuel Coleridge had called Louverture "a hero as much [Bonaparte's] superior in genius as in goodness."[3] But Bonaparte could not imagine a black man born into slavery as in any sense comparable to himself. If he later conceded that he should have worked with Louverture, it was only because the French expeditionary force he sent to Saint-Domingue ultimately ended in plague-stricken disaster, leading to the colony's independence and the disappearance of any hope for a renewed large-scale French imperial presence in the Americas.

In fact, although they had wildly different origins and did not come within four thousand miles of each other until the very end of Louverture's life, the two men had a surprising amount in common. Both, while born under French rule, initially saw France as an oppressor but, at the height of the French Revolution, fully embraced the French cause. Both made reputations as brilliant soldiers and rose through the highest ranks of the French army at a blistering pace. Both became supreme French commanders in their theaters of operations and soon started operating autonomously, disregarding or even openly flouting instructions from Paris. By 1800, both had reached positions of supreme political power, even if Louverture still formally acknowledged French sovereignty over Saint-Domingue. Both ruled in a decidedly authoritarian manner. Ultimately both fell from power and ended their days in miserable exile. But both, before this fate, had great success as charismatic leaders. Both were widely seen as possessing extraordinary natural gifts and enjoying an emotional bond with their followers that, along with the glory of their victories, legitimized their rule. Of course the differences were stark as well. Louverture, whatever his personal ambitions, remained a fierce opponent of slavery, committed to a principle of universal human equality. Bonaparte had powerful racial prejudices and ultimately forced free people back into slavery in the colonies over which he managed to keep control.

If Napoleon Bonaparte today is so much better remembered than the man Chateaubriand called "the black Napoleon," the reason does not lie solely in the scale of his conquests and the fact that they took place largely in Europe.[4] The chaos and destruction of the Haitian Revolution led to the loss or widespread scattering of much of the documentary material it generated, and Haitians have never had the resources to systematically collect and republish what survives, making research on the subject difficult. Until quite recently, most European and North American historians ignored the Haitian Revolution almost entirely.[5] As a result, some basic facts about Toussaint Louverture have come to light only in recent decades, as scholars have finally begun to recognize the key place of Haitian events in the age of revolution. And the tragic history of modern Haiti—a perennial victim of outside hostility, political instability, endemic poverty, and natural disaster—casts a deep shadow over the career of the man widely seen as its founding father. Yet these limitations should not distract us from acknowledging the extraordinary life of a man who overcame greater obstacles than any other charismatic leader of the age. As we will see, Toussaint Louverture was not a charismatic figure in the same way as Paoli, Washington, or Bonaparte, but he is just as important to charisma's modern history.

With hindsight, it is easy to think that a revolution in Saint-Domingue was inevitable. Few places on earth had such volatile, indeed explosive, social conditions in the late eighteenth century. Its economic dynamism was matched only by the unbelievably cruel conditions imposed on most of its population. The Western world was experiencing a consumer revolution, driven in large part by an insatiable demand for sugar, coffee, chocolate, cotton, and textile dyes, all of which Saint-Domingue produced in enormous volume. By 1790, it was the most lucrative of all the European powers' foreign colonies, producing close to half of the world's sugar and coffee. Its exports accounted for 40 percent of France's foreign trade.[6] But this wealth depended on the grueling labor of enslaved black people, whom plantation owners literally worked to death: losses in the enslaved population could reach 5 to 6 percent every year. French slave traders, however, met this hideous demand with such ruthless efficiency that between 1740 and 1789 the number of enslaved people in Saint-Domingue more than quadrupled, to well over 450,000. By 1789, this small colony with roughly the same surface area as Maryland held two-thirds as many enslaved people as did the entire United States of America. The enslaved outnumbered whites and free people of color (a category that included both freed black slaves and people of mixed race) by nearly ten to one. A majority of enslaved adults had been born in Africa.[7]

Adding to the volatility, Saint-Domingue was also in no sense isolated from the major cultural and intellectual currents of the century. By 1789 Le Cap Français (today Le Cap-Haïtien) had 15,000 inhabitants, making it larger than all but three towns in the United States. It was home to scientific and literary academies, at least five booksellers, several printing shops, a newspaper, and a theater that could seat 1,500 (seven other towns in the colony also had theaters). Just a few years after Franz Anton Mesmer introduced his fashionable theory of "animal magnetism" to credulous Parisians, wealthy colonists in Saint-Domingue were likewise letting practitioners "mesmerize" them—that is, cure them of disease by trying to adjust the "magnetic fluid" in their bodies.[8] Readers in Saint-Domingue could follow the events of the American Revolution in detail and even read admiring notices in their newspaper about the abbé Guillaume-Thomas Raynal, France's most prominent critic of slavery.[9] In short, the same cultural changes that helped bring about revolution in Europe and North America also reached these distant shores. They did not go unnoticed by the free people of color and even by some of the enslaved.[10]

Despite these volatile conditions, the plantation owners, supported by French military power, might yet have maintained control over the traumatized and fragmented slave population. The enslaved came from different parts of Africa and could sometimes barely communicate with one another. Other Caribbean colonies with broadly similar profiles (such as Jamaica) did not experience large-scale upheavals. In fact, before 1789 Saint-Domingue experienced less violent slave resistance than many other Caribbean colonies.[11] And in any case, throughout human history, slave revolts have had a distressingly low rate of success.

But the French Revolution of 1789 had massively destabilizing effects on Saint-Domingue. Wealthy white planters and poor whites were soon struggling for control of a new colonial assembly, while free people of color, many of whom themselves owned slaves, sought the civil rights seemingly promised by the Declaration of the Rights of Man and Citizen ("Men are born and remain free and equal in rights"). By 1791 the dissension had turned violent. Vincent Ogé, the leader of a rebellion by free people of color, received the hideous punishment the French legal system traditionally meted out to traitors: executioners tied him to a cartwheel and systematically crushed his bones with an iron bar. And then, in August 1791, as the civic order in Saint-Domingue trembled, enslaved blacks on its northern plain launched the largest slave rebellion in history. Over the next few months they killed thousands of white colonists, burned hundreds of plantations, organized themselves into armies, and gained control of a third of the colony. They did not demand independence and even claimed to be fighting in the name of the French king. At one point their leaders offered to lay down their arms in return for freedom only for themselves and their families and better working conditions for the rest. But the white colonists fought back brutally, massacring thousands in their turn.[12]

Over the next two years, conditions grew even more bloodily chaotic. In Paris, as the French Revolution moved to the left, Jacques-Pierre Brissot and his allies persuaded the Legislative Assembly to grant full civil rights to free people of color—both out of principle and in hopes the new citizens would help suppress the slave revolt. The French government sent a civil commission, accompanied by six thousand additional troops, to Saint-Domingue to implement the measure and take control of the French administration. Its arrival horrified white plantation owners, because commissioners Léger-Félicité Sonthonax and Étienne Polverel were abolitionists, and Sonthonax, a lawyer of modest birth, had even written newspaper articles prophesying that one day people of African descent would sit in the French National Assembly.[13] Then, in early 1793, as the European war expanded, British forces invaded Saint-Domingue from the sea, while the Spanish crossed the land border from Santo Domingo (the future Dominican Republic). Spain gave commissions to several leaders of the slave rebellion and wooed their armies over to its side with promises of freedom.[14] Meanwhile, following the execution of King Louis XVI, an important faction of white colonists broke with the French Revolutionary government altogether. In the spring, they tried to seize Le Cap Français, and in the subsequent fighting, most of the town burned to the ground.

Faced with this desperate situation, Sonthonax and Polverel took truly radical measures. First, they promised freedom to any rebel slaves who promised to fight for the French Republic. And then, with the colony still in flames, they went a giant step further and abolished slavery altogether, first in the northern province alone and then in all of Saint-Domingue. They did so out of conviction, but also for an eminently practical reason. They hoped that they could now enlist the overwhelming demographic mass of the black population to fight on their side, overcoming all their enemies at once: the Spanish, the British, and white counterrevolutionaries. In February, the National Convention in Paris confirmed their decision and voted for the abolition of slavery throughout the French overseas empire—the first time a European power had taken such a step.

At this decisive moment in the history of what we now call the Haitian Revolution, Toussaint Louverture came to the fore as the most important black leader. He did so, however, in a kind of partnership with another man who could not have been more different from him. Louverture had been born in slavery, the son of Africans forcibly transported across the ocean to Saint-Domingue. The other man, who had the formidably aristocratic name of Étienne Maynaud de Bizefranc de Laveaux, had been born to wealth and title in a Burgundian château.

Their relationship made for one of the most extraordinary stories of the age of revolution, because they became not just unlikely allies but also passionate friends—indeed, in a very real sense they came to love each other. The love was not sexual, but in this age of "sensibility," male relationships often throbbed with an intensity that is rarely seen in our own century. More surprising yet, it was the black former slave who emotionally dominated the white aristocrat. The relationship testifies to the explosive power of revolution to scramble established patterns of social life. It also testifies to Louverture's extraordinary charismatic appeal. His personality not only transfixed Laveaux but allowed the black man, with Laveaux's support, to rise to supreme power, defend his people's hard-won freedom from slavery, and permanently overturn racial hierarchies in Saint-Domingue. He would earn widespread support from across the Atlantic world and ultimately lead the colony to the brink of independence. More troubling, he would also develop a cult of personality and rule as a virtual dictator.

At the time of the slave revolt of 1791, the man then known as Toussaint Bréda, after the name of the plantation where he lived, was already in his late forties—old by the merciless standards of Caribbean slave societies. Frail and short, he had early on acquired the nickname of "Sickly Stick." In the 1790s he would lose most of his few remaining teeth. But he had already shown himself resourceful and ambitious. In the mid-1770s (as scholars only discovered two hundred years later) he had been one of the very small minority of enslaved people in Saint-Domingue to win manumission, probably because he had forged a close bond with a plantation manager. He then tried to establish a plantation of his own, complete with slave labor. After it failed, he returned as a free man to Bréda, where he served as a coachman, took care of animals, and held the trust of masters and the enslaved alike. He was particularly renowned for his horsemanship and would later be nicknamed "the Centaur of the Savanna." He had a manner that was calm but also authoritative—as befitted someone who claimed descent from West

African royalty. He played a key role in the 1791 slave revolt from the start—some sources even call him its mastermind, although the surviving evidence is fragmentary and uncertain. When the colonial authorities checked the revolt's progress, he did more than anyone else to keep it going and to provide the rebellious slaves with effective military organization, although he formally remained in a subordinate position to younger, more fiery leaders. He was one of the black leaders who received a commission from the Spanish government to fight the French under the Spanish flag.[15]

While Louverture came to a military role only late in his life, Laveaux was steeped in military culture from an early age.[16] Following the tradition of his French noble family, he enrolled as a dragoon officer in the French army at age seventeen, in 1768, and spent the next twenty years slowly working his way up its ranks. Most noble army officers in France turned against the French Revolution, but Laveaux embraced it—most likely out of a combination of ambition and genuine idealism. He might well have rethought this decision in September 1792, when his older brother, a priest, was arrested by the revolutionary government and then killed by radical *sans-culottes* during the Parisian prison massacres.[17] But by then Laveaux was on a ship approaching the coast of Saint-Domingue, accompanying Sonthonax and Polverel's civil commission. Over the course of the next months he performed effectively, earning the commissioners' trust and a promotion to brigadier general. Like Louverture, he was small and slight.

On August 29, 1793, the same day that Sonthonax and Polverel proclaimed the abolition of slavery, a proclamation of sorts was sent from one of the major rebel camps, most likely to white colonists and free people of color. It read: "Brothers and Friends. I am Toussaint Louverture. My name has perhaps become known to you. I have undertaken vengeance. I wish for liberty and equality to reign in Saint-Domingue. I am working to bring them into existence. Join us, brothers, and fight with us for the common cause."[18] The letter almost certainly did not amount to a call for slave emancipation—its author still held a commission in the army of a country (Spain) that permitted slavery. But it marked his emergence into the front rank of the rebel commanders and also his adoption of the name Louverture—"the opening" (most likely a reference to his ability to create openings for his forces on the battlefield).

Just a few weeks afterward, Laveaux stepped into the spotlight as well, when Sonthonax and Polverel named him interim governor-general of Saint-Domingue. They also gave him the assignment of wooing the rebel forces fighting for Spain over to the side of the French Republic, including those commanded by Louverture. The two men had not yet met, although in January 1793 they had found themselves on opposite sides of a battlefield, when Laveaux captured a mountain fortress held by the black armies, and Louverture led the retreat, holding his forces together in the process.

In the winter of 1793–94, Laveaux wrote to Louverture for the first time, and the two men began a correspondence that would eventually run to several hundred pages.[19] It was principally through these letters that their relationship would develop. Early on, the tone was cordial but decidedly formal. "I have received the honor of your letter," Louverture informed Laveaux in an early missive. "I can do nothing but express how much I was flattered by the way you received the deputies I sent to you."[20] The black commander was still wary. Despite the emancipation decree, he was not yet ready to switch sides and fight for the nation against which he had rebelled in 1791. Even after word came in the spring of 1794 of the Convention's confirmation of the decree, he remained hesitant. Only in mid-1794, after long negotiations with Laveaux, did he finally bring his army over to the Republic and accept an appointment as a French brigadier general.[21] In August 1794, the two men met in person for the first time. Laveaux boasted to his superiors in Paris that "since joining the republicans, Louverture has behaved in a superior fashion."[22] The written correspondence continued, with Louverture now acknowledging Laveaux as his commanding officer.

With most of the former slave troops now fighting for France, the Republic finally gained the upper hand over its many enemies in the colony. In mid-1795, a peace treaty ended the fighting with Spain, and the rebel commanders still fighting under its flag left the colony. The British withdrew from Saint-Domingue in 1798 after suffering massive losses. In his campaigns, Louverture demonstrated remarkable military acumen. He combined guerrilla tactics with conventional European maneuvers, imposed strict discipline, trained his soldiers exhaustively, and inspired great loyalty by sharing their privations and never hesitating to expose himself to danger. Like Napoleon's, his successes led him to believe that, as he later commented, "I felt I was destined for great things."[23] He and Laveaux exchanged letters almost daily and developed a remarkably effective military partnership.

Louverture's letters were long the subject of controversy.[24] Louverture did not write them himself but dictated them to white Frenchmen serving as his secretaries. Some hostile French observers later claimed that his letters were largely the secretaries' work. Louverture himself, they charged, barely spoke French. It is true that his first languages were Haitian Creole and the Ewe-Fon of his West African parents. But his long years as a favored slave, then as a free man working in proximity to whites, almost certainly left him with a high degree of French fluency. By 1793 at the latest he could read and write, and literacy in Saint-Domingue meant literacy in French. Moreover, some documents in Louverture's own hand have survived, and while their spelling is erratically phonetic, the language itself is a confident, even elegant, French. One author of an often strongly critical memoir insisted well after the revolution that Louverture would never have signed a letter without reworking every word of the text "until he had found the turn of phrase that gave proper expression to his thought."[25] We can therefore assume that the letters to Laveaux record Louverture's own words.

As Louverture won victories, Laveaux's admiration for his black colleague grew. In a letter to a parliamentary committee in Paris, he called Louverture "a citizen full of virtue, courage, and military talent; obedient to his superiors, accepting of the law beyond all measure, imbued with humanity; a true conqueror, tireless in his military capacity, knowing how to read and write, and thinking even better."[26] Meanwhile, Louverture's letters to Laveaux turned warmer and more personal. He praised Laveaux's exceptional love of the former slaves and began to use the sort of salutation normally employed between family members and close friends: "I embrace you with all my heart."[27] In October 1795 he wrote: "I have read all the good and wise advice you have given me with the most scrupulous attention. I accept it with gratitude, as a respectful son would receive it from his father. You may be sure that I have engraved it deeply in my heart."[28] Soon afterward, his language became even more openly emotional:

> It is impossible for me, General and dear papa, to find language strong enough to bear witness to the satisfaction I felt in my soul in reading your touching letter of the 26th. My heart has been so full, and still is so full, that I cannot . . . think of you without shedding tender tears. There no doubt exists such a thing as pure friendship, but I will not be persuaded that there are any that are more pure, or more sincere, than what I feel for you. Yes, General, Toussaint is your son. He cherishes you, your tomb will be his, he will support you at the risk of his own life; his hand and head are always at your disposition, and if ever he were to fall, he would take with him the sweet consolation of having defended a father, a virtuous friend, and the cause of liberty [29]

For the rest of the correspondence, Louverture would regularly address Laveaux, a man roughly eight years his junior, as "papa" (Laveaux does not seem to have reciprocated by calling Louverture "son," although far fewer of his letters have survived).

And then Louverture saved Laveaux's life—twice. The incidents involved free people of color, largely of mixed race, who had their own powerful armed detachments in Saint-Domingue, especially in the southern part of the colony. In theory these forces, like Louverture's, by now supported the French Republic, but they zealously defended their own interests and distrusted Laveaux, who favored Louverture and the former slaves over them. In April 1796 a group of mixed-race officers attempted a coup d'état against Laveaux. They sent soldiers to arrest him and his principal assistant in Le Cap and tried to rally formerly enslaved people to their side. The principal black commander in the ruined city refused to cooperate, however, and the coup quickly collapsed, for which Laveaux gave Louverture credit.[30]

But a few days later, during a meeting between Laveaux and Louverture in the town of La Petite Anse, mixed-race soldiers spread the rumor that Laveaux was planning to reestablish slavery. They even claimed he had stored a large supply of slave shackles in a local warehouse. Former slaves in the town believed the rumor, and a crowd surrounded the house where Laveaux was staying, bent on violence. But then Louverture intervened. The rumors were false, he shouted. Laveaux was a good friend to the blacks. In a dramatic gesture, he led the crowd to the warehouse and flung open the doors, showing that it was empty, at which point the crowd dispersed.[31] A relieved and jubilant Laveaux returned to Le Cap and staged an elaborate public ceremony to thank Louverture. To the accompaniment of cannon fire, he publicly embraced the former slave and named him lieutenant governor and major general—the highest civil and military ranks yet achieved by a person of African descent in the history of the Americas. With a nod to the popular French critic of slavery he declaimed, "Behold this Spartacus, the black man predicted by the abbé Raynal, whose destiny was to avenge all the harm done to his race."[32]

From here on, Louverture clearly functioned as the dominant partner in the relationship. "Be calm, my dear father," he wrote to Laveaux after the attempted coup, in an ironically paternal tone. "Toussaint your son will not cease keeping a watch over the bad men and will report to you about everything he does . . . I embrace you a million times."[33] In another letter he called Laveaux "my general, my father, my good friend . . . How happy I am to have such a true and sincere friend."[34] Laveaux responded just as exuberantly, and the correspondence continued in this vein. In August 1796, Louverture wrote: "I reread your letter every day. It will be a consolation for me in the deepest melancholy. I will keep it as the most sacred proof of our friendship, and in any place and in any circumstance at all you can count on the heart of Toussaint

Louverture, who will with God's grace always be your faithful friend, ready to die for you if need be." His conclusion turned even more passionate: "How happy I would be to be close to you, to hold you in my arms and to embrace you a thousand times!"[35]

Like many highly emotional relationships, Louverture and Laveaux's proved as short as it was intense. At the end of 1796, at Louverture's suggestion, Laveaux left Saint-Domingue, to serve as one of its deputies in the French parliament and to rejoin his family. The move gave Louverture a strong ally in Paris. It also left him, along with Civil Commissioner Sonthonax, the most powerful man in the colony, as Sonthonax recognized by promoting him to commander in chief of all French forces there in the spring of 1797.[36] Laveaux wrote a bittersweet letter to Louverture, expressing his sadness at parting from the man he now called "my most intimate friend." But he added, "I will taste the sweet pleasure of conversing with you [by letter], of telling you all the details of my trip, and making known to you the men who are the sincere friends of general liberty" (i.e., slave emancipation).[37] Indeed, after Laveaux's return home the correspondence continued, although not quite as passionately as before. When Louverture sent two sons to France for education, he commended them to Laveaux and asked the Frenchman to watch over them. He regretted the irregularity of the mail between the colony and France and asked Laveaux to give him the "infinitely sweet satisfaction" of letters as often as possible.[38]

The emotional power that Louverture gained over Laveaux was a remarkable phenomenon for the period. In part, of course, he gained it simply because Laveaux depended on him. Not only did Louverture save his life, but without the support of the thousands of black soldiers loyal to Louverture, the French Republic never would have regained control over Saint-Domingue. But this was not all. As Laveaux's effusive praise of Louverture to the French authorities suggests, the two men had forged a genuine bond. And one key reason was Louverture's letters. The mere fact that the two men communicated so intensively on paper was a key factor. Educated men and women in the late eighteenth-century Atlantic world relied on written correspondence to an extraordinary extent to forge bonds with one another. It was not unusual for them to spend two to three hours a day at a desk, writing letters, and their very sense of self was fundamentally shaped by the practice.[39] It was not only ships but paper and ink that bound the Atlantic world together.

Furthermore, in his letters Louverture used the language of "sensibility" and sentimental friendship that utterly pervaded the correspondence of Atlantic elites in this period, not to mention the novels they read and printed accounts written about men like Paoli and Washington. Louverture's decision to call Laveaux "papa" may have reflected African practices of "fictive kinship," as one historian has speculated, or perhaps the paternalistic customs of the slave plantation.[40] But it also allowed Louverture to address his superior officer in emotionally charged language that could have been taken directly from any of a hundred eighteenth-century sentimental novels and that Laveaux would have found familiar and comforting: "I cannot . . . think of you without shedding tender tears. There no doubt exists such a thing as pure friendship, but I will not be persuaded that there are any that are more pure, or more sincere, than what I feel for you."[41]

By the end of 1796, Toussaint Louverture had already established himself as a powerful charismatic leader—but his charisma took several very different forms, among several very different constituencies. The first consisted of his black soldiers. French observers claimed that he could speak Creole to these men with "mesmeric effect," often using homely metaphors.[42] On one occasion, to convince a black audience that they had nothing to fear from the small minority of surviving whites in Saint-Domingue, he ostentatiously mixed a handful of white corn kernels into a large container of black ones, until they disappeared from sight.[43] His extraordinary courage also clearly counted. He led bayonet charges in person and in 1795 wrote to Laveaux that he had taken part in combat for fifteen days without a break.[44] According to one French observer, "The soldiers regarded him as an extraordinary being, the field hands prostrated themselves before him as they would before a divinity."[45] Another commented that "the respect and obedience paid to him rises to the level of fanaticism."[46] In 1800, the French agent Philippe-Rose Roume de Saint-Laurent reported to the French government that in the course of the revolution, the "Africans" had developed a robust system of "popular assemblies" to debate political matters and that, in these assemblies, they expressed an "unconditional" loyalty to Louverture, whom they recognized as the chief defender of their rights and freedom.[47]

Beyond these observations, however, we know relatively little for certain about how Louverture interacted with his fellow former slaves. The relationship was built in person, orally, and for the most part did not leave the same written traces as did his relationships with whites. This aspect of Louverture's charisma, while fascinating and important, lies largely beyond the limits of this book. So does his considerable appeal to enslaved people throughout the Americas, who learned about him through rumors and tales told by fugitive slaves, sailors, merchants, and refugees, as well as through the printing press.[48]

But then there is the charismatic authority Louverture enjoyed over Europeans and white North Americans. This form of his charisma joins his story to the broader one of charisma in the revolutionary Atlantic world, and it had critical importance both for his own career and for the age of revolution more generally. Here, the relationship with Laveaux was foundational. It showed that a European could be convinced of Louverture's extraordinary personal qualities and could form an intense emotional attachment to him. In addition, it was in connection with Laveaux that a heroic, charismatic image of Louverture began to circulate in print throughout the world beyond Saint-Domingue, allowing readers in Europe and the Americas to see him in the same way.

Already during the attempted coup against Laveaux, Louverture had sent a letter of protest, written for publication, to the French ambassador to the United States, Saint-Domingue's largest trading partner (in the 1790s, close to five hundred ships a year from Saint-Domingue docked in American ports).[49] He denounced the "horrible plot" that not only threatened liberty and equality but that might lead to the "complete extinction" of the "white European race in this part of the Republic." He cast himself as nothing less than the instrument of the "Supreme Being," acting to save Laveaux and the whites. The French newspaper the *Gazette nationale* printed the letter, and an abridged version appeared in translation in London, while American newspapers reported on the affair in detail.[50] In an official report on the colonial situation, the Directory in Paris gave Louverture and his "army of blacks" full credit for restoring order, claiming they had acted out of gratitude for the abolition of slavery.[51] The Directors sent him a saber and a pair of pistols, and the gift gave Louverture the opportunity to publish another open letter, in which he not so subtly declared that it was his responsibility and no one else's to "secure tranquility" to Saint-Domingue.[52]

A few months later, back in France, Laveaux himself published a long pamphlet justifying his conduct as governor, describing the attempted coup against him, and heaping praise on Louverture. "The colonial journalists," he commented at one point, "have made it their mission to say that the blacks *have very few ideas about morality, and none about social organization.* Toussaint among others has been ripped to shreds by these gentleman. I will, in regard to these allegations, copy word for word a letter from this astonishing man; they will see that he at least has the spirit to defeat the enemies of his fatherland and the enemies of liberty." Laveaux then proceeded to quote two full pages of a letter from Louverture.[53]

In the spring and summer of 1797, the turbulent political climate in France created the conditions under which Louverture's charismatic reputation could rise even higher. At first, the rise of conservative political forces there seemed to threaten the gains that Louverture and the black population had made. They managed to bar Laveaux from taking his parliamentary seat, while a series of deputies demanded a reversal of French policies in the colony.[54] In late May a Saint-Domingue planter and deputy, Vincent-Marie Viénot-Vaublanc, launched a particularly scorching and deeply racist attack. He criticized the emancipation of the enslaved, while claiming that Louverture and his black followers had ruined the plantation economy and would soon massacre the remaining

FIG. 1. John F. Kennedy on the beach in
Santa Monica, California, in 1962

FIG. 2. An 1824 engraving
of Simón Bolívar by Samuel
William Reynolds

FIG. 3. *Napoleon Crossing the Alps,*
by Jacques-Louis David, circa 1801

FIG. 4. *The Reading of the Bulletin of the Grand Army,*
by Louis-Léopold Boilly, 1807

FIG. 5. A man and woman showing their children a portrait of
Simón Bolívar: "Here is your liberator."

FIG. 6. (*left*) *Pasqual Paoli [. . .] General of the Corsicans in St Antonio Della Casabianca*, by Richard Houston, after Pietro Gherardi, 1769; (*right*) *The illustrious Pascal Paoli, Gen.l of the Corsicans in the Military Habit of his Country*, anonymous, late eighteenth century

Nov. 2⁸. Last Monday arrived in this city His Excellency General WASH-INGTON, our victorious and illustrious commander in chief, with his Lady.

All panegyric is vain and language too feeble to express our ideas of his greatness. May the crown of glory he has placed on the brow of the genius of America, shine with untarnished radiance and lustre, and in the brightness of its rays be distinctly seen----WASHING-TON, THE SAVIOUR OF HIS COUNTRY!

ABOVE LEFT: FIG. 7. An image from a 1778 German-language Pennsylvania almanac hailing George Washington as "the father of the country"

ABOVE RIGHT: FIG. 8. A description of George Washington in the December 12, 1781, edition of *The Connecticut Journal*

RIGHT: FIG. 9. *George Washington, Esqr., General and Commander in Chief of the Continental Army in America,* 1775

ABOVE: FIG. 10. A bronze medal, known as the Voltaire Medal, depicting George Washington as general of the Continental Army

LEFT: FIG. 11. A locket displaying John Ramage's *Portrait of George Washington*, 1789

FIG. 12. *Apotheosis of Washington*, by David Edwin, after Rembrandt Peele, 1800

TOP LEFT: FIG. 13. Emmanuel Sieyès in his formal costume as a member of France's executive Directory, 1799

TOP RIGHT: FIG. 14. *Bonaparte at the Bridge of Arcole*, by Antoine-Jean Gros, 1796

ABOVE: FIG. 15. A 1798 engraving of a medal depicting Napoleon with Alexander and Hannibal, by Louis-Sébastien Berthet

RIGHT: FIG. 16. *Napoleon I on His Imperial Throne*, by Jean-Auguste-Dominique Ingres, 1806

TOUSSAINT L'OUVERTURE.

ABOVE: FIG. 17. (*left*) *Toussaint Louverture, Chief General in St. Domingue*, by François Bonneville, 1802; (*right*) *Portrait of Toussaint Louverture*, by Nicolas Eustache Maurin, 1832

LEFT: FIG. 18. Guillaume Guillon-Lethière's 1822 painting *Oath of the Ancestors*, which depicts Alexandre Pétion and Jean-Jacques Dessalines inaugurating the new state of Haiti in 1804

TOP: FIG. 19. Gran Colombia, 1819–1831

ABOVE LEFT: FIG. 20. *Simón Bolívar: Liberator and Father of the Nation*, by Pedro José Figueroa, 1819

ABOVE RIGHT: FIG. 21. *Sketch of Bolívar*, by José Maria Espinosa, completed shortly before Bolivar's death in 1830

whites.[55] In a pair of white-hot responses, Laveaux defended both his own record and that of the "incomprehensibly virtuous man" he had promoted, Toussaint Louverture: "He is a man gifted with every military talent . . . a republican full of feelings of humanity. To cite all his remarkable traits would mean wanting never to finish." Under Louverture's guidance, Laveaux insisted, the colony was actually flourishing.[56]

And then, from Saint-Domingue, Louverture himself—deeply upset by Viénot's speech—entered the fray in his single greatest piece of writing.[57] Were the blacks of Saint-Domingue "ignorant and crude," as Viénot had charged? Perhaps, Louverture admitted, since they lacked an education. "But," he continued, "should we indict them for this lack of education, or rather should we accuse those who kept them from obtaining an education by use of the most atrocious punishments?" Nor did the blacks' lack of education justify "putting them in a class separate from the rest of the human race, and confusing them with animals." Had they committed crimes in the course of their revolt? Yes, but what about "the monsters who taught these crimes to the blacks, and who, driven by barbaric greed, traveled to the coast of Africa to rip sons from mothers, brothers from sisters, and fathers from sons?" And were the French themselves so innocent? How would Viénot react if the people of Saint-Domingue called the French unworthy of liberty because the French Revolution had "produced Marats, Robespierres . . . the bloody scenes of the Vendée, the September Massacres, the slaughter of a large part of the National Convention"?[58] Never in the age of revolution had anyone denounced the hypocrisies of colonialism and racism more effectively. Louverture sent multiple copies of the pamphlet to France and asked his allies there to reprint it if need be. He wrote to the Directory that Viénot was plotting with exiled planters to restore slavery.[59]

Even before this response arrived in France, the Coup of Fructidor, which purged conservatives from the assemblies and executive Directory, removed the danger to Louverture. Viénot had to flee the country in disguise, and Laveaux took his seat in parliament and convinced the reconstituted government to renew its support for the policies of emancipation. A new law guaranteed that "any black individual, born in

Africa or in foreign colonies, and transported to the French islands, will be free as soon as he has set foot on the territory of the Republic, and can acquire the rights of a citizen."[60] Ironically, given the fact that Napoleon Bonaparte later sent an expedition to overthrow Louverture, on this occasion Bonaparte effectively saved him, because his military support proved crucial to the success of the coup. In Saint-Domingue, Louverture's position was now at least partially secured, and his reputation in the Atlantic world had grown considerably.

Now Louverture entered upon the most important five years of his career, in which he experienced epic success, then epic tragedy. He completed his defeat of the British and ended the military threat to French rule in the colony. He outmaneuvered a series of French officials, including Sonthonax, who tried to assert their own authority there. In the absence of effective local government, much of the colony remained under military control, with Louverture as the supreme military authority. By the end of 1799, one friendly official described Louverture matter-of-factly as "the absolute master of the island."[61] He overcame competing forces from the south of Saint-Domingue led by mixed-race officers in a short, brutal civil war and put down a rebellion in his own ranks. He attempted to revive Saint-Domingue's plantation economy through a harsh program that would have turned formerly enslaved people into virtual serfs, bound to the land if not to specific masters. Like Bonaparte, he frequently disregarded instructions from Paris and operated as an autonomous proconsul. Despite France's ongoing war with Britain, and the Quasi-War that erupted between France and the United States in 1798, he negotiated secret agreements on his own authority with both powers. Then, in direct defiance of French policy, he occupied the neighboring Spanish colony of Santo Domingo, which Spain had formally ceded to France five years before. In 1800, Napoleon Bonaparte's new regime decided that France would no longer treat its colonies as integral parts of the nation and that they would henceforth be governed by "special laws." In response, Louverture issued a constitution for Saint-

Domingue that made him governor-general for life and granted him absolute, untrammeled power. He was bringing the colony to the brink of independence, telling a British representative that "the power he possessed, he did not hold from France."[62] These last moves, however, proved too much for Bonaparte. In 1801, the First Consul sent his massive military expedition—three times as large as the one France had dispatched to help George Washington in the American Revolution—to restore full French power in Saint-Domingue.

Historians and biographers have never come to a consensus about this period of Louverture's career, and the sparseness of the source material has allowed them to stake out radically different interpretations. Was he, as the great Trinidadian writer C. L. R. James claimed, fundamentally an anti-imperialist freedom fighter, a model for the heroes of twentieth-century anti-colonial struggles? Or was he, rather, as the French diplomat Pierre Pluchon countered, a product of the plantation system who schemed to acquire land and wealth even as he struggled for liberty? Should we see him as a child of Africa best understood through the lens of the syncretic religion Vodou, as the novelist Madison Smartt Bell suggested? Or, instead, as the ruthless politician depicted by Philippe Girard, a man whose shortcomings prefigured Haiti's later political dysfunctionality? The newest biography, by Sudhir Hazareesingh, most convincingly presents him as a complex and sometimes contradictory figure, but first and foremost as an implacable enemy of slavery.[63]

Despite the disagreements, some facts about the period of Louverture's rule are clear. First, while Haitians today revere him as "the Great Precursor" of their independence, he himself never challenged French sovereignty over Saint-Domingue. In his writings and speeches, right down to the long, self-justifying "memoir" that he addressed to Bonaparte after his capture, he always posed as a faithful servant of the Republic.[64] He even liked to lecture his black supporters on everything the French had sacrificed for the cause of slave emancipation and the rights of man. His proclamations faithfully echoed the revolutionary rhetoric used by republican politicians thousands of miles away, and he referred knowledgeably to the French Revolution's principal events.

What distinguished Louverture's speeches and writings from those of most contemporary European revolutionaries was, rather, his blazingly eloquent insistence on the autonomy of all persons and their equal right to liberty. In 1800, he declared to the French government: "It is not just a freedom conceded to us alone that we want, but the absolute adoption of the principle that no man, whether born red, black or white, can be the property of another."[65]

But it is easy to overestimate the extent to which Louverture controlled events. Despite his genuinely extraordinary personal abilities, the political and military storms in which he operated often left him precious little room to maneuver. In this, he resembled Washington and Bonaparte at various moments of their careers, but with even less real autonomy. And just as in their cases, his success did not derive solely from his own abilities but from the need of desperate, fearful people to find—indeed, to half create—a leader they could trust and follow in the midst of explosive danger. As with Louverture's famous predecessors elsewhere in the Atlantic world, the charismatic authority that would prove so important in generating historical change was something of a joint enterprise between him and his willing admirers.

The years between 1796 and 1801 saw the full flowering of Louverture's charismatic reputation in the wider Atlantic world, and as before, it took two forms. Most immediately, it spread among French officials on the ground in Saint-Domingue who came to know Louverture personally. More broadly, stories and images circulated throughout the world of print. Like Napoleon Bonaparte, Louverture actively encouraged this circulation, although he did not have anywhere near as powerful a propaganda apparatus at his disposal.[66] But many others had an incentive to praise and support Louverture as well, including abolitionists trying to undermine the century's pervasive racism, and Britons and Americans hoping he might detach the colony from France. In many cases, these writers clearly imposed their own enchanted heroic vision on the man they themselves had encountered only on the printed page, barely glimpsing his all-too-human complexities through the thick gauze of their romantic preconceptions. And this heroic vision captivated others in turn.

White officials in Saint-Domingue had many reasons to support and admire Louverture. Like Laveaux, they were impressed by the reassuring familiarity of his rhetoric and his devotion to the Republic. Even more important were his repeated promises to safeguard the lives and interests of white colonists. The very first mention of Louverture in print anywhere had come in an early account of the 1791 revolt, written by a white lawyer who credited the rebel leader with risking his own life to save whites.[67] During Louverture's years in power, a French civil engineer named Charles-Humbert Vincent, who grew particularly close to him, described him to French superiors as "the friend and protector of the Europeans."[68] American newspapers frequently praised him in the same terms: "he is respected, cherished and admired by the whites"; "the unfortunate whites who have remained in St. Domingo call [him] father and protector."[69] In 1801, according to one newspaper story, Louverture threw into prison a dozen prominent French planters who had supported the British invasion. But then he brought them outside the prison and, before a large black audience, preached the virtues of forgiveness, explaining that he himself had once turned Spanish but had then become French again. Taking the hint, the planters exclaimed that they had turned British but were now ready, like Louverture, to resume their French identities. In front of the crowd, Louverture embraced them and set them free.[70] Of course, as in the case of Laveaux, any official who entered into an alliance with Louverture had every incentive to defend and praise him.

Virtually all the principal agents operating in Saint-Domingue in the late 1790s at least initially expressed enchantment with Louverture, although most also eventually fell out with him. In the late spring of 1796, soon after the attempted coup against Laveaux, civil commissioner Sonthonax described Louverture as a "hero of liberty" who had shown "heroic devotion" to Europeans.[71] In a conversation with a French general, Sonthonax contrasted Louverture with the other black officers he had encountered: "They want promotion solely to get their hands on an abundance of tafia [a rum-like alcohol], money and women. Toussaint is the only one who has rational ambitions, and some idea of the love of glory."[72] Roume de Saint-Laurent, a Caribbean native and a long-serving colonial official who became the chief French agent in early 1799, fell even harder for Louverture. Soon after meeting him, he wrote to a French general: "Whatever high opinion I had formed of his heart and mind before meeting him was far from the reality. He is a philosopher, a legislator, a general and a good citizen. Toussaint Louverture's merit is . . . transcendent."[73] A subordinate official, whom Louverture saved during the attempted coup against Laveaux, called him "this African genius."[74] The engineer Vincent called him "an astonishing man in every sense" who was "superior to everything that surrounded him" and whose "genius equaled his power."[75] These officials spoke with wonderment about what Vincent called "his great sobriety" and his apparently inexhaustible capacity for work. In their accounts, Louverture responded to hundreds of letters a day, exhausting five secretaries in a row, while sleeping only two hours and subsisting on a *galette* and a glass of water or perhaps a couple of bananas and a biscuit.[76]

Even Louverture's greatest detractors among the French officials could not keep notes of admiration from creeping into their reports and correspondence. General Charles Leclerc, Bonaparte's brother-in-law and the leader of the French expedition that captured Louverture, called him "no ordinary man . . . he has force of character."[77] Brigadier General François-Marie Perichou de Kerversau, who took part in the expedition and denounced Louverture as a master of deception, nonetheless credited him with "a superior intelligence and exemplary comportment."[78] General François-Joseph Pamphile de Lacroix, who served with Leclerc as well, and whose early history of the Haitian Revolution is peppered with acrid comments about Louverture's vanity and overreaching ambition, nonetheless called him a "genius" and praised his "discipline over barbarians."[79] With admiration, Pamphile recalled Louverture at the height of his power, dressed in a brilliantly colored, perfectly tailored military uniform, leading a parade of some fifteen thousand soldiers.

At that moment, Pamphile gushed, Louverture had "the radiance of a prince."[80]

It is important to note that these officials' expressions of admiration for Louverture did not for the most part challenge their prejudices against people of African descent. Indeed, something of the reverse was often at work: their admiration reflected and even heightened their prejudices, because they saw Louverture as a singular exception to the general pattern of his race. Even his friend Vincent casually drew a contrast between Louverture and the "mass of highly ignorant individuals" in the black armies, while Sonthonax's praise depended on casting the other black commanders as drunken, greedy lechers.[81] Indeed, after Sonthonax and Louverture fell out, the Frenchman denounced as ignorant and illiterate the man he had previously claimed to admire, insisting that "to avoid making the inhabitants of this land a horde of savages without laws or manners, the European must command."[82] In distinguishing Louverture from other blacks, the officials drew on a long literary tradition, for in the eighteenth century, even authors deeply opposed to slavery and committed to establishing bonds of sympathy between their readers and Africans tended to do so by inventing "exceptional" African characters. The hero of Aphra Behn's 1688 novel *Oroonoko*, which became hugely popular in French translation, was a "royal slave"—the son of an African king (Louverture himself claimed royal descent).[83] In the middle of the Haitian Revolution, the French writer Germaine de Staël, a staunch abolitionist, published an anti-slavery story with a male hero whose "features had none of the defects of men of his color . . . the shape of the Belvedere Apollo is not more perfect."[84]

These authors presented their exceptional black heroes as either noble savages or white people in black skins, and some officials in Saint-Domingue saw Louverture as white. In 1805, a French officer who had served in Saint-Domingue recounted a conversation he claimed to have overheard between Louverture and Sonthonax. "I am white, but I have the soul of a black man," Sonthonax supposedly remarked (Sonthonax had married a woman of color). "And I am black but have the soul of a white," Louverture supposedly replied.[85] We have no way of knowing if

Louverture actually spoke these words and, if so, whether he spoke them sincerely. But it is significant that the officer believed he had said them and gave the story a prominent place in his memoir.

As his power grew, Louverture also became increasingly sophisticated in the use of the printing press. In the summer of 1797, he used it to discredit the only person in the colony who could still rival his authority: his erstwhile supporter Sonthonax, who enjoyed great popularity in the black population, thanks to his role in the abolition of slavery. At the end of August, Louverture brought a major detachment of troops to Le Cap, supposedly for a military review, and then used their presence to force Sonthonax into immediately embarking on a ship for France. Louverture justified the action to the Directory with a lengthy report that denounced Sonthonax, a radical Jacobin, for having plotted to declare the colony independent and to slaughter wealthy planters. He also had printed a forty-page pamphlet that purported to reconstitute, verbatim, dialogues in French between Sonthonax and himself in which the civil commissioner had supposedly tried to enlist Louverture in his plot, while Louverture virtuously resisted. The pamphlet, which included stage directions, read like a script and most likely played a role in convincing the Directory tacitly to endorse Louverture's action.[86]

Louverture also continued to send out his own speeches and reports for publication. In an extraordinary 1797 speech to his soldiers, which appeared in several American and British newspapers after his promotion to commander in chief, he initially struck a Washingtonian pose. His promotion to high rank "never dazzled me," he insisted. He cared only about doing his duty to his men. He continued, however, in a vein Washington would have avoided and one that recalls Bonaparte's relentless self-promotion: "Now having become your Chief, I look upon you as my children . . . in return for my toils, sacrifices and my love for you, I only demand entire obedience to my orders." Yet the conclusion of the speech turned in a different direction again. In it, Louverture urged his men to swear eternal hatred to enemies of liberty, adding: "carrying death even to their haunts, let us go there to plant the tree of liberty, and break asunder the chains of such of our Brethren as they still hold under the shameful yoke of slavery. Let us associate them to the rights we now enjoy, to the imprescriptible and inalienable rights of free-men."[87] Never before in the history of the Western world had a person of African descent, commanding hundreds of thousands of soldiers, called for a general crusade against slavery in these terms. And thanks to the printing press, never before had such a call circulated so widely. Later, when Louverture issued his new constitution, he had pocket-sized copies of it distributed across the island.[88]

The extent to which Louverture and his allies consciously tried to shape his image in print comes through most clearly in a remarkable letter sent to him in 1799. Its author was most likely Henri Pascal, a Frenchman who had traveled to Saint-Domingue with the civil com-mission, married the daughter of the wealthy mixed-race commissioner Julien Raimond, worked as a secretary for Louverture, and then re-turned to France. He reported that he was forwarding to newspapers any letters received from Saint-Domingue "which do justice to you and which tell the truth," while being careful first to delete anything contro-versial. "In this way public opinion is formed," he commented. He im-plored Louverture to "correspond frequently with the government, but because it doesn't print anything, send me good news and we will spread it to the public by the path of print."[89]

One pair of articles, possibly written by Pascal himself, appeared in early 1799 in the *Gazette nationale*.[90] Attributed only to a "citizen re-cently returned from Saint-Domingue," they breathed with the spirit of James Boswell's pilgrimage to Paoli a quarter century earlier. The author explained that he had long nourished a desire to meet Louverture in person, and after giving a brief, largely inaccurate summary of Louver-ture's life, he devoted most of the account to a visit he had made to the general's home on a coffee plantation south of Le Cap. There, he had toured the property and spent an evening seated between Louverture and his wife—"the fattest woman I have seen in Saint-Domingue"—talking mostly about domestic matters. Louverture, taking the visitor by the hand, recounted his life story and chatted enthusiastically about his marriage. The general explained that he had resisted the attempts of his masters to marry him off to a younger, prettier woman because he wanted a happy union with a virtuous partner. The writer claimed to have seen, in the faces of the couple as they gazed at each other, "the sweet emotions felt by young lovers." As in the case of Mason Locke Weems's biography of Washington, the emphasis on Louverture's private life was no accident. It was a strategy with proven appeal to a reading public trained by novels and the culture of celebrity to dote on such behind-the-scenes glimpses of extraordinary men. In response to the articles, the *Gazette* also printed a letter from Louverture's former overseer, the Bréda plantation manager Antoine-François Bayon de Libertat, who praised Louverture for his steadfast attachment to his masters before the Revolution and for the way he strove to protect them thereafter. "Yes, I declare, it is to Toussaint Louverture, and the morality that he preached to his comrades, that I owe my continued existence."[91]

But it was not due only to conscious efforts by Louverture and his allies that information about him circulated widely beyond Saint-Domingue. The colony's economic and strategic importance, as well as its experience with slave revolt, made it a subject of intense interest in Europe and the Americas. Newspapers in Europe, Britain, and the United States reported regularly on the ongoing struggles and saw Louverture's most important declarations and speeches as inherently newsworthy. Many officials and travelers published melodramatic eyewitness accounts of events, devised for a public eager for tales of exotic violence, and gave considerable attention to Louverture. In 1802, a British periodical called him "the most interesting of all the public characters" of the present year anywhere in the world.[92] Hardly any of these accounts did very well in the fact-checking department. *The Times* of London did particularly badly, initially referring to the subject of their stories as "Poussaint Louverture" and repeatedly referring to him as a "mulatto."[93] But both the chaotic conditions in Saint-Domingue and linguistic obstacles made it difficult to receive accurate information. And many authors cared little for accuracy, especially when they played to the worst instincts of their readers, depicting the blacks of Saint-

Domingue as bloodthirsty savages intent on raping and murdering innocent whites.

In the United States especially, many of the reports on Saint-Domingue came infused with venomous hostility toward the black people who had carried out the largest slave revolt in history. They called Louverture ignorant and cruel, a "black monster."[94] Thomas Jefferson referred to the freed slaves of Saint-Domingue as "cannibals of the terrible republic."[95] But in the late 1790s, when the French and American republics stood on the edge of war, Louverture's willingness to pursue a separate foreign policy from France also earned him American applause, especially in the northern states. One American correspondent who met Louverture described him to *The Philadelphia Gazette* as "a wonderful man, sent by heaven . . . A word from his mouth moves to obedience and submission all the black citizens, and he is respected, cherished and admired by the whites."[96] At least twenty-four American newspapers printed translations of Louverture's constitution for Saint-Domingue, and in most cases they accompanied it with a highly laudatory sketch entitled "Character of the Celebrated Black General Toussaint Louverture."[97] Americans took note of Louverture in their diaries, with one Philadelphia matron referring to him as the "celebrated African Chief."[98] Strikingly, in 1803 two American wax artists added a life-size figure of Louverture (topped, most likely, with real human hair) to their traveling show, which toured through New Jersey, Pennsylvania, Maryland, and Rhode Island. While quite possibly employing racist tropes, the artists still gave the figure (which has not survived) the titles "General" and "Governor."[99]

In Britain, the combination of Louverture's willingness to make a separate peace, and growing abolitionist sentiment, produced even greater enthusiasm.[100] *The Annual Register* gushed about his "moderation, gratitude, and humanity," his "genius" and "great mind."[101] A London opposition paper, *The St. James's Chronicle*, offered him up as an object lesson in racial equality: "TOUSSAINT is a Negro; but, according to report, he is a Negro born to vindicate the claims of his species,

and to show that the character of man is independent of exterior color."
At least five other British newspapers, and two in the United States, reprinted this article.[102] And after Louverture's capture and deportation to
France, two of Britain's greatest poets took to the pages of London's
Morning Post to lament his fate. Samuel Coleridge charged that Bonaparte had acted out of "personal envy to a hero," while William Wordsworth composed a sad ode to Louverture, "the most unhappy Man of
Men," concluding with the lines: "There's not a breathing of the common wind / That will forget thee; thou hast great allies; / Thy friends are
exultations, agonies, / And love, and Man's unconquerable mind."[103]

Even as these accounts circulated, the first full-length biographies of
Louverture appeared. Some of them, sponsored by Bonaparte, or by
Saint-Domingue's dispossessed slaveholders, amounted to little more
than sustained exercises in racist character assassination. Bonaparte's prolific and reliable propagandist, Jean-Louis Dubroca, composed a particularly vicious account that maligned Louverture as "a vile assassin . . . a
deceiver . . . a hypocrite . . . a tiger avid for blood and carnage."[104] Happily transmitting any and all rumors obtained from exiled French planters, Dubroca's book consisted in large part of pure fiction. Another, even
more heavily fictionalized, biography attributed much of Louverture's
early success to the sponsorship of Robespierre, who supposedly recognized in him a kindred spirit—that is to say, a "criminal genius."[105] After
1800, Bonaparte's strict censorship of the French press and book trade
prevented any favorable treatments of Louverture from appearing in
France.

In Britain, however, growing abolitionist sentiment and long-
standing Francophobia provided a ready market for biographies that
spread the legend of Louverture, the charismatic black hero and liberator
who defied Bonaparte. The most interesting and extensive came from a
British career army officer named Marcus Rainsford, who had fought
against the American revolutionaries during the War of Independence
and subsequently attempted—with a spectacular lack of success—to
make a career as a poet. Back in the army, he deployed to the West Indies
and in 1798 quite literally washed up in Saint-Domingue, when bad

weather forced the ship he was on to land there. Arrested by the French authorities as a spy, he faced possible execution, only to have a merciful Louverture personally order his release. Upon his return to England, he published a short account of his adventures and then, in 1805, a full-blown history of the Haitian Revolution that gave pride of place to Louverture and included several engravings that depicted Louverture in heroic poses and graphically illustrated atrocities committed against black people.[106] Rainsford had large literary ambitions but much less literary talent. Melodramatic descriptions of his imprisonment, mostly spent lying on an uncomfortable bed of dried sugarcane, alternated with dubious comparisons of Louverture to a "gigantic oak, spreading its foliage with august grandeur above the minor growth of the forest, defending the humble shrub."[107] Rainsford drew much of his (inaccurate) information about Louverture's life from the 1799 *Gazette nationale* article and Dubroca's hostile biography, but he also included lengthy first-hand descriptions of Louverture's "bold and striking" countenance, his elegantly embroidered uniform, and the respect allegedly showed him everywhere by his black followers.[108] His book received generally favorable reviews and appeared in Dutch translation, and the German magazine *Minerva* published lengthy excerpts. Some scholars have even speculated that Rainsford's account of the slave rebellion influenced Hegel as he was developing his notion of the master-slave dialectic.[109]

Given the lack of reliable information, another admirer felt free to turn Louverture's life, quite literally, into a novel, drawing heavily on the literary tradition about enslaved Africans that stretched back to Aphra Behn and further. In Bavaria, in 1802, this anonymous author published a German-language book entitled *Toussaint Louverture's Early History*.[110] Supposedly a biography based on English newspaper reports, it was in fact pure invention from start to finish. It gave Louverture an African birthplace, a royal father, and a childhood in the household of a kindly priest who supposedly purchased him after his arrival in Saint-Domingue as a boy. It told how the priest had taught him to read and write and had given him a classical education. It also recounted a torrid love affair between the adolescent Louverture and one of the priest's relatives, who subsequently inherited the plantation. But this woman turned out to be a cruel mistress, and when Louverture protested her whipping of an elderly slave, she sold him across the border in Santo Domingo. From there, he escaped to live the life of a fugitive "maroon" until, in 1791, he descended from a mountain hideaway to take leadership of the slave rebellion. None of this was true. Still, there was something strangely appropriate about the anonymous author's transformation of Louverture, a man so adept at using the language of Enlightenment sentimentalism, into the hero of a sentimental novel. The book also included a fascinating disquisition upon the psychology of slavery, suggesting that the slaveholders' unremitting violence so completely paralyzed the mental powers of the enslaved "that they saw the words Master and Slave as the first principle in the code of nature" (if Haitian history did indeed influence Hegel, this German book probably mattered more for him than Rainsford's).[111]

Together, the biographies and newspaper accounts made Toussaint Louverture a celebrity in the Atlantic world. As yet another English biographer put it, "every body has heard of TOUSSAINT, the famous Negro General."[112] But how did "every body" envisage him? At least a dozen artists—only one of whom could have possibly met Louverture—produced engraved portraits, but like the early images of Paoli, Washington, and Bonaparte, these images varied enormously (see figure 17). Beyond all portraying Louverture in punctilious French military uniform, some gave him exaggeratedly African features, while others made him look nearly white.[113] And while the hostile accounts written about Louverture similarly emphasized his African descent, most of the favorable ones, like those of the French officials who had known him, contrasted him to other blacks and treated him as a white man in a black skin, or as a noble savage whose primitive purity raised him above most white people, in morality if not in learning. Wordsworth's ode did not even mention his race. One otherwise favorable review of Rainsford's book said that the author "forgets himself, by making the negro see with the eyes of a European."[114] But none of these accounts presented Louverture as an *ordinary* person. One French writer claimed that "he seems destined to become the Washington of the colonies," while Britain's *Annual*

Register said he was "considered the Washington or Bonaparte of St. Domingo."[115] The French writer Chateaubriand, as noted, later labeled him the "black Napoleon."

I n fact, these favorable accounts imbued Louverture with almost exactly the same characteristics attributed to figures like Paoli, Washington, and Bonaparte: extraordinary personal virtue, almost inhuman natural abilities—including, especially, mental "genius" and astonishing stamina—a special destiny, and the capacity to mold an entire people into a new nation. The authors did not use the words "father of his country," but the many descriptions by whites of the uncanny power he wielded over his black followers implicitly cast him in this role. And in the decades after his death, admirers would increasingly come to regard him as the father of modern Haiti. An anonymous Haitian poem from 1827–28, for instance, declared: "Invested in supreme power by heaven / TOUSSAINT delivered laws to the people of Haiti."[116] The French poet Alphonse de Lamartine put it more concisely: "This man is a nation."[117]

And in Louverture's own lifetime, just as in the case of the white charismatic leaders, the favorable accounts delighted in pulling aside the curtain and revealing the private, intimate man they invariably described in the language of sentimental novels. From the *Gazette nationale* article depicting him fawning over his wife like a young lover, to the fictitious German biography, it mattered to the authors to show, as the German author put it succinctly, that "a private history of the man who has swung himself up so high . . . must be welcome."[118] The authors all insisted on the moral spotlessness of Louverture's private life.[119] And they bolstered the argument with long, invented descriptions of his conduct toward his family. The English biographer James Stephen could rarely resist pulling at the heartstrings in this manner, notably in a long scene describing a tearful Louverture reuniting with two sons he had sent to school in France: "For a while the hero forgets that he is anything but a father. He presses first the elder boy, then the younger, to his heart, then locks them both in a long embrace."[120] The same mechanisms of celebrity that lay

behind the charismatic reputations of Paoli, Washington, and Bonaparte also operated for Louverture.

In short, Toussaint Louverture did end up gaining remarkable charismatic authority over Europeans and North Americans as well as over
his black followers. The pattern that began with Étienne Laveaux ultimately stretched far beyond Saint-Domingue. It brought Louverture to
the attention of men and women who had barely heard of the French
colony and had only the foggiest idea of its location, to say nothing of
the suffering and violence there or its ghastly record as a slave society.
They would not always gain more accurate knowledge from the accounts that reached them, for in these accounts fiction often pressed
hard upon fact and sometimes crushed it altogether. But, however dis-
torted the picture of Louverture that circulated around the Atlantic
world, it did convey the news that a former slave, of African descent,
could achieve the stature of a Paoli, a Washington, or a Bonaparte. This
circulation of Louverture's image, in turn, helped him consolidate his
position in Saint-Domingue—for a time.

The tragedy of Louverture's life is that as time passed, he seemed
increasingly to believe the more extreme versions of this charismatic legend and to feel that his special destiny entitled him to a special
status. The French officer Pamphile de Lacroix claimed that he often
remarked: "Since the first troubles in Saint-Domingue . . . A hidden
voice spoke to me and said: 'Since the blacks are free, they need a leader,
and it is I who must be this leader predicted by the abbé Raynal.'"[121] In
an address to his soldiers in 1801 he declared: "From the very dawn of
the revolution I wished to be free, and my conduct has sufficiently shown
to you that I did not wish to be so alone. I have always treated you as my
children, and as such, I have ever led you into the path of glory. You are
all free. Do you forget so great a blessing?"[122] Like Bonaparte and many
other charismatic leaders, he delighted in hearing himself praised. The
French agent Roume fed his ego at every opportunity, notably by giving
him a brochure about Bonaparte's Egyptian campaign and pointing out

to Louverture the two men's similarities: "the same courage, the same bravery, produced by genius, and the same capacity to be in all places at once, observing . . . and above all the same vision, embracing the past, the present, and the future." Roume told Louverture he was "greater even than Bonaparte."[123]

As he consolidated his rule between 1798 and 1801, Louverture came to expect more and more sumptuous displays of deference. He began to appear in public in elaborate, expensive military uniforms trimmed with gold. On his arriving in a town, the inhabitants often greeted him with lavish presents, displays of palm leaves and flowers, trumpet music, and the firing of cannon. In some cases the towns even built ceremonial arches for him to parade through, in the manner of a Caesar (or Washington, in his tour of the states in 1789). In one town the authorities gave him a medal with his image and the inscription "After God, it is he." According to some reports, he took to sitting in a gilded chair not unlike a throne. At grandiose ceremonies held to celebrate the promulgation of his new constitution in 1801, fawning orators compared him to classical figures—Spartacus, Hercules, and Alexander the Great—and also, of course, to Bonaparte.[124] As in other cases of charismatic leadership, it was not always Louverture himself who took the initiative in these matters. His followers did a great deal on their own, for the more Louverture seemed to rise above everyone else in Saint-Domingue, the more he could function as a reassuring symbol and source of unity in the midst of continuing violence and danger. His followers could also take pride in seeing a black man receiving such honors and deference, including from white colonists and foreign envoys. According to the great nineteenth-century Haitian historian Thomas Madiou, the adulation made Louverture himself uneasy, at least at the start. "Only God should be placed on a dais and sanctified with incense," he supposedly remarked at one ceremony in 1798.[125] But over time these expressions of humility and disquiet became increasingly rare. Like Bonaparte in Italy just a short time before, Louverture was behaving like an imperious proconsul, even a monarch.

To be sure, these tendencies did not represent a betrayal of his democratic political convictions; he never had these convictions in the first place. In May 1798 he sent a revealing letter to his old friend Laveaux, in France, which laid bare the heart of his political philosophy, and it was explicitly authoritarian: "Recall, my dear general, how often, conversing with you, I told you that it was both politic and necessary for the reins of the general administration of the colony to be held by a single European leader . . . I wanted a single leader, because I felt that in the hands of a single man, the reins of the colony would be less vulnerable to passions, and that the colony would be less exposed to internal quarrels . . . of the sort that grows so stealthily and easily in Saint-Domingue . . . and finally civil war."[126] By the time he issued his constitution three years later, Louverture had abandoned his insistence on the European origins of the leader (*chef*) but not his preference for one-man rule. On his own authority, in order to restore the colony's economy, he issued the regulations that reduced formerly enslaved people to virtual serfs, bound to their plantations. The constitution itself named him governor for life, with the right to choose his successor, and placed few constraints on his rule. The charismatic liberator was becoming an authoritarian, albeit one who still felt the need to have a constitution justifying his authority. A French colonial official sent to Paris the elaborate program devised for the official inauguration of the constitution in 1800 and in an accompanying letter accused Louverture of only pretending to consult the people, while in practice "usurping supreme power with tyranny . . . [in] a repetition of what we saw in France under the regime of the terror."[127]

But the greatest danger any figure like Louverture can face, in starting to believe his own charismatic legend, is to consider himself invincible. And there is much evidence that Louverture succumbed to this danger when he promulgated his constitution—and had it printed, confirming its official status—without first consulting Bonaparte, who had now taken power in France. The French engineer Vincent, who had grown close to Louverture, later wrote that the black leader, "puffed up by his own successes" and "falsely adulated," could not be saved from falling into error ("which I reproached him for more than anyone—

I was perhaps the only person to reproach this man to whom I always told the truth").[128] In believing his legend, Louverture brought the power of Napoleonic France down upon him. Bonaparte's own terse remark to Leclerc, when ordering the Saint-Domingue expeditionary force to depart, expressed his revulsion at the very idea that a man of African descent could possibly claim equal status to him in such a way: "Rid us of these gilded negroes."[129]

Louverture had no illusions about French racial attitudes in general but does not seem to have grasped the contempt that his fellow general Bonaparte felt, not merely toward ordinary blacks but even toward those who held high offices, wore French uniforms, protected whites and their property, and had risked their lives for the French republic. To his aides, Bonaparte expressed consternation that the Convention had freed "men who had no civilization . . . the point quite simply is that those who wanted the liberty of the blacks would like the slavery of the whites."[130] Bonaparte also reputedly remarked that "I am for the whites, because I am white."[131] And when he sent the Leclerc expedition, he was already contemplating the re-enslavement of blacks that he would soon impose on the French colonies he still controlled.[132]

For Louverture, the end came quickly. Upon first seeing Leclerc's massive fleet approaching the coast of Saint-Domingue in early 1802, he was heard to remark, "We must perish. All of France has come to Saint-Domingue."[133] Attempts at negotiation with Leclerc failed, and a short, sharp campaign ensued, during which the French won the critical engagements, and Louverture's forces crumbled, with one of his chief lieutenants, Henri Christophe, switching sides. In the spring, Louverture had no choice but to agree to a cease-fire and resign from the governorship. In June the French arrested him, after luring him to a meeting, and put him on a ship for France. His capture did not mark the end of the Haitian Revolution. The armed conflict soon resumed, and it degenerated into a race war, with the French resorting to mass drownings of blacks and even making use of man-eating dogs. It was now entirely clear that a French victory would lead to re-enslavement, which Napoleon formally implemented in Guadeloupe and Guyana in May 1802. But an

epidemic of yellow fever killed most of the French force, including Leclerc himself, and made a French victory in Saint-Domingue impossible.
At the end of 1803, the expedition's remnants evacuated, and on the first
day of 1804 Louverture's successor, Jean-Jacques Dessalines, proclaimed
the independence of the new state of Haiti (the name taken from the
original Indian name of the island). Louverture had not lived to see this
moment. On April 7, 1803, in a cold, miserable, isolated prison cell in
the Jura Mountains in France, his pleas to Bonaparte unacknowledged,
he had died.

Yet if Louverture did not survive into the era of independence, the
model of charismatic leadership he had established did. Jean-Jacques
Dessalines, who had lived in slavery until 1791 (and may have worked
on Louverture's short-lived plantation in the 1770s), did not hesitate to
assume dictatorial authority and to pose as a providential savior sent
from heaven to found the new nation.[134] In his first address to the Haitian people, after calling for "eternal hatred to France," he boasted that
"my happy fate preserved me to serve one day as the sentinel guarding
the idol to which you sacrifice: I have watched and fought, sometimes
alone." He accepted Louverture's title of "Governor General for Life,"
and his generals promised to "obey blindly the laws emanating from his
authority."[135] Eight months later, after receiving news of Bonaparte's assumption of an imperial title, he proclaimed himself Emperor Jean-
Jacques I of Haiti, but his empire lasted for only two years and ended
with his assassination. Throughout most of the nineteenth century, the
Haitian state would remain under the rule of authoritarian former generals who posed as providential saviors of their people, supported by a
powerful military caste.[136] An 1822 painting by the Guadeloupian Guillaume Guillon-Lethière brilliantly expressed this core early Haitian
political concept. It shows Dessalines and another general, Alexandre
Pétion, inaugurating the new state with an oath while shackles lie broken
on the ground and an approving Jehovah looms overhead (figure 18).[137]

This new state quickly fell into traps that have left it, today, the poorest in the western hemisphere. State expenditures went overwhelmingly
to the military. The plantation system never recovered from the revolu-

tionary upheaval of 1791–1804, and the bulk of the population, although freed from slavery, remained in poverty. Much of the blame for this misery lies with the European powers and the United States, which greeted the new state with unremitting hostility. France inflicted massive hardship when it insisted in 1825, in return for its diplomatic recognition, that Haiti pay reparations for the property—including human property—lost by white colonists during the Revolution. The United States, the dominant power in the hemisphere, recognized Haiti only in 1862. These conditions already made it fearsomely difficult for the Haitians to establish anything like a stable democratic regime. But the tradition of charismatic authoritarianism did not help.[138]

Louverture did not set off down this authoritarian path solely because of his own hubris and ambition. He was encouraged from the start by Europeans to see himself as a providential savior figure. It was Europeans and North Americans, as much as Louverture, who forged the charismatic legend of the man on horseback that he ultimately came to believe in. These whites did so in large part because of their own racial beliefs. A few of his admirers, like the unnamed British author of the article in *The St. James's Chronicle*, saw in him proof of the absurdity of racism: Louverture proved "that the character of man is independent of exterior color."[139] But most of the admirers, to the contrary, admired Louverture because he seemed so different from others of African descent, a noble savage or "a white man in a black skin." For these observers, the only government suited to people of African descent was indeed dictatorship. General Kerversau laid out this case explicitly in a remarkable memoir that he sent to the government in Paris before Bonaparte took power, advising the agents it was sending out to put all their influence behind Louverture (Kerversau himself, of course, would later change his opinion of the black leader):

> You will find the forces that are lacking in your close alliance with General Toussaint Louverture. He is a man of great common sense, whose loyalty to France cannot be doubted, whose religion guarantees his morality, whose firmness matches his prudence, who enjoys

the confidence of all the colors, and who has an ascendancy over his own color that no counterweight can offset. *With him, you are capable of everything; without him, you are capable of nothing.* You are arriving in a country whose inhabitants are very distant from the farthest limits of civilization. Fetishism was from all time and is still the religion of Africans. Here, more than elsewhere, enthusiasm for the leader is the sinew of authority; and the law, to be respected, depends on the credit of the man responsible for its execution.[140]

Kerversau's racially charged language implied that Africans, unlike Europeans, could not have a government without a "fetish" to follow.

Yet the word "fetish," tinged with racial condescension, in fact, recalls nothing so much as the words "idol" and "idolatry" used so insistently by John Adams and Benjamin Rush to explain the extraordinary reputation enjoyed by George Washington, even amid the disasters of the early Revolutionary War in America—and also to explain the rise of Napoleon Bonaparte. While Kerversau thought he was speaking about dark-skinned "savages" in a tropical island far removed from France, in fact he was describing a form of politics France itself was about to embrace with a vengeance, with Bonaparte's coup d'état. In claiming that "enthusiasm for the leader is the sinew of authority," he was describing a central principle of government by a charismatic leader, not just in Haiti but throughout the Atlantic world in the age of revolution. Napoleon Bonaparte might have contemptuously dismissed the very idea that a black man and former slave could resemble him. Yet, in many ways, no other figure in the age of revolution resembled him more closely than Toussaint Louverture.

FIVE

LIBERATOR AND DICTATOR

*During the last month of 1804 I saw the coronation of Napoleon in
Paris . . . [It] filled me with enthusiasm, but less because of the pomp than
because of the sentiments of love that an immense populace was showing towards
the French hero. That general effusion of every heart, that free and spontaneous
popular movement aroused by the glory, by the heroic deeds of Napoleon, who was
being cheered, at that moment, by more than a million individuals, seemed to
me . . . the ultimate ambition of man. The crown that Napoleon placed on his
head seemed to me a miserable thing . . . What seemed great to me was the
universal acclamation and interest that his person was inspiring.*

—Simón Bolívar, 1828

I n December 1815, a small ship sailed the two hundred miles from
Kingston, Jamaica, to the port of Les Cayes, on the southern coast
of Haiti, arriving the day before Christmas. Among the passengers
were five desperate men—South American revolutionaries whose hopes
of liberating Venezuela from Spanish rule had crumbled a year earlier.
Spurned by many of their own allies, and by the British authorities in
Jamaica, they had now come to their last, best hope for a base from
which to continue their struggle.

Haiti itself was still recovering, with difficulty, from the brutal final
stages of its own recent revolution. Shunned and under threat from
the Atlantic powers, its politics remained dangerously volatile. After

independence, Jean-Jacques Dessalines had ruled for barely two and a half years before falling victim to assassins' bullets during a revolt against his despotic rule. Subsequently, the revolt's leaders fell out among themselves, leading to the partition of Haiti into a northern state under Toussaint Louverture's former lieutenant Henri Christophe (who crowned himself its king in 1811), and a southern republic led after 1807 by Alexandre Pétion, the mixed-race son of a wealthy white planter. Christophe ruled as an autocrat, while Pétion, struggling to contain further secessionist tendencies, often violated his own constitution. Even so, Haiti, only the second country in the hemisphere successfully to have thrown off the colonial yoke, remained a powerful symbol of revolutionary hope.

The South Americans, along with an English aide-de-camp, quickly made their way to the southern capital of Port-au-Prince, where Pétion received them warmly.[1] In particular, he bonded with their leader, a strikingly handsome and intense man of thirty-two named Simón Bolívar, who spoke excellent French. Over the next three months, as more Venezuelan refugees washed up in Haiti, Pétion not only gave them shelter but agreed to equip an expedition to help them revive their revolution. Bolívar sailed back out of Les Cayes on March 31 in a flotilla of eight ships, bearing some 272 men (including perhaps 30 Haitians), and also 6,000 muskets, ammunition, and a printing press—all provided by Pétion. In return, in addition to Bolívar's friendship, Pétion asked the South American for a solemn promise to abolish slavery in Venezuela.[2]

In the event, the expedition proved an embarrassing failure, and by early September Bolívar had retraced his six-hundred-mile route across the Caribbean to Haiti. But Pétion was willing to give him a second chance. After another three-month respite in the black republic, at the end of 1816, Bolívar set out for his homeland with a new expedition outfitted much like the first. This time it had greater success. Many years of hard fighting would follow, but by 1825, thanks above all to Bolívar and his supporters, all of Spain's colonies on the South American continent had achieved independence.

Many have wondered how Bolívar's stay in Haiti influenced this white slaveholder who had been born into a society tightly stratified by race. Did he make his promise to Pétion out of genuine conviction or pragmatic necessity? Did his exposure to a republic of free black citizens lead him to question his own racial ideas? Like the voluble, irresistibly quotable Napoleon Bonaparte, the voluble, irresistibly quotable Simón Bolívar frequently contradicted himself, on this and many other issues.[3] Although he indeed declared the abolition of slavery upon his return home in 1816, conservative slaveholding elites resisted him, and Venezuela did not put a definitive end to the institution until 1854.[4]

There is evidence, though, that Haiti did provide a model for Bolívar in one particular area: personal political leadership.[5] During the first, abortive expedition from Haiti, he found it almost impossible to control the Venezuelan guerrilla chieftains known as *caudillos*.[6] Upon returning to Haiti, he found that Pétion, confronting his own political challenges, had revised the Haitian constitution to make himself president for life, on the model of Toussaint Louverture. It was an inspiration. On October 9, Bolívar wrote Pétion a remarkable note of congratulations:

The President of Haiti is the only leader who governs for the people. Only he commands equals. Other potentates are satisfied with being obeyed. They despise love, which is Your Excellency's glory. Your Excellency has been elevated to the perpetual dignity of the head of the Republic by the free acclamation of his fellow citizens, which is the sole legitimate source of all human power. Your Excellency is destined to erase even the memory of the great Washington.[7]

It would be easy enough to dismiss the letter as mere flattery of a desperately needed patron. Yet a decade later, in one of his most important pieces of political writing, Bolívar again cited Haiti as a political model. In his address to the Constituent Congress of the new Republic of Bolivia (named, of course, after him), he insisted on the need for a president for life, who would be "like the Sun, immovable at the center

of the universe, radiating life." And then Bolívar offered a lengthy di-
gression about Haiti, which had found itself "in a state of constant
insurrection" until Pétion created his life presidency, with the power to
choose his successor. "The people put their trust in him," Bolívar claimed,
"and the destinies of Haiti have not wavered since then."[8]

Bolívar's choice of words in his letter to Pétion was especially revealing. The "source of all legitimate power," in his view, was not simply the
consent of the citizens but something much stronger: their "acclamation," grounded in love. Biographers routinely note that over the course
of his revolutionary career, Bolívar moved from a classical republican
belief in the supremacy of law to a far more authoritarian stance.[9] But
his authoritarianism did not just amount to an insistence that an unruly
people obey their leader. It was grounded in the idea of an intense emotional bond between the leader and his country that in turn knit the
country itself together—the sort of bond that Bolívar believed he had
witnessed in Haiti and that could be traced back to the rule of Toussaint
Louverture.

Although Bolívar's experience in the postcolonial state of Haiti
weighed heavily with him, he also had another model for this authoritarianism of love. Throughout his adult life, like so many other people
in the Atlantic world in the nineteenth century, he nurtured an obsession with Napoleon Bonaparte, whom he had personally seen on at least
one occasion, in Italy, during early travels in Europe.[10] In 1828, he
boasted to a French aide that he had also personally witnessed Bonaparte's
coronation as emperor in the Cathedral of Notre Dame in 1804.[11] In
typically contradictory fashion, he told others that he had spurned the
event because of his disgust that a republican hero had placed a crown
on his head.[12] But regardless of what Bolívar actually did in 1804, the
language he used twenty-four years later was revealing, and strikingly
similar to what he had written to Pétion. He spoke of the "universal
acclamation" for Bonaparte on the occasion of the coronation, of "the
sentiments of love" that the French showed their leader, of the emotion
aroused by glory and heroism. Bolívar called "that general effusion of
every heart" nothing less than "the ultimate ambition of man."[13] It was a

vision of personal power that came very close to the one propounded by Bonaparte himself, and one that was frequently attributed to Louverture, Washington, and Paoli as well. It placed the South American firmly in a direct line of succession to these charismatic predecessors.

Spanish-speaking America makes the logical last stop in this story of how modern political charisma arose in the age of revolution. By the time the revolutions in the Spanish empire began, around 1810, charismatic leadership had become a dominant feature of political life throughout the Atlantic world, thanks to the experiences of the United States, France, and Haiti. As Spanish-speaking Americans began their own revolutionary struggles, they creatively and loquaciously debated the earlier examples. Bolívar, the most important of their revolutionary leaders, was compared to both Washington and Bonaparte, and he had his own definite, if not always entirely consistent, views of both men. He had spent time in the United States, France, and Haiti, was a voracious reader, and reflected deeply on forms of government and the role of powerful executives.

Furthermore, in Spanish-speaking America the tensions between charismatic democratic leadership and charismatic authoritarianism remained far more acute, for far longer, than elsewhere in the Atlantic world. Bolívar himself held executive power in several different states, with formal titles that included president, president for life, and dictator, setting an example that would remain influential in Spanish America long after his death in 1830. Under what conditions does charismatic democratic leadership become dangerous and threaten democratic republics? In Spanish-speaking America, the question has perhaps been posed more frequently than anywhere else.

The revolutions in Spanish-speaking America produced many charismatic leaders, from the fiery radical Mexican priest Miguel Hidalgo, to the enigmatic Argentinean José de San Martín, to the "precursor" of Venezuelan independence Francisco de Miranda, who among his other exploits witnessed George Washington's triumphal entry into Philadelphia in 1784 and served as a general in the French Revolutionary armies. But Bolívar was unquestionably the most important, the most fascinating, and the best documented, and his career puts the power and peril of charisma in sharp focus.

Bolívar's achievements certainly compared with those of the other great charismatic leaders of the era. He led to independence what would eventually become six separate countries (Venezuela, Colombia, Panama, Ecuador, Peru, and Bolivia), covering a combined surface area more than four times that of the United States in 1776. Among his many spectacular military feats was a grueling crossing of the high passes in the Andes, in 1819, that outdid even Napoleon's march over the Alps in 1800. Although born into the wealthiest stratum of the white Venezuelan elite, he forged a broad-based movement among poor, multiracial, and partially enslaved populations. By the 1820s, Bolívar's fame in Europe and the United States trailed only that of Washington and Bonaparte, despite the distance and unfamiliarity of South America. Engraved portraits and accounts of his exploits found an apparently insatiable market, and Americans in particular often included him in their civic celebrations as a sort of honorary founding father. Five American towns were named for him, and the future Confederate general and Kentucky governor Simon Bolivar Buckner was just one of at least two hundred American babies to suffer the same fate in the 1820s and 1830s.[14]

At Bolívar's birth, in 1783, this future would have looked fantastically unlikely (just as unlikely, it might be said, as Washington's, Louverture's, or Bonaparte's would have looked at their births). Despite the example of the recently concluded American War of Independence, little revolutionary fervor had as yet developed in Spain's enormous American empire, which in theory covered more than half the landmass of the western hemisphere, stretching from Cape Horn all the way to what is now the state of Montana.[15] Eighteenth-century reforms in imperial governance introduced, somewhat erratically, by Spain's Bourbon dynasty had disrupted older patterns of governance and shifted power from Creole (American-born white) elites to Spanish-born officials.

This change provoked resentment among the Creoles, and in places it triggered bouts of violent protests. Large-scale revolt in Peru in the 1780s, especially among indigenous people and led in one case by the self-proclaimed descendant of the Incas Túpac Amaru, shook Spanish rule even more deeply but did not unite the province's diverse populations into an independence movement.[16]

Nor was Venezuela the most obvious place in Spanish America for revolutionary fervor to evolve. Compared to the wealthy, cosmopolitan centers of Spanish civilization in the Americas, Mexico and Peru, it was something of a backwater. Five or six hundred white Creole slave-owning families, their wealth derived principally from cacao, coffee, and indigo, dominated a relatively stable colonial society whose population of eight hundred thousand included seventy thousand black slaves and four hundred thousand free people of mixed race known as *pardos* (unlike most of the South American states, Venezuela had few Native Americans). The leading families divided their time between vast plantations worked by slaves and Caracas mansions, bought imported consumer goods, and functioned very much as a local aristocracy. Otherwise, apart from a relatively small, mostly urban, middle class, the vast majority of Venezuelans were illiterate and poor. Catholicism was the sole permissible religion, and the church hierarchy feared and hated Enlightenment ideas. The colony had no printing presses, and royal censors and the Inquisition kept a close watch on imported books and periodicals.[17] After the beginning of the French Revolution, the anxious authorities prohibited the entry of any books or objects that made reference to events in France, "including coins, fans, clocks, engravings, and paintings."[18]

Yet even here it proved impossible to quarantine an entire society from revolutionary news. Some smugglers of prohibited materials— including texts published in North America in Spanish for the Latin American market—landed on remote, unguarded parts of the colony's 1,700-mile-long coastline. Others hid rolled-up papers inside boxes of hats and clocks, or wrapped books in waterproof cloths and dropped them overboard in crates from their ships when they docked, retrieving them once the Inquisition's inspectors had moved on. Young Creoles passed forbidden foreign books from hand to hand, translating French and English ones word for word with dictionaries if they did not speak the languages.[19] Then in the 1790s, thanks to the events in Saint-Domingue, both radical revolution and the specter of slave revolt came within a few hundred miles. They helped inspire a slave insurrection in the town of Coro in 1795 and, two years later, a small, abortive revolutionary conspiracy based in the port of La Guaira. Its Creole leaders distributed copies of the French Declaration of the Rights of Man and Citizen and called for the abolition of slavery.[20]

The adolescent Simón Bolívar, unlike the adolescent Napoleon Bonaparte, did not have grandiose literary and political ambitions. Born into one of the oldest and wealthiest Creole families in Venezuela, orphaned at a young age, he grew into a moody and recalcitrant teenager but not a revolutionary one. He did not attend university, but when he was sixteen, his family sent him to Europe to complete his education. In Spain, he met and married a beautiful young noblewoman and brought her back to Caracas, but after less than a year she died of yellow fever. Heartbroken, he returned to Europe in 1804, and there his life took a decisive turn when he came under the influence of a former tutor who became his teacher and close companion, Simón Rodríguez. A fervent admirer of Jean-Jacques Rousseau, Rodríguez had taken part in the 1797 conspiracy and subsequently fled Venezuela, calling himself Samuel Robinson, in honor of Robinson Crusoe (what better name for an alienated intellectual?). Under his tutelage, Bolívar, who would later salute him as "My master! My friend! My Robinson!," read deeply in the classics and Enlightenment philosophy, becoming a particular admirer of Montesquieu and also a fervent republican committed to South American independence.[21] In 1805, on the Monte Sacro in Rome, with Rodríguez at his side, he swore grandiloquently that he would not rest his body or soul "until I have broken the chains with which Spanish power oppresses us."[22]

But South America was still not much closer to revolution. In 1806, Francisco de Miranda, the Venezuelan-born itinerant revolutionary, took a small expedition back home with the intention of launching a war of liberation. An eccentric, seductive character, Miranda had become a close friend of Alexander Hamilton during his travels in the United States and boasted of having shared the bed of Catherine the Great while visiting Russia. In France, during his stint as a revolutionary general, his ties to the Brissotin faction nearly led him to the guillotine. Eventually acquiring some backing from the British, who were at war with Spain, he landed near Coro in the summer of 1806, bringing along, in addition to weaponry, a printing press to issue propaganda, as well as linen handkerchiefs printed with various portraits, including his own and George Washington's. But he failed to rally Venezuelan support, and the expedition quickly turned into a fiasco, from which he barely escaped. He ended up, like so many other failed freedom fighters of the era (including Paoli), in exile in London.[23]

The events that finally triggered Spanish America's long revolutionary wars took place not in a Venezuelan equivalent of Lexington and Concord but at the heart of the empire.[24] The person responsible was not a Spanish-speaking Jefferson or Adams but Napoleon Bonaparte. He counted Spain as an ally, but as he struggled without success to strangle Britain economically by closing off continental Europe to its trade, he found the Spanish increasingly unreliable. In the spring of 1808, after Spanish crown prince Ferdinand staged a coup against his ailing and erratic father, King Carlos IV, Bonaparte summoned both men to the French frontier town of Bayonne, forced both to abdicate, and took them prisoner. He then installed his own brother Joseph as king in Madrid, with the help of large French military contingents already deployed in the country. Much of Spain immediately burst into revolt and established "juntas" loyal to Ferdinand, setting off the long, brutal Peninsular War that ultimately helped destroy Bonaparte's empire.

When news of these events reached Venezuela (in issues of *The Times* of London), the local elites, like their counterparts throughout Spain's American empire, immediately and enthusiastically pledged their loyalty to Ferdinand, the captive, "longed-for king." But they balked at giving Spanish juntas authority over the colony, arguing that they answered directly to the monarch. More than a year and a half of rising tensions and confused maneuvering followed, during which the loyalists fighting Bonaparte in Spain refused to give the Americans representation in their councils, and Bonaparte himself seemed to consolidate his control of the peninsula. Finally, in April 1810, popular demonstrations in Caracas led to the overthrow of the Spanish colonial administration and the creation of a Venezuelan Junta that professed its loyalty to Ferdinand alone.

Bolívar had only a small role in these events, because he favored complete independence, but he agreed to take part in a diplomatic mission to seek aid for the Venezuelan Junta from the British government. The discussions in London accomplished little, but they did give Bolívar the chance to meet the sixty-five-year-old Miranda, and when he returned to Caracas in December, he did so in the role of a political John the Baptist, proclaiming the advent of the savior. Miranda soon followed him, and the two quickly took on key roles in a new political club, the Patriotic Society, where they agitated for a full-scale declaration of independence. With the Spanish Juntas still opposing any concession of authority, their arguments carried the day, and on July 5, 1811, the First Venezuelan Republic was born. Bolívar, still shy of his twenty-eighth birthday but already noted for his commanding personality and apparently unlimited energy, already counted as one of its leading figures.

To say that Venezuela's independence struggle did not go smoothly, however, would be a massive understatement.[25] The disasters that beset the American revolutionaries in 1776 look minor by comparison. The Creole elites who created the First Republic, and wanted to maintain their social dominance, found it difficult to attract the support of poor whites and *pardos*, many of whom rallied to the Spanish side. Then, on March 26, 1812, came a hammer blow when a massive earthquake came close to leveling Caracas, killing thousands. A month later, the Republic invested Miranda with dictatorial powers, but he could not hold back the advancing Spanish. An overwhelmed Bolívar had to surrender control of a key fort. Finally, in July 1812, Miranda took it upon himself to negotiate a surrender. Bolívar, who wanted to continue the struggle, had him arrested. The man later called the "Precursor" of independence ended up in Spain as a prisoner and died there in 1816. Bolívar himself fled to the port town of Cartagena in neighboring New Granada (present-day Colombia).

With Miranda gone, Bolívar now came to the fore as the unquestioned leader of the Venezuelan struggle. In Cartagena, he issued a manifesto, written in stern, classical republican language, blaming the failure of the First Republic on its weak federalist constitution, designed, in his words, by "certain worthy visionaries who, imagining ethereal republics [*repúblicas aéreas*] for themselves, and presupposing the perfection of the human race, tried to achieve political perfection." In place of "exaggerated maxims of the rights of man," he insisted, in language reminiscent of Robespierre's justifications for the Reign of Terror, that Venezuela needed centralization and a firm hand: "The government . . . must appear terrifying and gird itself with a strength equal to the dangers, without regard for laws, or constitutions, until happiness and peace have been restored."[26]

The level of bloodshed that followed matched anything previously seen in the age of revolution. Bolívar persuaded the leaders of Cartagena, then involved in its own, somewhat more successful fight for independence, to provide him with soldiers and equipment for a new campaign. By March 1813 he had reached the Venezuelan border, liberating territory from the Spanish as he went. In response to his advance, the Spanish started shooting prisoners and civilians. Bolívar retorted with a "Decree of War to the Death," ordering his forces to kill as a traitor any Spaniard who did not actively side with them.[27] He fought brilliantly, and increasing numbers of Venezuelans, compelled to choose a side, joined his army. Even as atrocities multiplied, Bolívar's campaign succeeded, and in August 1813 he entered Caracas in triumph and declared the republic reestablished. Two months later, the city conferred on him the title "Liberator of Venezuela."[28]

Still, the war continued, and it turned even bloodier. On the vast interior plains of the country—the *llanos*—an adventurer and convicted smuggler named José Tomás Boves raised a large irregular force to fight for Spain. He recruited primarily from among the *pardos* and blacks, promising plunder and revenge against the white Creoles who had exploited them, and freedom to slaves. Sadistic, brave, fiercely loved by his men, Boves was one of the first great South American *caudillos*, and like Bolívar he promised a war to the death. When Boves's deputy Francisco Rosete took the town of Ocumare in February 1814, his troops cut down civilians indiscriminately, "slicing off noses, ears, breasts and sexual organs, leaving the town littered with body parts as a deterrent to rebels."[29] The same month, Bolívar himself ordered the cold-blooded execution of eight hundred Spanish prisoners after the Spanish commander in chief refused his demands.[30] All in all, the body count may have risen to as high as eighty thousand republican victims and a smaller number on the Spanish side.[31]

Boves's ruthlessness, combined with his undeniable military talent and his appeal to the blacks and *pardos*, had an effect. The Republic's Assembly formally granted Bolívar dictatorial powers, as its predecessor had done with Miranda, but Boves won a decisive action in June 1814, and amid further massacres, Bolívar and the republican government fled Caracas. Boves himself died in battle in December, but his victories allowed the royalists again to take complete control of Venezuela. Bolívar himself sailed back to Cartagena in September 1814 after issuing another manifesto in which he took responsibility for defeat while insisting he could have done no better. "Man is the feeble plaything of fortune," he wrote.[32] From Cartagena, he made another attempt to invade Venezuela. When it, too, quickly failed, he fled the South American continent altogether, arriving in Jamaica in May 1815. At the end of the year he would sail on to Haiti.

An epic series of disasters had destroyed two Venezuelan republics within barely three years, and Bolívar could hardly escape a large share of the blame. Nor was it at all obvious, as he solicited support in Jamaica and Haiti, that he would remain at the head of his country's independence struggle. In Venezuela itself, away from the coast and the major cities, that struggle continued, led by rough-hewn soldiers—the *caudillos*—who maintained their hold over their multiracial troops through force of personality and sheer physical strength and skill. They were genuine "men on horseback" who needed to use "the lance with both hands, to fight on wild horses and to break them in during actual battle, to swim and to fight while swimming in swollen rivers, to lasso and kill wild beasts simply to get food."[33] They engaged in frequent duels and epic drinking contests. José Antonio Páez typified them: a poor, illiterate *llanero* (cowboy) subject to epileptic fits, he did not even know how to use a knife and fork, but he possessed enormous physical strength and managed to shape hundreds of other *llaneros* into an effective guerrilla band. He had charismatic authority of a classically premodern sort.[34] Could Bolívar control such unruly subordinates? He necessarily functioned as something of a *caudillo* himself during the campaigns of 1811–15, gaining respect by spending whole days in the saddle without tiring. In the Spanish-American armies, commanders won support soldier by soldier, in campaigns fought on a very small scale compared to the titanic conflicts taking place at the same moment on the other side of the Atlantic. Even one of the largest battles—Araure, on December 5, 1813—had only about 6,500 total combatants. Two months earlier, in the Battle of Leipzig, between Napoleon and a large allied coalition, more than 500,000 had taken part.[35]

But Bolívar was not just a *caudillo*, and by 1815 he had developed his own powerful form of charisma, which came much closer to Washington's, Bonaparte's, or Louverture's than to Páez's. He could do so in large part because political culture in South America had evolved with startling speed since the start of the century. It was no accident that Miranda had brought a printing press with him during his 1806 expedition. In his London exile, the "Precursor" published a Spanish-language newspaper called *El Colombiano*, which supporters smuggled back across the Atlantic. In 1808, Caracas finally acquired its own printing press and a bi-weekly newspaper. Overall, in the years immediately after independence, the typical Spanish-American periodical had ten times more subscriptions than in the late colonial period, came out six times as frequently, and cost half as much.[36] Cafés, reading circles, libraries, and other venues for reading and political debate multiplied, with the Patriotic Society playing a particularly important role.[37] The *Gaceta de Caracas*, speaking for the Creole elite, positioned itself as the voice of a rational, educated public opinion that could restrain what it called "the maneuvers of the ignorant, passionate and licentious mob."[38] But the expansion of the public sphere meant that printed works could now reach significantly beyond the wealthiest five or six hundred Venezuelan families and could help construct a broad-based independence movement.

From the earliest days of the independence struggle, Simón Bolívar understood the power of the press. He himself published articles in the *Gaceta de Caracas* and sent false reports of victories for publication in newspapers in London to counter royalist sympathies there.[39] The *Gaceta de Caracas* and other papers printed his speeches and proclamations to his soldiers.[40] And he devoted particular care to the grandiose "Manifestos" in which he defended his record, diagnosed the political situation, and laid out a program for his movement. Several of them quickly appeared in pamphlet form.

Meanwhile, much as literate Americans had seized on Washington as a focus of their hopes and dreams even after his worst defeats, elite Creoles began to treat Bolívar as an idol of sorts as early as 1813. When he entered the city at the end of his so-called Admirable Campaign on August 6, the municipality helped arrange a Roman-style triumph reminiscent of Washington's entries into Trenton and Philadelphia in 1789. Printers published books of songs to be sung on the occasion in honor of the Hero Liberator (one set of lyrics compared him to the Athenian Miltiades, hero of Marathon, giving a strong hint as to the social class of the intended singers).[41] Some thirty thousand people thronged the streets to see him. Young women dressed in white, holding flowers, grasped the bridle of Bolívar's horse as he dismounted, and then they crowned him with laurel wreaths. He made his way to the center of the town on foot, walking under ceremonial arches through streets strewn with flowers, accompanied by the ringing of church bells, salvos of artillery, and shouts of "Long Live the Liberator!"[42] The *Gaceta* described the festivities at length and offered its own extravagant praise for Bolívar as the "guardian angel who freed the people of Caracas, broke their chains, and returned to them their honor and glory."[43] Significantly, it devoted just as much coverage to the emotions shown by the crowd toward Bolívar as it did to Bolívar himself:

> At the news of the arrival of the Hero Liberator, the city of Caracas sprang into motion, and individuals of every age and sex flew to meet the Father of their Country. What a grand spectacle! Thirty thousand souls ran to express their gratitude towards the Conqueror. All broke out in acclamations. All voices spoke in concert: Long live General Bolívar, Long live the Liberator! . . . All is jubilation, all is enthusiasm. Bolívar's entry is a day of joy that every citizen feels happily obligated to celebrate.[44]

It was a classic depiction of charismatic authority as grounded in the emotional bond between the founding "father" and the people he had saved and unified. It was precisely the language of "acclamation" that Bolívar would evoke three years later in his letter to Alexandre Pétion, when his triumph had turned to dust and blown away in the Caribbean wind.

During the year and a half Bolívar spent crisscrossing the Caribbean after the fall of Venezuela's Second Republic (from May 1815 to the end of 1816), the outlook for the independence struggle only seemed to turn more dire. In Europe, as Bonaparte's empire crumbled, Ferdinand VII returned to rule in Madrid. But the king was not in a forgiving mood. He abrogated the liberal constitution that the parliament in Cádiz had drafted in 1812 and that had granted full citizenship to whites and native peoples in the Americas although still maintaining an unequal relationship between the metropole and the colonies. He also sent one of the largest military expeditions in Spanish history across the Atlantic to crush the insurgents. It besieged Cartagena and starved it into submission, with a third of the population dying in the process.

After the Spanish captured the New Granadan capital of Santa Fe de Bogotá (present-day Bogotá), they displayed the heads of defenders on stakes and in cages.[45]

When Bolívar returned from Haiti for the second time at the end of 1816, his prospects seemed especially faint. Not only did he lack the strength to challenge the Spanish, who occupied most of the country, including Caracas; he could not even control his allies among the fractious *caudillos*. But he did have the arms provided by Pétion, and over the next few months he began to reestablish his leading position. He moved his forces deep into the remote, impenetrable swamps of the Orinoco River delta, safe from Spanish attack. In keeping with his pledge to Pétion, he promised freedom to black slaves who would fight for him and reached out as well to *pardos* who had previously flocked to Boves. And he started to organize a ramshackle collection of colonial militias and *caudillo*-led war bands into a professional army. Despite the classical republican prejudices against such forces, Bolívar recognized, as had George Washington before him, that he could not achieve victory against a powerful European professional military without a professional military of his own. He forged a close alliance with the most prominent *caudillo* who was willing to accept his authority—José Antonio Páez—and moved ruthlessly against the most vulnerable *caudillo* who was not, a *pardo* named Manuel Piar. In early autumn 1817 he had Piar arrested, court-martialed, and shot by firing squad. With the *Gaceta de Caracas* in enemy hands, he also established a new newspaper of his own: *El correo del Orinoco*.

The year 1817 marked the beginning of the most extraordinary period in Bolívar's extraordinary life. In July he captured the city of Angostura, on the Orinoco (today it is called Ciudad Bolívar). The military situation remained difficult, with the fledgling Venezuelan army unable to liberate other major towns. But Bolívar now stood as the undisputed "Supreme Leader" (*Jefe Supremo*) of the independence struggle. The Spanish commander even claimed, in a report to Madrid, that Bolívar was planning on proclaiming himself King Simón I.[46] This was false, but Bolívar did feel confident enough to call for elections for a new

Congress, and at the start of 1819 it assembled in Angostura, effectively marking the foundation of a new, Third Republic. On February 8, it named Bolívar president with almost unlimited emergency powers.

In an address to the Congress a week later, building on ideas first developed during his exile in Jamaica, Bolívar laid out a major new political vision for the country.[47] He began with a distinctly Washingtonian note of republican renunciation, insisting that he wanted no title or position other than "good citizen." He praised Venezuelans for having struggled to build a "democratic republic" that respected the "rights of man" and civil equality and that had removed the country from under "the black veil" of slavery.[48] But he also insisted that Venezuela needed a system built around a charismatic leader. The best solution would not be "pure democracy" but a mixed, moderate regime that, in keeping with Montesquieu's teachings, would suit the character of the people. That character was both passive, thanks to the long centuries of Spanish despotism, and also fragile, because of the country's volatile racial mixture ("our people is neither European, nor North American, and more a blend of Africa and America than an emanation of Europe"). South Americans, in his view, did not, unlike North Americans, yet have the virtues necessary for republican self-government. Bolívar insisted that teaching them such virtues would require "infinite tact" and, still more, "an infinitely firm hand."[49] He therefore rejected the idea of adapting to Venezuela the federal constitution of the United States with what he perceived as its relatively weak central power. Venezuela did need a constitution of some sort, to provide a stable framework in which a republican society could mature. But because of its historical circumstances, it needed something resembling the British constitution, with a hereditary senate for stability and, above all, a powerful chief executive. Significantly, Bolívar declared that the only passions a republican needed to feel were "love of the fatherland, love of the laws, and love of the leaders."[50] A classical republican like the young John Adams would not have included "the leaders" in this phrase. Bolívar also advocated the creation of a "moral power," on the model of the ancient Roman office of censor, to police and reform private behavior.

In doing so, he counted on the support of the Catholic Church—an institution he took pains to cultivate throughout his years in power, despite his own lax religious beliefs, and which supported him in turn.[51]

Yet none of these elaborate plans would matter if Bolívar could not break the military stalemate. In the spring of 1819, he decided upon a high-risk gamble. New Granada was far more weakly defended by the Spanish than Caracas and the Venezuela coastlands. If he could strike there and take Santa Fe de Bogotá, he could deal the Spanish a major blow and acquire a powerful base. But getting there, via the only open route—the high passes through the Andes mountains—would be nearly impossible. Nonetheless, in late May he set out with an army of 2,100, including several hundred foreign mercenaries, mostly British veterans of the Napoleonic Wars (overall, at least 5,300 British and Irish volunteers fought in the South American independence struggles).[52] The army forded wide rivers and crossed the savannas of central New Granada in the monsoon season. It then climbed through narrow, treacherous passes, still under ceaseless driving rain, high into the Andes, crossing over the Páramo de Pisba pass at the dizzying height of thirteen thousand feet, with temperatures near freezing. Boots wore through, and clothing turned to rags held together by string. A quarter of the British troops died of disease, exhaustion, or accident.

But two thousand survivors made it through, regrouped, and reequipped themselves. And then, on August 7, they defeated a larger Spanish force at Boyacá, seventy miles from the New Granadan capital. Three days later, disheartened Spanish officials having fled, Bolívar and his army entered the city in triumph. A British veteran recalled a series of celebratory balls, at which every toast honored the Liberator. "In the plenitude of enthusiasm, up sprung three or four Venezuelan patriots, and seizing Bolívar, they bore him on a seat of entwining hands around the board, amidst vociferous *vivas*."[53] Bolívar himself staged a victory procession, reenacting the 1813 liberation of Caracas by having twenty girls dressed in white crown him with laurel wreaths.[54]

But these were not laurels Bolívar was prepared to rest on. In fact, following the victory, his ambitions soared far higher. Although he still did not control the major cities of Venezuela, he now proposed uniting the country with New Granada and what would become Ecuador into a single great republic, to be called Colombia (historians now refer to it as Gran Colombia, to distinguish it from the later, smaller state of that name; see figure 19). Roughly the size of the United States at independence, it would cover nearly all the northern part of the continent, with the possibility of extending even farther. In December 1819, Bolívar returned to Angostura, where the Congress duly proclaimed the new state. The next month, he received help from an unexpected quarter when a liberal revolution broke out in Spain, forcing King Ferdinand to restore the liberal constitution of 1812 and weakening his ability to re-supply Spanish forces in the Americas. On June 24, 1821, Bolívar's men won the Battle of Carabobo, one of the bloodiest of the war, thanks in large part to the heroism of José Antonio Páez, whom Bolívar promoted to general-in-chief on the spot. Five days later, Bolívar finally marched into Caracas. In September, the Congress elected him president of Gran Colombia under a new constitution, which, tailored to his wishes, established a powerful central government dominated by the chief executive. Bolívar accepted his election, while also warning the Congress, in Washingtonian style, against giving him excessive power. "A man like me," he told them, meaning a successful and charismatic military leader, "is a dangerous citizen in a popular government."[55]

More still was to come. Bolívar now determined to march south and complete the new state by liberating all of what would become Ecuador, and doing so before his Argentinean counterpart, José de San Martín, could snatch the prize away. In early 1822 his armies marched south, paying for supplies with a paper scrip bearing an image of the leader swathed in laurel leaves. While troops under his direct command met fierce Spanish resistance, his young protégé, the brilliant, talented, and vain Antonio José de Sucre, won a decisive victory at Pichincha on May 24. Three weeks later, Bolívar entered the city of Quito, re-creating the familiar entry ceremony by having himself greeted by women in white carrying laurel wreaths. In Quito, Bolívar also met the brilliant, beautiful and strong-willed Manuela Sáenz, who would become his companion and supporter (but not his wife, although he had now spent twenty years as a widower). He was now what one of his generals called the *hijo predilecto de la Gloria*—the favorite son of glory.[56]

The events of 1817 to 1822 had changed the history of the Americas and utterly transformed Bolívar's reputation. At the start of the period, he had been one independent chieftain among many, failing to make headway in his campaign and struggling to hold together a fractious group of *caudillos*. By the end, he had become the most successful leader the western hemisphere had seen since Washington, a commander whose exploits and conquests rivaled those of Bonaparte. In the process, he attracted intensive, obsessive attention, not only in South America but throughout the Atlantic world. He was celebrated and adulated, denounced and reviled, and everywhere commentators compared him to the other great charismatic leaders of the era. This attention had an impact on politics in Gran Colombia and, increasingly, on Bolívar himself.

In Gran Colombia, and throughout Spanish-speaking South America, the idolization of Bolívar followed very closely the pattern we have seen with his charismatic predecessors elsewhere. Adulatory short biographies began to materialize, along with breathless accounts of the Boyacá campaign.[57] Poetry and songs appeared in profusion, with unimaginative lines such as "Gloria! Gloria! Bolívar. / Gloria, Libertador."[58] Bolívar was everywhere hailed as a genius and the father of his country. The Ecuadorean writer (and future president) Vicente Rocafuerte praised him as "the hero of America, the Washington of the South, the sublime Bolívar . . . the immortal Bolívar."[59] At the same time, Spanish and loyalist American poets were denouncing him, with one Colombian priest damning him as a "cruel Nero" and Herod.[60]

Changes in civic celebrations underlined Bolívar's new, more exalted status. After the liberation of Caracas in 1821, the city chose, as the day for major festivities, October 28—Bolívar's saint's day (which traditional Catholic societies celebrated in preference to birthdays). In addition to the usual artillery salvos, church bells, triumphal arches, and nocturnal illuminations, there was displayed a giant painted allegory showing Minerva and Hercules placing a bust of Bolívar on a pedestal in the presence of a representation of Colombia, shown holding her broken chains.[61] A year later, on the same occasion, the American traveler (and future Treasury Secretary) William Duane observed the proceedings. "The streets of Caracas are usually very still, and seldom crowded," he wrote. "On this day they appeared like ant-hills with their inhabitants in motion."[62] After a high mass, a band and choir performed in front of the cathedral, with songs written for the occasion. "Whenever the name of Bolivar occurred," Duane continued, "and it was the whole theme, the air resounded with acclamations, not only from the soldiery, but from the vast concourse assembled." Duane also recounted that at a dinner party in the city, he complimented the wealthy host on the splendor of his home and told him he need not envy anyone on earth. The man replied, "Yes, there is one man whom I envy, though I love," and he pointed to the only picture in the room: Bolívar's.[63] These were the days, as Gabriel García Márquez wrote in a fine novel about Bolívar (*The General in His Labyrinth*), when "people would grasp his horse by the halter and stop him . . . simply to feel themselves close to the radiance of greatness."[64]

As these anecdotes suggest, not only did at least some Venezuelans genuinely adulate Bolívar, but visual representations of the man had become common. In 1819, the *pardo* painter Pedro José Figueroa portrayed Bolívar in a striking primitivist manner, pairing him with a girl in an Indian headdress representing America, thereby casting the Liberator as the father of his country (figure 20). Figueroa presented the work to Bolívar himself during the festivities after Bogotá's liberation.[65] Many other painters rushed to do more conventional portraits, and by 1822 several dozen engravings had appeared as well, mostly produced in Europe but often meant for the South American market. At some point there also appeared the remarkable engraving showing black or *pardo* parents displaying a portrait of an unusually dark-skinned Bolívar to their children, with the caption "Here is your liberator" (figure 5). It suggests how widely such engraved portraits may have circulated in South America and how printed works helped extend the cult of Bolívar beyond the Creole elite.

Bolívar's legend now also took hold in Europe and North America. Newspapers there reported regularly on him and published short accounts of his life.[66] Travelers to South America, and veterans of Bolívar's British legion, rushed into print with vividly written accounts of the war that nearly always, in the style of Boswell, included detailed physical descriptions of Bolívar and highlighted personal traits such as his incessant womanizing and his absolute detestation of tobacco smoke.[67] It was now that Bolívar's name and image began to appear in patriotic festivities in the United States, with the Liberator cast as a new George Washington spreading a gospel of freedom from the northern to the southern hemisphere. Not all the coverage was adulatory. George Chesterton, a British soldier who grew disillusioned with Bolívar, left an especially acid portrait: "He is short and meagre: his hair is now grey, and his mustachios quite white. His eyes are large and very light, and the general effect of his countenance is in the highest degree unprepossessing. His voice is harsh and disagreeable, and his manners are cold and forbidding in the extreme."[68] Edward Everett, the American writer and statesman now best remembered for sharing the podium with Abraham Lincoln at Gettysburg (and orating for more than two hours), composed a magazine essay that nastily dismissed South America as unworthy of sustained attention, thanks to its "odious confusions of Spanish bigotry and indolence, with savage barbarism and African stupidity . . . Not all the treaties we could make," Everett commented, "nor the commissioners we could send out, nor the money we could lend them, would transform their . . . Bolivars into Washingtons."[69]

But the adulation dominated, and it certainly did not escape Bolívar's own attention. George Chesterton caustically noted in 1820:

> His manner evidently betrays the effect produced upon him by the extracts, carefully copied into the *Orinoko Courier*, from the English and French papers, in which the appellations of a "second Washington," "hero," and "liberator of his country," are frequently found.

These compliments seem to have been dwelt upon by him, till he fancied himself the first man of the age; at least, such was the impression made not only upon myself, but upon others of my countrymen.[70]

Other foreign observers also noted the expanding Bolivarian ego. A German veteran of Boyacá described his character as "cold, domineering and limitlessly proud. Those around him suffer from his . . . practically childlike vanity."[71] The brother of a British officer who helped lead the Colombian army called him "insatiably covetous of fame."[72] Well before his great victories, Bolívar had come, like Bonaparte and Louverture before him, to believe he had a unique, extraordinary destiny. In his speeches and manifestos he routinely described himself as the chosen instrument of Providence bringing freedom to South America.[73] After arriving in Quito in 1822 he climbed the 20,564-foot-high Mount Chimborazo (then thought to be the tallest mountain in the world) and wrote an extraordinary sort of prose poem he called "My Delirium on Chimborazo," in which he spoke of having "the God of Colombia take possession of me" and having encountered the spirit of Time itself, which accused him of vanity. He responded: "I have surpassed all men in good fortune, as I have risen above the heads of all. I dominate the earth."[74]

At the same time, Bolívar's sense of himself as a world-historical figure, and his experience of the long, hard labor of war, were leading him to reject even more of his optimistic early republicanism. In a letter to his soon-to-be vice-president Francisco de Paula Santander in June 1821, he poured scorn on liberals who imagined that the Colombian population consisted wholly of "coddled patricians" (lanudos) sitting around comfortable fireplaces. These liberals, he continued, had not taken into account the ungovernably wild variety of peoples in the country, including "savage hordes from Africa and America." The true people of Colombia, he insisted, were to be found in the army: "This is the people that expresses its will, the people that labors and the people that can act. Everyone else merely vegetates, with more or less malignity, or with more or less patriotism, and in any case without any right to be anything but passive citizens." He added, rather unnecessarily, "This is certainly not the politics of Rousseau."[75] Much like Bonaparte and Louverture before him, Bolívar was moving toward a fusion of military and political authority, in which the nation only found full expression in the army and its charismatic supreme commander, who alone had the ability to unite a fractious population.[76] The next and final stage of his career would see him attempt to implement this vision. He would firmly reject Bonaparte's monarchical strategy, however, and instead embrace a distinctly Latin American model that followed most directly from the Haitian example first developed by Toussaint Louverture.

In 1822, Bolívar was thirty-nine and had just eight more years to live. In those eight years, he would first soar even higher than before but then tumble into what South Americans often termed a political "labyrinth," as his new state of Gran Colombia failed to consolidate and stabilize. In his last years he would grow ever more frustrated, ever more despairing of South Americans learning the art of self-government, and ever more drawn to the lure of authoritarianism.

The last of his great triumphs began in July 1822 with a meeting in Guayaquil, in what is now southern Ecuador, with his counterpart from the southern part of the continent, the cool, reserved Argentinean José de San Martín. The subject was Peru, which had declared its independence the year before, with Argentinean support, but had not managed to overcome powerful Spanish forces. San Martín took a quick dislike to Bolívar, finding him intolerably ambitious and vain. It did not help that Bolívar, at a dinner, offered a toast to "the two greatest men of South America—to General San Martín, and to me," or that he gave San Martín a portrait of himself as a present.[77] Still, San Martín had no choice but to ask Bolívar for help in Peru, and Bolívar readily assented. He arrived in the country by sea in September 1823 and received a delirious welcome. "BOLÍVAR is with us," the *Gaceta de Lima* proclaimed, "and there is no reason to fear. He is worth more than an army . . . Let the world see that South America also has its Washington."[78] Local poets hailed the "immortal Bolívar" as a "sublime genius."[79]

The welcome was extravagant, but Bolívar entirely fulfilled the Peruvians' hopes. His campaign suffered early reverses, but he had no doubt about ultimate victory. In typically grandiose style, he wrote to Sucre: "I am driven by the demon of war and am embarked upon ending this struggle in one way or another. It seems as if the guiding spirit of America and the guiding spirit of my destiny have both intruded into my head."[80] In the second half of 1825 he and Sucre won the last great battles of the South American revolutions and secured Peru's independence. During the campaign, the Peruvian Congress gave him the formal title of Dictator, which, in South America, still retained its original Roman associations of temporary, honorable emergency powers.[81]

After the victories, Bolívar embarked on a triumphal tour of Peru and received a torrent of adulation that out-drenched anything even he had previously experienced. The town of Arequipa served him dinner on plates of gold and presented him with precious jewels on silver platters during a banquet in his honor.[82] In Cuzco, he received a gold key to the city, while a contributor to the local newspaper hailed him in the voice of an Inca: "From the tomb, O illustrious regenerator of my country, avenger of the blood of my children, I salute you . . . The Sun my father, the father of light, the god of the day, is shining, it appears, with more splendor than in the years of my glory, because it is pleased with your deeds."[83] A visiting British merchant later recalled:

> Every where he was received with princely honors: at the entrance of each town, were erected arches to victory, and ladies of the first class, dressed in white for the occasion, strewed flowers before his charger's path as he advanced . . . In Arequipa, and Puno, Oruro, La Paz, &c. improvisatore toasts in verse, as long as the ballad of "Chevy Chase," were drunk with nine times nine of "hip-hip-hurras"—that shook the massive buildings of Peru something similar to its earthquakes.[84]

In a Washingtonian gesture, Bolívar ostentatiously declared that he would resign both from the Peruvian dictatorship and the Colombian presidency. In both countries, the legislative bodies refused to agree. In a distinctly un-Washingtonian gesture, Bolívar graciously deferred to their wishes.[85]

There was one nation left to liberate: what the Spanish had called Upper Peru, mountainous home to the fabulous silver mines of Potosí and an impoverished, largely Indian population. At the start of 1825, Sucre took his army there and fought a campaign culminating, on April 1, with one final victory. The Spanish-American wars of independence were now complete. In just a quarter century, Spain had lost all its vast mainland American empire to the new nations, although it still retained Caribbean island colonies—most importantly, Cuba. So great was Bolívar's standing as liberator of the continent that Upper Peru's leaders (who also had much to gain from flattering him) immediately changed the country's name to Bolivar, soon modifying it to Bolivia. By this date, the United States had of course named its capital and many other places after George Washington. In the 1790s, a department in Saint-Domingue had taken the name of Toussaint Louverture. But neither of these men, or Bonaparte, had given their name to an entire country.

Not only was Bolívar the metaphorical father of this new country, he was also its lawgiver, and the constitution he personally designed for it clearly shows how his political thought had continued to evolve in an authoritarian direction. Although Bolivia would have a government divided into different branches, one branch would tower above the others: a powerful presidency whose occupant would serve for life, with the ability to choose his successor. Bolívar did not want the Bolivian presidency for himself—he saw his protégé Sucre in the role—but he hoped that the other new South American states would adopt the Bolivian constitution as the blueprint for their own governments. He took great pride in it, personally writing a circular explaining its benefits and having no fewer than five editions printed and distributed throughout the continent.[86] Although Bolívar continued to profess, throughout his life, his admiration for Britain and its moderate, parliamentary system of government, the Bolivian constitution looked much more like Alexandre Pétion's in Haiti, or like Bonaparte's 1802 charter for a so-called life consulate.[87] It also included his long-standing proposition for a branch of government responsible for upholding public morality.

With the liberation of Peru and Bolivia, Bolívar had reached the peak—the Chimborazo, so to speak—of his career. His friend José Joaquín Olmedo, at his request, composed an epic poem on his Peruvian triumphs to serve as a sort of South American *Aeneid,* celebrating the birth of a new nation. The poem hailed Bolívar as the continent's Aeneas and also as a successor to the Incas.[88] Yet even as it appeared, Bolívar's charismatic authority already showed signs of fracturing. Even before leaving for Peru, he had been forced to suppress a small revolt in New Granada. After his victories in Peru, he dreamed of uniting all the new Spanish-American nations into a grand federation, and he invited them to a congress in Panama for this purpose. But many of them failed to attend, and the congress accomplished little. Worse, centrifugal forces were straining Gran Colombia itself. With the Spanish threat largely dissipated, the Creole elites of its component countries, historically distinct and distant from one another, now had little inclination toward unity. They also distrusted Bolívar, both for his heavy-handed style of rule and also for his promises to abolish slavery, as well as for his readiness to seek support among *pardos* and Indians. Ironically, the distrust had grown particularly great in Bolívar's native Venezuela, where he had spent precious little time in the previous decade. He had little taste or talent for the daily grind of government, and the Venezuelans—their institutions and economy disrupted by a decade and a half of warfare—had reason to feel neglected.

Already in October 1825, in an anxious letter from Caracas, the former *caudillo* José Antonio Páez warned Bolivar of the growing unrest in Venezuela and urged him to follow the example of a charismatic European predecessor. "The situation in this country," he wrote, proudly displaying the education he had acquired since his days as a *llanero*:

> greatly resembles the way things stood in France when Napoleon was in Egypt, and was called upon by those leading men of the revolution, who were convinced that a government that had fallen

into the hands of the lowest rabble was not one that could save that
nation. You are now in a position to say what that famous man said
at the time: the intriguers are going to ruin the country. Let us go
and save it . . . General, this is not the land of Washington. Here
people bow down to power out of terror and self-interest.[89]

A Venezuelan newspaper editor who brought the letter to Peru suggested that Bolívar should follow Bonaparte's example and take a crown.
Bolívar reacted with indignation. Writing to his vice president Santander,
he called Páez and his allies demagogues and claimed that, according to
them, "no one can be great except in the manner of Alexander, Caesar
and Napoleon." Again, he implicitly cast himself as more of a Washington, insisting on his own "detachment" and "moderation." "My life will
serve as the rule," he continued, rather less modestly. "The people will
adore me, and I will be the ark of their covenant."[90] To Páez himself,
Bolívar responded sternly:

> Colombia is not France and I am not Napoleon . . . Napoleon was
> great and unique, and besides, exceedingly ambitious. Here things
> are very different. I am not Napoleon and do not want to be. Nei-
> ther do I want to imitate Caesar . . . Such examples seem to me
> unworthy of my glory. The title of liberator is superior to all those
> that human pride has received. Therefore it is impossible to demean
> it. Furthermore, our population is not, not, not at all French [*nues-
> tra populación no es de franceses en nada, nada, nada*].

He added that if he tried to crown himself king, "equality would be
broken and the people of color would see all their rights lost to a new
aristocracy."[91] Gran Colombia needed a firm hand, but a Bolivian-style
constitution would provide all the firmness necessary.

Despite the increasingly authoritarian tendencies on display in this
constitution, Bolívar still had not fundamentally broken with the broadly
democratic conception of charismatic power he had developed in his Haitian exile, ten years before. South American countries needed powerful,

charismatic leaders whose rule rested not only on the consent and obedience of the governed but on their enthusiastic "acclamation," as expressed in the sort of public festivities that had accompanied his triumphs throughout his career. Only such rulers could exert sufficient emotional gravitational attraction to keep their fractious, racially divided countries from spinning apart. But the leaders still needed to avoid the temptations of monarchy and despotism and to stand ready to surrender their power as soon as the public interest demanded such a renunciation.

Yet even as Bolívar's letter slowly made its way back to Venezuela, Páez himself, tired of waiting for a Bolivarian Eighteenth Brumaire, was taking matters into his own hands and assuming leadership of a secessionist movement. Gran Colombia now seemed on the point of breaking up, and the news sent Bolívar into despair. In one of his more extraordinary pieces of writing—a long, anguished letter to Santander—he repeated three times, "all is lost." And he continued:

> The journalists proclaim that heroes should live under the law, and principles should be higher than men. That is ideology . . . Virgins and saints, angels and cherubim will be the citizens of this new paradise. Bravo! Bravissimo! . . . I am tired of wielding this abominable arbitrary power, but at the same time I am convinced, deep in my bones, that only a skillful despotism can rule America. We are very far from the beautiful days of Athens and Rome and should not compare ourselves to anything European. Our very being has the most impure origin possible . . . We are the abominable compound of those tiger-like hunters who came to America to shed blood and to crossbreed with their victims before sacrificing them, and then to mix the impure offspring of those liaisons with the offspring of slaves torn out of Africa. With such physical mixtures, with such moral elements, how can we place laws above heroes, and principles above men? All right, let these ideological gentlemen govern and fight and then we will see the fine ideal of Haiti, and new Robespierres will be the worthy stewards of this great liberty.[92]

Haiti now stood for political chaos, not orderly presidential government, in Bolívar's mind, and the people of color to whom he had
promised freedom and equality now seemed to him a curse and a bur-
den. Indeed, in the letter he predicted that without his "skillful despotism," Gran Colombia would fall victim to a Haitian-style race war in
which not a single white would survive. Two months later, he frankly
argued that "a dictatorship solves everything . . . with constitutional
laws we can do nothing more in this business of Páez except to punish
the rebellion. But authorized by the nation, I will be able to do anything."[93] Here, Bolívar seems to have given up on many of his earlier
positions, including his constitutionalism and his belief that, despite the
sorry state of South America, a firm hand could guide it toward enlightened republicanism. Previously he had only condemned "despotism."
Now he seemed to be commending it.

As the letters exchanged between Bolívar and Páez demonstrate, it
had become impossible for anyone to discuss Bolívar's leadership
without invoking the shades of his most famous charismatic predecessors, George Washington and Napoleon Bonaparte. As Bolívar's own
charismatic reputation had grown, the comparisons became ubiquitous.
Other figures were invoked as well, of course. A single writer, the Peruvian Manuel Lorenzo de Vidaurre, at various times compared Bolívar to
William Tell, Alexander the Great, Julius Caesar, Charles V of Spain,
Jesus Christ, and also (after undergoing a dramatic change of heart)
Satan.[94] But Washington and Bonaparte dominated.

In most cases, the discussions built upon the comparisons of Washington and Bonaparte to each other by Byron, Coleridge, and Chateaubriand.[95] These authors had mostly established a simple, blunt dichotomy:
Washington the self-sacrificing political angel versus Bonaparte the political Lucifer, tempted, corrupt, and fallen. As the Venezuelan writer Cristóbal Mendoza wrote to Bolívar in 1827, "Your enemies are always
searching for your model in Bonaparte, and you have done seven times

more than Washington."[96] Indeed, like Mendoza, Bolívar's most ardent admirers felt the need to go beyond merely calling him the "Washington of the South" or the "image" or "follower" of Washington, to insist that he actually outshone the original. As one besotted English traveler argued, Bolívar had after all entirely lacked Washington's advantages: "No France had tendered her armies and her wealth to aid him. No Franklins, and Henrys, and Jeffersons were at his right hand, nor the stern, uncompromising virtue of a New England race."[97] In contrast, an American diplomat reported contemptuously to President John Quincy Adams that "without a ray of true political knowledge or a hint of morality, [Bolívar] apes the style and claims the character of Washington."[98] The *North American Review*, like many other publications, claimed that the dictatorial Bolívar found his true model in Bonaparte.[99] In 1827 the Cuban poet José María Heredia, after first praising "immortal Bolivar," issued a dire warning: "Brilliant Lucifer, will you fall from the sky? . . . Thus the earth saw dispelled the glory of Napoleon."[100]

Virtually the only North American or European to break out of this rigid and simplistic political grammar was Richard Bache, a grandson of Benjamin Franklin (and brother of George Washington's critic Benjamin Franklin Bache) who traveled to South America in 1822–23 with his stepfather, William Duane. Bache noted that "it is customary to compare Bolivar with Washington," and he argued that if the Venezuelan's career continued as brilliantly as it had begun, history would justify the comparison. But he also insisted on the men's different circumstances. Washington, he claimed, had operated in a society accustomed to self-government and so always deferred to public opinion or tried to persuade it by rational argument. Bolívar, by contrast, "controls and forces opinion." While Washington had tried "to secure ascendancy over the understanding" (in other words, to place his hopes in reason), Bolívar aimed "to move the passions, to excite enthusiasm, and govern by the *prestige* of his name."[101] The passage well captures the form of charismatic authority Bolívar embraced and which Washington had resisted, even as it was thrust upon him.

Bolívar himself, driven by both his intense self-regard and his intense curiosity about the world beyond South America, took an obsessive interest in these comparisons. Given the general preference for Washington over Bonaparte—especially among Americans and Britons—in public he mostly tried to align himself with the North American. To a visiting American naval officer, he declared that "I would rather walk in the footsteps of Washington and die the death of Washington than to be the monarch of the whole earth."[102] He repeatedly declared that although he had initially admired Bonaparte, the Corsican lost his respect when he crowned himself emperor and became an "ambitious tyrant."[103] Still, by dating his disillusionment to the creation of the First Empire in 1804, Bolívar implicitly signaled his approval of Bonaparte's highly authoritarian "Consulate" of the preceding five years. Bolívar also could not resist measuring his military reputation against Bonaparte's. A French-born shoemaker chattered, as he helped Bolívar to try on boots, about his time in the French army, repeatedly exclaiming, "What a great general Napoleon was!" Finally, the *Libertador* gave the man a kick, exclaiming, "So what am I then?"[104]

But during the 1820s, Bonaparte's reputation was itself undergoing a rapid metamorphosis. He died of stomach cancer, on the island of Saint Helena in the South Atlantic, in 1821. Barely a year later, one of his aides, Emmanuel de Las Cases, published a long, digressive, first-person account of this exile, interspersed with transcriptions of Bonaparte's rambling reminiscences, entitled *The Memorial of Saint Helena*. The book was disorganized and verbose, but the abundant personal details, and the pathos-filled contrast between Bonaparte's memories of glory and the petty tribulations imposed on him by his British captors, made it utterly absorbing. It quickly became one of the great bestsellers of the century.[105] It cast Bonaparte not as a tyrant but as a martyr whose career illustrated the potential of humanity and whose glorious regime shone in bright colors compared to the gray, depressed, and disillusioned society of the subsequent decade. Upon hearing of the book, Bolívar tried to obtain a copy, and in 1826 Las Cases himself sent him one.[106] "To make known to Bolivar the features and intimate details of Napoleon," the Frenchman wrote in an accompanying note, "does that not amount to bringing close and bringing together two great men?"[107] Numerous accounts testify that Bolívar read the *Memorial* with passionate interest.[108]

In 1828, a Spanish-speaking French veteran of the Napoleonic Wars, Louis Perú de Lacroix, serving as an aide to Bolívar, spent three months living in close quarters with him. He took extensive notes and eventually wrote up a narrative of the period under the title *Journal of Bucaramanga*. The diaristic style, the attention to small physical details, and the inclusion of long, supposed transcriptions of Bolívar's conversation, as well as Perú's explicit references to the *Memorial*, make clear that he hoped to produce its Bolivarian equivalent, although his text did not actually appear in print until many years after his death.[109] In prose that recalled Boswell as well as Las Cases, Perú praised Bolivar as "an extraordinary man, a great genius, an immense intelligence, a profound observer and thinker." He recounted numerous instances of Bolívar's courage and moral strength, including a moment when everyone except the Liberator rushed out of a church in the middle of Mass, fearing that an earthquake had started. Bolívar remained calm and composed. Perú also stressed the leader's personal frugality and his remarkable horsemanship and stamina in the saddle. And he carefully noted that while Bolívar's aides always wore impeccable uniforms, Bolívar himself wandered around Bucaramanga dressed in peasant style with a handkerchief around his neck, plain white shirt and trousers, and a straw hat.[110]

The *Journal* also left no doubt about which charismatic predecessor Bolívar saw as a model. It quotes him speaking frequently of Bonaparte, at one point even claiming that he deliberately concealed his true opinion of the man, "to avoid the opinion arising that I am imitating Napoleon ... that I want to ... dominate South America as he dominated Europe." In fact, Bolívar insisted, "I am a great admirer of the French hero ... *The Memorial of Saint Helena*, the campaigns of Napoleon, and everything of his have made most agreeable and profitable reading for me. This is where you should study the art of war, of politics, and of government."[111] It was to Perú that Bolívar claimed to have witnessed the emperor's coronation and the "universal acclamation" that accompanied it.

But could Bolívar still attract this sort of "universal acclamation"? The years from 1827 to 1830 revealed, all too painfully, the limits of his charismatic authority. He could still command remarkable displays of public enthusiasm, and he could still sometimes overawe the Creole elites he had led to independence. But what his Irish-born aide Daniel O'Leary called the "magic of his prestige" was flickering unevenly and could not light a path for Gran Colombia out of civil strife. Worse, Bolívar himself was ill with tuberculosis and subject to spells of what one confidant called "ruinous apathy."[112] The last sketch drawn from life, by José María Espinosa in 1830, shows a man worn and aged far beyond his forty-seven years (figure 21).[113] As García Márquez put it in his novel, "The glory had left his body."[114] In December 1826, a Venezuelan newspaper wrote: "Only Providence can lead us out of the inextricable labyrinth of ideas and passions into which certain ill-intentioned persons wished to place us so as to ruin us." Bolívar liberated the continent from Spanish domination, it continued, but now we have "a much more powerful and dangerous enemy: ourselves."[115]

The last great show of acclamation took place in the first days of 1827. To deal with Páez's rebellion in Venezuela, Bolívar planned to depart from his base in Peru and return to the country by force. But, recognizing that his erstwhile protégé enjoyed widespread support, he agreed to negotiate. Páez ended up submitting to him, but in return for complete amnesty and a promise of constitutional reform. The two men then staged an elaborate, largely hypocritical reconciliation. "From the center of Peru," Páez declared with monumental insincerity, "the Liberator has heard our cries, and has flown to our rescue . . . Let us prepare to receive him as the dry earth receives the dew . . . Venezuela now owes Bolivar an apotheosis."[116]

The apotheosis duly took place on January 10, 1827, when Bolívar arrived back in his birthplace. He entered Caracas through a series of ornamental arches covered with ribbons and pennants bearing slogans of praise. As crowds cheered "the Genius of War and Peace," a carriage took him to the cathedral, where he received laurel wreaths from two of his great-nieces.[117] The British consul in Caracas wrote in his diary that

> triumphal Arches . . . rose almost at every fifty yards, all entwined with laurels and palms . . . [There were] crowds of rejoicing people all wild in screaming Viva Bolívar! Viva Páez! Viva Colombia! firing pistols, guns, rockets, and showing various other demonstrations of joy and loyalty—or more properly, affection. The windows, balconies and temporary platforms were crowded by ladies dressed in their gayest and richest attire—showering flowers of all kinds upon him—and not a few libations of rose water was [sic] poured on both the heroes.[118]

There followed what amounted to a contest to praise Bolívar as extravagantly as possible, with the undoubted winner a learned doctor of the University of Caracas, José Hernández Sanavria. He praised Bolívar as a "sovereign deity! Divine emanation, which has descended to earth from heaven . . . You are the powerful magnet for the hearts which seek you out and gaze on you in a single simultaneous movement!"[119] Another author called Bolívar, rather contradictorily, both "the most idolized son of the fatherland" and "father of the fatherland."[120] As in previous festivities, the emphasis fell heavily on demonstrating the unbreakable emotional bond between the charismatic leader and his people.

Yet for all the real emotion on display in the streets of Caracas, the centrifugal tendencies within the unwieldy amalgam of Gran Colombia did not diminish, and the state's future remained very much in doubt. The reconciliation with Páez outraged the more legalistic Vice-President Santander, a native of New Granada who had effectively served as chief executive during Bolívar's absence in Peru. There followed a break between Bolívar and Santander, who now turned secessionist in his turn. An exhausted Bolívar wrote to an English friend that "I am tired of

public service" and compared himself to Sisyphus. "How can a single
man build half a world?" he asked grandiosely.[121] Finally, the Colombian congress summoned a Great Convention to revise the 1821 constitution. It met in April 1828 in the town of Ocaña in northern New
Granada, not far from the Venezuelan border. Bolívar himself waited for
it to conclude in Bucaramanga, a hundred miles to the south, and it was
during this enforced idleness that Perú de Lacroix took the notes for his
Journal.

Yet if Bolívar was idle, his supporters were not. Despite the continuing civil unrest and looming threats of violence, by this point, nearly
twenty years after the beginning of the independence struggles, political
life in the new nations revolved tightly around the printed word. During
the first months of 1828, the Bolivarian party mounted an extraordinary propaganda effort to persuade their fellow citizens that only by
granting Bolívar even greater power could they save Gran Colombia
from collapse. Hundreds of municipalities, militia companies, and army
regiments produced printed petitions demanding that he have the
chance, in the words of the Civic Squadron of Caracas, to "save Colombia from anarchy, regenerate it and give it laws, customs, dignity, splendor, liberty, and new glories."[122] These texts spoke the classic language of
charismatic idolization. They hailed Bolívar as the father of his country
and added, "He is the man we most love."[123]

In response, Bolívar's opponents, led by Santander, responded in
print in the language of classical republicanism deployed half a century
before by John Adams when he warned against the "superstitious veneration" of Washington. "The nation is only subject, or if you wish, slave
to the laws, not to men," declared a pamphlet entitled *Political Faith of
a Colombian*, and it added a warning from Cicero that obviously applied to Bolívar: "The more notable a man is for his greatness of spirit,
the more ambitious is he to be . . . the sole ruler."[124] The author insisted
that Cromwell, Robespierre, and Bonaparte had all proven that honorable, Roman-style dictatorship was not an institution compatible with
"modern customs." Of modern figures, only George Washington could
possibly have served as dictator, because of the "unlimited confidence

people held in his virtues."[125] Bolívar himself replied, in June, that "dictatorships are glorious when they close the abyss of revolutions," although he added that people should not become overly accustomed to dictatorial authority.[126] But he did not resort solely to arguments to prevail over his opponents. Pro-Bolívar soldiers burned issues of a pro-Santander newspaper called *The Bullwhip* (*El zurriago*), and when its editors published a new edition the next day under the title *The Incombustible* (*El incombustible*), they shut down its printing house.[127]

The debate in fact involved two starkly opposed political visions. Bolívar, as he had written many times before, did not trust South Americans to govern themselves and therefore advocated enlightened authoritarianism. His opponents, by contrast, did not trust any South American leader to govern in a genuinely enlightened manner and therefore advocated democratic republicanism. In the event, the Convention of Ocaña ended in deadlock, even as the danger rose of new revolts or of war with Spain or Peru. Finally, on August 28, 1828, Bolívar cut the Gordian knot and issued a so-called Organic Decree that accorded him sweeping dictatorial powers. He did not adopt "Dictator" as a formal title (as he had done in Peru) but now called himself "Liberator President." Referring to the printed petitions, he argued that "the national will has pronounced itself unanimously" in favor of his action, but of course he had undertaken it entirely on his own authority.[128] A new wave of repression followed, and it intensified after an assassination attempt on him—possibly instigated by Santander—took place on September 25. Fully thirty conspirators took part in the plot, with one group fighting their way into the Palace of San Carlos. Bolívar survived only because his companion, Manuela Saénz, persuaded him to escape out a window, and then misled the killers, who beat her badly. Bolívar himself hid for three hours under a bridge. In the aftermath, fourteen alleged plotters were executed. Santander was also sentenced to death, but the council of ministers commuted the sentence to exile.[129]

Like Bonaparte before him, the charismatic leader had finally broken decisively with the law, acting on the basis of his own personal authority. Unlike Bonaparte, however, he did not have the resources to hold his crumbling state together. He could count on the support of some Creole elites, especially in the army, the government administration, and the church, but despite his rhetoric of inclusion he offered the *pardos* and other peoples of color little of substance in return for their support. Although he remained loyal in theory to the principle of slave emancipation, he did little to make it a reality.[130] And his health continued to decline. By the spring of 1829 he was discussing resignation with his ministers, some of whom argued that if he left office, the only possible successor would be a European prince, arriving with the title of king. Bolívar rejected the idea, but the discussions themselves helped prompt a new revolt by a general from New Granada.

The collapse of the union soon came to seem inevitable. "Venezuelans," Páez insisted in a December 1 letter to Bolívar, "have a heartfelt hatred for the union with Bogotá."[131] One Venezuelan municipality after another issued declarations in favor of secession. Bolívar raged, like many an authoritarian since, about the false news he blamed for his plight. In response, he instructed a Colombian official to "publish articles in the *Gazette* and other papers with the object I indicate. They should be written with candor, but also with the fire of indignation."[132] But it was too late. To another correspondent he wrote dejectedly that "I long for the desperate moment when this shameful life may end."[133]

The end came quickly, both for Gran Colombia and for Bolívar himself. In the early months of 1830, first Venezuela and then Ecuador formally seceded, bringing the federation to an end. The crowds that had once shouted their *vivas* for Bolívar now jeered him and called for his death. On April 27 he resigned the presidency and left Bogotá for Cartagena, where he had issued his first great manifesto and launched his first great military campaign eighteen years before. In the summer the news came that rebels had murdered his protégé Sucre, driving him further into the labyrinth of despair. In November he wrote to the new president of Ecuador, saying that in twenty years of rule he had learned several lessons: "1. America is ungovernable for us. 2. He who serves a revolution is plowing the sea. 3. The only thing one can do in America is emigrate. 4. This country will inevitably fall into the hands of the unchained masses, and then, almost imperceptibly, into those of petty tyrants of every race and color," et cetera.[134] On December 17, in a small town on the coast of the Caribbean Sea, racked by tuberculosis, he died. "How will I escape from this labyrinth?" he asked on his deathbed.[135]

In this last period of his life, Bolívar attracted as much curiosity and attention as ever across the world. More biographies appeared, as well as the first extensive histories of the South American revolutions, and the first massive collections of documents relative to the Liberator's life (many more would follow, down to the digital collection of more than 13,000 documents prepared by order of President Hugo Chávez).[136] Foreign travelers and soldiers like Perú de Lacroix continued to write accounts of their encounters with the great man, which fit perfectly into the adulatory, voyeuristic style of portraits of charismatic leaders pioneered by Boswell and continued most famously by Mason Locke Weems for George Washington and by Emmanuel de Las Cases for Napoleon Bonaparte.

True, the admiration Bolívar had elicited around the Atlantic world faded noticeably after his 1828 coup d'état. In Britain and the United States, much of the newspaper press that had hailed him as a liberator now denounced him, although one British Tory paper still called him "plainly not a hero, saint, or philosopher, but . . . a capital managing fellow."[137] In France, the great liberal thinker Benjamin Constant excoriated him as a dictatorial usurper like Bonaparte.[138] Citizens of the United States were naming fewer babies after Bolívar and drinking fewer toasts to him, but not just because of events in South America. By the late 1820s, Americans—especially the southerners who controlled American foreign policy—were less likely to see other countries in the hemisphere as partners in a universal crusade for liberty and more as sites for the expansion of American territory, American influence, and slavery.[139]

Regardless, in 1830 it was easy to view Bolívar's principal legacy as what one historian has called South America's "predatory militarism," in which charismatic *caudillos* competed for control of the new nations in an unending series of coups and civil wars.[140] The pattern would certainly prevail for part of the continent's subsequent history, especially in the countries Bolívar himself had governed.[141] And it is tempting to depict Bolívar in his final days—despairing, impotent, lamenting lost glories, and unable to find his way out of the "labyrinth"—as a symbol of sorts for Latin American politics as a whole. Gabriel García Márquez succumbed a little too easily to this temptation in *The General in His Labyrinth*, which is one reason why this novel, for all its beauty, does not live up to its author's greatest works.

But then, none of the charismatic leaders of the age of revolution had gloriously charismatic deaths. George Washington at least left this world at the height of his charismatic reputation, passing away in an odor of patriotic sanctity at Mount Vernon as an entire nation—or at least that part of it not in bondage—prepared to mourn. Bolívar, coughing out his lungs on the Caribbean coast, died in a lonely manner more similar to Bonaparte in his windswept tropical exile on Saint Helena, or Louverture in his miserable mountain prison in eastern France. Yet as Bolívar himself knew, from reading *The Memorial of Saint Helena*, pathos, sacrifice, and martyrdom had their own charismatic sheen. However low and defeated he felt in his last days, his legend, like those of the others, would survive his tribulations. In fact, in much of South America, the legend of the "divine Bolívar" would eventually grow to mammoth proportions. In Venezuela itself, President Hugo Chávez would turn it into the gospel of a quasi-religious cult, to the point of renaming the country the "Bolivarian Republic of Venezuela" upon seizing power in 1999.[142]

CHARISMA AND DEMOCRACY

The History of the world is but the Biography of great men.

—*Thomas Carlyle, 1841*

History is not the biography of great men . . . The great men
of the earth are but the marking stones on the road of humanity;
they are the priests of its religion . . . There is yet something greater,
more divinely mysterious, than all the great men—and that is the earth
which bears them, the human race which includes them, the thought
of God which stirs within them, and which the whole human
race collectively can alone accomplish.

—*Giuseppe Mazzini, 1843*

In 1840 and 1842, two strikingly similar ceremonies took place some 4,500 miles apart. On December 15, 1840, a solemn procession wound its way through the streets of Paris from a river dock in the suburb of Courbevoie to the church of the Invalides on the Left Bank, carrying Napoleon Bonaparte to his final resting place. The coffin rode in a gigantic wagon, thirty feet long and thirty feet tall, decorated with fourteen plaster figures commemorating the emperor's victories. Two months before, a delegation from the French government had presided over his exhumation in Saint Helena, noting the astonishingly well-preserved condition of the cadaver. Between seven hundred thousand and one million people lined the Parisian streets as he passed, including thousands of veterans of his Grande Armée, some dressed in their old uniforms for the occasion, many of them convulsed in tears. On its way, the wagon passed through the Arc de Triomphe, which Bonaparte had commissioned and which was topped for the occasion with a statue of the man, dressed in his coronation robes, staring out at the city below. Over the next two weeks, as he lay in state in the Invalides, more than a million people would file past to pay their respects. He remains in the church to this day, inside a massive sarcophagus of porphyry upon which visitors can stare down from a circular balustrade.[1]

Two years and two days after the ceremony in Paris, Simón Bolívar's body came home to Caracas from the Colombian coastal town of Santa Marta, where he had died exactly twelve years earlier. The Venezuelan government followed the French example very closely. It sent an official delegation to preside over Bolívar's exhumation and to report on the condition of the corpse ("the skull was partly exposed to view," a British newspaper reported ghoulishly, "as were also some of the ribs, which had fallen in").[2] The government even commissioned a small Arc de Triomphe of its own from Parisian artisans, shipped in pieces across the Atlantic and reassembled on the other side, for Bolívar to pass under in Caracas. He, too, rode through city streets in a massive wagon (emblazoned with a great letter *B*), past silent crowds that included many of his former soldiers. His journey ended at the Cathedral of San Francisco, where solemn funeral services took place. He would remain there for thirty-four years, before moving on to Venezuela's National Pantheon, where he has lain ever since (except for a brief moment in 2010 when President Chávez had the body exhumed in a futile attempt to prove that the Liberator's enemies had assassinated him). A painting on the ceiling shows Bolívar ascending to heaven, recalling the painting of George Washington's heavenly apotheosis in the dome of the United States Capitol.[3]

Both these ceremonies were the product, in part, of pragmatic political calculation. In both countries, the regime dated only from 1830, when Venezuela declared independence from Gran Colombia and when the so-called July Revolution in France replaced the conservative Bourbon Restoration monarchy with the moderate King Louis-Philippe. In both countries, these new regimes remained fragile: multiple revolts plagued the Venezuelan government of the legendary *caudillo* José Antonio Páez between 1830 and 1835, while major urban uprisings took place in France in 1832 (Victor Hugo's *Les misérables* immortalized the one in Paris). In both countries, opponents of the regime had seized on the legendary leaders as useful symbols, and the ceremonies were designed in large part to co-opt those symbols for the government. In both cases, however, the political benefits proved fleeting. In February 1848 yet another French Revolution overthrew Louis-Philippe and brought into being the short-lived Second Republic. The same year, Páez began a revolt against his successor, which failed and led to his lengthy exile (he died in New York City in 1873). The ceremonies ended up doing more for Bonaparte and Bolívar themselves than for their successors.

In the United States and Haiti, no such ceremonies ever took place. George Washington, in accordance with his wishes, has never left his burial place at Mount Vernon. Toussaint Louverture's French jailers interred him where he died, at the Fort de Joux in the Jura Mountains, and renovation work there destroyed his grave in 1879. Only in 1982 did the Haitian government stage a symbolic "return of the remains," bringing back a shovelful of earth from the fort's grounds for burial in Haiti.[4]

Even so, the 1840s marked important steps in the posthumous careers of both Washington and Louverture as well. After Washington's death, the United States Congress had initially balked at commissioning a memorial to him in the capital that bore his name, with Democratic-Republican opponents of his Federalist party claiming that it would smack too much of monarchy. But on July 4, 1848, a private society laid the cornerstone of the Washington Monument, whose height of more than 550 feet would make it the tallest man-made structure in the world (it took until 1884 to complete, however, and lost the height record to the Eiffel Tower after just five years).[5] In Haiti, in 1847, the historian Thomas Madiou published his monumental, pioneering history of his country, with abundant attention given to Toussaint Louverture. Despite belonging to the mixed-race community whose leaders had struggled against Louverture, Madiou presented a generally admiring picture of the man. He claimed that a meeting with Louverture's son Isaac first inspired him to undertake the project, and the work included vivid accounts of the revolution based on oral testimony from Louverture's followers.[6]

Despite this convergence, the posthumous reputations of the four men had not always evolved in the same ways in the decades after their disappearances from the political scene. While Bolívar's cult prospered in Venezuela itself after 1840 (notably with the renaming of Angostura as Ciudad Bolívar in 1846), it never again acquired the broader international resonance it had enjoyed in the 1820s, thanks to the dissolution of Gran Colombia, the political turmoil of its successor states, and South America's own diminished place in geopolitical affairs. The 1842 ceremonies in Caracas received only a tiny fraction of the voluminous coverage that Napoleon's return to Paris did in newspapers across the Western world.[7] As for Toussaint Louverture, his refusal to break openly with France, and his conflicts with the largely mixed-race groups whose political descendants dominated the country in the nineteenth century, left many Haitians, especially in the governing elite, unwilling to celebrate him as a founding father. International attention to him, meanwhile, declined dramatically as the Atlantic powers effectively quarantined the black state. His international renown remained strongest, as during his lifetime, among abolitionists, and especially among African-Americans. Frederick Douglass revered him as the greatest of all emancipators. A Union chaplain during the American Civil War claimed that among southern slaves, "the name of Toussaint Louverture has been passed from mouth to mouth until it has become a secret household word."[8]

In contrast with these two figures from the global South, George Washington, as we have seen, remained a key symbol of political virtue and republican heroism across the Western world. And despite the criticism from Democratic-Republicans, white Americans mostly continued to revere him. Already in the year after his death, during a presidential election whose vicious partisanship led some observers to fear imminent civil war, Mason Locke Weems's biography encouraged Americans to seize on Washington as a symbol of national unity rather than of the Federalist party.[9] By 1812, John Adams was again lamenting "the idolatrous worship paid to the name of George Washington . . . manifested in the impious applications of names and epithets to him which are ascribed in scripture only to God and to Jesus Christ."[10] Twenty years after that, the French jurist Gustave de Beaumont, who toured America in the company of Alexis de Tocqueville, remarked that he saw monuments to no one other than Washington in the country, "because Washington, in America, *is not a man but a God.*"[11] All this reverence, however, had the effect of turning Washington, already famous for his reserve and self-control, into something of an alabaster saint, curbing the intense, sexually tinged emotions that had inflected responses to him during his lifetime. Although applauded for his impeccable respect for constitutional norms, despite the treatment of him by Weems he did not serve as a democratic symbol in the sense of someone ordinary people could easily identify with. Only in the second half of the nineteenth century did Americans generally start to see Washington less as a god and more as a heroic but fundamentally ordinary man who exemplified the democratic qualities Americans wanted to see in themselves.[12]

Throughout the Western world, it was Bonaparte, far more even than Washington, who remained the single greatest model of charismatic heroism between his fall in 1815 and the 1840s. Unlike Washington, he continued to elicit intense emotional reactions. The spectacle of the glorious emperor in miserable exile—presented so powerfully by Las Cases in *The Memorial of Saint Helena*—generated enormous pathos. Both in France and elsewhere, Bonaparte also served as more of a democratic symbol than might have been predicted from his actual record, thanks largely to the fact that during his brief return to power in 1815 he tried to rally support by recasting himself as the true heir to the

French Revolution.[13] Although widely reviled as well as widely admired, his name drew attention like no other. The Harvard University library system contains more than 2,500 books and articles devoted to Bonaparte in the English language, published in just the thirty years after his final defeat. For Louverture and Bolívar, in the thirty-year periods after their departures from the political scene, the figures are 30 and 47, respectively.[14] In France, the magic of the Bonaparte name allowed his nephew Louis-Napoleon (1808–1873), despite a record as a farcically incompetent coup plotter, to win election as president under the Second Republic in 1848. Three years after that, the man Victor Hugo derisively labeled "Napoleon the Little" staged a coup against his own government, albeit with considerable popular support. In 1852 he crowned himself Emperor Napoleon III (Napoleon's son and namesake had died twenty years previously without issue).

If all four of the leaders continued to loom over political life in one way or another throughout so much of the Western world through the 1840s, the reason lies partly in the contrast so many contemporaries perceived between the age of revolution and what followed. Everywhere, the struggles of 1775–1825 had been titanic: they freed most of two continents from imperial rule, created new republics grounded on radically new political principles, altered the government and/or boundaries of every major European state, overthrew the institution of slavery in the place of its greatest cruelty (Saint-Domingue), and in that place proclaimed the equality of all men (though not of men and women), regardless of race. In contrast, the subsequent development of political life in the West generally looked distinctly unheroic. Reactionary governments came to power in much of Europe, seeking to quarantine and eliminate the contagion of revolution. Most of the postrevolutionary states, including France, Haiti, and Venezuela, reeled as governments and constitutions succeeded one another at a dizzying pace, often with considerable violence. The United States experienced relative political stability, accompanied by furious economic, demographic, and geographical expansion. But the even more furious growth of slavery, and the increasingly aggressive stance of the southern slave power, already hinted at the cataclysm that would come in the 1860s.

Bonaparte, above all, symbolized the contrast between the glorious recent past and the gray present, and by the 1830s, even some of his sharpest critics could not resist the overwhelming nostalgia his name evoked. One of them, the great Romantic author François-René de Chateaubriand, wrote beautifully that "to fall from Bonaparte and the Empire into what followed them is to fall from reality into nothingness, from the summit of a mountain into an abyss. Did not everything come to an end with Napoleon? . . . What person can evoke interest other than him?"[15] The poet Gérard de Nerval put the same thought more concisely: "Down with little men! We have seen Napoleon."[16] "With the emperor," exclaimed the German poet Heinrich Heine in yet another lyrical lament, "died the last hero of the old stamp, and our new Philistine world can breathe, as if released from a brilliant nightmare."[17]

Because of the emotions Bonaparte continued to elicit and the contrasts he symbolized, he would tower above culture and politics in these decades, and for many years to follow, in a way that none of the other revolutionary figures did, including Washington. He suffuses the Western literature of the century, featuring in many of its greatest and most famous works: *Les misérables, War and Peace, Crime and Punishment, The Red and the Black*. Victor Hugo, the son of a Napoleonic general, and almost certainly the most popular writer of the century, worldwide, nourished an obsession with Bonaparte throughout his life.[18] Writers as different as Walter Scott, Ralph Waldo Emerson, and Alexander Pushkin all wrote about him at length.[19] Goethe, who met him, later enthused: "His life was the march of a demi-god . . . His destiny was as brilliant as any that the world had seen before him, and perhaps will ever see after him."[20] The philosopher Hegel saw Bonaparte ride past his window after the destruction of the Prussian army at Jena in 1806 and in a letter dubbed him "the world-soul . . . who, sitting here astride a horse, reaches out across the world and dominates it."[21] Hegel would devote many pages of his philosophy to Bonaparte as a "world-historical figure."

Very few of these authors had an entirely positive view of the French emperor, but like Chateaubriand, they believed that the man possessed a grandeur that stood apart from—and possibly even canceled out—his many moral and political failings.

A s this book has shown, modern forms of charismatic leadership, although made imaginable by the cultural and intellectual changes of the eighteenth century, only fully emerged in the crucibles of revolutionary crisis, the founding of new states, and warfare on a titanic scale. In the following decades, in the absence of such circumstances—at least on the same dramatic scale as before—it became far harder for new charismatic figures to emerge and receive the same sort of acclamation that had been showered on Washington, Bonaparte, Louverture, and Bolívar. And the widespread sense so many had of having been born too late, into a pale, unheroic age, only added to the difficulty.

Charismatic leaders still did arise throughout the Western world, but they no longer necessarily fit the older model of the man on horseback, the military savior. Political charisma is a protean, fluid, dynamic phenomenon, always evolving, and as the revolutions that had begun in 1775 receded into the past, that phenomenon continued to evolve. As in the eighteenth century, it did so under the influence of changing media environments, changing literary and artistic forms, changing ideas, and changing political practices.

The media environment of the nineteenth century greatly facilitated the process by which leaders could forge emotional bonds with ordinary readers. Everywhere in the Atlantic world both literacy and the circulation of newspapers continued to expand. In Venezuela, which had not possessed a single printing press before its revolution, more than a dozen towns had newspapers by 1850.[22] The introduction of new industrial methods of paper production made printed periodicals far cheaper to produce than in the eighteenth century, and railroads made them far cheaper to distribute. Papers carried more illustrations than before, including, after the invention of photography, engravings produced directly from photographs. The telegraph allowed for the transmission of news instantaneously. In 1858, the first telegraph cable connected the Americas and Europe.

The growth and spread of organized political parties in the decades after the age of revolution also had important implications. Already in the 1760s, the existence of the Whig party in Great Britain had facilitated the emergence of John Wilkes as a political celebrity, but in most other Western countries a party system did not develop until after the revolutionary moment (in the United States, in the 1790s). But after it did, political parties could provide a cadre of supporters primed by both ideological conviction and self-interest to demonstrate their attachment to charismatic leaders: as voters, as leaders of party organs, as marchers and rioters, as militants and organizers.

The cult of all charismatic leaders in these decades also benefited enormously from the Romantic movement in the arts and literature. Artists and writers associated with it delighted in the portrayal of wild, untamed, elemental natural forces. They celebrated individual expressiveness and the apparent ability of especially gifted individuals to break the bonds of terrestrial existence to touch divine knowledge—a quality that Goethe called "daemonic."[23] They strove to capture ceaseless movement on the still page or canvas. Arguably, these aspects of Romanticism themselves took considerable inspiration from the charismatic leaders of the revolutionary era, whose supporters had seen them in very similar terms. Goethe early on called Bonaparte an example of the daemonic.[24] The Romantics eagerly contributed to the idolization of the revolutionary leaders, especially Bonaparte, but also looked for new, living figures they could celebrate in similar terms, even if in doing so they abetted the rise of new Caesars.

New visions of history also helped shape this continuing process of idolization. The most consequential philosopher of the age, Hegel, insisted on the importance of "world-historical figures" in the unfolding of humanity's story—especially Caesar and Bonaparte.[25] The British writer Thomas Carlyle, in the year of Bonaparte's reburial in Paris, gave a series of six lectures elaborating on his claim that "the History of the world is but the Biography of great men." He called Bonaparte "our last great man."[26] The views of Hegel and Carlyle were in no sense identical. Hegel cast world-historical figures as the instruments of much greater, impersonal historical forces—although not purely passive instruments: "It is theirs to know . . . the necessary next stage of their world, to make it their own aim and to put all their energy into it."[27] But he believed they set a larger plan in motion. Carlyle, by contrast, attributed more creative force to "great men" themselves in actively shaping the course of history according to their own personalities and ambitions.

Most history writing before the nineteenth century had likewise highlighted the deeds of "great men." Hegel and Carlyle, however, did not just write about such figures but developed coherent philosophies that cast the entire development of humanity as dependent upon such men's actions. Particularly in Carlyle's case, moreover, what made the men "great" was not the way they served a cause greater than themselves— God's plan, the good of their country—but how they themselves actively shaped the causes for which they fought, putting something of their very essence into them. These new visions of history reinforced the idea that certain leaders, by virtue of their extraordinary charismatic qualities, deserved unqualified and unanimous acclamation.

At the same time, much as in the age of revolution, the exaltation of great men also evoked a strong reaction from critics who decried such "idol-worship" and warned of Caesars trampling on the rights of the people. The Italian revolutionary and statesman Giuseppe Mazzini wrote one of the most eloquent retorts to his friend Thomas Carlyle's "great man" theory of history. "Mr. Carlyle," he argued in 1843, "comprehends only the *individual*; the true sense of the unity of the human race escapes him . . . In the name of the democratic spirit of the age, I protest against such views." And Mazzini continued:

> History is not the biography of great men . . . The great men of the
> earth are but the marking stones on the road of humanity . . . There

is yet something greater, more divinely mysterious, than all the great men—and that is the earth which bears them, the human race which includes them, the thought of God which stirs within them, and which the whole human race collectively can alone accomplish.[28]

Similarly, the great French historian Jules Michelet insisted later that peoples as a whole were the truly great, collective actors of history. In his brilliantly lyrical history of the French Revolution, he endorsed the eloquent warnings of Jacobin radicals against a Caesar and seized with particular pleasure on Anacharsis Cloots's plea for France to cure itself of individuals. Writing in the shadow of Louis-Napoleon, Michelet lamented "this poor France, sickened with the strange need to make and remake gods for itself."[29]

As Mazzini's and Michelet's comments suggest, by the mid-century the spread of explicitly "democratic" ideas was also influencing the evolution of political charisma. As I have already argued, despite the frequent modern description of the revolutions of 1775 through the 1820s as "democratic," the label is not really appropriate. The period did not actually see the birth of stable democratic governments, and few of its leading figures used the word "democracy" in a positive sense. Most of them identified it with the ancient Greek past, and John Adams expressed the most common viewpoint when he associated it with chaos and mob violence. The American founders envisioned their new state as a republic, not a democracy. Only after 1800 did the word "democracy" acquire desirable connotations in the United States, and most of the Atlantic world took several decades longer to follow.[30] The first decades of the nineteenth century in fact saw renewed suspicion of "democracy" across the Atlantic world, because of what the revolutions had supposedly revealed about the dangerously uncontrollable nature of democratic passions.

By 1840, however, liberal writers throughout the West were beginning to develop new, broader, and more favorable definitions of democracy, characterizing it not merely as popular self-rule but as self-rule rooted in egalitarian social practices that gave ordinary people control over many different aspects of their lives. They saw these practices, to quote the historian Stephen Sawyer, as "a positive means of building a collective order."[31] And nowhere did they find democracy at work more powerfully than in the United States, which became the subject of Alexis de Tocqueville's great study *Democracy in America*, completed in 1840. It offered a sweeping portrait of American society as a whole, not just American politics, and, despite the strong reservations Tocqueville expressed about the pathologies of democratic governance, he nonetheless presented democratic egalitarianism as an irresistible force sweeping the modern world.[32]

Was charismatic political leadership compatible with democratic egalitarianism? While liberals like Mazzini and Michelet implied that it was not, some writers insisted that no contradiction in fact existed between democracy and authoritarian one-man rule if the latter was backed by a popular majority. Louis-Napoleon Bonaparte himself made this argument succinctly in an 1839 book entitled *Napoleonic Ideas*. "The nature of democracy," the future emperor wrote, "is to personify itself in a man."[33] A doctrine often referred to as Caesarism was taking shape and would flourish for much of the next century. It amounted to an elaboration of the ideas put forth by Bolívar and others that large modern states needed a single powerful executive leader, legitimized by popular "acclamation," to bind their fractious peoples together. "Caesarists" put little stock in parliaments or the separation of powers, instead favoring systems in which popular plebiscites granted sweeping powers to charismatic executives backed by powerful political parties.[34]

The mid-nineteenth century did see a number of new charismatic political figures arise in the West, some in revolutionary circumstances and some not. The list included Benjamin Disraeli in Britain, Alphonse de Lamartine in France, Lajos Kossuth in Hungary, Otto von Bismarck in Germany, Giuseppe Garibaldi in Italy, and Andrew Jackson in the United States. In keeping with the essence of modern political charisma, each of these leaders became a celebrity and the object of intense emotional attachment on the part of his followers. Disraeli in particular, following the model of his compatriot John Wilkes (although they were poles apart in their political beliefs), excelled in making a grand political spectacle of his own exuberant personality. Not coincidentally, he was also a successful novelist whose works exhibited a powerful streak of sentimentalism.[35] Many of these leaders, however, did not fit the model of the "man on horseback," the military hero and savior. It was becoming possible for national leaders to have a powerful charismatic appeal without the military qualities that had proven so necessary during the great revolutionary crises.

But these military qualities still had enormous appeal, and some charismatic leaders of the period did fit the old model quite closely. One was Garibaldi, a friend and protégé of Mazzini. Born in 1807, he had to flee Italy while still in his twenties after receiving a death sentence for revolutionary activities. He landed in South America, where he learned the art of irregular warfare and also became an excellent horseman in the style of the *gauchos* of Brazil and Uruguay. Returning to Europe during the revolutions of 1848, he first achieved fame for his heroic defense of the newborn Roman Republic against a counterrevolutionary French army. After the republic's defeat, he spent five more years roaming the world—including a stint working in a candle factory on Staten Island—before coming home to fight for Italian unification. In 1860, the volunteer force he led, known as the Redshirts, carried out a spectacular conquest of the island of Sicily and then joined with the Kingdom of Piedmont to subdue the rest of southern Italy. The profusion of Garibaldi newspaper stories, biographies, poetry, images, statuettes, and trinkets of every conceivable variety throughout Europe and the Americas exceeded in volume anything seen in the period of 1775–1825, while praise for the hero reached a similar level of hyperbole. The *Gazzetta di Palermo* went so far as to call Garibaldi "the real Messiah."[36] Later admirers described him as an incarnation of the "world spirit" straight out of Hegel.[37] Like so many of his charismatic predecessors, Garibaldi had an ambiguous relationship to revolutionary democracy, especially after he seemed to put nationalism above revolutionary principle by pledging his loyalty to Piedmont's King Victor Emmanuel during his final campaigns.

In the United States, the creation of a presidency with sweeping executive powers, and Washington's example in the office, guaranteed that charisma would always play a central role in the country's political life. But after Washington, none of the next five presidents enjoyed anything like Washington's degree of adulation. None had served as a military leader, and two—John Adams and his son, John Quincy Adams—expressed active distrust for charismatic personal leadership.[38] But the seventh president, Andrew Jackson, had been a general—and yet another first-class horseman. His spectacular victory in the 1815 Battle of New Orleans had led admirers to hail him, to quote one of the more florid, as "an instrument reserved by a munificent Providence to save the political Israel of God."[39] As a politician in the 1820s, he explicitly tried to forge a direct bond with voters, presenting himself as the personification of the country's collective will in opposition to a privileged, corrupt elite. This image only gained in strength after the House of Representatives chose John Quincy Adams as president in 1824 despite the fact that Jackson had won a large plurality of the popular vote. Jackson finally triumphed in 1828, thanks to a raucous campaign in which the Democratic Party played a decisive role, especially in promoting the image of Jackson as a "man of the people."[40] As president, Jackson frequently displayed contempt for the formal mechanisms of government, leading opponents to tar him as a despot and dictator—a Caesar. But despite some claims that he would found the United States anew by returning it to the republican purity of its earlier days, his political career remained within well-established constitutional bounds. He could not acquire the aura of a revolutionary founding father, as Garibaldi would do a few years later (also Kossuth and Bismarck in the new states of Hungary and Germany, respectively).

The period after the mid-nineteenth century lies largely beyond the scope of this book. But to state an entirely obvious point, political charisma has continued to play a central role in world history, in both democratic and authoritarian states. Think only of the names Lincoln, Gladstone, Lenin, Stalin, Hitler, Churchill, Roosevelt, de Gaulle, Gandhi, Mao, Castro, Kennedy, Reagan, Mandela, to say nothing of men and women still alive. Of course, these figures differed wildly from one another and from the men studied in this book. But in each case, fervent followers believed they possessed extraordinary natural gifts and felt a powerful emotional bond with them.

Since the mid-nineteenth century, the technologies, cultural norms, political institutions and ideas shaping political charisma have all changed again, at often bewildering speed. In the decades after World War I, radio and film (and then television) made possible powerful new, vivid connections between charismatic leaders and their followers, taking the illusion of a personal connection to a new level. Mass political parties, in tandem with state apparatuses controlling education and media, provided means of mobilization and indoctrination that exceeded the wildest disciplinary fantasies of the eighteenth century.

A thread of continuity still linked the forms of political charisma that arose in the twentieth century—even in totalitarian states—to the earlier cases I examined in this book. Adolf Hitler and Joseph Stalin, for instance, were both, like the men I have studied here, exalted by their followers as sublime, quasi-sacred, redemptive figures possessed of absolutely extraordinary natural abilities.[41] Nazi propaganda relentlessly praised Hitler as a "genius" and compared him to the great artistic geniuses of the past, making much of his training as an artist and his supposed artistic temperament.[42] Both Hitler and Stalin successfully posed, for a long time, as founding fathers of a sort, who had given their states a new birth. For both, the perceived legitimacy of their regimes depended on the ecstatic devotion they claimed to have inspired (and, to a frightening extent, actually did inspire) in their populations. Propaganda operations in both Nazi Germany and the Stalinist USSR often depicted the supreme leaders meeting with awestruck ordinary men and women. And the example of the earlier revolutionary leaders loomed large for them. One of the most haunting photographs from World War II shows Adolf Hitler in the Invalides, staring down from the balustrade at the porphyry tomb of Napoleon Bonaparte.

In the totalitarian regimes, however, a key aspect of the charismatic bond fundamentally shifted. In earlier periods, followers had imagined themselves having an individual relationship with a charismatic leader—a relationship akin to friendship or romantic love. The followers, in other words, did not feel a need to sacrifice their individuality. They saw their devotion to the leader as, ultimately, proceeding from their own free choice. The totalitarian states, by contrast, sought to dissolve the individuality of the followers, to fuse these men and women metaphorically into a single great mass summoned forth by the leader's talismanic powers. In Leni Riefenstahl's disturbingly powerful Nazi propaganda film of 1935, *The Triumph of the Will*, depicting the Nuremberg rallies, the camera does close in on individual faces, but all are frozen into an identical rictus of ecstasy at the sight of the Führer. And always the camera pulls back to dissolve these faces into vast crowds of paramilitary and civilians, all deployed in perfect order, marching as one in massive formation, apparently invincible. In Hitler's Germany, all pretense of democratic rule of course dropped away, and acclamation of the charismatic leader became an organizing principle of all social and political life, right down to the most common of social interactions. "Every child says 'Heil Hitler!' from 50 to 150 times a day, immeasurably more often than the old neutral greetings," wrote Thomas Mann's daughter Erika in her 1938 book *School for Barbarians*. "The formula is required by law . . . 'Heil Hitler!' says the postman, the street-car conductor, the girl who sells you notebooks at the stationery store; and if your parents' first words when you come home for lunch are not 'Heil Hitler!' they have been guilty of a punishable offense and can be denounced."[43]

The experience of the totalitarian regimes also shows how indoctrination through state-controlled media, party organizations, and the threat of repression can fabricate a sort of charisma for almost any individual, regardless of their actual personal qualities. The regime in North Korea has taken this process to the absurd extreme with the cult of Kim Il-Sung's son and grandson. Already in the 1950s Kim himself, the founder of North Korea, was treated as a virtual god, and the regime today enforces worship of the grandson Kim Jong-un with comically relentless fanaticism. The largest propaganda sign on earth, stretching more than a third of a mile in length, each letter in its short slogan "the size of a small building," hails Kim Jong-un as "the shining sun."[44] It may seem absurd to call this most recent Kim charismatic, when, like dynastic monarchs of old, his principal qualification for his position has been his choice of ancestor. Surely the fabrication of charisma requires more than propaganda, even the industrial-strength propaganda of a totalitarian state. If some North Koreans feel something like love for Kim, it is surely a love born out of indoctrination and coercion. Yet as countless visitors to the "Hermit Kingdom" report, the feelings are nonetheless genuine and strong and help keep the regime in power.[45]

In the democratic West in the twentieth century, the story of charismatic authority took a different path. There, acclaim for charismatic leaders remained closer to the model I have examined in these pages, but by 1900 it had largely lost the quasi-religious resonance so prevalent in the cults of the earlier revolutionary leaders and that had remained commonplace through at least the lifetime of Garibaldi; language such as "godlike," "savior," "redeemer," and so forth was largely abandoned. American evangelical Christians even today still extol particular politicians as chosen by God, but such claims have generally ceased to appear in the secular media. Indeed, especially in the United States, it has become more important than ever—in a trend going back at least to Andrew Jackson's day—for charismatic leaders to appear as men or women of the people, comfortable in ordinary company, sharing ordinary tastes (especially culinary), understanding ordinary struggles. The popularization of the word "charisma" itself, which occurred in the 1950s and 1960s, may well have come in part as a reaction to these recent tendencies.[46] Even in popular usage it has a religious resonance (albeit a weak and unspecific one). Praising figures as "charismatic" provides a way of hinting at a transcendental quality—a departure from ordinary life—without actually invoking the deity or offending secular sensibilities.

In stable democratic states, political charisma cannot of course be linked to revolutionary disruption, or to the founding of new regimes, as it was in the age of revolution. Social scientists often argue that in these states charisma has become "routinized"—transferred from the revolutionary founders to stable constitutional offices. In this view the charisma of George Washington, for instance, has transferred itself to the American presidency.[47] It is an intriguing argument. But it is worth noting that if the reality of revolutionary disruption and the refounding of states has disappeared from the life of stable democracies, the rhetoric has not. It arises very predictably with every election cycle and remains key to the charismatic appeal of many politicians. It is no coincidence that among John F. Kennedy's most famous words is the line "the torch has been passed to a new generation of Americans," from his inaugural address, rhetorically signaling an American rebirth. In every election, American presidential candidates promise regenerative change, a breaking with "politics as usual," even (as for Bernie Sanders in 2016) a "revolution." Although Barack Obama governed as a moderate Democrat, his campaign in 2008 also promised epochal change and in many ways exemplified the operation of political charisma in American democracy. So powerful was his bond with his followers that his Republican opponents took to mocking him as "the chosen one" and the "messiah." Meanwhile, in France, no president of the Fifth Republic has been a purer product of the country's political, educational, and business establishments than the exquisitely centrist Emmanuel Macron. Yet the book that Macron, frequently described as France's most charismatic politician in decades, published as the centerpiece of his presidential campaign in 2017 had the title *Révolution*.[48]

I n the twenty-first century, the factors shaping charismatic leadership have changed dramatically yet again, especially with the rise of the Internet and social media. These technologies provide yet another way for ordinary people to imagine an intimate, emotional relationship with political figures they do not know personally. Indeed, one of the most striking features of social media is that powerful, distant political figures appear in the same feeds, in exactly the same format, as friends and relatives. Their posts can be responded to, forwarded, and debated in precisely the same manner. Furthermore, the format has encouraged many of the most prominent political figures to post in an informal, freewheeling, casual, utterly untutored manner, complete with bad jokes, crude insults, name-calling, and even (for some) spelling and grammatical errors, further lowering the perceived barrier between the holder of an august office and a dyspeptic relative, and furthering the illusion of a personal relationship. At the same time, social media has demonstrated an unparalleled ability to function as a conduit for rumor, conspiracy theories, outrage, and panic, stoking the impression that only the intervention of a savior figure wielding extraordinary powers can prevent imminent catastrophe. Scholars are still grappling with the political implications of social media—including the extraordinary fact that so large a proportion of the news and opinions reaching billions of people now passes through social-media portals controlled by just two massively wealthy corporations.

These new information technologies of course do not operate in a vacuum but rather in tandem with older media that have undergone important transformations of their own in recent years, especially in the United States. Here, twenty-first century elections have demonstrated the enormous political power of constellations of television and radio programs that incessantly repeat the same lines, and promote the same political candidates, every waking hour—especially on the political right. These programs, in combination with social media, have a particular impact upon audiences of people in retirement, on disability, or who spend many hours a day in their cars—categories to which belong a large portion of the Republican party's "base."[49] In the American election of 2016, the victorious candidate demonstrated an uncanny ability to combine social media with radio and television to arouse fanatical support. He was not lying when he boasted that, unlike his opponent Hillary Clinton, he did not need celebrities to fill large stadiums with his supporters.[50] His charismatic appeal among his most fervent followers broke in many other ways from recent American patterns, too. Notably, these followers resorted quite frequently to explicitly religious language. His own secretary of state compared him to a biblical figure, while his campaign manager asserted that "only God could deliver such a savior to our nation."[51]

Is the new media environment, combined with rising illiberal and xenophobic sentiment across the world, helping a new wave of charismatic strongmen rise up at the expense of democratic freedoms? Since 2016, prophecies of this doom have proliferated, and Cassandra has proven a popular—indeed, profitable—model to emulate.[52] And while, as of the writing of this book, these prophecies have proven overly alarmist (or at least premature), the experience of many countries gives credence to them. Should we, then, beware, and seek to mute the effects of political charisma, given the destructive power that the phenomenon seems to have recently acquired? As we have seen time and again in these pages, political charisma can indeed help ambitious leaders destroy constitutional regimes. The emotional bond that can arise between charismatic leaders and their followers has often proven more powerful than those followers' attachment to constitutional norms. A "despotism of love" can lead to despotism, pure and simple.

Yet as I have also argued here, charisma is an integral, inescapable part of modern political life—democracy's shadow self. Its modern forms arose out of the same cultural and intellectual universe that gave birth, in the age of revolution, to modern constitutional, democratic regimes. It is fused into the very structure of cultures where celebrity remains such a potent force. And while charismatic leaders have often threatened constitutional orders, they were also important in the initial creation of those orders. The emotional connection between them and their public might even have helped bond that public to the new regime. It is easier to love a person than to love a constitution, but the love for one can help promote love for the other.

In the twenty-first century, charismatic leaders can still have a constructive role to play. Rallying people behind democratic causes has become more difficult than ever, given rising inequalities, the massive economic power that resides in a small number of hands, and the frighteningly strong ability of illiberal forces to misinform, distract, and deceive. Fighting these forces requires more than principles and causes—it requires leaders who can elicit emotions powerful enough to impel people to action. The fact that illiberal politicians have proven so successful, in the early twenty-first century, in impelling their own followers to action by stoking anger at elites should not discredit the use of a charismatic politics for democratic, liberal ends. Political charisma is indeed a dangerous, combustible force, but we cannot dispense with it.

But the story told in this book also underlines just how much the individuals themselves matter. True, as I have argued here, the charismatic bond between leaders and followers is not shaped solely by the leader's own qualities. The leader fills a role shaped, in large part, by the hopes, desires, and fantasies of his or her followers. Indeed, in all the cases I have studied in this book—Paoli, Washington, Bonaparte, Louverture, and Bolívar—the legends around the charismatic leader sometimes seemed to take on lives of their own, until the connection with the real person appeared to break almost entirely. But, in fact, all of these men were also genuinely extraordinary (if not always admirable) historical figures. The same has been true of the most important subsequent examples of democratic political charisma, through Abraham Lincoln down to Nelson Mandela and Barack Obama. Their followers and admirers may have desperately longed for saviors, but it was no accident that they fastened on these men, rather than others, to play the role of the charismatic hero. And this role, while it constrained these men in some ways, in other ways gave them enormous freedom of action—enormous power. Still, however desperately we may hope for charismatic figures who can, by sheer force of personality, unite our nations and cut through impossibly tangled problems, charisma by itself is not enough. To what ends will it be used? For which purposes? By what sort of person? We will always have charismatic leaders. They are part of the fabric from which our political societies are woven. Our task is to choose these charismatic leaders wisely, by judging as carefully as possible both the individuals themselves and the causes for which they stand.

WRITING CHARISMA
INTO HISTORY

s I noted in the introduction, while social scientists have generated a massive literature on charisma, historians have made
relatively little use of the concept. With some important excep-
tions, they have engaged with it principally in the writing of biography—
for instance, Ian Kershaw's important studies of Adolf Hitler.[1] Yet as I
have tried to show in these pages, the concept can help us better understand some broader important aspects of modern history. In this brief
excursus, I will try to make the case for why historians should pay more
attention to charisma, and I will discuss which aspects of the social-
scientific literature have proved most useful to me in writing this book.

To begin with, a very simple point is worth noting. Historians today
have surprisingly few analytical tools to help them understand the role of
key individuals in history. Ever since the professionalization of the discipline in the nineteenth century, historians have quite understandably
rejected Thomas Carlyle's mystical "great man theory of history," which
I discuss in the epilogue. But in doing so they have often rushed pell-mell
to the other extreme, sometimes playing down the autonomous role of
powerful individuals almost entirely and thereby eliminating it as a topic
in need of investigation.

This tendency was especially true of the most influential single current
of historical thought of the past century and a half—namely, Marxism.
The long Marxist intellectual tradition has been anything but monolithic,

but it has always stressed the predominance of social forces over individual action in the unfolding of the human story. Karl Marx himself put it most eloquently, and most famously, in a work that alludes to Napoleon Bonaparte in its first paragraph. "Men make their own history," he wrote in 1852, "but they do not make it just as they please . . . The tradition of all the dead generations weighs like a nightmare on the brain of the living." Bonaparte, Robespierre, and Caesar, Marx wrote, "performed the task of their time."[2]

In a strange irony, among the political figures whose individual personalities and autonomous decisions have arguably had the greatest effect on the history of the past century, the largest share have been Communists who pledged fealty to Marx's ideas: Vladimir Lenin, Joseph Stalin, Mao Zedong, Ho Chi Minh, Fidel Castro, Kim Il-Sung, Josip Broz Tito, and many others (adding to the irony, they often virtually deified Karl Marx himself). Stephen Kotkin's magisterial biography of Joseph Stalin forcefully emphasizes the decisive impact of Stalin's particular personality and choices upon the course of Soviet—and, therefore, world—history.[3] The Soviet propaganda that hailed Stalin as "the great driver of the locomotive of history," whatever its putative basis in Marxist theory, arguably had far more in common with Carlyle's vision of history than with Marx's.[4] Yet Stalin himself explicitly subscribed to a theory of history that denied the importance of such individual factors.

In the discipline of history, Marxism as an all-encompassing system of explanation has lost most of its allure (as opposed to Marx's own writings, which remain justly influential, as do those of many of his intellectual heirs). But the principal historical schools of the later twentieth and early twenty-first centuries have largely shared Marxism's stance toward the role of powerful individuals. Fernand Braudel, the leading figure of the *Annales* school of social history, the most significant historical school of the mid-twentieth century, wrote, in an explicit echo of Marx: "Men do not make history. Rather it is history above all that makes men and thereby absolves them from blame."[5]

Much of the most influential work in cultural history and global history that arose as the *Annales* school faded could have adopted the same motto. As an example, *A World Connecting*, a prestigious history of the globe from 1870 to 1945, written and edited by some of the best-known and most talented representatives of the "new global history," paid strikingly little attention to individuals. In its 1,168 pages the name of one of the most prominent individual leaders of the period, Winston Churchill, appeared precisely three times (fewer than that of the explorer David Livingstone).[6] Since the 1960s, the discipline of history as a whole has also devoted much of its energy to rescuing from "the enormous condescension of posterity" groups of people—women, workers, people of color, sexual minorities, the "subaltern" subjects of imperialism—whom earlier generations of historians, in their concentration on influential white men, had unjustly disregarded or found impossible to acknowledge.[7] These new schools of history have in no sense always neglected individual lives, but they have attended to them most powerfully in "microhistories" that highlight particular life stories for what they reveal about larger patterns of change, not for the changes the men and women themselves brought about.[8] These trends in historical writing have had enormously salutary and important effects. I could not have even started my chapter on the Haitian Revolution without them.[9] But the result has still been to leave the study of powerful charismatic individuals disproportionately to biographers and writers of popular history.

Yet even as historians kept their distance from anything like a "great man" theory, the social-scientific disciplines continued to ponder the relationship of prominent individuals to society. Émile Durkheim, one of the founders of modern sociology, and an inheritor of the French republican tradition, explained the influence of such individuals in much the same way that he famously explained the origins of religion. In both cases, society was worshipping idols of its own making: "In the present day just as much as in the past, we see society constantly creating sacred things out of ordinary ones. If it happens to fall in love with a man and if it thinks it has found in him the principal aspirations that move it, as well as the means of satisfying them, this man will be raised above the others and, as it were, deified."[10]

But it was Durkheim's German contemporary Max Weber who reflected most systematically and productively on the subject. Weber did not ground his reflections in a fully elaborated philosophy of history (and he certainly did not consider history as nothing more than the biography of great men). Nonetheless, he insisted that key ruptures in history, the revolutionary passage from one stage to another in the life of a people or a religion, could happen by means of particular individuals gaining recognition as extraordinary and sublime, as possessing some quality of the divine, and thereby achieving the particular sort of authority that he labeled "charismatic."

The word "charisma" itself comes from the Greek. It literally means a gift of divine grace, and it appears both in the New Testament and in the earliest Greek translations of the Old Testament. In the scriptures, charisma could belong to groups as well as to individuals, and while it could denote an ability to bring others to God, it also implied an utter subjection to God's will. The charismatic figure was not a disruptive figure but a slavishly obedient one.[11] In the late nineteenth century, the German theologian Rudolph Sohm argued that charisma, rather than church law, provided the basis for church organization in the first centuries of Christianity.

Weber borrowed the word "charisma" from Sohm but radically altered its meaning. In his work it came to mean a revolutionary, highly personal form of political authority or domination (the German word *Herrschaft* has both connotations), which he contrasted both to traditional, patriarchal forms of authority of the sort enjoyed by kings and prelates, and also to the forms of rule-bound authority that arise within bureaucratic systems. His emblematically charismatic figures—the list included everyone from Native American shamans to Napoleon and the Mormon prophet Joseph Smith—were seen by their followers as possessing divine gifts and godlike powers. They were wild, disruptive figures, not in the least submissive, and the intense emotional bond between them and their followers trumped all ordinary political rules and restraints.[12]

Weber's thinking, it is crucial to note, owed an enormous amount to the very changes I have examined in this book. With charisma, he gave a name to the sort of political authority that had developed a century earlier, in the age of revolution. As I have discussed in the epilogue, the appearance of Washington, Bonaparte, Louverture, and Bolívar, and the sheer sense of human potential they seemed to represent, had powerful echoes in the main lines of Western thought. It helped shape and drive forward what we now call Romanticism in art and literature, and it mesmerized philosophers and social theorists alike. The philosopher Hegel called both Bonaparte and Caesar "world-historical spirits" who incarnated and channeled entire epochs of humanity. Friedrich Nietzsche, who likewise had a fascination with Napoleon, celebrated the powerful superman (*Übermensch*) who existed beyond the limits of ordinary morality.[13] In a brilliantly evocative phrase, he called Napoleon "this synthesis of *Unmensch* and *Übermensch*."[14]

It was against this background that Weber developed his concept of charisma. He did not develop it principally as a tool of historical analysis. Rather, he did so in the process of examining what he saw as some of the greatest dangers in modern society. His most important sociological work traced the rise of rational, bureaucratic forms of social organization, which he warned could trap men and women within what he termed an "iron cage" of administrative domination. And although no reactionary, in his later years (particularly following the German Revolution of 1918 and the chaotic birth of the Weimar Republic), Weber worried deeply about what would happen to democracy if it was left "headless," without strong individual leadership. Charismatic authority offered a possible solution—if a volatile and potentially dangerous one—to both these challenges. In the tradition of the nineteenth-century Caesarists, whom I discuss in the epilogue, Weber believed that modern bureaucratic states needed a charismatic, powerful chief executive—albeit, he added, one constrained by a parliament and subject to recall—to function effectively.[15]

Weber's concept of charisma, like his earlier description of a "Protestant ethic" that drove the rise of capitalism, inflamed the imagination of

social scientists worldwide.[16] It also provided material for numerous debates, not least because, as the cultural anthropologist Clifford Geertz
once delicately remarked, "there are multiple themes in Weber's concept
of charisma . . . almost all of them . . . more stated than developed."[17]
Indeed, the concept soon became the subject of an academic cottage
industry of sorts. Subsequent generations of scholars have exhaustively—
and sometimes exhaustingly—dilated upon, developed, and argued
about how charisma functions in the modern world. Does it have a
significant place in democratic, as opposed to authoritarian, political
systems? Some scholars, in my view underestimating the power of personality in democratic politics, have argued that it does not.[18] Should
we see charisma principally as a harmful force, or can it help constitutional democracies function better, by breaking through the paralysis
and partisan strife that afflicts so many contemporary societies? The
French political philosopher Jean-Claude Monod argued the latter case
in one of the most stimulating recent works to deal with charisma,
Qu'est-ce qu'un chef en démocratie? ("What is a leader in democracy?").[19]
He published it, however, in 2012, before the waves of populism that
subsequently swept across so much of the Western world.

And there have been other important discussions. The political theorist Karl Loewenstein maintained that since charisma was a fundamentally religious form of authority, it made little sense to speak of it in the
context of secular societies. Most subsequent scholars have disagreed,
noting that even in supposedly secular societies, ideas of transcendence,
the supernatural, and the sacred can remain enormously powerful.[20]
Many writers have pursued Weber's suggestion that charismatic authority can be institutionalized ("routinized"), with something of the original appeal transferred from individuals to offices such as the American
presidency.[21] Does such "routinization" represent a surrender to the
"iron cage" or, to the contrary, a means of tempering its effects?[22] For the
sociologists Edward Shils and Shmuel Eisenstadt, charisma's routinization, and its place in the ordinary functioning of society, has greater
significance than the revolutionary effects that Weber himself put such
stress on.[23]

Then there is the question of whether charisma is primarily an exceptional, magnetic quality possessed by individuals or, rather, something projected onto them by their followers, which is to say, a fiction invented to serve a social and political purpose. Some of Weber's successors, influenced by Durkheim's sociology and the psychology of Sigmund Freud, have preferred to define charisma primarily in these terms, occasionally to the point of describing the great charismatic leaders of the past as little but puppets of their own followers.[24] Others, such as Ann Ruth Willner, the author of an influential survey of charismatic modern politicians, *The Spellbinders*, insist on a more active, dynamic role for the charismatic figures themselves.[25]

Complicating the debates yet further has been the broad popularization of the concept that began in the mid-twentieth-century United States. American intellectuals who had encountered the word "charisma" in the social-scientific literature began to use it in general-interest publications in this period, notably to describe that paradigmatically charismatic American politician, John F. Kennedy.[26] From there charisma spread into the worlds of popular culture and marketing, where it rapidly lost its definitional specificity and came to signify little more than glamour, excitement, and personal magnetism. Since the 1960s, the word has been attached to brands of everything from yachts to perfume to soap to lingerie, and it has even found its way into the food pages. To quote a 2007 article on iceberg lettuce: "Revisit a retro classic with dressings that add charisma to its crunch."[27] This popularization makes the hesitation of historians to engage with the concept of charisma even more understandable.

Yet historians should put the salad dressing aside and write charisma into their work nonetheless. Weber's original concept, enriched by the subsequent discussions and debates, in fact provides an enormously useful and suggestive tool for understanding the role of prominent and powerful individual leaders in the historical process and the emotional bonds they form with their followers, especially in moments of crisis and revolution. The literature on charisma does not provide an overall theory of the role of individual leaders in history. But it provides crucial insights into the dynamics of leadership and the relationship between political leaders and the societies in which they operate.

In this book, I have tried to provide a case study of sorts, by looking at how the concept of charisma can illuminate the history of political leadership in the age of revolution. I have done so by trying to integrate the concept into what could be considered a cultural history of this leadership. This is an approach that has come naturally to me as a historian of political culture, in the style of the post-*Annales* "new cultural history."[28] The Weberian concept is in fact quite compatible with this cultural historical approach and provides a way to redirect it from the study of broad, impersonal cultural shifts to the lives and actions of particular individuals. Weber's insistence that the charisma depends not just on the individual, but also on the social "recognition" of that individual's qualities, of necessity directs attention to the cultural context in which this recognition is given.[29]

In writing this book, I have followed Weber in seeing charismatic figures as people "considered extraordinary and treated as endowed with supernatural, superhuman, or at least specifically exceptional powers or qualities."[30] Followers are connected to these figures by an intense emotional bond that can potentially overwhelm any other loyalties. I have been particularly concerned with charismatic political leaders who were seen as capable of giving a country a new birth simply by virtue of their extraordinary qualities. And in keeping with my focus on revolutionary moments, I have treated charisma principally as a disruptive, revolutionary force, not as the "routinized" one of Shils and Eisenstadt. Like the sociologists M. Rainer Lepsius and Philip Smith, I fear that an excessive focus on routinization risks conflating charisma with the elements and symbolism of ordinary political leadership.[31] I also believe that it distracts from the way even the most conventional of politicians in democratic political systems so often find themselves obliged to pose as disruptive, revolutionary, charismatic figures in order to win electoral support. While of course charisma exists outside the political sphere, in this book I have not dealt with charismatic figures in such fields as the arts, literature, or science. That said, the cultural environment in which figures in these fields achieved a new sort of fame in the eighteenth century has an important place in my story.

I have also followed Weber in seeing charisma as something deeply bound up with what societies consider sacred—although not just premodern ones. It is no coincidence that followers of charismatic leaders in the age of revolution so often reached for religious language to describe them: "godlike," "divine," "heavenly," "savior." They did not mean these words literally—that would have been blasphemy for observant Christians—but the words still suggested that the person in question existed at least partly beyond the profane world and possessed qualities best described as transcendent. If the intense interest shown in every aspect of the charismatic leaders' lives had a precedent from before the mid-eighteenth century, it was above all in the cult of the saints in the lands of the Roman Catholic Church. It was no coincidence that the word most often chosen by those who wished to bring charismatic leaders back to earth, exposing the legends around them as nothing but fictions and frauds, was "idol": a material object made by human hands and worshipped as a god. Associating charismatic figures with the sacred did not mean that the admiration of these figures in any sense replaced established Christian worship as part of a process of "secularization." As I emphasize in chapter 1, none of the societies that experienced revolution in this period turned "secular" in any simple sense. But in all of these societies, what was considered sacred became the subject of bitter, and sometimes deadly, conflict and underwent radical change. In the process, political leaders could find themselves treated as sacred, not because of the office they held but because of their supposedly transcendent personal qualities.

Where I have departed from Weber, and from most of the social scientists who followed him, is that I have little interest in charisma as an abstract, timeless, universal phenomenon. I have been concerned about how it took on a particular form in a particular time and place: the eighteenth- and early nineteenth-century Atlantic world. This concern has led me to put considerably more emphasis than has most of the literature on the specific cultural, social, and political contexts in which it became possible to perceive figures as charismatic and perhaps even to project charismatic qualities onto them. Weber, despite his attention to the "recognition" of charismatic figures, did little to explore what actually led people to bestow this "recognition." In contrast, especially in chapter 1, I have made this question central to my analysis, turning from the charismatic individuals themselves to their societies. I have also paid considerable attention to those observers, like John Adams, who themselves, at the time, understood and commented upon the issue of recognition, usually as they sought to knock a leader off his charismatic pedestal and reveal him as nothing but an idol cast by the hands of those who worshipped him.

I have also moved beyond the existing literature on charisma by introducing a distinction between the way charisma operates with respect to a leader's active followers on the one hand and distant admirers on the other. Nearly all the existing work on charisma has concerned the first of these—the bond with partisans, with members of a movement. But the perception of charisma also matters for admirers who are not in a position actively to support the object of their affections and who indeed may live in an entirely different country—or a different time. Obviously, this second sort of relationship does not benefit the leaders in the same way or produce the same sort of potentially dramatic and immediate consequences. But the bond felt by admirers toward a distant charismatic leader can still be an intense one. And it has enormous significance, since it shapes their sense of what charismatic leadership should be and what they will look for in leaders of their own. Think of the appeal, in the twentieth century and even now, of figures like Gandhi and Mandela, far beyond their own homelands. If we hope to understand why communities perceive certain figures as charismatic, the models they have for charisma in other places and times become a crucial factor. The charisma of the figures I study in these pages did not matter only in their own countries or in their own times but throughout the Western world for long afterward, providing a model that many others would try to imitate and that many followers would look for in their own countries. A central theme of the book has also been just how much these men mattered to one another and how much they copied one another.

I recognize that in putting such strong emphasis on the cultural contexts that defined charisma, I have moved back toward a deterministic approach, emphasizing in my turn, and in my manner as a cultural historian, the weight of dead generations on the brains of the living. I have not gone as far as the social scientists who treat charisma as essentially a fiction, a projection onto a leader of qualities that followers and admirers would desperately like the leader to possess. In this book, charisma is not akin to Shakespeare's "hollow crown that rounds the mortal temple of a king," which fools monarchs into believing they are something more than ordinary men.[32] In the cases I have looked at, the actual character and abilities of the leader did matter, considerably. Yet the book does suggest that political and cultural circumstances tightly shaped collective hopes and desires and fantasies, and that these in turn shaped a very specific sort of leadership role, one that only a very specific sort of person could play.

But not, I hope, entirely. Because in the end, the stories of the actual individuals I have studied here were considerably stranger, and less predictable, than such a rigid analysis might suggest. Yes, they had an instinctive sense of the hopes, desires, and fantasies of their followers, and they worked hard to fulfill them, to craft their personae accordingly. Yes, they could not have succeeded unless they fit plausibly into a role that had been sketched out for them: the role of the man on horseback. But, like great improvisational actors, they could also appropriate and modify this preordained role, reach beyond it, and begin writing the script for themselves. Their revolutionary careers testify to the power of culture and circumstance to shape even the most extraordinary of lives. But they testify as well to the power of extraordinary personalities to rewrite culture and circumstance in unpredictable ways.

NOTES

INTRODUCTION: CHARISMA

1. *Psychology Today: Basics*, https://www.psychologytoday.com/us/basics/charisma, accessed June 20, 2019.

2. I am drawing here on the large social-scientific literature on charisma. For a guide to it, see the excursus, "Writing Charisma into History."

3. On this point, see notably Ann Ruth Willner, *The Spellbinders: Charismatic Political Leadership* (New Haven, CT: Yale University Press, 1984), pp. 128–50.

4. See, though, the pioneering collection edited by Edward Berenson and Eva Giloi, *Constructing Charisma: Celebrity, Fame, and Power in Nineteenth-Century Europe* (New York: Berghahn Books, 2010), and Edward Berenson, *Heroes of Empire: Five Charismatic Men and the Conquest of Africa* (Berkeley: University of California Press, 2010). On Hitler, see especially the work of Ian Kershaw, including *Hitler: A Biography* (New York: W. W. Norton, 2008) and "Hitler and the Uniqueness of Nazism," *Journal of Contemporary History*, vol. 39, no. 2 (2004), pp. 239–54. A prominent work that uses the concept of charisma to understand John F. Kennedy and his family is Garry Wills, *The Kennedy Imprisonment: A Meditation on Power* (Boston: Mariner, 2002), especially pp. 163–218.

5. Max Weber, *Economy and Society: An Outline of Interpretive Sociology*, eds. Guenther Roth and Claus Wittich, trans. Ephraim Fischoff et al., 2 vols. (Berkeley: University of California Press, 1978), vol. 1, p. 244.

6. The phrase is associated above all with the work of R. R. Palmer, *The Age of the Democratic Revolution: A Political History of Europe and America, 1760–1800* (Princeton, NJ: Princeton University Press, 2014).

7. For reflections on the concept of democracy in Western history, see James Miller, *Can Democracy Work? A Short History of a Radical Idea from Ancient Athens to Our World* (New York: Farrar, Straus and Giroux, 2018).

8. Jean-Jacques Rousseau to Victor de Riqueti, marquis de Mirabeau, July 26, 1767, in Jean-Jacques Rousseau, *Collection complète des œuvres de J. J. Rousseau*, 24 vols. (Geneva: n.p., 1782), vol. 24, pp. 475–76.

9. See Blair Worden, "Providence and Politics in Cromwellian England," *Past and Present*, no. 109 (1985), pp. 55–99.

10. See Antoine Lilti, *Figures publiques: L'invention de la célébrité, 1750–1850* (Paris: Fayard, 2014).

11. Louis-Marcelin de Fontanes, "Éloge de Washington," in *Éloges funèbres de Washington*, ed. Isaiah Townsend (Paris: Casimir, 1835), pp. 25–26; Simón Bolívar, quoted in Paul Verna, *Pétion y Bolívar: Cuarenta años (1790–1830) de relaciones haitano-venezolanas y su aporte a la emancipación de Hispanoamérica* (Caracas: Oficina Central de Información, 1969), p. 271; James Boswell, *An Account of Corsica, the Journal of a Tour to That Island, and Memoirs of Pascal Paoli* (Glasgow: Robert and Andrew Foulis, 1768), p. 162.

12. See notably Claude Mossé, *L'antiquité dans la Révolution française* (Paris: Albin Michel, 1989); Eran Shalev, *Rome Reborn on Western Shores: Historical Imagination and the Creation of the American Republic* (Charlottesville: University of Virginia Press, 2009); Carl J. Richard, *The Founders and the Classics: Greece, Rome, and the American Enlightenment* (Cambridge, MA: Harvard University Press, 1994).

13. Quoted in David A. Bell, *The First Total War: Napoleon's Europe and the Birth of Warfare as We Know It* (Boston: Houghton Mifflin, 2007), p. 139.

14. See Melissa Schwartzberg, "Shouts, Murmurs and Votes: Acclamation and Aggregation in Ancient Greece," *The Journal of Political Philosophy*, vol. 18, no. 4 (2010), pp. 448–68. On this theme see also Jason Frank, "The People as Popular Manifestation," in Bas Leijssenaar and Neil Walker, eds., *Sovereignty in Action* (Cambridge: Cambridge University Press, 2019), pp. 65–90, drawing on Carl Schmitt, *Constitutional Theory*, trans. Jeffrey Seitzer (Durham, NC: Duke University Press, 2008).

15. James Harrington, *The Oceana of James Harrington and His Other Works* (Dublin: J. Smith and W. Bruce, 1737), p. 37.

16. Fontanes, *Éloge funèbre de Washington*; Dominique de Pradt, *Les trois âges des colonies, ou De leur état passé, présent et à venir*, 2 vols. (Paris: Giguet, 1801), vol. 2, p. 103; *The Annual Register; or, A View of the History, Politics, and Literature of the Year 1802* (London, Wilks, 1803), p. 211; Marie Arana, *Bolívar: American Liberator* (New York: Simon & Schuster, 2013), p. 4.

17. On the shared culture, see Nathan Perl-Rosenthal, "Atlantic Cultures and the Age of Revolution," *The William and Mary Quarterly*, vol. 74, no. 4 (2017), pp. 667–96. On the connections between the revolutions, see David A. Bell, "The Atlantic Revolutions," in David Motadel, ed., *Waves of Revolutions* (Cambridge: Cambridge University Press, forthcoming 2020).

18. See Richard S. Wortman, *Scenarios of Power: Myth and Ceremony in Russian Monarchy: From Peter the Great to the Death of Nicholas I*, 2 vols. (Princeton, NJ: Princeton University Press, 1995–2000), vol. 1, pp. 110–44.

19. On changing views of masculinity in this period, see notably Brian Joseph Martin, *Napoleonic Friendship: Military Fraternity, Intimacy, and Sexuality in Nineteenth-Century France* (Lebanon, NH: University Press of New England, 2011); George L. Mosse, *The Image of Man: The Creation of Modern Masculinity* (New York: Oxford University Press, 1998); Alain Corbin, Jean-Jacques Courtine, and Georges Vigarello, eds., *A History of Virility*, trans. Keith Cohen (New York: Columbia University Press, 2016).

20. See notably Brenda Meehan-Waters, "Catherine the Great and the Problem of Female Rule," *The Russian Review*, vol. 34, no. 3 (1975), pp. 293–307; Anthony Cross, "Catherine II Through Contemporary British Eyes," *Russica Romana*, vol. 4 (1997), pp. 55–65.

21. See Samuel E. Finer, *The Man on Horseback: The Role of the Military in Politics* (New York: Praeger, 1962).

22. Thomas Jefferson to Walter Jones, Monticello, January 2, 1814, in *Founders Online*, https://founders.archives.gov/documents/Jefferson/03-07-02-0052, accessed June 20, 2019.

23. See Sudhir Hazareesingh, *Black Spartacus: The Epic Life of Toussaint Louverture* (London: Allen Lane, 2020).

24. See, for instance, Luis Perú de Lacroix, *El diario de Bucaramanga*, ed. Nicolás E. Navarro, 2 vols. (Caracas: Bohemia, 1949), vol. 1, pp. 76–80.

25. See Carolina Vanegas Carrasco, "Iconografía de Bolívar: Revisión historiográfica," *Ensayos: Historia y teoría del arte*, vol. 22 (2012), pp. 112–34.

26. See especially William M. Reddy, *The Navigation of Feeling: A Framework for the History of Emotions* (Cambridge: Cambridge University Press, 2001); Monique Scheer, "Are Emotions a Kind of Practice (and Is That What Makes Them Have a History?): A Bourdieuian Approach to Understanding Emotion," *History and Theory*, vol. 51, no. 2 (2012), pp. 193–220.

27. See Lynn Hunt, *Inventing Human Rights: A History* (New York: W. W. Norton, 2007), and Timothy Tackett, *The Coming of the Terror in the French Revolution* (Cambridge, MA: Harvard University Press, 2015). Both authors, however, assume a little too quickly that the experience

of a particular emotion necessarily led men and women to take a particular political action as a result, and neither gives sufficiently close attention to the larger political and intellectual contexts in which those actions were decided upon.

28. See discussion in Dawn Ades, *Art in Latin America: The Modern Era, 1820–1980* (New Haven, CT: Yale University Press, 1989), pp. 16–17.

ONE: MR. BOSWELL GOES TO CORSICA

1. James Boswell, *Boswell's London Journal, 1762–1763* (New Haven, CT: Yale University Press, 2004), p. 155.

2. On the young Boswell, see Peter Martin, *A Life of James Boswell* (New Haven, CT: Yale University Press, 2000), quote from p. 165; Frederick A. Pottle, *James Boswell: The Earlier Years, 1740–1769* (New York: McGraw-Hill, 1966); James Boswell, *Boswell on the Grand Tour: Italy, Corsica, and France, 1765–1766* (Melbourne: W. Heinemann, 1955); Douglas Day, "Boswell, Corsica, and Paoli," *English Studies*, vol. 45, no. 1 (1964), pp. 1–20; Francis Beretti, *Pascal Paoli et l'image de la Corse au dix-huitième siècle: Le témoignage des voyageurs britanniques* (Oxford: Voltaire Foundation, 1988); Pierre Carboni, "Boswell et Paoli: Un Plutarque écossais et son Lycurgue corse," in Jackie Pigeaud and Jean-Paul Barbé, eds., *Le culte des grands hommes au XVIIIe siècle* (Nantes: Institut Universitaire de France, 1996), pp. 109–18; Dominique Colonna, *Le vrai visage de Pascal Paoli en Angleterre* (Nice: self-published, 1969); Leo Damrosch, *The Club: Johnson, Boswell, and the Friends Who Shaped an Age* (New Haven, CT: Yale University Press, 2019).

3. See most recently Luke Paul Long, "Britain and Corsica 1729–1796: Political Intervention and the Myth of Liberty," unpublished Ph.D. dissertation, University of Saint Andrews, 2018.

4. Jean-Jacques Rousseau, *The Social Contract,* ed. Maurice Cranston (London: Penguin Books, 1968), p. 96. The principal source for Boswell's trip is Boswell, *An Account of Corsica.* Modern edition: James Boswell, *An Account of Corsica, the Journal of a Tour to That Island, and Memoirs of Pascal Paoli,* eds. James T. Boulton and T. O. McLoughlin (Oxford: Oxford University Press, 2006).

5. Quoted in Michel Vergé-Franceschi, *Paoli: Un Corse des Lumières* (Paris: Fayard, 2005), p. 270.

6. On Paoli, see most recently Vergé-Franceschi, *Paoli,* conditions of poverty on p. 278; Antoine-Marie Graziani, *Pascal Paoli: Père de la patrie corse* (Paris: Tallandier, 2002).

7. Peter Martin, p. 206.

8. Fanny Burney to Samuel Crisp, October 15, 1782, in Fanny Burney, *The Early Journals and Letters of Fanny Burney,* eds. Lars E. Troide and Stewart J. Cooke, 5 vols. (Montreal: McGill University Press, 2012), vol. 5, p. 125.

9. Boswell, *An Account of Corsica* (1768), p. 351.

10. Pascal Paoli, *Lettres de Pascal Paoli,* ed. Pietro Perelli, 5 vols. (Bastia: Ollagnier, 1884–1899), vol. V, pp. 62, 77, 85, 166.

11. Peter Martin, p. 217.

12. Vergé-Franceschi, p. 338.

13. Day, p. 10.

14. E.g., "The Corsicans are . . . extremely violent in their tempers. This is certainly the effect of a warm climate." Boswell, *An Account of Corsica* (1768), p. 133.

15. Ibid., p. 302.

16. Ibid., p. 328.

17. Ibid., pp. 332, 328.

18. See Day, p. 11.

19. Vergé-Franceschi, pp. 336–40; Beretti, pp. 119–20; James Boswell, *Letters of James Boswell: Addressed to . . . W. J. Temple: Now First Published from the Original Mss.; with an Introduction and Notes* (London: Bentley, 1857), p. 60; Moray McLaren, *Corsica Boswell: Paoli, Johnson and Freedom* (London: Secker & Warburg, 1966), p. 163.

20. Paoli, *Lettres de Pascal Paoli*, vol. V, p. 166.

21. *The Cambridge Magazine; or, The Universal Repository of Arts, Sciences, and the Belles Lettres . . . . By a Society of Gentlemen, of the University of Cambridge* (London, 1769), p. 350; *The London Magazine; or, The Gentleman's Monthly Intelligencer*, September 1770, p. 455; Thomas Davies, *Memoirs of the Life of David Garrick, Esq. Interspersed with Characters and Anecdotes of His Theatrical Contemporaries*, vol. 2 (Dublin: Joseph Hill, 1780), pp. 2, 161; William C. Dowling, *The Boswellian Hero* (Athens: University of Georgia Press, 1979), p. 20.

22. Poems include George Cockings, *The Paoliad* (London: n.p., 1769); Anna Aikin, *Corsica: An Ode* (London: Ridley, 1769); Anna Letitia Barbauld, *Poems* (London: Joseph Johnson, 1773), p. 11; Michael Bruce, *Poems on Several Occasions by Michael Bruce* (Edinburgh: J. Robertson, 1770), p. 101; Robert Colvill, *The Cyrnean Hero: A Poem* (London: n.p., 1772); *The Conquest of Corsica by the French: A Tragedy. By a Lady.* (London, n.p., 1771); Capel Lofft, *The Praises of Poetry: A Poem* (London: W. Owen, 1775); Timothy Scribble, *The Weeds of Parnassus, a Collection of Original Poems* (Rochester: T. Fisher, 1774), p. 11; Thomas Tournay, *Ambition. An Epistle to Paoli* (London: Edward and Charles Dilly, 1769); "Poetry to Pascal Paoli" and "On the Dejection of the Corsicans," cited in Colonna, pp. 32–33. Portraits appeared inter alia in *The Gentleman's Magazine*, April 1768, p. 172; *The London Magazine*, January 1769, pp. 36–7. For "Chicken Paoli," see *The Lady's Magazine; or The Entertaining Companion for the Fair Sex, Appropriated Solely to Their Use and Amusement*, 3 vols. (London, 1771), vol. 2, p. 35. Racehorses in *The Sporting Calendar*, 1769, pp. 258, 259, 286. Mentions of volunteering to fight in Corsica: *Miss Melmoth; or, The New Clarissa*, 3 vols. (London: T. Lowndes, 1771), vol. 3, p. 256; *The History of Jack Wilks, a Lover of Liberty . . .* , 2 vols. (London: n.p., 1769), p. 246.

23. *Pride: A Poem. Inscribed to John Wilkes, Esquire. By an Englishman* (London: J. Almon, 1766), pp. 11–12.

24. *The London Magazine*, January 1769, pp. 36–7; also in *The Political Register*, January 1769, p. 31. See also *Corsica: A Poetical Address* (London: n.p., 1769); Catherine Macaulay, *Loose Remarks on Certain Positions to Be Found in Mr. Hobbes' Philosophical Rudiments of Government and Society with a Short Sketch of a Democratical Form of Government in a Letter to Signior Paoli* (London: T. Davies, 1769).

25. James Boswell, ed., *British Essays in Favour of the Brave Corsicans* (London: Edward and Charles Dilly, 1769); Day, p. 16; reports of donations also in *The London Magazine*, May 1769, p. 275; *The Court Miscellany; or, The Ladies' New Magazine*, 1769, p. 674; *Critical Memoirs of the Times: Containing a Summary View of the Popular Pursuits, Political Debates, and Literary Productions of the Present Age* (London: n.p., 1769), p. 277. See also Beretti, p. 75.

26. Quoted in Damrosch, p. 242.

27. See Franco Venturi, *The End of the Old Regime in Europe, 1776–1789,* Part II: *Republican Patriotism and the Empires of the East* (Princeton, NJ: Princeton University Press, 1991), pp. 502–509.

28. McLaren, pp. 152–53.

29. James Boswell, *Boswell's "The Life of Samuel Johnson"* (New York: Scribner's Sons, 1917).

30. George P. Anderson, "Pascal Paoli: An Inspiration to the Sons of Liberty," *Publications of the Colonial Society of Massachusetts: Transactions*, vol. 26 (1924), pp. 180–210, at p. 188; extracts in Thomas More, *Poor Thomas Improved: Being More's Country Almanack for the Year of Christian Account 1770* (New York: Alexander and James Robertson, 1770), unpaginated. See also Pauline Maier, *From Resistance to Revolution: Colonial Radicals and the Development of American Opposition to Britain, 1765–1776* (London: W. W. Norton, 1991), pp. 161–82.

31. Paoli's letter in *The Newport Mercury*, March 27, 1775; *The Connecticut Courant*, March 27, 1769; *The Boston Gazette*, April 10, 1769; *The New York Journal*, March 16, 1769; *The Georgia Gazette*, March 22, 1769; *The Essex Gazette* (Salem, MA), March 21–28, 1769; *The Providence Gazette and Country Journal*, April 1, 1769. *Pride: A Poem*, published in *The Quebec Gazette*, January 26, 1769; *The Essex Gazette*, November 29–December 6, 1768; *The Boston Evening Post*, November 28, 1768; three further references in Maier, *From Resistance to Revolution*, p. 181.

32. *The Newport Mercury*, March 27, 1775, p. 1.

33. Quoted in Maier, *From Resistance to Revolution*, p. 162.

34. Anderson, "Pascal Paoli," pp. 189, 200, 204, 209.

35. See Graziani, p. 149.

36. Quoted in Boswell, *An Account of Corsica* (1768), p. 382.

37. See, notably, on this subject, Thomas E. Kaiser, "Louis le Bien Aimé and the Rhetoric of the Royal Body," in *From the Royal to the Republican Body: Incorporating the Political in Seventeenth-and Eighteenth-Century France*, eds. Sara E. Melzer and Kathryn Norberg (Berkeley: University of California Press, 1998), pp. 131–61.

38. See, for instance, Peter Burke, *The Fabrication of Louis XIV* (New Haven, CT: Yale University Press, 1992); Kevin M. Sharpe, *Rebranding Rule: The Restoration and Revolution Monarchy, 1660–1714* (New Haven, CT: Yale University Press, 2013).

39. Immanuel Kant, "On the Common Saying, That May Be Correct in Theory, but It Is of No Use in Practice," in *Practical Philosophy*, trans. and ed. Mary J. Gregor (Cambridge: Cambridge University Press, 1996), p. 291.

40. Boswell, *An Account of Corsica* (1768), p. 304.

41. Ibid., pp. 153, 162.

42. Ibid., p. 312.

43. See Sinclair Thomson, "Sovereignty Disavowed: The Tupac Amaru Revolution in the Atlantic World," *Atlantic Studies*, vol. 13, no. 3 (2016), pp. 407–31; Charles F. Walker, *The Tupac Amaru Rebellion* (Cambridge, MA: Harvard University Press, 2014). A Google Ngram search suggests that even in the years of the Túpac Amaru rebellion, Paoli was mentioned more frequently in English-language publications.

44. Franco Venturi, *The End of the Old Regime in Europe, 1768–1776: The First Crisis*, trans. R. Burr Litchfield (Princeton, NJ: Princeton University Press, 1979), p. ix.

45. On the image of Peter in the West, see Anthony Glenn Cross, *Peter the Great Through British Eyes: Perceptions and Representations of the Tsar Since 1698* (Cambridge: Cambridge University Press, 2000); Albert Lortholary, *Le mirage russe en France au XVIIIe siècle* (Paris: Boivin, 1951); Christiane Mervaud and Michel Mervaud, "Le Pierre le grand et la Russie de Voltaire: Histoire ou mirage?" in *Le mirage russe au XVIIIe siècle*, ed. Serguei Karp and Larry Wolff (Ferney-Voltaire: Centre International d'Étude du XVIIIe siècle, 2001), pp. 11–35; Emmanuel Waegemans, *Peter de Grote in de Oostenrijkse Nederlanden* (Antwerp: Koninklijke Bibliotheek Albert I, 1998); Rudolf Minzloff, *Catalogue raisonné des Russica de la Bibliothèque impériale publique de Saint-Pétersbourg: Pierre le grand dans la littérature étrangère* (Saint Petersburg: Glasounow, 1872); Antoine-Léonard Thomas, *Œuvres complètes de Thomas, de l'Académie française; précédées d'une notice sur la vie et les ouvrages de l'auteur*, 6 vols. (Paris: Verdière, 1825), vol. 5, pp. 53–336. Much of this work was based on the developing cult of Peter in Russia itself. See Nicholas V. Riasanovsky, *The Image of Peter the Great in Russian History and Thought* (New York: Oxford University Press, 1985); Paul Bushkovitch, *Peter the Great* (Lanham, MD: Rowman & Littlefield, 2001).

46. Thomas, vol. 5, p. 95.

47. Quoted in Cross, *Peter the Great*, 50. See also W. H. Dilworth, *The Father of His Country; or, The History of the Life and Glorious Exploits of Peter the Great, Czar of Muscovy* (London: Woodgate and Brooks, 1760), p. 135. See also Voltaire, *Histoire de l'empire de Russie sous Pierre-le-Grand* (*Œuvres complètes de Voltaire*), 25 vols. (Paris: Antoine-Augustin Renouard, 1817), vol. 22, p. 90.

48. Dilworth, pp. 134–35.

49. James Thomson, *The Seasons* (Philadelphia: n.p., 1764), p. 200.

50. Aaron Hill, *The Northern Star, a Poem: On the Great and Glorious Actions of the Present Czar of Russia* (London: T. Payne, 1724), p. 24.

51. John Mottley, *The Life of Peter the Great, Emperor of All Russia*, 3 vols. (London: M. Cooper, 1725), vol. I, p. 91.

52. Dilworth, p. 22.

53. The work on Frederick's image, both in Prussia itself and throughout the West, is voluminous. See especially Ute Frevert, *Gefühlspolitik: Friedrich II. als Herr über die Herzen?* (Göttingen: Wallstein Verlag, 2012); Stephanie Kermes, *Creating an American Identity: New England, 1789–1825* (New York: Palgrave Macmillan, 2008), pp. 57–85; Eckhart Hellmuth, "Die 'Wiedergeburt' Friedrichs des Grossen und der 'Tod fürs Vaterland': Zum patriotischen Selbstverständnis in Preussen in der zweiten Hälfte des 18. Jahrhunderts," *Aufklärung*, vol. 10, no. 2 (1998), pp. 23–54; Thomas Biskup, *Friedrichs Grösse: Inszenierungen des Preussenkönigs in Fest und Zeremoniell, 1740–1815* (Frankfurt: Campus Verlag, 2012); Hans Dollinger, *Friedrich II. von Preussen: Sein Bild im Wandel von zwei Jahrhunderten* (Munich: List, 1986); Hans Marcus, *Friedrich der Grosse in der englischen Literatur* (Leipzig: Mayer & Mueller, 1930); Manfred Schlenke, *England und das Friderizianische Preussen, 1740–1763: Ein Beitrag zum Verhältnis von Politik und öffentliche Meinung im England des 18. Jahrhunderts* (Freiburg: Verlag Karl Alber, 1963).

54. See Schlenke, especially pp. 234–37. W. H. Dilworth, *The Life and Heroick Actions of Frederick II King of Prussia* (London: G. Wright, 1758).

55. See Kermes, p. 67; Frevert, passim.

56. Frederick II, King of Prussia, *Examen du Prince de Machiavel, avec des notes historiques & politiques*, 2 vols. (The Hague: Jean van Duren, 1741), vol. II, p. 12.

57. *Acta Borussica: Denkmäler der Preussischen Staatsverwaltung im 18. Jahrhundert*, 6 vols. (Berlin: Paul Parey, 1901), vol. 6, p. 42. On this text, see Frevert, especially pp. 50–51 and passim on what she calls Frederick's "politics of sentiment" (*Gefühlspolitik*).

58. Quoted in Kermes, p. 69.

59. Ibid., p. 84.

60. See most recently Miller, *Can Democracy Work?*

61. See James T. Kloppenberg, *Toward Democracy: The Struggle for Self-Rule in European and American Thought* (New York: Oxford University Press, 2016).

62. Denis Diderot, article "Autorité politique," from the *Encyclopédie* (1751), in https://gallica.bnf .fr/essentiels/diderot/encyclopedie/article-autorite-politique, accessed October 1, 2018.

63. One strain of this research puts the emphasis on cultural institutions and was shaped above all by the 1962 work of Jürgen Habermas, published in English as *The Structural Transformation of the Public Sphere: An Inquiry into a Category of Bourgeois Society*, trans. Thomas Burger and Frederick Lawrence (Cambridge, MA: MIT Press, 1989). A second strand looks particularly at the literary sphere and notions of sensibility and sentimentalism. See here above all Hunt, *Inventing Human Rights*.

64. See, for instance, Moshe Sluhovsky, *Patroness of Paris: Rituals of Devotion in Early Modern France* (Leiden: Brill, 1998); Hannah Williams, "Saint Genevieve's Miracles: Art and Religion in Eighteenth-Century Paris," *French History*, vol. 30, no. 2 (2016), pp. 322–53.

65. B. Robert Kreiser, *Miracles, Convulsions and Ecclesiastical Politics in Early Eighteenth-Century Paris* (Princeton, NJ: Princeton University Press, 1978); Catherine-Laurence Maire, *Les convulsionnaires de Saint-Médard: Miracles, convulsions et prophéties à Paris au XVIIIe siecle* (Paris: Gallimard, 1985).

66. See especially Douglas L. Winiarski, *Darkness Falls on the Land of Light: Experiencing Religious Awakenings in Eighteenth-Century New England* (Chapel Hill: University of North Carolina Press, 2017); Harry S. Stout, *The Divine Dramatist: George Whitefield and the Rise of Modern Evangelicalism* (Grand Rapids: William D. Eerdmans, 1991).

67. For a good overview, see Charly Coleman, "Resacralizing the World: The Fate of Secularization in Enlightenment Historiography," *The Journal of Modern History*, vol. 82, no. 2 (2010), pp. 368–95. See also David A. Bell, *The Cult of the Nation in France: Inventing Nationalism, 1680–1800* (Cambridge, MA: Harvard University Press, 2001), pp. 22–49.

68. Paul-Henry Thiry, baron d'Holbach, *Système de la nature, ou Des loix du monde physique et du monde moral*, 2 vols. (London: n.p., 1781), vol. 2, p. 350. On this subject, see Coleman, "Re-

sacralizing the World," and Charly Coleman, *The Virtues of Abandon: An Anti-Individualist History of the French Enlightenment* (Stanford, CA: Stanford University Press, 2014).

69. See Darrin M. McMahon, *Divine Fury: A History of Genius* (New York: Basic Books, 2013).
70. Quoted in ibid., p. 98.
71. Barbauld, *Poems*, p. 11; *Pride: A Poem*, p. 12; Bruce, *Poems on Several Occasions*, p. 101.
72. Boswell, *An Account of Corsica* (1768), p. 328.
73. See Geneviève Bollème et al., *Livre et société dans la France du XVIIIe siècle*, 2 vols. (Paris: Mouton, 1965–70); Lucien Febvre and Henri-Jean Martin, *The Coming of the Book: The Impact of Printing, 1450–1800*, trans. David Gerard, eds. Geoffrey Nowell-Smith and David Wootton (London: Verso, 1976).
74. See on this subject notably Andrew Pettegree, *The Invention of News: How the World Came to Know About Itself* (London: Yale University Press, 2014), pp. 251–325.
75. See Jeremy Black, *The English Press in the Eighteenth Century* (London: Croom Helm, 1987); Michael Warner, *The Letters of the Republic: Publication and the Public Sphere in Eighteenth-Century America* (Cambridge, MA: Harvard University Press, 1990).
76. Warner, p. 68.
77. On France, the best survey remains Roger Chartier, *The Cultural Origins of the French Revolution*, trans. Lydia G. Cochrane (Durham, NC: Duke University Press, 1991). On Spain's American colonies, see notably Cristina Soriano, *Tides of Revolution: Information, Insurgencies, and the Crisis of Colonial Rule in Venezuela* (Albuquerque: University of New Mexico Press, 2018); Rebecca Earle, "Information and Disinformation in Late Colonial New Granada," *The Americas*, vol. 54, no. 2 (1997), pp. 167–84.
78. This opinion follows above all from Habermas's tremendously influential *Structural Transformation of the Public Sphere*.
79. Jean-Marie Goulemot, *Ces livres qu'on ne lit que d'une main: Lecture et lecteurs de livres pornographiques au XVIIIe siècle* (Paris: Alinéa, 1991).
80. On these subjects, see notably David Denby, *Sentimental Narrative and the Social Order in France, 1760–1820* (Cambridge: Cambridge University Press, 1994); Jessica Riskin, *Science in the Age of Sensibility: The Sentimental Empiricists of the French Enlightenment* (Chicago: University of Chicago Press, 2002); Anne C. Vila, *Enlightenment and Pathology: Sensibility in the Literature and Medicine of Eighteenth-Century France* (Baltimore: Johns Hopkins University Press, 1998); Nicole Eustace, *Passion Is the Gale: Emotion, Power, and the Coming of the American Revolution* (Chapel Hill: University of North Carolina Press, 2008); Sarah Knott, *Sensibility and the American Revolution* (Chapel Hill: University of North Carolina Press, 2009).
81. Denis Diderot, "Éloge de Richardson" (1761), https://fr.wikisource.org/wiki/%C3%89loge_de_Richardson, accessed November 2, 2017.
82. Robert Darnton, "Readers Respond to Rousseau: The Fabrication of Romantic Sensitivity," in *The Great Cat Massacre and Other Episodes in French Cultural History* (New York: Basic Books, 1984), pp. 215–56.
83. Boswell, *An Account of Corsica* (1768), p. 126.
84. Ibid., pp. 314, 133, 326.
85. See Jean-Claude Bonnet, *Naissance du panthéon: Essai sur le culte des grands hommes* (Paris: Fayard, 1998); Bell, *The Cult of the Nation in France*, pp. 107–39.
86. See the classic work of Donald A. Stauffer, *The Art of Biography in Eighteenth-Century England*, 2 vols. (Princeton, NJ: Princeton University Press, 1941); also Brian Cowan, "News, Biography, and Eighteenth-Century Celebrity," *Oxford Handbooks Online*, http://www.oxfordhandbooks.com/view/10.1093/oxfordhb/9780199935338.001.0001/oxfordhb-9780199935338-e-132?rskey=RFtadH&result=1402, accessed January 24, 2018.
87. Samuel Johnson, *The Rambler*, eds. W. J. Bate and A. B. Straus, 3 vols. (New Haven, CT: Yale University Press, 1969), vol. I, p. 321, quoted in Cowan, "News, Biography."
88. See Chartier, pp. 89–91.
89. Figures are taken from soundings in the Burney Collection of seventeenth- and eighteenth-century

British newspapers, and from the Early American Imprints collection, accessed November 2, 2017.

90. See Lilti, *Figures publiques*, pp. 84–87; Cowan, "News, Biography"; John Brewer, *The Pleasures of the Imagination: English Culture in the Eighteenth Century* (New York: Farrar, Straus and Giroux, 1997), pp. 47–49, 120, 328.

91. Images found through the British Museum research collection online, http://www.british museum.org/research/collection_online/search.aspx?searchText=Paoli&images=true, accessed November 2, 2017.

92. Boswell, *An Account of Corsica* (1768), p. 351.

93. See Geoffrey Holmes, *The Trial of Doctor Sacheverell* (London: Methuen, 1973); Brian Cowan, ed., *The State Trial of Doctor Henry Sacheverell* (Oxford: Wiley-Blackwell, 2012).

94. See Kathleen Wilson, "Empire, Trade and Popular Politics in Mid-Hanoverian Britain: The Case of Admiral Vernon," *Past and Present*, vol. 121 (1988), pp. 74–109.

95. See John Shovlin, "Selling American Empire on the Eve of the Seven Years' War: The French Propaganda Campaign of 1755–56," *Past and Present*, vol. 206 (2010), pp. 121–49; Bell, *Cult of the Nation*, pp. 78–106.

96. On Wilkes, see above all John Brewer, *Party Ideology and Popular Politics at the Accession of George III* (Cambridge: Cambridge University Press, 1976), pp. 163–200.

97. Day, "Boswell, Corsica, and Paoli," p. 18; William Kenrick, "A Parallel Between Pascal Paoli, General of the Corsicans, and John Wilkes Esq., Member of Parliament for Middlesex," in Kenrick, *An Epistle to James Boswell, Esq. Occasioned by His Having Transmitted the Moral Writings of Dr. Samuel Johnson, to Pascal Paoli, . . . With a Postscript, Containing Thoughts on Liberty* (London: Fletcher and Anderson, 1768), pp. 49–55; *Pride: A Poem*, passim.

98. On Wilkes's reputation in America, see Maier, *From Resistance to Revolution*, pp. 161–79.

99. See Bell, *The First Total War*, pp. 53–78; Voltaire quoted in Lilti, p. 125.

100. George Washington to François-Jean de Beauvoir de Chastellux, April 25, 1788, in W. B. Allen, ed., *George Washington: A Collection* (Indianapolis: Liberty Fund, 1988), p. 395.

101. Immanuel Kant, *Kritik der Urteilskraft*, trans. and ed. Karl Vorländer (Leipzig: Felix Meiner, 1922), p. 109.

102. See on this subject, Bell, *The First Total War*, pp. 78–83; also Yuval Noah Harari, *The Ultimate Experience: Battlefield Revelations and the Making of Modern War Culture, 1450–2000* (London: Palgrave Macmillan, 2008).

103. On this subject, see especially Robert Morrissey, *The Economy of Glory: From Ancien Régime France to the Fall of Napoleon* (Chicago: University of Chicago Press, 2014).

104. François-Martin Poultier d'Elmotte, "Sur l'illustre Washington," *Almanach littéraire, ou Étrennes d'Apollon* (Paris: n.p., 1789), pp. 69–70.

105. Boswell, *An Account of Corsica* (1768), p. 351.

106. Although see Nancy Harding, Hugh Lee, Jackie Ford, and Mark Learmonth, "Leadership and Charisma: A Desire That Cannot Speak Its Name?" *Human Relations*, vol. 64, no. 7 (2011), pp. 927–49.

107. There has been a very large literature on this subject, going back to Eve Kosofsky Sedgwick, *Between Men: English Literature and Male Homosocial Desire* (New York: Columbia University Press, 2016). See also especially George Haggerty, *Men in Love: Masculinity and Sexuality in the Eighteenth Century* (New York: Columbia University Press, 1999); Kenneth Loiselle, *Brotherly Love: Freemasonry and Male Friendship in Enlightenment France* (Ithaca, NY: Cornell University Press, 2014).

108. Machiavelli notoriously wrote that it was better for monarchs to be feared than loved, and kings were routinely described as the "terror of their enemies." On this subject, see Ronald Schechter, *A Genealogy of Terror in Eighteenth-Century France* (Chicago: University of Chicago Press, 2018).

109. See especially Hunt, *Inventing Human Rights*.
110. See, for example, Lynn Hunt, "The Many Bodies of Marie Antoinette: Political Pornography and the Problem of the Feminine in the French Revolution," in Hunt, ed., *Eroticism and the Body Politic* (Baltimore: Johns Hopkins University Press, 1990), pp. 108–30; John T. Alexander, "Amazon Autocratrixes: Images of Female Rule in the Eighteenth Century," in Peter I. Barta, ed., *Gender and Sexuality in Russian Civilization* (London: Routledge, 2001), pp. 33–53; Anthony Cross, "Catherine II Through Contemporary British Eyes," pp. 55–65.
111. Boswell, *An Account of Corsica* (1768), p. 291.
112. Napoleon Bonaparte to Carlo Bonaparte (Buonaparte), September 12 or 13, 1784, in Napoleon Bonaparte and Fondation Napoléon, *Correspondance générale de Napoléon Bonaparte*, 12 vols. (Paris: Fayard and Fondation Napoléon, 2004), vol. I, p. 45; Fernand Ettori, "Pascal Paoli modèle du jeune Bonaparte," *Annales historiques de la Révolution française*, vol. 203 (1971), pp. 45–55, at p. 50; Aimé Dupuy, "Un inspirateur des juvenilia de Napoléon: L'Anglais James Boswell," *Bulletin de l'Association Guillaume Budé*, vol. 3 (1966), pp. 331–39, at pp. 337–38.
113. Bonaparte to Pascal Paoli, June 12, 1789, in Bonaparte, *Correspondance générale*, vol. I, p. 76.
114. Stendhal (Marie-Henri Beyle), *Vie de Napoléon, par Stendhal* (Paris: Calmann-Levy, 1877), p. 12.
115. *The Pennsylvania Ledger*, February 18, 1775, p. 3; *The Newport Mercury*, March 27, 1776, p. 1; *New England Chronicle; or, Essex Gazette*, March 14, 1776, p. 1 (the last with a slightly different quote).
116. *Maryland Journal and Baltimore Advertiser*, July 28, 1778, p. 4.
117. *The Norwich Packet and the Weekly Advertiser*, Thursday, July 27, 1780, p. 1, with reference to previous publication in *The New Jersey Journal*.

TWO: AMERICAN IDOL

1. The best account of this period is to be found in David Hackett Fischer, *Washington's Crossing* (New York: Oxford University Press, 2004); 10 percent figure on p. 5.
2. George Washington to Lund Washington, Harlem, September 30, 1776, in *The Papers of George Washington: Digital Edition*, at https://rotunda.upress.virginia.edu/founders/default.xqy?keys=GEWN-search-1-5&expandNote=on#match1, accessed October 20, 2018.
3. Quoted in Ron Chernow, *Washington: A Life* (New York: Penguin Press, 2010), p. 264.
4. Thomas Paine, *The Crisis*, December 23, 1776, at http://www.ushistory.org/paine/crisis/c-01.htm, accessed November 3, 2015.
5. *Henry V*, act 4, scene 1.
6. John Adams to Abigail Adams, October 8, 1776, in *The Adams Papers: Digital Edition*, at https://rotunda.upress.virginia.edu/founders/default.xqy?keys=ADMS-print-04-02-02-0096, accessed October 20, 2018.
7. Joseph Reed to Charles Lee, November 21, 1776, in *American Archives: Documents of the American Revolutionary Period, 1774–1776*, at http://amarch.lib.niu.edu/islandora/object/niu-amarch%3A104417, accessed November 3, 2015.
8. Charles Lee to Horatio Gates, December 13, 1776, in ibid., at http://amarch.lib.niu.edu/islandora/object/niu-amarch%3A104112, accessed November 3, 2015.
9. Admiral John Byng, court-martialed and shot in 1757 for failing to defend Minorca against the French, and Thomas-Arthur de Lally, tried for treason and decapitated in 1766 after losing Pondicherry to the British.
10. The essential works on the image of George Washington are Paul K. Longmore, *The Invention of George Washington* (Berkeley: University of California Press, 1988); Barry Schwartz, *George Washington: The Making of an American Symbol* (New York: Free Press, 1987); François Furstenberg, *In the Name of the Father: Washington's Legacy, Slavery, and the Making of a Nation* (New

York: Penguin Press, 2006); Wendy C. Wick, *George Washington, an American Icon: The Eighteenth-Century Graphic Portraits* (Washington, DC: Smithsonian Institution, 1982). For the advertisements, see, for instance, *The Virginia Gazette*, no. 1281, February 24, 1776, p. 3; *The Constitutional Gazette*, no. 74, April 13, 1776, p. 4; *The Pennsylvania Evening Post*, no. 184, March 28, 1776.

11. Chernow, p. 228; Longmore, p. 195.

12. Jonathan Mitchell Sewall, *Gen. Washington a New Favourite Song, at the American Camp: To the Tune of the British Grenadiers* (n.p., 1776).

13. Phillis Wheatley, *Complete Writings*, ed. Vincent Carretta (New York: Penguin, 2001), p. 90.

14. Quoted in Longmore, p. 201.

15. John Leacock, *The Fall of British Tyranny; or, American Liberty Triumphant, a Tragi-Comedy* (Philadelphia: Styner and Cist, 1776). See Francis James Dallett Jr., "John Leacock and the Fall of British Tyranny," *Pennsylvania Magazine of History and Biography*, vol. 78, no. 4 (1954), pp. 456–75; Sarah E. Chinn, *Spectacular Men: Race, Gender, and Nation on the Early American Stage* (New York: Oxford University Press, 2017).

16. *The Pennsylvania Evening Post*, January 21, 1777, p. 29.

17. "Honour, I Obey Thee!," *The Virginia Gazette*, January 24, 1777, p. 1. The article was widely reprinted. See, for instance, *The Freeman's Journal*, April 12, 1777, p. 1.

18. William Hooper to Robert Morris, Baltimore, February 1, 1777, in John Kaminski, ed., *George Washington: A Man of Action* (Madison: Wisconsin Historical Society Press, 2017), p. 9.

19. [Francis Hopkinson], "A New Catechism," in *The Pennsylvania Journal and the Weekly Advertiser*, no. 1777 (February 19, 1777), pp. 2–3.

20. Kathryn Gehred, "Did George Washington's False Teeth Come from His Slaves?: A Look at the Evidence, the Responses to That Evidence, and the Limitations of History," *Washington Papers*, October 19, 2016, at http://gwpapers.virginia.edu/george-washingtons-false-teeth-come-slaves-look-evidence-responses-evidence-limitations-history/, accessed November 13, 2018; Erica Armstrong Dunbar, *Never Caught: The Washingtons' Relentless Pursuit of Their Runaway Slave, Ona Judge* (New York: Simon & Schuster, 2017).

21. Quoted in Leland S. Person, *The Cambridge Introduction to Nathaniel Hawthorne* (Cambridge: Cambridge University Press, 2012), p. 100.

22. Gordon S. Wood, "The Greatness of George Washington," *Virginia Quarterly Review*, vol. 68, no. 2 (1992), p. 207.

23. Quoted in Colleen J. Shogan, "George Washington: Can Aristotle Recapture What His Countrymen Have Forgotten," in Ethan M. Fishman, William D. Pederson, and Mark J. Rozell, *George Washington: Foundation of Presidential Leadership and Character* (Westport, CT: Greenwood Publishing Group, 2001), p. 53.

24. Abigail Adams to John Adams, July 16, 1775, in *Adams Family Papers*, Massachusetts Historical Society, at https://www.masshist.org/digitaladams/archive/doc?id=L17750716aa, accessed November 4, 2015. The lines ("*she's* a temple . . .") come from Dryden's *Don Sebastian*, act 2, scene 1.

25. James Thacher, *A Military Journal During the American Revolutionary War* (Boston: Cottons and Barnard, 1827), p. 33 (July 20, 1775).

26. Ibid., p. 150 (October 1778).

27. Quoted in Schwartz, *George Washington*, p. 19. On Rush, see David Freeman Hawke, *Benjamin Rush, Revolutionary Gadfly* (Philadelphia: Ardent Media, 1971); Alyn Brodsky, *Benjamin Rush: Patriot and Physician* (New York: Truman Talley Books, 2004).

28. Lydia Minturn Post, *Personal Recollections of the American Revolution: A Private Journal*, ed. Sidney Barclay (New York: Rudd and Carleton, 1859), pp. 53–54. See also Schwartz, p. 19.

29. See Shovlin, "Selling American Empire"; Bell, *Cult of the Nation*, pp. 78–106.

30. See on this point especially Jack Rakove, *Revolutionaries: A New History of the Invention of America* (Boston: Houghton Mifflin Harcourt, 2010), pp. 112–56.

31. Adams to Rush, Quincy, March 19, 1812, in *Founders Online*, National Archives, at http:// founders.archives.gov/documents/Adams/99-02-02-5768, accessed November 8, 2015.

32. Adams to Rush, Quincy, November 11, 1807, in *The Gilder Lehrman Institute of American History*, at https://www.gilderlehrman.org/sites/default/files/inline-pdfs/T-00424.pdf, accessed November 8, 2015.

33. Adams to Benjamin Rush, Quincy, April 22, 1812, in *Founders Online*, National Archives, at http://founders.archives.gov/documents/Adams/99-02-02-5777, accessed November 8, 2015.

34. See Brendan McConville, *The King's Three Faces: The Rise and Fall of Royal America, 1688–1776* (Chapel Hill: University of North Carolina Press, 2006); Eric Nelson, *The Royalist Revolution: Monarchy and the American Founding* (Cambridge, MA: Harvard University Press, 2014); Louise Burnham Dunbar, *A Study of "Monarchical" Tendencies in the United States, from 1776 to 1801* (Urbana: University of Illinois Studies in the Social Sciences, 1922).

35. On toasting, see David Waldstreicher, "Rites of Rebellion, Rites of Assent: Celebrations, Print Culture, and the Origins of American Nationalism," *Journal of American History*, vol. 82, no. 1 (1995), pp. 37–61.

36. See Eran Shalev, *American Zion: The Old Testament as a Political Text from the Revolution to the Civil War* (New Haven, CT: Yale University Press, 2013), pp. 15–49; Robert P. Hay, "George Washington: American Moses," *American Quarterly*, vol. 21 (1969), pp. 780–91.

37. See McConville and Nelson.

38. See McConville, pp. 306–309.

39. On this subject, see Nathan Perl-Rosenthal, "The 'Divine Right of Republics': Hebraic Republicanism and the Debate over Kingless Government in Revolutionary America," *The William and Mary Quarterly*, vol. 66, no. 3 (2009), pp. 535–64.

40. Thomas Paine, *Common Sense; Addressed to the Inhabitants of America* (Philadelphia: W. and T. Bradford, 1776), pp. 19, 55.

41. "Oration Delivered at Boston, March 5, 1777, by Benjamin Hichborn, Esq.," in *Orations Delivered at the Request of the Inhabitants of the Town of Boston, to Commemorate the Evening of the Fifth of March, 1770* (Boston: Peter Edes, 1785), p. 87.

42. Quoted in Nelson, p. 182.

43. See Robert G. Parkinson, "Print, the Press, and the American Revolution," in *Oxford Research Encyclopedias: American History*, http://americanhistory.oxfordre.com/view/10.1093/acrefore /9780199329175.001.0001/acrefore-9780199329175-e-9, accessed November 19, 2018. See also the not-quite-complete list of revolutionary newspaper titles at https://www.readex.com /titlelists/early-american-newspapers-1690-1779, accessed November 19, 2018.

44. On the sales of *Common Sense*, see Trish Loughran, *The Republic in Print: Print Culture in the Age of U.S. Nation Building, 1770–1870* (New York: Columbia University Press, 2007), pp. 37–44.

45. *The Pennsylvania Evening Post*, February 13, 1776, p. 77.

46. Ambrose Serle to the Earl of Dartmouth, July 25, 1776, quoted in Parkinson, "Print, the Press, and the American Revolution."

47. On the birth of celebrity culture, see above all Lilti, pp. 39–121.

48. On Franklin's celebrity, see ibid., pp. 89–95.

49. See, for instance, *The London Chronicle*, October 24–26, 1775; *The Morning Post*, June 1, 1779; *The English Magazine*, August 1777; *Lloyd's Evening Post*, August 17, 1778; *The London Chronicle*, September 21–28, 1779. Many of these early texts are collected in William S. Baker, ed., *Early Sketches of George Washington, Esquire, Commander in Chief of the Armies of the United States of America* (Philadelphia: Lippincott, 1894). On British wartime views of Washington, see Troy O. Bickham, *Making Headlines: The American Revolution as Seen Through the British Press* (DeKalb: Northern Illinois University Press, 2009), p. 185.

50. It appeared as an appendix to Charles Henry Wharton's *A Poetical Epistle to His Excellency George Washington* (London: C. Dilly and J. Almon, 1780). The reference in this volume to a previous printing in Annapolis appears to be false. Wharton himself was English. The first American editions only followed in 1781.

51. Story about Martha Washington in *The London Packet*, reprinted in Frank Moore, ed., *Diary of the American Revolution from Newspapers and Original Documents*, 2 vols. (New York: Charles Scribner, 1860), vol. I, p. 201. Story about Washington's daughter in Bickham, p. 188. On the letters, see Worthington Chauncey Ford, ed., *The Spurious Letters Attributed to Washington* (Brooklyn: Privately printed, 1889); George Washington to Richard Henry Lee, Valley Forge, February 15, 1778, in *The Papers of George Washington*, https://founders.archives.gov/documents /Washington/03-13-02-0463, accessed November 14, 2018. For more, see Paul R. Misencik, *The Original American Spies: Seven Covert Agents of the Revolutionary War* (Jefferson, NC: Mc-Farland, 2014), p. 145. A French-language report had Washington betrayed by his loyalist lover: *Mercure historique et politique de Bruxelles*, March 31, 1777, p. 459.

52. See Bell, *The First Total War*, pp. 21–51.

53. See David Meschutt, "Life Portraits of George Washington," in Barbara J. Mitnick, ed., *George Washington: American Symbol* (New York: Hudson Hills Press, 1999), pp. 25–35.

54. See Chernow, p. 721. Wick, pp. 18–19, also discusses the images.

55. *Pennsylvania Journal and Weekly Advertiser*, August 28, 1776, p. 5.

56. Christopher Marshall, *Extracts from the Diary of Christopher Marshall*, ed. William Duane (Albany: Joel Munsell, 1877), p. 111 (January 5, 1777).

57. For instance, *New-York Gazette and Weekly Mercury*, February 3, 1777, p. 2; *The Philadelphia Gazette and Universal Daily Advertiser*, May 3, 1777, p. 2; *The London Packet; or, New Lloyd's Evening Post*, March 19, 1777, p. 1.

58. The remarks were not recorded in the terse *Journals of the Continental Congress* but rather in Benjamin Rush's diary. See Benjamin Rush, *A Memorial Containing Travels Through Life; or Sundry Incidents in the Life of Dr. Benjamin Rush* (Lanoraie, QC: Louis Alexander Biddle, 1905), p. 104.

59. *Constitution of the Commonwealth of Massachusetts* (1780), Part the First, article XXX.

60. See Longmore, p. 174; Chernow, p. 220.

61. Joseph J. Ellis, *His Excellency: George Washington* (New York: Vintage Books, 2005), p. 148.

62. On this subject, see, especially, Garry Wills, *Cincinnatus: George Washington and the Enlightenment* (Garden City, NY: Doubleday, 1984). Cincinnatus had the Roman title "dictator."

63. Ibid., p. 3.

64. See most recently Holger Hoock, *Scars of Independence: America's Violent Birth* (New York: Crown, 2017).

65. Quoted in Chernow, p. 305.

66. Benjamin Rush to John Adams, Reading, October 21, 1777, in *Founders Online*, at https:// founders.archives.gov/documents/Adams/06-05-02-0187, accessed November 21, 2018.

67. Cited in note from Continental Congress Intelligence Committee to George Washington, Philadelphia, September 2, 1777, in ibid., https://founders.archives.gov/documents/Washington /03-11-02-0121, accessed November 20, 2018.

68. "Thoughts of a Freeman," reproduced in annex to Henry Laurens to George Washington, Yorktown (PA), January 27, 1778, in ibid., https://founders.archives.gov/documents/Washington /03-13-02-0322, accessed November 20, 2018.

69. See, for instance, *The Pennsylvania Evening Post*, October 16, 1777, p. 499; *The Virginia Gazette*, October 17, 1777, p. 1.

70. John Williams Austin, March 5, 1778, in Kaminski, *George Washington*, p. 14.

71. Samuel Shaw to John Eliot, near Philadelphia, April 12, 1778, in ibid., p. 16.

72. *Song of Washington* (n.p., 1778).

73. Anthony Sharp, *Der gantz neue verbesserte Nord-Americanische Calendar auf das 1779ste Jahr Christi* (Lancaster: Francis Bailey, 1778).

74. Simon P. Newman, "Principles or Men? George Washington and the Political Culture of National Leadership, 1776–1801," *Journal of the Early Republic*, vol. 12, no. 4 (1992), pp. 477–507,

at p. 482; James Thomas Flexner and George Washington, *George Washington in the American Revolution, 1775–1783* (Boston: Little, Brown, 1968), p. 490.

75. Rush to Adams, Reading, October 21, 1777, in *Adams Family Papers*, http://www.masshist.org/publications/apde2/view?id=ADMS-06-05-02-0187, accessed November 8, 2015.

76. John Adams to Abigail Adams, York Town, October 26, 1777, in ibid., http://www.masshist.org/publications/apde2/view?id=ADMS-04-02-02-0289, accessed November 8, 2015.

77. Quoted in Hawke, *Benjamin Rush*, p. 231. The article mostly consisted of a blistering attack on the Congress.

78. Nathanael Greene to George Washington, Charleston, August 8, 1783, in *Founders Online*, https://founders.archives.gov/?q=greene%20washington%20adored&s=1111311111&sa=&r=2&sr=, accessed November 27, 2018.

79. *The Connecticut Journal*, December 12, 1781, p. 3.

80. See, for instance, *A Poem, Spoken Extempore, by a YOUNG LADY, on Hearing the Guns Firing and Bells Chiming* . . . (Boston: E. Russell, 1781); *A Poem Composed July 4, 1783, Being a Day of General Rejoicing, for the Happy Restoration of Peace and Independence to the United States of America* (n.p., 1783), unpaginated: "But most I adore Great Godlike WASHINGTON; . . ."; Philip Freneau, "To His Excellency George Washington," "On the Fall of Cornwallis," and "Verses Occasioned by General WASHINGTON's arrival in Philadelphia, on his way to his seat in Virginia, December, 1783," in Philip Freneau, *The Poems of Philip Freneau* (Philadelphia: Francis Bailey, 1786).

81. Kathleen Bartoloni-Tuazon, *For Fear of an Elective King: George Washington and the Presidential Title Controversy of 1789* (Ithaca, NY: Cornell University Press, 2014), pp. 44–45.

82. See, for instance, Josiah Meigs, *An Oration Pronounced Before a Public Assembly in New-Haven, On the 5th Day of November 1781, at the Celebration of the Glorious Victory over Lieutenant-General Earl Cornwallis* (New Haven, CT: Thomas and Samuel Green, 1782); John Murray, *Jerubbaal; or, Tyranny's Grove Destroyed and the Altar of Liberty Finished* (Newburyport: John Mycall, 1784); more generally, Ellis Sandoz, ed., *Political Sermons of the American Founding Era*, 2 vols. (Indianapolis: Liberty Fund, 1991); Bartoloni-Tuazon, pp. 35–43.

83. "A Moderate Whig," in Sandoz, ed., vol. I, p. 715.

84. Ezra Stiles, *The United States Elevated to Glory and Honor: A Sermon Preached Before His Excellency Jonathan Trumbull, Esq. L.L.D., Governor and Commander in Chief, May 8th, 1783* (New Haven, CT: Thomas & Samuel Green, 1783).

85. Quoted in Schwartz, *George Washington*, p. 42.

86. Murray, p. 37.

87. Ibid., pp. 43, 44.

88. Timothy Dwight, *The Conquest of Canaan* (Hartford: Elisha Babcock, 1785), pp. 4, 134.

89. Joel Barlow, *The Vision of Columbus* (Paris: English Press, 1793). The book would later be reworked into an even longer epic poem entitled *The Columbiad*.

90. Quoted in Gilbert Chinard and P. J. Conkwright, *George Washington as the French Knew Him* (Princeton, NJ: Princeton University Press, 1940), p. 40.

91. Charles-César Robin, *New Travels Through North America, in a Series of Letters* (Philadelphia: Robert Bell, 1783), p. 35.

92. Editor's note in *The Papers of George Washington*, from Gerard Vogels to George Washington, March 10, 1784, https://founders.archives.gov/documents/Washington/04-01-02-0148, accessed November 27, 2018.

93. Francisco de Miranda, *Colombeia*, 20 vols. (Caracas: Ediciones de la Presidencia de la Republica, 1978), vol. III, p. 103.

94. Editor's note in *The Papers of George Washington*, from Gerard Vogels to George Washington, March 10, 1784, https://founders.archives.gov/documents/Washington/04-01-02-0148, accessed November 27, 2018.

95. Louis-Edme Billardon de Sauvigny, *Vashington, ou La liberté du Nouveau Monde* (Paris: Maillard d'Orivelle, 1791). In general on the cult of Washington in France, see Chinard; Durand Echeverria, *Mirage in the West; A History of the French Image of American Society to 1815* (Princeton, NJ: Princeton University Press, 1957), especially pp. 98–143; Julia Osman, "Cincinnatus Reborn: The George Washington Myth and French Renewal During the Old Regime," *French Historical Studies*, vol. 38, no. 3 (2015), pp. 421–46.

96. For instance, *Gazette de Leyde*, September 30, 1777, quoted in Julia Osman, "Ancient Warriors on Modern Soil: French Military Reform and American Military Images in Eighteenth-Century France," *French History*, vol. 22, no. 2 (2008), p. 193. For the engravings, see Wick, pp. 18–19; medal in George Fuld, "Early Washington Medals," *American Journal of Numismatics*, vol. 14 (2002), pp. 105–63.

97. "General Washington auf der Reise: Eine ganz neue Anecdote," *Literatur und Völkerkunde*, vol. 6 (1785), p. 176. The same anecdote appeared the same year in France: "Affabilité du Général Washington," *Almanach littéraire ou Etrennes d'Apollon* (Paris: Laurent Jeune, 1785), p. 75.

98. Lucretia Wilhelmina van Winter, "Poem for George Washington," ed. H. A. Höweler, *Tijdschrift voor Nederlandse Taal-en Letterkunde*, vol. 52 (1933), pp. 70–77; *Washington en Necker* (Amsterdam: n.p., 1790).

99. Bickham, *Making Headlines*, pp. 185–205, quote from p. 189.

100. John Price to John Jay, Great Bourton, Oxfordshire, October 29, 1783, in Kaminski, p. 29.

101. Lafayette to the duc d'Ayen, Gulph, Pennsylvania, December 16, 1777, in Kaminski, p. 16.

102. Lafayette, quoted in Wick, p. xvi.

103. François-Jean de Beauvoir de Chastellux, *Voyages de M. le marquis de Chastellux dans l'Amérique septentrionale dans les années 1780, 1781 et 1782*, 2 vols. (Paris: Prault, 1786), vol. I, especially pp. 118–23. On Chastellux, see Fanny Varnum, *Un philosophe cosmopolite du XVIIIe siècle: Le chevalier de Chastellux* (Paris: Rodstein, 1936).

104. Honoré-Gabriel de Riqueti, comte de Mirabeau, *Considérations sur l'ordre de Cincinnatus, ou Imitation d'un pamphlet anglo-américain par le comte de Mirabeau* (London: J. Johnson, 1785), p. 305.

105. The translation, by Richard Price, appeared as *Reflections on the Observations on the Importance of the American Revolution, and the Means of Making It a Benefit to the World* (Philadelphia: T. Seddon, 1786), quotation on p. 3. For echoes, see Noah Webster, *Collection of Essays and Fugitive Writings* (Boson: I. Thomas and E. T. Andrews, 1790), p. 23; Edmund Bacon to George Washington, Augusta, Georgia, May 20, 1791, in *The Papers of George Washington*, https://founders.archives.gov/documents/Washington/05-08-02-0152, accessed November 28, 2018; anonymous letter included in Post, *Personal Recollections of the American Revolution*, p. 222; recollections of Washington's step-grandson quoted in Albanese, *Sons of the Fathers*, p. 150.

106. Freneau, "To His Excellency George Washington," p. 213. He had first mentioned Washington in verse in 1772 and praised him extensively in his 1775 poem "American Liberty."

107. Meigs, *An Oration*, p. 11.

108. On these debates, see Palmer, *The Age of the Democratic Revolution*, and David A. Bell, "The Atlantic Revolutions," in Motadel, *Waves of Revolutions*.

109. See Jean-Nicolas Démeunier, *L'Amérique indépendante, ou Les différentes constitutions des treize provinces qui se sont érigées en républiques sous le nom d'États-Unis de l'Amérique* (Ghent: P. F. de Goesin, 1790). Searches for quotations from the Declaration of Independence were conducted in the Gallica online database of French publications (gallica.bnf.fr) and the Stanford online database of French parliamentary debates (frda.stanford.edu), November 28, 2018.

110. See Lilti, pp. 89–95; Simon Schama, *Citizens: A Chronicle of the French Revolution* (New York: Alfred A. Knopf, 1989), pp. 42–45.

111. William R. Staples and Reuben Aldridge Guild, eds., *Rhode Island in the Continental Congress*

(Providence: Providence Press Company, 1870), p. 303. See also Philip Schuyler to Alexander Hamilton, Poughkeepsie, September 16, 1780, in *The Papers of Alexander Hamilton*, https:// rotunda.upress.virginia.edu/founders/default.xqy?keys=ARHN-search-1-7&expandNote =on#match1, accessed November 30, 2018.

112. Quoted in John C. Fitzpatrick, ed., *The Writings of George Washington from the Original Manuscript Sources, 1745–1799*, 39 vols. (Washington, DC: Government Printing Office, 1931), vol. 18, p. 211.

113. Quoted in Chernow, pp. 435–36. For contrasting views of the "Newburgh Conspiracy," see the exchange between C. Edward Skeen and Richard H. Kohn, "The Newburgh Conspiracy Reconsidered," *The William and Mary Quarterly*, vol. 31, no. 2 (1974), pp. 273–98. David Head's *A Crisis of Peace: George Washington, the Newburgh Conspiracy, and the Fate of the American Revolution* (New York: Pegasus Books, 2019) appeared too late for me to consult here.

114. Quoted in Wood, "The Greatness of George Washington," p. 197.

115. George Washington, "Circular to State Governments," June 8, 1783, http://founding.com /founders-library/american-political-figures/george-washington/circular-to-state-governments, accessed November 29, 2018.

116. Quoted in Chernow, p. 531.

117. On the ratification debates, see Pauline Maier, *Ratification: The People Debate the Constitution, 1787–1788* (New York: Simon & Schuster, 2010).

118. James Monroe to Thomas Jefferson, Fredericksburg, Virginia, July 12, 1788, in *Founders Online*, https://founders.archives.gov/documents/Jefferson/01-13-02-0256, accessed November 30, 2018.

119. Ibid.

120. An unnamed British correspondent sent the poem to John Adams in a letter dated March 2, 1786. *Adams Family Papers*, https://rotunda.upress.virginia.edu/founders/FOEA-03-01-02 -0547, accessed November 30, 2018. It subsequently appeared in the *Columbian Magazine* and the Charleston *City Gazette*. See John P. Kaminski and Jill Adair McCaughan, eds., *A Great and Good Man: George Washington in the Eyes of His Contemporaries* (Madison, WI: Madison House, 1989), p. 39.

121. Thomas Jefferson to Edward Carrington, Paris, May 27, 1788, in Kaminski, *George Washington*, p. 48.

122. Monroe to Jefferson, op. cit. On the poetry, see Bartoloni-Tuazon, p. 43.

123. This is the position, notably, of Gordon S. Wood. See Wood, "The Greatness of George Washington."

124. See T. H. Breen, *George Washington's Journey: The President Forges a New Nation* (New York: Simon & Schuster, 2016).

125. Newman, p. 482; Bartoloni-Tuazon, p. 51.

126. Bartoloni-Tuazon, p. 51; Breen, pp. 35–36. Breen says the laurel-dropper was a boy.

127. Breen, pp. 39, 113.

128. Ibid., p. 37.

129. Quoted in Bartoloni-Tuazon, p. 51. The passage is from Revelation 6:2.

130. Quoted in Schwartz, *George Washington*, p. 51.

131. Quoted in Breen, p. 37.

132. *The Salem Mercury*, November 3, 1789, p. 2.

133. Jedidiah Morse, *A True and Authentic History of His Excellency George Washington* (Philadelphia: n.p., 1790), p. 7.

134. Ibid., p. 8.

135. Thomas Thornton, "Ode on General Washington's Birth-Day," in ibid., p. 21.

136. "Letter Describing Washington's Visit to Salem in 1789," in *Historical Collections of the Essex Institute*, vol. 67 (1931), pp. 299–300. It is signed "N. Fisher." Breen (p. 122) describes her

only as an "obscure young woman." But the letter was written in Beverly and says that the brother had enjoyed seeing Washington "in a much higher degree" than she did, and Washington's own diary of the trip describes meeting in Beverly with the managers of the Cotton Manufactory there, including Joshua Fisher. See *Founders Online*, "October 1789," http://founders.archives.gov/documents/Washington/01-05-02-0005-0002, accessed November 30, 2018.

137. *The Roanoke Times*, January 24, 2016.

138. *A Monody in Honor of the Chiefs Who Have Fallen in the Cause of American Liberty, Spoken at the Theatre in Philadelphia, December 7, 1784* (Philadelphia: Thomas Bradford, 1784), p. 8.

139. Robert F. Haggard, "The Nicola Affair: Lewis Nicola, George Washington, and American Military Discontent During the Revolutionary War," *Proceedings of the American Philosophical Society*, vol. 146, no. 2 (2002), pp. 139–69. Haggard demonstrates that Nicola did not, as has often been thought, urge Washington to establish a monarchy in the United States itself.

140. Quoted in Bartoloni-Tuazon, p. 25.

141. Quoted in Breen, p. 34.

142. Chernow, p. 743.

143. Thomas Paine, "Letter to George Washington, 30 July 1796," in *The Writings of Thomas Paine*, ed. Moncure Daniel Conway, 4 vols. (New York: G. P. Putnam's Sons, 1894–1908), vol. 3, p. 252.

144. Chernow, pp. 686–87, 696.

145. Quoted in Sophia Rosenfeld, *Democracy and Truth: A Short History* (Philadelphia: University of Pennsylvania Press, 2019), p. 13.

146. See, especially, Gordon Wood, *The Radicalism of the American Revolution* (New York: Vintage, 1993).

147. On American newspapers in the 1790s, see Pettegree, p. 370.

148. On the "apotheosis of George Washington," see Furstenberg, pp. 25–70.

149. Quoted in ibid., p. 26.

150. *Washington Eulogies: A Checklist of Eulogies and Funeral Orations on the Death of George Washington* (New York: New York Public Library, 1916). See also James H. Smylie, "The President as Republican Prophet and King: Clerical Reflections on the Death of Washington," *Journal of Church and State*, vol. 18, no. 2 (1976), pp. 232–52.

151. Furstenberg, p. 26, and more generally pp. 25–30.

152. Quoted in ibid., p. 106.

153. On Weems, see ibid., pp. 105–46. Weems continued to revise the book, which only appeared in a definitive edition in 1809.

154. Mason Locke Weems, *The Life of George Washington: With Curious Anecdotes, Equally Honourable to Himself, and Exemplary to His Young Countrymen* (Philadelphia: Joseph Allen, 1837).

155. Ibid., p. 4.

156. Ibid., p. 49.

157. Ibid., pp. 82, 170.

158. Ibid., p. 5.

159. Ibid., p. 3.

THREE: WAITING FOR CAESAR IN FRANCE

1. See Félix Faulcon, *Mélanges législatifs, historiques et politiques*, 3 vols. (Paris: Henrichs, 1801), vol. 3, pp. 293–98; *Gazette nationale, ou Le moniteur universel*, February 4, 1800, p. 3. On the reception of Washington's death in France, see Bronislaw Baczko, *Politiques de la Révolution française* (Paris: Gallimard, 2008), pp. 535–693; Echeverria, *Mirage in the West*, pp. 253–55.

2. François-Xavier Pagès de Vixouse, *Histoire secrète de la Révolution française*, 3 vols. (Paris: Dentu, 1800), vol. III, p. 54.

3. Baczko, p. 607; Alphonse Aulard, *Paris sous le Consulat: Recueil de documents pour l'histoire de l'esprit public à Paris*, 4 vols. (Paris: Cerf, 1903), vol. 1, pp. 133–34; Fontanes, pp. 9–31.

4. Fontanes, p. 18. Bronislaw Baczko is wrong to interpret Fontanes's oration as republican. Fontanes himself was a noble who had been banished from France and owed his return to Bonaparte's patronage.

5. Ibid., p. 25.

6. Ibid., p. 31.

7. Emmanuel de Las Cases, *Le mémorial de Sainte-Hélène, par le comte de Las Cases*, 4 vols. (Paris: Garnier Frères, 1823), vol. 1, p. 308.

8. Germaine de Staël, *Considérations sur la Révolution française*, 2 vols. (Paris: Charpentier, 1862), vol. 2, p. 33; Benjamin Constant, *Mémoires sur les cent-jours* (Paris: Pauvert, 1961), p. 21; François-René de Chateaubriand, *Œuvres complètes*, 38 vols. (Paris: Desrez, 1837–41), vol. 2, p. 23; George Gordon, Lord Byron, "Ode to Napoleon Buonaparte," at http://www.bartleby .com/333/543.html, accessed December 9, 2015; Samuel Taylor Coleridge, "To the Editor of the Courier, Letter VI, December 21, 1809," in *Essays on His Own Times*, 3 vols. (London: William Pickering, 1850), vol. 2, pp. 644–47; José María Heredia, *Niágara y otros textos* (Caracas: Biblioteca Ayacucho, 1990), pp. 62–64.

9. Napoleon Bonaparte, *Œuvres littéraires et écrits militaires*, ed. Jean Tulard, 3 vols. (Paris: Claude Tchou, 2001), vol. 2, p. 227.

10. Louis-Antoine de Saint-Just, *Fragments sur les institutions républicaines*, ed. Charles Nodier (Paris: Techener, 1831), p. 30.

11. Anacharsis Cloots, *Appel au genre humain* (n.p., 1793), p. 12n.

12. Jacques-Bénigne Bossuet, *Politique tirée des propres paroles de l'ecriture sainte*, ed. Jacques Le Brun (Geneva: Droz, 1967), pp. 178–79; Keith Michael Baker, ed., *The Old Regime and the French Revolution* (Chicago: University of Chicago Press, 1987), p. 49.

13. On this subject, see Pierre Rosanvallon, *Good Government: Democracy Beyond Elections*, trans. Malcolm DeBevoise (Cambridge, MA: Harvard University Press, 2018), p. 33. The medieval fiction of the "king's two bodies"—one humanly fallible and frail, the other transcendentally majestic and undying, the two bound together by the magic of royal ritual—had been largely discarded by the eighteenth century, but the office of king remained widely seen as mystical and sacred.

14. Félix-Sébastien Feuillet de Conches, ed., *Louis XVI, Marie-Antoinette et Madame Élisabeth: Lettres et documents inédits*, 6 vols. (Paris: Plon, 1864–73), vol. 1, p. 82n.

15. On Louis, see John Hardman, *The Life of Louis XVI* (New Haven, CT: Yale University Press, 2016).

16. Quoted in Durand Echeverria, *The Maupeou Revolution: A Study in the History of Libertarianism: France, 1770–1774* (Baton Rouge: Louisiana State University Press, 1985), p. 32.

17. See, for instance, Pierre-Jean-Baptiste Nougaret, *Anecdotes du règne de Louis XVI*, 6 vols. (Paris: n.p., 1791), collecting earlier material. A well-known 1785 painting by Louis-Philibert Debucourt, showing the king giving alms to a poor family in Versailles, was engraved and widely distributed.

18. "Declaration des Droits de l'Homme et du Citoyen de 1789," in *Legifrance*, https://www .legifrance.gouv.fr/Droit-francais/Constitution/Declaration-des-Droits-de-l-Homme-et-du -Citoyen-de-1789, accessed December 13, 2018.

19. Quoted in Alphonse Aulard, *Les grands orateurs de la Révolution: Mirabeau, Vergniaud, Danton, Robespierre* (Paris: F. Rieder, 1914), p. 58.

20. *The Times* of London, July 16, 1794, p. 2.

21. Of the numerous biographies of Robespierre, see most recently Peter McPhee, *Robespierre: A Revolutionary Life* (New Haven, CT: Yale University Press, 2012) and Jean-Clément Martin,

Robespierre: La fabrication d'un monstre (Paris: Perrin, 2016). The most trenchant analysis of Robespierre's political role is Marcel Gauchet, *Robespierre: L'homme qui nous divise le plus* (Paris: Gallimard, 2018).

22. Weber, *Economy and Society*, vol. 2, p. 1209. Weber added that this glorification of reason "is the last form charisma has adopted in its fateful historical course."

23. *Archives parlementaires de 1787 à 1860: Recueil complet des débats législatifs et politiques des chambres françaises,* ed. Jérôme Maridal (Paris: Librairie administrative de Paul Dupont, 1879), vol. 9, pp. 79–83 (September 21, 1789). Robespierre did not actually deliver the speech but had it printed and distributed to the Assembly.

24. See Amy Freund, "The Legislative Body: Print Portraits of the National Assembly, 1789–1791," *Eighteenth-Century Studies*, vol. 41, no. 3 (2008), pp. 337–58; Lilti, *Figures publiques*, pp. 245–56.

25. Sigismond Lacroix, ed., *Actes de la commune de Paris pendant la Révolution*, 8 vols. (Paris: L. Cerf, 1894), vol. 6, p. 458. On Marat, see the forthcoming biography by Keith Michael Baker.

26. Jean-Paul Marat, *Œuvres de J. P. Marat*, ed. A. Vermorel (Paris: Décembre-Alonnier, 1869), e.g., pp. 155, 254.

27. Ibid., p. 61.

28. See Annie Jourdan, "L'éclipse d'un soleil: Louis XVI et les projets monumentaux de la Révolution," in Ian Germani and Robin Swales, eds., *Symbols, Myths and Images of the French Revolution: Essays in Honor of James A. Leith* (Regina: Canadian Plains Research Center, 1998), pp. 135–48.

29. See M. L. Batiffol, *Les journées des 5 et 6 octobre 1789 à Versailles* (Versailles: Aubert, 1891), pp. 72–73.

30. See, for instance, *Le triomphe de la nation, ou Louis XVI au milieu de son peuple* (Paris: n.p., 1789).

31. See on this subject Paul Friedland, *Political Actors: Representative Bodies and Theatricality in the Age of the French Revolution* (Ithaca, NY: Cornell University Press, 2002).

32. For instance, Marat, p. 97. See more generally Wolfgang Kruse, *Die Erfindung des modernen Militarismus: Krieg, Militär und Bürgerliche Gesellschaft im politischen Diskurs der französischen Revolution 1789–1799* (Munich: Oldenbourg, 2003), pp. 58–66.

33. Lafayette to Washington, Paris, August 23, 1790, *Founders Online*, https://founders.archives .gov/documents/Washington/05-06-02-0146, accessed January 3, 2019.

34. *Révolutions de Paris*, no. 115, September 17–24, 1791, p. 519.

35. Louis de la Vicomterie, *Les crimes des rois de France* (Paris: Adolphe Havard, 1834), p. 362. The book was originally printed in 1791, went through numerous editions during the Revolution, and was translated into English.

36. Maximilien Robespierre, *Discours de Maximilien Robespierre sur la guerre, prononcé à la société des amis de la constitution, le 2 janvier 1792* (Paris: Imprimerie Nationale, 1792), p. 38.

37. "Je suis peuple moi-même." Quoted in Gauchet, pp. 76, 82.

38. Quoted in ibid., p. 80.

39. Quoted in ibid., p. 84.

40. *Mercure universel*, April 13, 1791, p. 199.

41. Edmond-Louis-Alexis Dubois-Crancé, in Maximilien Robespierre, *Œuvres complètes de Maximilien Robespierre*, 11 vols. (Paris: Various publishers, 1910–2007), vol. 5, p. 132.

42. Maximilien Robespierre, *Plan d'éducation nationale de Michel Lepelletier* (Paris: Imprimerie Nationale, 1793).

43. Quoted in Geneviève Boucher, "Le héros robespierriste, entre l'incarnation du peuple et la victime sacrificielle," *PostScriptum.org*, vol. 10 (Autumn 2010), p. 1. The words echoed Matthew 23:12 and Luke 14:11.

44. On this period, a useful reference is still Robert R. Palmer, *Twelve Who Ruled: The Year of the Terror in the French Revolution* (Princeton, NJ: Princeton University Press, 1989 [1939]).

45. Bernard Vinot, *Saint-Just* (Paris: Fayard, 1985), p. 218.

46. Maximilien Robespierre, *Discours prononcé par Robespierre à la Convention nationale dans la séance du 8 thermidor* (Paris: Imprimerie Nationale, 1794), p. 15.

47. See, for instance, the History Channel documentary *The French Revolution*, dir. Doug Shultz (2005).
48. Colin Jones in McPhee, back cover.
49. Cited in Ernest Hamel, *Histoire de Robespierre d'après des papiers de famille, les sources originales et les documents entièrement inédits*, 3 vols. (Paris: A. Lacroix, 1865), vol. 2, p. 522.
50. Bertrand Barère, April 5, 1793, in *Archives parlementaires*, vol. 61, p. 343. On the use of the word "dictator" in the French Revolution, see Cesare Vetter, "Dictature: Les vicissitudes d'un mot. France et Italie (XVIII et XIX siècles)," Révolution-Française.net (2008), http://revolution -francaise.net/2008/03/01/212-dictature-vicissitudes-mot-france-italie-xviii-xix-siecles, accessed March 2, 2018.
51. Marat, 1790, in *Œuvres*, p. 90; Marat, September 25, 1792, in *Archives parlementaires*, vol. 52, p. 138.
52. Jean-Marie Roland de la Platière, September 30, 1792, in *Archives parlementaires*, vol. 52, pp. 235–36.
53. Jean-Baptiste Louvet de Coudrai, October 29, 1792, in *Archives parlementaires*, vol. 53, p. 53.
54. Bertrand Barère, November 5, 1792, in *Archives parlementaires*, vol. 53, p. 171; December 16, 1792, in *Archives parlementaires*, vol. 55, p. 85.
55. Many of these were found after his death: *Papiers inédits trouvés chez Robespierre, Saint-Just, Payan, etc., supprimés ou omis par Courtois* (Paris: Baudouin Frères, 1828).
56. See Louis Jacob, *Robespierre vu par ses contemporains* (Paris: Armand Colin, 1938), pp. 127–28; Hamel, vol. 3, p. 523.
57. Cited in Hamel, vol. 3, p. 524.
58. Ibid., p. 405. Englishman quoted in J. M. Thompson, *English Witnesses of the French Revolution* (Oxford: Blackwell, 1938), p. 254.
59. Saint-Just to Robespierre, August 19, 1790, in *Œuvres de Saint-Just, représentant du peuple à la Convention nationale* (Paris: Prévot, 1834), p. 359.
60. Saint-Just, *Fragments d'institutions républicaines*, p. 74.
61. Bertrand Barère, *Mémoires de Bertrand Barère*, eds. Hippolyte Carnot and Pierre-Jean David (d'Angers), 2 vols. (Paris: J. Labitte, 1842), vol. 2, pp. 214–55.
62. See Bronislaw Baczko, *Comment sortir de la Terreur: Thermidor et la Révolution* (Paris: Gallimard, 1989), pp. 15–56; Martin, *Robespierre*, pp. 240–61.
63. Étienne Barry, *Discours sur les dangers de l'idolâtrie individuelle dans une république* (n.p., 1794), pp. 3, 10–11.
64. See Howard G. Brown, *Ending the French Revolution: Violence, Justice, and Repression from the Terror to Napoleon* (Charlottesville: University of Virginia Press, 2006).
65. For instance, in the Bibliothèque Nationale de France's database of French Revolutionary en-gravings, two-thirds of those of Sieyès date from 1789–91, as opposed to the period of the Directory. frda.stanford.edu, accessed January 12, 2019.
66. Rafe Blaufarb, *The French Army 1750–1820: Careers, Talents, Merit* (Manchester: Manchester University Press, 2002), pp. 8–12.
67. T. C. W. Blanning, *The French Revolutionary Wars, 1787–1802* (London: Arnold, 1996), p. 126.
68. Of the plethora of Napoleon biographies, the most authoritative at present for the early period of Napoleon's life are Patrice Gueniffey, *Bonaparte, 1769–1802*, trans. Steven Rendall (Cam-bridge, MA: Harvard University Press, 2015), and Michael Broers, *Napoleon: Soldier of Destiny* (New York: Pegasus, 2014). See also my own *Napoleon: A Concise Biography* (New York: Oxford University Press, 2015). On the image of Napoleon, see especially Natalie Petiteau, *Napoléon: De la mythologie à l'histoire* (Paris: Seuil, 1999), and Annie Jourdan, *Napoléon: Héros, imperator, mécène* (Paris: Aubier, 1998).
69. On this side of Napoleon, see Andy Martin, *Napoleon the Novelist* (London: Polity, 2001).
70. Quoted in J. M. Thompson, *Napoleon Bonaparte* (Oxford: Blackwell, 1988), p. 37.
71. The campaign against popular "emotion" is noted by Guillaume Mazeau in "Émotions poli-tiques: La Révolution française," in Alain Corbin et al., *Histoire des émotions*, 3 vols. (Paris:

Seuil, 2016–17), vol. 2, p. 123. Mazeau misses the fact that the regime encouraged precisely such emotions in the patriotic context of military victory.

72. Cited in Alphonse Aulard, *Paris pendant la réaction thermidorienne et sous le Directoire*, 5 vols. (Paris: Léopold Cerf et al., 1898–1902), vol. 3, p. 749 (February 14, 1797), vol. 3, p. 780 (March 3, 1797).

73. *French Revolution Digital Archive*, https://frda.stanford.edu, accessed December 20, 2016.

74. *Épitre à Buonaparte* (Paris: Le Normant, 1796), pp. 3–4.

75. Quoted in Philip G. Dwyer, "Napoleon Bonaparte as Hero and Saviour: Image, Rhetoric and Behaviour in the Construction of a Legend," *French History*, vol. 18, no. 4 (2004), pp. 379–403, at p. 393.

76. Joseph Charron, *Discours prononcé à Châlons le 10 prairial an V, fête de la reconnaissance* (Châlons-sur-Marne: Mercier, 1797), p. 10.

77. Archives Nationales (France), AD VIII 25, no. 15: Jean-Louis Dubroca, *Discours sur divers sujets de morale et sur les fêtes nationales* (Paris: Dessessarts, 1798), p. 272. On Dubroca, see Albert Mathiez, *La théophilanthropie et le culte decadaire, 1796–1801* (Paris: Félix Alcan, 1903).

78. See L.-Henry Lecomte, *Napoléon et l'empire racontés par le théâtre, 1797–1899* (Paris: Jules Raux, 1900), pp. 2–47.

79. *Some Account of the Early Years of Buonaparte, at the Military School of Brienne; and of His Conduct at the Commencement of the French Revolution* (London: Hookham and Carpenter, 1797). See Peter Hicks, "Late 18th-Century and Very Early 19th-Century British Writings on Napoleon: Myth and History," *Napoleonica: La revue*, vol. 9 (2010), pp. 105–17.

80. *Épitre à Buonaparte*, p. 4.

81. Dubroca, *Discours*, p. 273.

82. *Journal de Bonaparte et des hommes vertueux* (1797).

83. Charron, p. 10.

84. Ibid., p. 11; *Épitre à Buonaparte*, p. 4.

85. *Le conservateur*, no. 313 (22 Messidor, Year VI, July 10, 1798), p. 2512.

86. Quoted in Aulard, *Paris pendant la réaction*, vol. 4, p. 253.

87. Quoted in Bell, *The First Total War*, p. 206.

88. Lucien Bonaparte to Joseph Bonaparte, June 24, 1792, in Frédéric Masson and Guido Biagi, eds., *Napoléon inconnu: Papiers inédits, 1786–1793*, 2 vols. (Paris: Ollendorff, 1895), vol. 2, p. 397.

89. André-François Miot de Melito, *Mémoires du comte Miot de Melito*, 2 vols. (Paris: Calmann-Lévy, 1873–4), vol. 1, p. 154.

90. *The Whitehall Evening Post*, July 6–8, 1797.

91. Quoted in Dwyer, "Napoleon Bonaparte as Hero and Saviour," p. 389. See also Wolfgang Kruse, "La formation du discours militariste sous le directoire," *Annales historiques de la Révolution française*, vol. 360 (2010), pp. 77–102.

92. On the propaganda in general, see Philip Dwyer, *Napoleon: The Path to Power* (New Haven, CT: Yale University Press, 2008), and Wayne Hanley, *The Genesis of Napoleonic Propaganda, 1796–1799* (New York: Columbia University Press, 2005).

93. On the painting, see especially Christopher Prendergast, *Napoleon and History Painting: Antoine-Jean Gros's La bataille d'Eylau* (Oxford: Oxford University Press, 1997), pp. 145–49.

94. See Miot de Melito, vol. 1, pp. 150–56; Dwyer, "Napoleon Bonaparte as Hero," pp. 390–92.

95. "A l'armée," 26 Messidor, Year V, July 14, 1797, in Napoléon Bonaparte, *Correspondance de Napoléon 1er, publiée par ordre de l'empereur Napoléon III*, 20 vols. (Paris: Imprimerie Impériale, 1858–60), vol. 3, p. 239 (no. 2010); *Le courrier de l'armée d'Italie*, no. 1 (July 20, 1797), p. 4.

96. Quoted in Philippe Roger, "Mars au Parnasse," in Jean-Claude Bonnet, ed., *L'empire des muses: Napoléon, les arts et les lettres* (Paris: Belin, 2004), p. 384.

97. In general, on Bonaparte's cultivation of his own soldiers, see Bell, *The First Total War*, pp. 196–99.

98. *Le courrier de l'armée d'Italie*, no. 48 (October 23, 1797), p. 206. The author was Marc-Antoine Jullien.

99. On the Egyptian expedition, see Juan Cole, *Napoleon's Egypt: Invading the Middle East* (New York: Palgrave Macmillan, 2007).

100. Quoted in Steven Englund, *Napoleon: A Political Life* (New York: Scribner, 2004), p. 157.

101. See Dwyer, "Napoleon Bonaparte as Hero," p. 395; Aulard, *Paris pendant la réaction thermidorienne et sous le Directoire*, vol. 5, p. 763.

102. See Nicole Gotteri, "L'esprit public à Paris avant le coup d'état de brumaire an VIII," in Jacques-Olivier Boudon, ed., *Brumaire: La prise de pouvoir de Bonaparte* (Paris: Éditions SPM, 2001), pp. 15–25.

103. Quoted in Aulard, *Paris pendant la réaction*, vol. 5, p. 763.

104. *Ami des lois*, quoted in ibid., p. 766.

105. Quoted in Jérémie Benoît and Bernard Chevallier, *Marengo: Une victoire politique* (Paris: Editions de la Réunion des Musées Nationaux, 2000), p. 79. On the coup in general, see Patrice Gueniffey, *Le dix-huit brumaire: L'épilogue de la Révolution française (9–10 novembre 1799)* (Paris: Gallimard, 2008).

106. de Staël, *Considérations sur la Révolution française*, vol. 2, p. 8.

107. See, for instance, the many variations quoted in Jourdan, *Napoléon*, pp. 109–14.

108. See especially the biography by Jean Tulard, *Napoléon, ou Le mythe du sauveur* (Paris: Fayard, 1983).

109. See Katia Sainson, "'Le Régénérateur de la France': Literary Accounts of Napoleonic Regeneration, 1799–1805," *Nineteenth-Century French Studies*, vol. 30, nos. 1–2 (2001–2002), pp. 9–25. The phrase "second founder" comes from an address to Bonaparte by French troops in *Le miroir de la France: Recueil historique, politique et littéraire*, no. 8 (Tübingen: Cotta, 1804), p. 85.

110. Jean-Louis Dubroca, *La vie de Bonaparte, depuis sa naissance jusqu'au 18 brumaire an X* (Paris: Dubroca, 1802). The English translation appeared as *Life of Bonaparte, First Consul of France* (London: G. and J. Robinson, 1802).

111. A. Lavant, *Éloge de Bonaparte* (Nîmes: B. Farge, 1800), p. 14.

112. Dubroca, *La vie de Bonaparte*, p. 7. The line about Washington was actually plagiarized from Pagès de Vixouse, *Histoire secrète*, p. 54.

113. Jean-Louis Dubroca, "Éloge de Washington," in Townsend, *Éloges funèbres*, pp. 33–72.

114. Charles-Antoine Saladin, *Coup d'oeil politique sur le continent* (Paris: Honnert, 1800), quote from p. 163. The work went through several editions. Much the same arguments were found in Joseph Balthazar Bonet de Treyches, *Tableau politique de la France régénérée* (Paris: Pillardeau, 1800).

115. *Parallèle entre César, Cromwel* [sic], *Monck* [sic] *et Bonaparte   fragment traduit de l'anglais* (Paris: n.p., 1800). On the pamphlet, see Thierry Lentz, "Vers le pouvoir héréditaire: Le 'parallèle entre César, Cromwell, Monck et Bonaparte' de Lucien Bonaparte," *Revue du souvenir napoléonien*, vol. 431 (2000), pp. 3–6.

116. *Parallèle*, p. 1.

117. Ibid., pp. 10–11.

118. Ibid., p. 12.

119. Fontanes, p. 25.

120. This analysis is indebted to Morrissey, *The Economy of Glory*.

121. *Journal de Paris*, July 30, 1807, p. 1490.

122. See the sensible analysis by Englund, in *Napoleon*, pp. 170, 235, and Claude Langlois, "Le plebiscite de l'an VIII, ou Le coup d'état du 18 pluviôse an VIII," *Annales historiques de la Révolution française*, vol. 207 (1972), pp. 43–65.

123. See Natalie Petiteau, *Napoléon Bonaparte: La nation incarnée* (Paris: Armand Colin, 2015), pp. 129–35, quote from p. 131.

124. See Sudhir Hazareesingh, *The Legend of Napoleon* (Cambridge: Granta, 2005); Jean-Lucas Dubreton, *Le culte de Napoléon, 1815–1848* (Paris: Albin Michel, 1960).

125. Alfred de Vigny, *Servitude et grandeur militaires* (Paris: F. Bonnaire and V. Magen, 1835), p. 309.

126. See Eugene (Evgeny) Tarle, *Napoleon's Invasion of Russia* (Oxford: Oxford University Press, 1942).

127. See Stuart Semmel, *Napoleon and the British* (New Haven, CT: Yale University Press, 2004).

128. Henry Redhead Yorke, *France in Eighteen Hundred and Two*, ed. J.A.C. Sykes (London: Heinemann, 1906), p. 119.

129. Antoine-Claire Thibaudeau, *Mémoires sur le Consulat par un ancien conseiller d'état* (Paris: Ponthieu, 1827), pp. 391–92.

130. Las Cases, *Mémorial de Sainte-Hélène*, vol. 3, p. 370. The remark "the state was me" of course played off Louis XIV's famous remark "l'état c'est moi." Italics in original.

131. See Lentz, p. 6.

132. See the collection of speeches in *Le miroir de la France*, no. 8.

133. Jean-Louis Dubroca, *Les quatre fondateurs des dynasties françaises* (Paris: Dubroca and Fantin, 1810).

134. Frank Bowman, "Napoléon et le Christ," *Europe*, vol. 480 (1969), p. 83.

135. See Sudhir Hazareesingh, *The Saint-Napoleon: Celebrations of Sovereignty in Nineteenth-Century France* (Cambridge, MA: Harvard University Press, 2004).

136. Weber, *Economy and Society*, vol. 2, pp. 1111–56.

137. Daniel Arenas, "Fuit Imperator: Towards a Critical Interpretation of the Malet Coup of October 23, 1812," paper presented at the Western Society for French History, Bozeman, Montana, October 4, 2019.

FOUR: THE SPARTACUS OF THE CARIBBEAN

1. Las Cases, *Mémorial de Sainte-Hélène*, vol. 2, pp. 522–24.

2. Some of these letters allegedly bore the salutation "from the first of the blacks to the first of the whites," but this is most likely a later invention. See François-Joseph Pamphile de Lacroix, *Mémoires pour servir à l'histoire de la Révolution de Saint-Domingue*, 2 vols. (Paris: Pillet aîné, 1819), vol. 2, p. 51.

3. Coleridge, "To the Editor of the Courier," December 21, 1809, in Coleridge, *Essays on His Own Times*, vol. 2, p. 647. See also, for similar remarks, Samuel Coleridge, "Letter to Mr. Fox," *The Morning Post*, November 9, 1802.

4. Quoted in Victor Schoelcher, *Vie de Toussaint Louverture* (Paris: Karthala, 1982 [1889]), p. 289.

5. On the "silencing" of the Haitian Revolution, see Michel-Rolph Trouillot, *Silencing the Past: Power and the Production of History* (Boston: Beacon Press, 2015).

6. David Patrick Geggus, "Toussaint Louverture and the Haitian Revolution," in *Profiles of Revolutionaries in Atlantic History, 1700–1850*, eds. R. William Weisberger, Dennis P. Hupchick, and David L. Anderson (Boulder: Social Science Monographs, 2007), pp. 115–35, at p. 116.

7. See Trevor Burnard and John Garrigus, *The Plantation Machine: Atlantic Capitalism in French Saint-Domingue and British Jamaica* (Philadelphia: University of Pennsylvania Press, 2016), pp. 43, 250; Laurent Dubois, *Avengers of the New World: The Story of the Haitian Revolution* (Cambridge, MA: Harvard University Press, 2004), pp. 39–40. In general on the Haitian Revolution, see also Carolyn E. Fick, *The Making of Haiti: The Saint Domingue Revolution from Below* (Knoxville: University of Tennessee Press, 1990).

8. See Burnard and Garrigus, pp. 51–54; François Regourd, "Lumières coloniales: Les Antilles françaises dans la république des lettres," *Dix-huitième siècle*, vol. 33 (2001), pp. 183–99 (material on mesmerism on p. 194).

9. *Affiches américaines*, July 24, 1784, p. 462.
10. See Laurent Dubois, "An Enslaved Enlightenment: Rethinking the Intellectual History of the French Atlantic," *Social History*, vol. 31, no. 1 (2006), pp. 1–14.
11. See Burnard and Garrigus, pp. 101–36.
12. On the Haitian Revolution, see above all Dubois, *Avengers of the New World*. On this early period, and the abolition of slavery in Saint-Domingue, see Jeremy D. Popkin, *You Are All Free: The Haitian Revolution and the Abolition of Slavery* (Cambridge: Cambridge University Press, 2010).
13. Robert Louis Stein, *Léger Félicité Sonthonax: The Lost Sentinel of the Republic* (Rutherford, NJ: Fairleigh Dickinson University Press, 1985), p. 21.
14. On the role of Spain in the revolution in Saint-Domingue, see Ada Ferrer, *Freedom's Mirror: Cuba and Haiti in the Age of Revolution* (Cambridge: Cambridge University Press, 2014).
15. The principal biographies of Toussaint Louverture have been C. L. R. James, *The Black Jacobins: Toussaint L'Ouverture and the San Domingo Revolution* (New York: Vintage Books, 1963); Pierre Pluchon, *Toussaint Louverture: Un révolutionnaire noir d'Ancien Régime* (Paris: Fayard, 1989); Madison Smartt Bell, *Toussaint Louverture: A Biography* (New York: Pantheon, 2007); Jacques de Cauna, *Toussaint Louverture: Le grand précurseur* (Bordeaux: Sud-ouest, 2012); Philippe R. Girard, *Toussaint Louverture: A Revolutionary Life* (New York: Basic Books, 2016); and Charles Forsdick and Christian Høgsbjerg, *Toussaint Louverture: A Black Jacobin in the Age of Revolutions* (London: Pluto Press, 2017). These have now been surpassed by Hazareesingh, *Black Spartacus*. See also the invaluable essay by David Geggus, "The Changing Faces of Toussaint Louverture: Literary and Pictorial Depictions," John Carter Brown Library (2013), http://www.brown.edu/Facilities/John_Carter_Brown_Library/exhibitions/toussaint/pages/historiography.html, accessed March 21, 2017. The principal guide to primary sources is the handwritten finding aid compiled by Joseph Boromé and available at the Schomburg Center, New York Public Library, Joseph Boromé Papers, MG 714, Box 2. This list has recently been digitized as a spreadsheet by Julia Gaffield, and I am grateful to her and Nathan Perl-Rosenthal for sharing it with me. See as well David A. Bell, "Haiti's Jacobin," *The Nation*, November 2, 2016.
16. On Laveaux, see Bernard Gainot, "Le général Laveaux, gouverneur de Saint-Domingue, député néo-jacobin," *Annales historiques de la Révolution française*, vol. 278 (1989), pp. 433–54; Paul Montailot, "Mayneaud de Laveaux," in *Mémoires de la Société éduenne*, vol. 39 (Autun: Dejussieu and Demasy, 1911), pp. 73–86.
17. "Le bienheureux Claude Mayneaud de Bisefrance," http://paroissedigoin7116.wixsite.com/paroissedigoin/bienheureux-claude-sylvain-martyr, accessed March 21, 2017.
18. Quoted in Schoelcher, p. 94. On the "Proclamation of Camp Turel," see Girard, p. 137.
19. The original manuscript correspondence from the Bibliothèque Nationale de France is now online at http://www.patrimoines-martinique.org/ark:/35569/a0113504825123aLaGx/1/1, accessed March 17, 2017. There are two printed editions: Gérard M. Laurent, ed., *Toussaint Louverture à travers sa correspondance, 1794–1798* (Madrid: Industrias Gráficas, 1953), and Antonio Maria Baggio and Ricardo Augustin, eds., *Toussaint Louverture, Lettres à la France, 1794–1798: Idées pour la libération du peuple noir d'Haïti* (Bruyères-le-Châtel: Nouvelle Cité, 2011).
20. Louverture to Laveaux, July 19, 1794, in Laurent, p. 121.
21. See David Geggus, "The 'Volte-Face' of Toussaint Louverture," in Geggus, *Haitian Revolutionary Studies* (Bloomington: Indiana University Press, 2002), pp. 119–36.
22. Quoted in Gainot, "Le général Laveaux," p. 442.
23. Quoted in Pamphile de Lacroix, vol. 1, p. 404.
24. See, for instance, Michel-Etienne Descourtilz, *Voyages d'un naturaliste, et ses observations faites sur les trois règnes de la nature, dans plusieurs ports de mer français*, 3 vols. (Paris: Dufart, 1809), vol. 3, p. 245. On this issue, see Deborah Jenson, "Toussaint Louverture, Spin Doctor?

Launching the Haitian Revolution in the French Media," in Doris Garraway, ed., *Tree of Liberty: Cultural Legacies of the Haitian Revolution in the Atlantic World* (Charlottesville: University of Virginia Press, 2008), pp. 41–62; John Patrick Walsh, *Free and French in the Caribbean: Toussaint Louverture, Aimé Césaire and Narratives of Loyal Opposition* (Bloomington: Indiana University Press, 2013), pp. 80–98; Philippe R. Girard, "Quelle langue parlait Toussaint Louverture?: Le *Mémoire* du Fort de Joux et les origines du kreyòl haïtien," *Annales: Histoire, Sciences Sociales*, vol. 68, no. 1 (2013), pp. 107–30.

25. Pamphile de Lacroix, vol. 2, p. 206.
26. Quoted in Gainot, "Le général Laveaux," p. 442n.
27. Louverture to Laveaux, August 31, 1795, and December 7, 1795, in Laurent, p. 250.
28. Louverture to Laveaux, October 20, 1795, in ibid., p. 241.
29. Louverture to Laveaux, March 18, 1796, in ibid., pp. 347–48.
30. See Gainot, "Le général Laveaux," pp. 443–44. Laveaux himself recounted the incident at length in Étienne Laveaux, *Compte rendu par le général Laveaux à ses concitoyens, à l'opinion publique, aux autorités constituées* (Paris: Imprimerie du Bureau Central d'Abonnement à tous les Journaux, 1797), pp. 76–88. See also Henry Perroud, *Précis des derniers troubles qui ont eu lieu dans la partie du nord de Saint-Domingue* (Le Cap Français: P. Roux, 1796).
31. This incident is recounted in Thomas Madiou, *Histoire d'Haiti*, 3 vols. (Port-au-Prince: J. Courtois, 1847), vol. 1, p. 237.
32. Madiou, vol. 1, p. 359; Gainot, "Le général Laveaux," p. 443. The abbé Raynal was the principal compiler of a massive—and massively popular—work about European overseas expansion, which, in one passage, predicted the coming of a black Spartacus who would free his people.
33. Louverture to Laveaux, April 10, 1796, in Laurent, p. 366.
34. Louverture to Laveaux, August 31, 1796, in ibid., p. 427.
35. Louverture to Laveaux, August 31, 1796, in ibid., p. 428.
36. Pluchon, *Toussaint Louverture*, p. 173; Frédéric Régent, *La France et ses esclaves: De la colonisation aux abolitions (1620–1848)* (Paris: Grasset, 2007), p. 255. Sonthonax had left Saint-Domingue in 1794 but returned as a member of a new civil commission in 1796.
37. Laveaux to Louverture, December 11, 1796, quoted in Schoelcher, p. 184.
38. Louverture to Laveaux, May 23, 1797, in Laurent, p. 433.
39. See, notably, Dena Goodman, *Becoming a Woman in the Age of Letters* (Ithaca, NY: Cornell University Press, 2009).
40. David Patrick Geggus, *The Haitian Revolution: A Documentary History* (Indianapolis: Hackett, 2014), p. 128. Other black commanders, while fighting for Spain, had called their Spanish commanders "godfather." See Ferrer, p. 141.
41. Louverture to Laveaux, March 18, 1796, in Laurent, pp. 347–48.
42. Geggus, "Toussaint Louverture and the Haitian Revolution," p. 116.
43. Girard, *Toussaint Louverture*, pp. 195–96.
44. See Hazareesingh, *Black Spartacus*, p. 75.
45. Pamphile de Lacroix, vol. 1, p. 408.
46. Charles-Humbert Vincent, *Du seul parti à prendre à l'égard de Saint-Domingue* (Paris: Delaunay and Pelicier, 1819), p. 55.
47. Philippe-Rose Roume de Saint-Laurent, "Moyens proposés au gouvernement français par son agent à Saint-Domingue pour la réorganisation de cette colonie, sans recourir aux voies de rigueur," 22 prairial an VIII, June 11, 1800, Archives Nationales d'Outre-Mer (Aix-en-Provence), CC9B2.
48. On this subject, see especially Julius S. Scott, *The Common Wind: Afro-American Currents in the Age of the Haitian Revolution* (London: Verso, 2018). See also Geggus, *The Haitian Revolution*, p. 188.
49. See Manuel Covo, "Baltimore and the French Atlantic: Empires, Commerce and Identity in a Revolutionary Age, 1783–1798," in A. B. Leonard and David Pretel, eds., *The Caribbean and*

the Atlantic World Economy: Circuits of Trade, Money and Knowledge, 1650–1914 (New York: Palgrave Macmillan, 2015), pp. 87–107, at p. 98.

50. Both letters appeared in the *Gazette nationale, ou Le moniteur universel*, no. 310, July 28, 1796, pp. 1238–39. English translation in *The Oracle and Public Advertiser*, August 2, 1796, no. 1938. American coverage in *Le courrier français*, May 10, 1796, and *The Independent Gazeteer*, May 14, 1796.

51. Quoted in *The Telegraph* (London), December 6, 1796, p. 2.

52. Letter reprinted in *The Morning Chronicle* (London), June 19, 1797, p. 2.

53. Laveaux, *Compte rendu*, p. 59. Italics in original.

54. See Gainot, "Le général Laveaux," pp. 446–47.

55. Vincent-Marie Viénot-Vaublanc, *Discours sur l'état de Saint-Domingue et sur la conduite des agens du Directoire* (Paris: Imprimerie Nationale, 1797), especially pp. 14–17, 28. See also Pluchon, *Toussaint Louverture*, pp. 179–80.

56. Étienne Laveaux, *Réponse d'Étienne Laveaux, général de division, ex-gouverneur de St.-Domingue, aux calomnies que le citoyen Viénot Vaublanc, colon de St. Domingue et membre du Conseil des Cinq Cents s'est permis de mettre dans son discours prononcé dans la séance du 10 prairial dernier* (Paris: J. F. Sobry, 1797), p. 15; Étienne Laveaux, *Discours prononcé par C. Lavaux, député de Saint-Domingue* (Paris: Imprimerie Nationale, 1797), p. 7. See also Marie Jacobie-Sophie de Laveaux, *Réponse aux calomnies coloniales de Saint-Domingue: L'épouse du républicain Lavaux, gouverneur-général (par intérim) des isles françaises sous le vent, à ses concitoyens* (Paris: Imprimerie de Pain, 1797).

57. On Louverture's reaction, see Hazareesingh, *Black Spartacus*, p. 119.

58. Toussaint Louverture, *Réfutation de quelques assertions d'un discours prononcé au corps législatif le 10 prairial, an cinq, par Viénot Vaublanc* (Le Cap Français: n.p., 1797), pp. 5, 18, 25.

59. See Hazareesingh, *Black Spartacus*, p. 123.

60. Quoted in Marcel Dorigny, *Léger-Félicité Sonthonax: La première abolition de l'esclavage: La Révolution française et la révolution de Saint-Domingue* (Paris: Société française d'histoire d'outre-mer, 1997), p. 102n.

61. Vincent, p. 55.

62. Quoted in Hazareesingh, *Black Spartacus*, p. 209.

63. See the biographies cited above by James, Pluchon, Bell, Girard, and Hazareesingh.

64. Toussaint Louverture, *Mémoires du général Toussaint Louverture*, Daniel Desormeaux, ed. (Paris: Classiques Garnier, 2011).

65. Joseph Allen Prince, *Toussaint Louverture: Anthologie poétique*, 2 vols. (Paris: Publibook, 2013), vol. 1, p. 79. In this context "red" referred to people of mixed race.

66. See on this subject Deborah Jenson, "Toussaint Louverture, Spin Doctor?" and Deborah Jenson, *Beyond the Slave Narrative: Politics, Sex, and Manuscripts in the Haitian Revolution* (Liverpool: Liverpool University Press, 2011).

67. Gabriel Le Gros, *An Historick Recital of the Different Occurrences in the Camps of Grande-Riviere, Dondon, Sainte-Suzanne, and Others, from the 26th of October 1791, to the 24th of December, of the Same Year* (Baltimore: John and Samuel Adams, 1792). The work appeared in France and Saint-Domingue the next year. See Ashli White, *Encountering Revolution: Haiti and the Making of the Early Republic* (Baltimore: Johns Hopkins University Press, 2010), pp. 156–57.

68. Charles-Humbert Vincent, "Précis sur l'état actuel de la colonie de Saint-Domingue" (November 1799), manuscript report in Archives Nationales d'Outre-Mer, CC9A22, "Rapports de divers sur Saint-Domingue."

69. "Extract of a Letter from Cape-François," *The Philadelphia Gazette and Universal Daily Advertiser*, March 12, 1799, p. 3; *The Independent Gazeteer*, May 14, 1796.

70. "Character of the Celebrated Black General Toussaint L'Ouverture," *American Intelligencer*, June 11, 1801, p. 1.

71. Quoted in Pluchon, *Toussaint Louverture*, p. 144.

72. Pierre Pluchon, "Toussaint Louverture d'après le général de Kerversau," in *Toussaint Louverture et l'indépendance de Haïti*, Jacques de Cauna, ed. (Paris: Karthala, 2004), at p. 168.

73. Prince, vol. 2, p. 124.

74. Perroud, p. 14.

75. Vincent, *Du seul parti à prendre*, p. 55; Vincent, "Précis." On Vincent, see Christian Schneider, "Le colonel Vincent, officier du génie à Saint-Domingue,"*Annales historiques de la Révolution française*, no. 329 (2002), pp. 101–22.

76. "Mémoire secret," possibly by Henri Pascal, in New York Public Library, Schomburg Center for Research in Black Culture, Kurt Fisher Haitian Collection, Microfilm 2228, Reel 8.

77. Charles Leclerc, ed., *Lettres du général Leclerc: Commandant en chef de l'armée de Saint-Domingue en 1802* (Paris: Leroux, 1937), p. 118.

78. Quoted in Pluchon, "Toussaint Louverture d'après le général de Kerversau," p. 162.

79. Pamphile de Lacroix, vol. 1, pp. 303, 348.

80. Ibid., p. 405.

81. Vincent, p. 55.

82. Quoted in Stein, *Léger Félicité Sonthonax*, p. 154.

83. See on this subject Pratima Prasad, *Colonialism, Race, and the French Romantic Imagination* (New York: Routledge, 2009), pp. 109–19.

84. Germaine de Staël, "Mirza, ou Lettre d'un voyageur," in *Œuvres complètes de madame la baronne de Staël-Holstein*, 3 vols. (Paris: Firmin-Didot, 1871), vol. 1, pp. 72–78, quote from p. 73.

85. Philippe-Albert de Lattre, *Campagnes des Français à Saint-Domingue, et réfutation des reproches faits au capitaine-général Rochambeau* (Paris: Locard, 1805), p. 46.

86. Toussaint Louverture, *Extrait du rapport adressé au Directoire exécutif par le citoyen Toussaint Louverture, général en chef des forces de la République française à Saint-Domingue* (Le Cap Français: P. Roux, 1797).

87. Speech to the soldiers of the army, May 11, 1797, in *Bulletin officiel de Saint-Domingue*, 29 Floréal, Year V (May 18, 1797); in *Greenleaf's New York Journal*, June 17, 1797, p. 2; *Argus* (London), June 17, 1797; *Charleston Gazette and Daily Advertiser*, July 8, 1797 (*Argus* and *Charleston Gazette* cited in the Joseph Boromé Finding Aid). Quotes are from *Greenleaf's New York Journal*.

88. See Hazareesingh, *Black Spartacus*, p. 259.

89. New York Public Library, Schomburg Center for Research in Black Culture, Kurt Fisher Haitian Collection, Microfilm 2228, Reel 5.

90. *Gazette nationale, ou Le moniteur universel*, no. 110, 20 Nivôse, Year VII (January 9, 1799), p. 448; *Gazette nationale, ou Le moniteur universel*, no. 121, 1 Pluviôse, Year VII (January 20, 1799), p. 492.

91. "Au rédacteur," *Gazette nationale, ou Le moniteur universel*, no. 135, 15 Pluviôse, Year VII (February 3, 1799), p. 555. The name of the author is not given, but it is clearly Bayon.

92. *The Annual Register; or, A View of the History, Politics, and Literature for the Year 1802* (London: Wilks, 1803), p. 211.

93. See Geggus, "The Changing Faces of Toussaint Louverture."

94. "Copy of a Letter from a Gentleman in St. Domingo, to the Editors of This Gazette," *The Commercial Register*, Norfolk, Virginia, October 18, 1802, p. 2.

95. Thomas Jefferson to Aaron Burr, Philadelphia, February 11, 1799, in *Founders Online*, https://founders.archives.gov/documents/Jefferson/01-31-02-0015, accessed July 23, 2019.

96. "Extract of a Letter from Cape-François," *The Philadelphia Gazette and Universal Daily Advertiser*, March 12, 1799, p. 3.

97. "Character of the Celebrated Black General Toussaint L'Ouverture." On this subject see Michael J. Drexler and Ed White, "The Constitution of Toussaint: Another Origin of African-American Literature," in *A Companion to African-American Literature*, Gene Andrew Jarrett, ed. (Chichester, U.K.: Wiley-Blackwell, 2010), pp. 59–74.

98. Quoted in James Alexander Dun, *Dangerous Neighbors: Making the Haitian Revolution in Early America* (Philadelphia: University of Pennsylvania Press, 2016), p. 149. See also White, *Encountering Revolution*.

99. See Ashli White, "The Materiality of the Haitian Revolution in the Atlantic World," *Proceedings of the American Philosophical Society*, forthcoming. I am grateful to Professor White for sharing a pre-publication copy of the article with me.

100. See David Patrick Geggus, "British Opinion and the Emergence of Haiti, 1791–1805," in *Slavery and British Society, 1776–1846*, James Walvin, ed. (Baton Rouge: Louisiana State University Press, 1982), pp. 123–50.

101. *The Annual Register; or, A View of the History, Politics and Literature for the Year 1798* (London: Burton, 1800), p. 249.

102. C. L. R. James used this quote as an epigraph to his book *The Black Jacobins*, but unfortunately misattributed it. The first appearance of it I have found is in *The St. James's Chronicle*, November 29–December 1, 1798, where it is attributed to "an opposition newspaper." Versions of the same article appeared in *Lloyd's Evening Post*, November 30–December 3, 1798, *E. Johnson's British Gazette and Sunday Monitor*, December 2, 1798, and *The Star*, December 1, 1798. In the United States it appeared in *Gazette of the United States*, February 1, 1799; *Aurora*, February 2, 1799, and again in *Gazette of the United States*, August 22, 1799.

103. Coleridge, "Letter to Mr. Fox"; William Wordsworth, "To Toussaint Louverture," originally published in *The Morning Post*, February 2, 1803.

104. Jean-Louis Dubroca, *La vie de Toussaint-Louverture, chef des noirs insurgés de Saint-Domingue; contenant son origine, les particularités les plus remarquables de sa jeunesse* (Paris: Dubroca, 1802), p. 44.

105. René Périn, *L'incendie du Cap, ou Le règne de Toussaint-Louverture* (Paris: Chez les Marchands de Nouveautés, 1802), p. 133.

106. Marcus Rainsford, *St. Domingo; or, An Historical, Political and Military Sketch of the Black Republic, with a View of the Life and Character of Toussaint L'Ouverture* (London: R. B. Scott, 1802); Marcus Rainsford, *An Historical Account of the Black Empire of Hayti*, Paul Youngquist and Grégory Pierrot, eds. (Durham, NC: Duke University Press, 2013).

107. Rainsford, *An Historical Account of the Black Empire of Hayti*, pp. 145, 153.

108. Ibid., p. 157.

109. See Youngquist and Pierrot's Introduction to Rainsford, and Grégory Pierrot, "'Our Hero': Toussaint Louverture in British Representations," *Criticism*, vol. 50, no. 4 (2008), pp. 581–607; also Susan Buck-Morss, *Hegel, Haiti and Universal History* (Pittsburgh: University of Pittsburgh Press, 2009), pp. 43–44.

110. *Toussaint-Louverture's frühere Geschichte nach englischen nachrichten bearbeitet* (Fürth: Im bureau für litteratur, 1802).

111. Ibid., pp. 87–88. The book was widely noticed in Germany. A version was reprinted in *Archiv für Geographie, Historie, Staats- und Kriegskunst*, September 16 and 19, 1814, pp. 465–67; September 21, pp. 477–80; September 28, pp. 484–88. Another version appeared in *Annalen menschlicher Grösse und Verworfenheit*, 2 vols. (Leipzig: Johann Friedrich Hartknoch, 1804), vol. 1, p. 76. Reviews appeared in *Kaiserlich privilegirter Reichs-Anzeiger*, September 22, 1802, p. 3212, and in *Intelligenzblatt der Zeitung für die elegante Welt*, August 14, 1802, p. 1. On Hegel and Haiti, see Buck-Morss.

112. James Stephen, *Buonaparte in the West Indies; or, The History of Toussaint Louverture, the African Hero*, 3 vols. (London: J. Hatchard, 1803), vol. 1, p. 2.

113. See Geggus, "The Changing Faces of Toussaint Louverture."

114. Quoted in Rainsford, *An Historical Account*, p. xl.

115. Pradt, *Les trois âges des colonies*, p. 103; *The Annual Register* (1802), p. 211.

116. "Haïtiade" in Doris Y. Kadish and Deborah Jenson, eds., Norman R. Shapiro, trans., *Poetry of Haitian Independence* (New Haven, CT: Yale University Press, 2015), p. 122.

117. Quoted in Isabell Lammel, *Der Toussaint-Louverture-Mythos: Transformationen in der französischen Literatur, 1791–2012* (Bielefeld: Transcript Verlag, 2015), p. 13.

118. *Toussaint-Louverture's frühere Geschichte*, p. ix.

119. Rainsford, *An Historical Account*, 156; Stephen, vol. 1, p. 4.

120. Stephen, p. 28.

121. Pamphile de Lacroix, vol. 1, pp. 404–405.

122. Quoted in George F. Tyson Jr., *Toussaint Louverture* (Englewood Cliffs, NJ: Prentice-Hall, 1973), p. 56.

123. Quoted in Hazareesingh, *Black Spartacus*, p. 189.

124. Girard, *Toussaint Louverture*, p. 217; Decourtilz, p. 247; Claude Moïse, *Le projet national de Toussaint Louverture et la Constitution de 1801* (Port-au-Prince: Editions Mémoire, 2001), pp. 22–27; Philippe R. Girard, *The Slaves Who Defeated Napoleon: Toussaint Louverture and the Haitian War of Independence, 1801–1804* (Tuscaloosa: University of Alabama Press, 2011), pp. 14–15; Hazareesingh, *Black Spartacus*, p. 228.

125. Madiou, vol. 1, p. 307.

126. Louverture to Laveaux, May 22, 1798, in Laurent, p. 442.

127. Letter from unknown official to the Directory, June 30, 1800, Archives Nationales d'Outre-Mer, CC9B9.

128. Vincent, p. 56.

129. Quoted in Dubois, *Avengers of the New World*, p. 255.

130. Thibaudeau, *Mémoires sur le Consulat*, p. 120.

131. Quoted in Pierre Branda and Thierry Lentz, *Napoléon, l'esclavage et les colonies* (Paris: Fayard, 2006), p. 117.

132. See Yves Bénot, *La démence coloniale sous Napoléon* (Paris: La Découverte, 1992). Bénot argues that Bonaparte intended a full-scale reestablishment of the colonial regime from the start, while Branda and Lentz suggest that his actions were mainly dictated by pragmatic geopolitical considerations.

133. Quoted in Girard, *The Slaves Who Defeated Napoleon*, p. 4.

134. On Dessalines and Louverture, see Hazareesingh, *Black Spartacus*, p. 38. On Dessalines as a savior, see, for instance, "Hymme Haytienne," in Kadish, Jenson, and Shapiro, p. 2; Carlo Celius, "Neoclassicism and the Haitian Revolution," in Norman Fiering and David Geggus, eds., *The World of the Haitian Revolution* (Bloomington: Indiana University Press, 2009), pp. 352–92; Robert Fatton Jr., *The Roots of Haitian Despotism* (Boulder, CO: Lynne Rienner, 2007).

135. *Armée indigene* (Port-au-Prince, [1804]), pp. 6, 8.

136. On this subject, see above all Dubois, *The Aftershocks of History*.

137. In Celius, and see figure 18.

138. See Dubois, *The Aftershocks of History*.

139. *The St. James's Chronicle*, November 29–December 1, 1798, and see other printings of the article referred to above.

140. Quoted in Pluchon, "Toussaint Louverture d'après le général de Kerversau," p. 169. Italics in the original.

FIVE: LIBERATOR AND DICTATOR

1. The fundamental work on Bolívar in Haiti remains Verna, *Pétion y Bolívar*. See also the important article by Sybille Fischer, "Bolívar in Haiti: Republicanism in the Revolutionary Atlantic," in *Haiti and the Americas*, eds. Carla Calarge, Rafael Dalleo, Luis Duno-Gottberg, and Clevis Headley (Jackson: University Press of Mississippi, 2013), pp. 25–53.

2. See Verna, pp. 192–221.

3. See, for instance, the "Discurso de Angostura" of February 15, 1819, in Simón Bolívar, *Doc-*

trina del Libertador, ed. Manuel Pérez Vila (Caracas: Biblioteca Ayacucho, 1976), pp. 101–27. Also Bolívar's notorious letter to Francisco Paula Santander, Magdalena (Peru), July 8, 1826, in the online *Archivo del Libertador*, http://www.archivodellibertador.gob.ve/escritos/buscador /spip.php?article3318, accessed February 15, 2019, and his remarks to the British officer Thomas Malling in José María Rojas, *Tiempo perdido* (Paris: Garnier, 1905), p. 9.

4. See on this issue Michael Zeuske, *Simón Bolívar: History and Myth*, trans. Steven Rendall and Lisa Neal (Princeton, NJ: Markus Wiener, 2013).

5. The following analysis is indebted to Fischer's "Bolívar in Haiti."

6. See John Lynch, "Bolívar and the Caudillos," in *Latin America Between Colony and Nation: Selected Essays* (Houndmills, U.K.: Palgrave Macmillan, 2001), pp. 163–93; Clément Thibaud, "Entre les cités et l'état: Caudillos et pronunciamientos en Grande-Colombie," *Genèses*, vol. 62, no. 1 (2006), pp. 5–26; Clément Thibaud, *Républiques en armes: Les armées de Bolívar dans les guerres d'indépendance du Venezuela et de la Colombie* (Rennes: Presses Universitaires de Rennes, 2006), pp. 241–76.

7. Quoted in Verna, p. 271.

8. Simón Bolívar, "Mensaje al Congreso de Bolivia," May 25, 1826, in Bolívar, *Doctrina del Libertador*, pp. 233–34.

9. See, for instance, John Lynch, *Simón Bolívar: A Life* (New Haven, CT: Yale University Press, 2006), especially p. 201. On Bolívar, see also Arana, *Bolívar*, and Rafael Rojas, *Las repúblicas de aire: Utopía y desencanto en la revolución de Hispanoamérica* (Madrid: Taurus, 2009).

10. Luis Perú de Lacroix (Louis Pérou de Lacroix), *El diario de Bucaramanga*, ed. Nicolás E. Navarro, 2 vols. (Caracas: Bohemia, 1949), vol. 1, p. 57; Daniel Florence O'Leary, *Bolívar y la emancipación de Sur-América: Memorias del general O'Leary*, 32 vols. (Madrid: Sociedad Española de Librería, 1915), vol. 1, pp. 86–87. This occasion was Napoleon's coronation as king of Italy in Milan in 1805.

11. Perú de Lacroix, vol. 1, p. 67.

12. O'Leary, vol. 1, p. 83; Daniel Florence O'Leary, *The "Detached Recollections" of General D. F. O'Leary*, ed. R. A. Humphreys (London: Athlone Press, 1969), p. 28; Hiram Paulding, "Bolivar in His Camp" (1831), in Rebecca Paulding Meade, *Life of Hiram Paulding* (New York: Baker & Taylor, 1910), p. 71. For a thorough analysis of the issue see Manuel Pérez Vila, "Entusiasmo y desencanto: Un joven criollo ante Napoleón," in Alfredo Boulton et al., *Bolívar en Francia* (Caracas: Comité Ejecutivo del Bicentenario de Simón Bolívar, 1984), pp. 109–44.

13. Perú de Lacroix, vol. 1, pp. 67–68.

14. On Bolívar's reputation in the United States, see above all Caitlin Fitz, *Our Sister Republics: The United States in an Age of American Revolutions* (New York: W. W. Norton, 2016), especially pp. 116–55. His reputation in Europe is exhaustively chronicled in Alberto Filippi, ed., *Bolívar y Europa en las crónicas, el pensamiento político y la historiografía*, 3 vols. (Caracas: Ediciones de la Presidencia de la República, 1986).

15. In addition to nearly all the South American continent besides Brazil, Spain also claimed all of Central America, Mexico, what is now the southwest United States, and, thanks to the 1763 Treaty of Paris, what became the Louisiana Purchase, covering roughly an additional third of the continental United States.

16. See Walker, *The Tupac Amaru Rebellion*; Sinclair Thomson, *We Alone Will Rule: Native Andean Politics in the Age of Insurgency* (Madison: University of Wisconsin Press, 2002).

17. On late colonial Venezuelan society, see P. Michael McKinley, *Pre-Revolutionary Caracas: Politics, Economy, and Society 1777–1811* (Cambridge: Cambridge University Press, 1985); Lynch, *Simón Bolívar*, pp. 1–15; Soriano, *Tides of Revolution*. On literacy and print culture, note also Earle, "Information and Disinformation in Late Colonial New Granada," pp. 167–84.

18. Soriano, p. 56.

19. Ibid., pp. 30–39.

20. See Carmen Michelena, *Luces revolucionarias: De la rebelión de Madrid (1795) á la rebelión de La Guaira (1797)* (Caracas: Fundación Centro de Estudios Latinoamericanos Rómulo Gallegos, 2010); Victor M. Uribe Uran, "The Birth of a Public Sphere in Latin America During the Age of Revolution," *Comparative Studies in Society and History*, vol. 42, no. 2 (2000), pp. 425–57; Michael Zeuske, "The French Revolution in Spanish America," in *The Routledge Companion to the French Revolution in World History*, eds. Alan Forrest and Matthias Middell (London: Routledge, 2015), pp. 77–96.

21. On Bolívar's early intellectual formation, see especially Manuel Pérez Vila, *La formación intelectual del Libertador* (Caracas: Ediciones de la Presidencia de la República, 1979), quote about Rodríguez on pp. 75–76 (letter of January 24, 1824).

22. Quoted in Lynch, *Simón Bolívar*, p. 26.

23. On Miranda, see, especially, Karen Racine, *Francisco de Miranda: A Transatlantic Life in the Age of Revolution* (Wilmington, DE: Scholarly Resources, 2003). See also John Charles Chasteen, *Americanos: Latin America's Struggle for Independence* (New York: Oxford University Press, 2008), pp. 36–7.

24. On the Spanish-American independence struggles, see especially Jeremy Adelman, *Sovereignty and Revolution in the Iberian Atlantic* (Princeton, NJ: Princeton University Press, 2006); Jaime E. Rodríguez O, *The Independence of Spanish America* (Cambridge: Cambridge University Press, 1998); John Lynch, *The Spanish American Revolutions, 1808–1826* (New York: W. W. Norton, 1973).

25. For the most recent comprehensive survey of the wars of independence, see Anthony McFarlane, *War and Independence in Spanish America* (London: Routledge, 2013).

26. "Manifiesto de Cartagena," December 15, 1812, in Bolívar, *Doctrina del Libertador*, pp. 9, 12. On Robespierre, see especially Maximilien Robespierre, *Rapport sur les principes du gouvernement révolutionnaire* (Paris: Imprimerie des Administrations Nationales, 1793).

27. "Decreto de Guerra a Muerte," June 15, 1813, in Bolívar, *Doctrina del Libertador*, pp. 20–22.

28. Lynch, *Simón Bolívar*, p. 79.

29. Adelman, *Sovereignty and Revolution*, p. 265.

30. Lynch, *Simón Bolívar*, p. 80.

31. Arana, *Bolívar*, p. 165.

32. Simón Bolívar, "Manifiesto de Carúpano," September 7, 1814, in Bolívar, *Doctrina del Libertador*, p. 44.

33. José de Austria, quoted in Lynch, *Simón Bolívar*, p. 98.

34. See on this subject Thibaud, "Entre les cités et l'état"; Thibaud, *Repúbliques en armes*, pp. 266–71; Lynch, *Simón Bolívar*, p. 114.

35. Bartolomé Mitre, *The Emancipation of South America*, trans. William Pilling (London: Chapman and Hall, 1893), p. 339; Bell, *The First Total War*, p. 7. The largest single Venezuelan army of the period was the one raised by Boves, which numbered roughly 31,000. See Zeuske, *Simón Bolívar*, p. 34.

36. Stephen M. Hart, "Blood, Ink and Pigment: Simón Bolívar as Proteus," *Bulletin of Spanish Studies*, vol. 82, nos. 3–4 (2005), pp. 335–52; Stephen M. Hart, "Literary Print Culture in the Spanish Colonies," *Forum for Modern Language Studies*, vol. 36, no. 1 (2000), pp. 92–107.

37. See Adelman, *Sovereignty and Revolution*, pp. 181–209; Earle, "Information and Disinformation in Late Colonial New Granada"; Uribe Uran, "The Birth of a Public Sphere"; Véronique Hébrard, *Le Venezuela indépendant: Une nation par le discours, 1808–1830* (Paris: L'Harmattan, 1996); Véronique Hébrard, "Opinión pública y representación en el Congreso Constituyente de Venezuela (1811–1812)," in *Los espacios públicos en Iberoamérica: Ambigüedades y problemas. Siglos XVIII–XIX*, eds. François-Xavier Guerra et al. (Mexico City: Centro de Estudios Mexicanos

y Centroamericanos, 2013), pp. 196–224; François-Xavier Guerra, *Modernidad y independencias: Ensayos sobre las revoluciones hispánicas* (Madrid: MAPFRE, 1992); José Ratto Ciarlo, *El correo del Orinoco: Expresión periodística de ecumenismo bolivariano* (Caracas: Oficina Central de Información, 1968).

38. *Gaceta de Caracas*, April 27, 1810, p. 1; June 22, 1810, p. 1.

39. Ratto Ciarlo, p. 17; Earle, p. 180.

40. For instance, *Gaceta de Caracas*, October 14, 1813, almost entirely devoted to Bolívar's bulletins and speeches.

41. José Felix Blanco et al., eds., *Documentos para la historia de la vida publica del Libertador*, 15 vols. (Caracas: Imprenta de "La Opinión Nacional," 1875–1879), vol. 5, pp. 128–34.

42. *Gaceta de Caracas*, August 26, 1813, p. 4. On the festival, see José María Salvador, *Efímeras efemérides: Fiestas cívicas y arte efímero en la Venezuela de los siglos XVII XIX* (Caracas: Universidad Católica Andrés Bello, 2001), p. 193. Two months later, the spectacle repeated itself when Bolívar led a procession into Caracas, accompanying the heart of a New Granadan officer who had fallen heroically in battle. See *Gazeta Extraordinaria* (*Gaceta de Caracas*), October 14, 1813, pp. 1–2; Salvador, p. 194.

43. *Gaceta de Caracas*, August 26, 1813, p. 4.

44. *Gazeta Extraordinaria* (*Gaceta de Caracas*), October 14, 1813, p. 2.

45. See Adelman, *Sovereignty and Revolution*, pp. 273–75.

46. Pablo Morillo to the Ministry of War, April 2, 1818, in Filippi, *Bolívar y Europa*, vol. I, pp. 73–74.

47. "Oración inaugural del Congreso de Angostura," February 15, 1819, in Bolívar, *Doctrina del Libertador*, pp. 101–27. It built upon thoughts first developed in a public letter of September 6, 1815, usually known as the "Carta de Jamaica" in ibid., pp. 55–75.

48. "Oración inaugural," pp. 102, 107, 110, 121.

49. Ibid., pp. 110–11.

50. Ibid., pp. 108, 121. Bolívar used the word *magistrados*, or magistrates, which in early modern political theory meant civil leaders.

51. See the still-useful article of Mary Watters, "Bolívar and the Church," *Catholic Historical Review*, vol. 21, no. 3 (1935), pp. 299–313.

52. Lynch, *Simón Bolívar*, p. 122.

53. George Laval Chesterton, *Peace, War, and Adventure: An Autobiographical Memoir*, 2 vols. (London: Longman, 1853), vol. 2, p. 137.

54. Lynch, *Simón Bolívar*, p. 130.

55. Simón Bolívar, "Discurso pronunciado ante el Congreso de Cúcuta," October 3, 1821, in Bolívar, *Doctrina del Libertador*, pp. 160–61.

56. Quoted in Lynch, *Simón Bolívar*, p. 167.

57. See, for instance, "Noticia biográfica de Don Simón de Bolívar, generalissimo de Venezuela," *Variedades o Messagero de Londres*, no. 1, January 1823, pp. 1–14; *El general Simón Bolívar en la campaña de la Nueva Granada en 1819* (Bogotá: Imprenta del C.B.E., 1820).

58. Quoted in Richard Longeville Vowell, *Campaigns and Cruises in Venezuela and New Granada and in the Pacific Ocean*, 3 vols. (London: Longman, 1831), vol. 2, p. 218.

59. Vicente Rocafuerte, *Bosquejo ligerísimo de la revolución de Mégico: Desde el grito de Iguala hasta la proclamación imperial de Iturbide* (Philadelphia: "Teracrouef and Naroajeb," 1822), pp. 162, 223.

60. Quoted in Emilio Rodríguez Demorizi, *Poetas contra Bolívar: El Libertador a través de la calumnia* (Madrid: Gráficas Reunidas, 1966), p. 20.

61. Salvador, *Efímeras efemérides*, pp. 148–49.

62. William Duane, *A Visit to Colombia in the Years 1822 & 1823 by Laguayra and Caracas over the Cordillera to Bogota and Thence by the Magdalena to Cartagena* (Philadelphia: Thomas Palmer, 1826), p. 98.

63. Ibid., p. 111.

64. Gabriel García Márquez, *The General in His Labyrinth*, trans. Edith Grossman (New York: Vintage International, 1990), p. 40.

65. On the visual representations of Bolívar, see above all Alfredo Boulton, *Iconografía del Libertador*, ed. Enrique Uribe White (Caracas: Ediciones Lerner, 1967); Ades, *Art in Latin America*, pp. 1–27, especially pp. 16–17; Hart, "Blood, Ink and Pigment."

66. See Fitz, *Our Sister Republics*, pp. 116–55; Filippi, *Bolívar y Europa*, passim.

67. See, for instance, George Laval Chesterton, *A Narrative of Proceedings in Venezuela in South America in the Years 1819 and 1820* (London: John and Arthur Arch, 1820); Richard Bache, *Notes on Colombia Taken in the Years 1822–3. With an Itinerary of the Route from Caracas to Bogotá* (Philadelphia: H. C. Carley and I. Lea, 1827); Duane, *A Visit to Colombia*; Gaspard Théodore Mollien, *Travels in the Republic of Colombia. In the years 1822 and 1823* (London: C. Knight, 1824); C. Richard, *Briefe aus Columbien an seine Freunde von einem hannoverischen Officier* (Leipzig: Brockhaus, 1822).

68. Chesterton, *A Narrative*, p. 130. By the time he came to write his autobiographical memoir thirty-odd years later, Chesterton's attitude toward Bolívar had softened (Chesteron, *Peace, War and Adventure*).

69. Edward Everett, "South America," *North American Review*, vol. 3, no. 2 (1821), pp. 433–34, 438.

70. Chesterton, *A Narrative*, p. 131.

71. Richard, *Briefe*, p. 222.

72. John Miller, *Memoirs of General Miller in the Service of the Republic of Peru*, 2 vols. (London: Longman et al., 1829), vol. 2, p. 333.

73. On this theme, see Frank Safford, "Bolívar as Triumphal State Maker and Despairing 'Democrat,'" in David Bushnell and Lester D. Langley, eds., *Simón Bolívar: Essays on the Life and Legacy of the Liberator* (Lanham, MD: Rowman & Littlefield, 2008), pp. 99–120.

74. For a full English translation, see Simón Bolívar, *El Libertador: Writings of Simón Bolívar*, ed. David Bushnell, trans. Frederick H. Fornhoff (New York: Oxford University Press, 2003), pp. 135–36). The authenticity of the document has been contested.

75. Simón Bolívar to Francisco de Paula Santander, June 13, 1821, in Francisco de Paula Santander and Símon Bólivar, *Cartas Santander-Bolívar*, 6 vols. (Bogotá: Fundación para la Conmemoración del Bicentenario del Natalicio y el Sesquicentenario de la Muerte del General Francisco de Paula Santander, 1988), vol. 3, p. 114.

76. See on this subject Adelman, *Revolution and Sovereignty*, p. 286.

77. Arana, *Bolívar*, p. 302; Lynch, *Simón Bolívar*, p. 174.

78. *Gaceta de Lima*, excerpted in Blanco et al., vol. 9, p. 71.

79. "Oda al Libertador de Colombia," in ibid., p. 101. See also the remarkable description in Robert Proctor, *Narrative of a Journey Across the Cordillera of the Andes, and of a Residence in Lima, and Other Parts of Peru, in the Years 1823 and 1824* (London: Constable, 1825), pp. 245–51.

80. "Parece que el genio de América y el de mi destino se me han metido en la cabeza," Simón Bolívar to José Antonio de Sucre, Huaraz, June 9, 1824, in O'Leary, *Memorias*, vol. 30, p. 507.

81. See the Congress's declaration of the need for a *poder dictatorial* in Blanco et al., vol. 9, p. 212.

82. Samuel Haigh, *Sketches of Buenos Ayres, Chile, and Peru* (London: Effingham Wilson, 1831), p. 364; José Luis Businche, *Bolívar visto por sus contemporáneos* (Mexico City: Fonda de Cultura Económica, 1960), p. 169.

83. O'Leary, *Memorias*, vol. 30, p. 178; *El sol de Cuzco*, July 16, 1825.

84. Haigh, pp. 364–65.

85. Lynch, *Simón Bolívar*, p. 194; see also Blanco et al., vol. 9, p. 574.

86. Blanco et al., vol. 9, p. 242; Lynch, *Simón Bolívar*, p. 203.

87. See John Lynch, "Simón Bolívar and the Age of Revolution," in *Latin America Between Colony and Nation*, pp. 134–62.

88. José Joaquín Olmedo, *La victoria de Junín: Canto a Bolívar* (Guayaquil: Imprenta Municipal, 1917). See also Christopher B. Conway, *The Cult of Bolívar in Latin American Literature* (Gainesville: University Press of Florida, 2003), pp. 27–28.

89. José Antonio Páez to Símon Bólivar, October 1, 1825, in O'Leary, *Memorias*, vol. 11, pp. 58–59.

90. Simón Bolívar to Francisco de Paula Santander, February 21, 1826, in Bolívar, *Doctrina del Libertador*, p. 221.

91. Simón Bolívar to José Antonio Páez, March 6, 1826, in ibid., p. 222.

92. Simón Bolívar to Francisco de Paula Santander, July 8, 1826, in http://www.archivodellibertador .gob.ve/escritos/buscador/spip.php?article3318, accessed April 14, 2019. The concept of "ideology" had been invented in the 1790s by French thinkers who mostly rallied to Bonaparte after the Eighteenth Brumaire.

93. Simón Bolívar to Francisco de Paula Santander, September 19, 1826, in *Archivo Santander*, 24 vols. (Bogotá: Aguila Negra, 1913–24), vol. 15, pp. 188–89.

94. See Ronald Briggs, "A Napoleonic Bolívar: Historical Analogy, *Desengaño*, and the Spanish/ Creole Consciousness," *Journal of Spanish Cultural Studies*, vol. 11, nos. 3–4 (2010), pp. 337–52.

95. See above, chapter 3, pp. 91–132.

96. Cristóbal Mendoza to Simón Bolívar, December 1, 1827, in O'Leary, *Memorias*, vol. 2, p. 295.

97. Joseph Andrews, *Journey from Buenos Ayres Through the Provinces of Cordova, Tucuman, and Salta, to Potosi*, 2 vols. (London: John Murray, 1827), vol. 2, p. 91. See also, for instance, Dominique-Georges-Frédéric Dufour de Pradt, *Congrès de Panama* (Paris: Béchet, 1825), p. 83. For the more conventional view, see Rocafuerte, *Bosquejo*, p. 162; poems in Blanco et al., vol. IX, pp. 193–95; Businche, p. 123; correspondence from Lafayette in Filippi, *Bolívar y Europa*, vol. 1, pp. 236–40.

98. Quoted in Arana, *Bolívar*, p. 260.

99. Briggs, p. 339.

100. José María Heredia, "A Bolivar," in José María Heredia, *Poesía completa*, ed. Carmen Almany Bay (Madrid: Verbum, 2004), pp. 225–30.

101. Bache, *Notes on Colombia*, p. 122.

102. Paulding, "Bolivar in His Camp," p. 72.

103. See ibid., p. 77; O'Leary, *The "Detached Recollections,"* p. 28; Robert Ker Porter, *Sir Robert Ker Porter's Caracas Diary: 1825–1842*, ed. Walter Dupouy (Caracas: Walter Dupouy, 1966), p. 208; cf. Pérez Vila, "Entusiasmo y desencanto."

104. J. Boussingault, reprinted in Filippi, *Bolívar y Europa*, vol. 1, p. 226.

105. See Morrissey, *The Economy of Glory*, pp. 147–80; Hazareesingh, *The Legend of Napoleon*.

106. Pérez Vila, *Formación intellectual*, pp. 147–48.

107. Emmanuel de Las Cases to Simón Bolívar, December 3, 1826, in Blanco et al., vol. 11, p. 36.

108. See Thibaud, *Républiques en armes*, p. 112.

109. Péru de Lacroix, *Diario*. For Péru's evocation of Las Cases, see p. 193. The first, partial edition only appeared in 1869.

110. Péru de Lacroix, *Diario*, pp. 102, 110–11, 124–26, and passim.

111. Ibid., pp. 120–21. See also, on Bonaparte, ibid., pp. 33, 54–56, 67.

112. Quoted in Porter, *Caracas Diary*, January 19, 1828, p. 352.

113. Vanegas Carrasco, "Iconografía," p. 124.

114. García Márquez, *The General in His Labyrinth*, p. 16.

115. Quoted in Hébrard, *Le Venezuela indépendant*, p. 332.

116. Quoted in ibid.

117. See Salvador, *Efímeras efemérides*, pp. 196–98.

118. Porter, *Caracas Diary*, January 10, 1827, pp. 196–97.

119. José Hernández Sanavria, "Discurso que la Universidad de Caracas dedica á su protector el

guerrero político SIMON BOLÍVAR, Libertador de tres Repúblicas y Presidente de la de Co-lombia," in Blanco et al., vol. 11, pp. 159–63.

120. Santiago Mariño, quoted in Hébrard, *Le Venezuela indépendant*, p. 333.

121. Bolívar to Robert Wilson, May 26, 1827, quoted in Rojas, *Las repúblicas de aire*, p. 339.

122. Quoted in Hébrard, *Le Venezuela indépendant*, p. 334. Many of the petitions were collected in *El voto de Venezuela* (Caracas: G. F. Devisme, 1828).

123. See, for instance, Hébrard, *Le Venezuela indépendant*, pp. 334–5; *El voto de Venezuela*, p. 260.

124. *Fe política de un Colombiano, o tres cuestiones importantes para la política del día* (Bogotá: Salazar, 1827), pp. 5, 14. The Cicero quote was from *De Officiis*: ". . . ut quisque animi magnitudine maxime excellet, ita maxime vult princeps omnium vel potius solus esse."

125. Ibid., pp. 14–16.

126. Quoted in José Antonio Aguilar Rivera, "The Liberal Cloak: The Constant–De Pradt Con-troversy on Bolívar's Last Dictatorship," *Jahrbuch für Geschichte Lateinamerikas / Anuario de historia de América latina*, vol. 55 (2018), pp. 84–107, quote from p. 89.

127. See David Bushnell, "The Last Dictatorship: Betrayal or Consummation?" *The Hispanic American Historical Review*, vol. 63, no. 1 (1983), p. 66.

128. The decree is reproduced in Bolívar, *Doctrina del Libertador*, pp. 271–77, quote from p. 273.

129. See Lynch, *Simón Bolívar*, pp. 240–41.

130. See Bushnell, "The Last Dictatorship," pp. 104–105.

131. Quoted in Lynch, *Simón Bolívar*, p. 268.

132. Simón Bolívar to Estanislao Vergara, December 16, 1828, in Bolívar, *Doctrina del Libertador*, p. 279.

133. Quoted in Lynch, *Simón Bolívar*, p. 268.

134. Simón Bolívar to Juan José Flores, November 9, 1830, in Bolívar, *Doctrina del Libertador*, p. 323.

135. Quoted in Lynch, *Simón Bolívar*, p. 277.

136. Most important, José Manuel Restrepo, *Historia de la revolución de Colombia*, 10 vols. (Paris: Libreria Americana, 1827); Francisco Javier Yanes and Cristóbal Mendoza, eds., *Colección de documentos relativos a la vida pública del Libertador de Colombia y del Perú, Simón Bolívar*, 22 vols. (Caracas: Imprenta de Devisme hermanos, 1826–33). The electronic archive is available at http://archivodellibertador.gob.ve.

137. See Calvin P. Jones, "The Images of Simón Bolívar as Reflected in Ten Leading British Periodi-cals, 1816–1830," *The Americas*, vol. 40, no. 3 (1984), pp. 377–97, quote from p. 396; David Sowell, "The Mirror of Public Opinion: Bolívar, Republicanism and the United States Press, 1821–1831," *Revista de historia de América*, no. 134 (2004), pp. 165–83.

138. See Aguilar Rivera, "The Liberal Cloak."

139. See Fitz, *Our Sister Republics*, pp. 240–48; Matthew Karp, *This Vast Southern Empire: Slavehold-ers at the Helm of American Foreign Policy* (Cambridge, MA: Harvard University Press, 2016), pp. 10–31.

140. Alain Rouquié, *The Military and the State in Latin America* (Berkeley: University of California Press, 1987), p. 43.

141. Rodríguez O, *The Independence of Spanish America*, pp. 243–44.

142. See on these points Elías Pino Iturrieta, *El divino Bolívar* (Caracas: Alfadil, 1988); German Carrera Damas, *El culto a Bolívar: Esbozo para un estudio de la historia de las ideas en Venezuela* (Caracas: Grijalbo, 1989).

EPILOGUE: CHARISMA AND DEMOCRACY

1. See Philip Dwyer, *Napoleon: Passion, Death and Resurrection, 1815–1840* (London: Blooms-bury, 2018), pp. 196–231; Hazareesingh, *The Legend of Napoleon*, pp. 151–83. The tomb was only completed in 1861.

2. *Lloyd's Weekly London Newspaper*, February 5, 1843, p. 8.

3. See Salvador, *Efímeras efímérides*, pp. 291–307; Conway, *The Cult of Bolívar*, pp. 29–37; Pino Iturrieta, *El divino Bolívar*, pp. 27–30; Zeuske, *Simón Bolívar*, pp. 71–72.

4. Roland Lambalot, *Toussaint Louverture au château de Joux* (Pontarlier: Office du Tourisme, 1989), p. 37.

5. See Kirk Savage, "The Self-Made Monument: George Washington and the Fight to Erect a National Memorial," *Winterthur Portfolio*, vol. 22, no. 4 (1987), pp. 225–42.

6. Madiou, *Histoire de Haïti*; Arthur Lescouflair, *Thomas Madiou* (Port-au-Prince: Pan-American Institute of Geography and History, 1950).

7. On the image of Bolívar in nineteenth-century Venezuela, see Conway, *The Cult of Bolívar*, pp. 18–45; Zeuske, *Simón Bolívar*, pp. 68–72; Pino Iturrieta; and especially Carrera Damas, *El culto a Bolívar*.

8. Quoted in Matthew J. Clavin, *Toussaint Louverture and the American Civil War: The Promise and Peril of a Second Haitian Revolution* (Philadelphia: University of Pennsylvania Press, 2010), p. 136. See also Hazareesingh, *Black Spartacus*, chapter 12.

9. See Furstenberg, *In the Name of the Father*, especially pp. 8–13, 25–70.

10. Quoted in Kaminski, *George Washington: A Man of Action*, p. 104.

11. Quoted in Schwartz, *George Washington*, p. 195, italics in original. On Washington's posthumous reputation, see in general Schwartz, pp. 193–207.

12. On this point, see Barry Schwartz, "Social Change and Collective Memory: The Democratization of George Washington," *American Sociological Review*, vol. 56, no. 2 (1991), pp. 221–36.

13. On this point, see above all Hazareesingh, *The Legend of Napoleon*.

14. A search for "Bonaparte" or "Napoleon" returns some 2,911 articles and books in English, but a small portion relates to people other than Napoleon Bonaparte or represents duplicates.

15. François-René de Chateaubriand, *Mémoires d'outre-tombe*, ed. Edmond Biré, 6 vols. (Paris: Garnier Frères, 1910), vol. 4, p. 139.

16. Quoted in Jean-Baptiste Decherf, *Le grand homme et son pouvoir: Histoire d'un imaginaire de Napoléon à de Gaulle* (La Tour d'Aigues: Éditions de l'Aube, 2017), p. 62.

17. Heinrich Heine, January 6, 1841, in Heine, *Heinrich Heines sämmtliche Werke*, 12 vols. (Hamburg: Hoffman and Campe, 1876), vol. 5, p. 276.

18. See Graham Robb, *Victor Hugo: A Biography* (New York: W. W. Norton, 1997); David Bellos, *The Novel of the Century: The Extraordinary Adventure of "Les Misérables"* (New York: Farrar, Straus and Giroux, 2017).

19. On the literary afterlife of Bonaparte, see notably Elizabeth Duquette, "The Man of the World," *American Literary History*, vol. 27, no. 4 (2015), pp. 635–64; Robert L. Jackson, "Napoleon in Russian Literature," *Yale French Studies*, vol. 26 (1960), pp. 106–18; Lucas-Dubreton, *Le culte de Napoléon*; Dwyer, *Napoleon: Passion, Death and Resurrection*.

20. Johann Wolfgang von Goethe to Johann Peter Eckermann, March 11, 1828, quoted in Werner Telesko, *Napoleon Bonaparte: Der "moderne Held" und die bildende Kunst 1799–1815* (Vienna: Bohlau, 1998), p. 217.

21. Georg Wilhem Friedrich Hegel, *Briefe von und an Hegel*, ed. Johannes Hoffmeister, 4 vols. (Hamburg: Felix Meier, 1952), vol. 1, p. 120.

22. See Pedro Grases, ed., *Materiales para la historia del periodismo en Venezuela durante el siglo XIX* (Caracas: Escuela de Periodismo, 1950).

23. See Angus Nicholls, *Goethe's Concept of the Daemonic: After the Ancients* (London: Boydell and Brewer, 2006).

24. See Decherf, *Le grand homme*, p. 65.

25. See Georg Wilhelm Friedrich Hegel, *Reason in History: A General Introduction to the Philosophy of History* (New York: Bobbs-Merrill, 1953).

26. Thomas Carlyle, *On Heroes, Hero-Worship and the Heroic in History: Six Lectures* (New York: John Wiley & Sons, 1866), pp. 26, 217. See Darrin M. McMahon, "The Fate of Nations Is the Work of Genius: The French Revolution and the Great Man Theory of History," in David A. Bell and Yair Mintzker, eds., *Rethinking the Age of Revolutions: France and the Birth of the Modern World* (New York: Oxford University Press, 2018), pp. 134–53.

27. Hegel, *Reason in History*, p. 40.

28. Giuseppe Mazzini, "On the Genius and Tendency of the Writings of Thomas Carlyle," in *Life and Writings of Joseph Mazzini*, 6 vols. (London: Smith, Elder, 1864–70), vol. 4, pp. 75, 78. The essay was originally published in English.

29. Jules Michelet, *Histoire de la Révolution française*, 2 vols. (Paris: Gallimard, 1952), vol. 2, p. 668. In his 1869 essay "Le tyran," Michelet again cited Clootz, but this time in a more hopeful vein: "Happily the age advances. We are a little less imbecilic. The mania for incarnation . . . messianism, is passing." Quoted in Decherf, p. 15.

30. See Joanna Innes and Mark Philp, eds., *Re-imagining Democracy in the Age of Revolutions: America, France, Britain, Ireland, 1750–1850* (Oxford: Oxford University Press, 2013); Miller, *Can Democracy Work?*

31. Stephen W. Sawyer, *Demos Assembled: Democracy and the International Origins of the Modern State* (Chicago: University of Chicago Press, 2018), p. 1.

32. Alexis de Tocqueville, *De la démocratie en Amérique*, 4 vols. (Paris: Charles Gosselin, 1835–40).

33. Louis-Napoléon Bonaparte, *Des idées Napoléoniennes* (Brussels: Jules Géruzet, 1839), p. 21n.

34. See Peter Baehr and Melvin Richter, eds., *Dictatorship in History and Theory: Bonapartism, Caesarism, and Totalitarianism* (Cambridge: Cambridge University Press, 2004). For a contemporary example of "Caesarist" theory, see Auguste Romieu, *L'ère des Césars* (Paris: Ledoyen, 1850).

35. See most recently David Cesarani, *Disraeli: The Novel Politician* (New Haven, CT: Yale University Press, 2016).

36. See Lucy Riall, *Garibaldi: Invention of a Hero* (New Haven, CT: Yale University Press, 2007); *Gazzetta di Palermo* quoted in *Il divin Salvatore*, April 26, 1882, p. 956.

37. See Giacinto Stiavelli, *Garibaldi nella letteratura italiana* (Rome: Enrico Voghera, 1901), especially pp. 37–67, 167–89.

38. See on this subject Nancy Isenberg and Andrew Burstein, *The Problem of Democracy: The Presidents Adams Confront the Cult of Personality* (New York: Random House, 2019).

39. Quoted in John William Ward, *Andrew Jackson: Symbol for an Age* (New York: Oxford University Press, 1955), p. 109. On Jackson's charisma, see Thomas Brown, "From Old Hickory to Sly Fox: The Routinization of Charisma in the Early Democratic Party," *Journal of the Early Republic*, vol. 11, no. 3 (1991), pp. 339–69.

40. See Lynn Hudson Parsons, *The Birth of Modern Politics: Andrew Jackson, John Quincy Adams, and the Election of 1828* (New York: Oxford University Press, 2009).

41. See Jan Plamper, *The Stalin Cult: A Study in the Alchemy of Power* (New Haven, CT: Yale University Press, 2012); Stephen Kotkin, *Stalin: Waiting for Hitler, 1929–1941* (New York: Penguin Press, 2017); Kershaw, *Hitler*.

42. See McMahon, *Divine Fury*, pp. 208–14.

43. Erika Mann, *School for Barbarians: Education Under the Nazis* (New York: Dover, 2014), p. 21.

44. "Half-Kilometre Long Kim Jong-un Propaganda Message Visible from Space," *National Post*, November 23, 2012, at https://nationalpost.com/news/half-kilometre-long-kim-jong-un-propaganda-message-visible-from-space, accessed May 11, 2019.

45. See notably Choe Sang-Hun and Norimitsu Onishi, "North Korea's Tears: A Blend of Cult, Culture and Coercion," *The New York Times*, December 20, 2011.

46. See the excursus, "Writing Charisma into History."

47. See ibid. For a recent exposition of the thesis in the American context, see Bruce Ackerman,

Revolutionary Constitutions: Charismatic Leadership and the Rule of Law (Cambridge, MA: Harvard University Press, 2019).

48. Emmanuel Macron, *Révolution: C'est notre combat pour la France* (Paris: XO Éditions, 2016).

49. See Rosenfeld, *Democracy and Truth*, pp. 137–76; David A. Bell, "When the Farce Is Tragedy," *Dissent* magazine online, February 1, 2018; David A. Bell, "Fake News Is Not the Real Media Threat We're Facing," *The Nation* magazine online, December 22, 2016.

50. Emma Stefansky, "Trump Says Clinton's Beyoncé and Jay Z Concert Is 'Almost Like Cheating,'" *Vanity Fair* magazine online, November 6, 2016.

51. Andrew Restuccia, "The Sanctification of Donald Trump," *Politico*, April 30, 2019.

52. See, for instance, Timothy Snyder, *The Road to Unfreedom: Russia, Europe, America* (New York: Tim Duggan Books, 2018); Robert Kagan, "The Strongmen Strike Back," *The Washington Post*, March 14, 2019.

EXCURSUS: WRITING CHARISMA INTO HISTORY

1. See Berenson and Giloi, *Constructing Charisma*; Berenson, *Heroes of Empire*; Kershaw, *Hitler*; Wills, *The Kennedy Imprisonment*.

2. Karl Marx, *The Eighteenth Brumaire of Louis Bonaparte* (New York: International Publishers, 1963), pp. 15–16.

3. Stephen Kotkin, *Stalin: Paradoxes of Power, 1878–1928* (New York: Penguin Press, 2014); Kotkin, *Stalin: Waiting for Hitler*.

4. Quoted in Jeffrey Brooks, *Thank You, Comrade Stalin! Soviet Public Culture from Revolution to Cold War* (Princeton, NJ: Princeton University Press, 2000), p. 66.

5. Fernand Braudel, *The Identity of France*, trans. Siân Reynolds, 2 vols. (New York: HarperCollins, 1989–91), vol. 2, p. 679.

6. Emily S. Rosenberg, ed., *A World Connecting: 1870–1945* (Cambridge, MA: Harvard University Press, 2012). See also David A. Bell, "This Is What Happens When Historians Overuse the Idea of the Network," *The New Republic*, October 25, 2013.

7. The reference of course is to E. P. Thompson, *The Making of the English Working Class* (London: Victor Gollancz, 1963), p. 12.

8. See David A. Bell, "Total History and Microhistory," in Sarah Maza and Lloyd Kramer, eds., *The Blackwell Companion to Historical Thought* (Oxford: Blackwell, 2002), pp. 262–76.

9. On the silencing of the Haitian Revolution, see Trouillot, *Silencing the Past*.

10. Émile Durkheim, *The Elementary Forms of the Religious Life: A Study in Religious Sociology* (London: G. Allen & Unwin, 1915), pp. 212–13.

11. On the history of the word, see John Potts, *A History of Charisma* (London: Palgrave Macmillan, 2009), and Philip Rieff, *Charisma: The Gift of Grace, and How It Has Been Taken Away from Us* (New York: Pantheon, 2007).

12. See, especially, Weber, *Economy and Society*, vol. 1, pp. 241–45; vol. 2, pp. 1111–56; Max Weber, "Politics as a Vocation," in *From Max Weber: Essays in Sociology*, trans. and eds. H. H. Gerth and C. Wright Mills (New York: Oxford University Press, 1946), pp. 77–128.

13. On Hegel, Nietzsche, and Weberian "charisma," see notably Jean-Claude Monod, *Qu'est-ce qu'un chef en démocratie? Politiques du charisme* (Paris: Seuil, 2012), pp. 171–72; Charles Lindholm, *Charisma* (Oxford: Blackwell, 1990), pp. 22–23.

14. Friedrich Nietzsche, *Zur Genealogie der Moral* (Berlin: Hofenberg, 2016), p. 218.

15. See Peter Baehr, *Caesarism, Charisma and Fate: Historical Sources and Modern Resonances in the Work of Max Weber* (New Brunswick, NJ: Transaction Publishers, 2008); Gerhard Casper, "Caesarism in Democratic Politics—Reflections on Max Weber," lecture delivered at the Kluge Center, Library of Congress (2007), online at https://ssrn.com/abstract=1032647, accessed July 1, 2019.

16. The literature on charisma is immense. In addition to the works by Lepsius, Lindholm, Monod,

Potts, Rieff, and Willner, I have found the following particularly useful both for their own insights and as guides to the debates: Christopher Adair-Toteff, "Max Weber's Charisma," *Journal of Classical Sociology*, vol. 5, no. 2 (2005), pp. 189–204; Baehr, *Caesarism*; Vanessa Bernadou et al., eds., *Que faire du charisme? Retours sur une notion de Max Weber* (Rennes: Presses Universitaires de Rennes, 2014); Stefan Breuer, *Max Webers Herrschaftssoziologie* (Frankfurt: Campus Verlag, 1991); Joshua Derman, *Max Weber in Politics and Social Thought: From Charisma to Canonization* (Cambridge: Cambridge University Press, 2012); Eva Horn, "Introduction: Narrating Charisma," *New German Critique*, vol. 38, no. 3 (2011), pp. 1–16; Philip Smith, "Culture and Charisma: Outline of a Theory," *Acta Sociologica*, vol. 43, no. 2 (2000), pp. 101–111.

17. Clifford Geertz, "Centers, Kings and Charisma: Reflections on the Symbolics of Power," in Sean Wilentz, ed., *Rites of Power: Symbolism, Ritual and Politics Since the Middle Ages* (Philadelphia: University of Pennsylvania Press, 1999), pp. 13–38, quote from p. 14.

18. Notably Arthur M. Schlesinger Jr., *The Politics of Hope* (Boston: Houghton Mifflin, 1963).

19. Monod, *Qu'est-ce qu'un chef?* In the same vein, see also Vincent Lloyd, *In Defense of Charisma* (New York: Columbia University Press, 2018).

20. On this debate, see Reinhard Bendix, "Reflections on Charismatic Leadership," in Ronald M. Glassman and William H. Swatos Jr., eds., *Charisma, History and Social Structure* (New York: Greenwood Press, 1986), pp. 17–25.

21. See, notably, Ackerman, *Revolutionary Constitutions*.

22. See Thomas Dow, "The Theory of Charisma," *The Sociological Quarterly*, vol. 10, no. 3 (1969), pp. 306–18.

23. Edward Shils, "Charisma, Order, and Status," *American Sociological Review*, vol. 30, no. 2 (1965), pp. 199–213; Shmuel Eisenstadt, ed., *Max Weber on Charisma and Institution Building* (Chicago: University of Chicago Press, 1968). A recent addition to this literature is Ackerman, *Revolutionary Constitutions*.

24. See, for instance, Lindholm, *Charisma*; Irvine Schiffer, *Charisma: A Psychoanalytical Look at Mass Society* (Toronto: University of Toronto Press, 1973); Bryan R. Wilson, *The Noble Savages: The Primitive Origins of Charisma and Its Contemporary Survival* (Berkeley: Quantum Books, 1975).

25. Willner, *The Spellbinders*; also Adair-Toteff, "Max Weber's Charisma."

26. See Derman, pp. 176–215; Potts, pp. 137–81. One of these intellectuals was my father, Daniel Bell.

27. Quoted in Potts, p. 190.

28. See Lynn Hunt, ed., *The New Cultural History* (Berkeley: University of California Press, 1989). My own somewhat more "linguistically turned" approach has, throughout my career, been particularly influenced by Keith Michael Baker, *Inventing the French Revolution: Essays on French Political Culture in the Eighteenth Century* (Cambridge: Cambridge University Press, 1990).

29. Weber, *Economy and Society*, vol. 1, p. 242.

30. Ibid.

31. Lepsius, "Charismatic Leadership"; Smith, "Culture and Charisma."

32. *Richard II*, act 3, scene 2.

BIBLIOGRAPHY

NEWSPAPERS AND MAGAZINES

Affiches américaines
American Intelligencer
El amigo del pueblo: Periódico semanario literario, científico, de política y comercio
Annalen menschlicher Grösse und Verworfenheit
Archiv für Geographie, Historie, Staats-und Kriegskunst
Aurora
The Bermuda Gazette
The Boston Evening Post
The Boston Gazette
The Cambridge Magazine; or, The Universal Repertory of Arts, Sciences and the Belles Lettres
The Christian Observer, Conducted by Members of the Established Church
The Commercial Register
The Connecticut Courant
Le conservateur
The Constitutional Gazette
El correo del Orinoco
Le courrier de l'armée d'Italie, ou Le patriote français à Milan
Le courrier français
The Court Miscellany; or, The Ladies New Magazine
The Crisis
Le décade philosophique, littéraire et politique
Il divin Salvatore
E. Johnson's British Gazette and Sunday Monitor
La France vue de l'armée d'Italie
The Freeman's Journal
Gaceta de Caracas
Gazette nationale, ou Le moniteur universel
Gazette of the United States
The Georgia Gazette
Greenleaf's New York Journal
The Independent Gazetteer
Intelligenzblatt oder Zeitung für die elegante Welt
Journal de Bonaparte et des hommes vertueux
Journal de Paris
Journal des défenseurs de la patrie
Kaiserlich Privilegirter Reichs-Anzeiger

The Lady's Magazine; or, The Entertaining Companion for the Fair Sex, Appropriated Solely to Their Use and Amusement
The London Chronicle
The London Magazine; or, The Gentleman's Monthly Intelligencer
Lloyd's Evening Post
Lloyd's Weekly London Newspaper
Maryland Journal and Baltimore Advertiser
Mercure universel
Le messager du soir, ou La gazette générale de l'Europe
Le miroir de la France: Recueil historique, politique et littéraire
The Morning Chronicle
The Morning Post
New England Chronicle; or, Essex Gazette
The New-Jersey Journal
The New York Journal
The Newport Mercury
The Norwich Packet and Weekly Advertiser
The Oracle and Public Advertiser
The Pennsylvania Evening Post
The Pennsylvania Journal and Weekly Advertiser
The Pennsylvania Ledger
The Philadelphia Gazette and Universal Daily Advertiser
The Political Register
The Providence Gazette and Country Journal
The Quebec Gazette
Révolutions de Paris
The Roanoake Times
The St. James's Chronicle
El sol de Cuzco
Le spectateur du nord
Sporting Calendar: Containing an Account of the Plates, Matches, and Sweepstakes That Have Been Run for in Great Britain, Ireland, and Jamaica
The Star
The Telegraph
The Times of London
The Virginia Gazette
The Whitehall Evening Post

PRINTED SOURCES

Ackerman, Bruce, *Revolutionary Constitutions: Charismatic Leadership and the Rule of Law* (Cambridge, MA: Harvard University Press, 2019).
Acta Borussica: Denkmäler der Preussischen Staatsverwaltung im 18. Jahrhundert (Berlin: Paul Parey, 1901), vol. 6.
Adair-Toteff, Christopher, "Max Weber's Charisma," *Journal of Classical Sociology*, vol. 5, no. 2 (2005), pp. 189–204.
Adams, John, et al., *Microfilms of the Adams Papers: Owned by the Adams Manuscript Trust and Deposited in the Massachusetts Historical Society* (Boston: Massachusetts Historical Society, 1954).
Adams, John, and Benjamin Rush, *The Spur of Fame: Dialogues of John Adams and Benjamin Rush, 1805–1813*, eds. John A. Schutz and Douglass Adair (San Marino, CA: Huntington Library, 1966).

Addison, Joseph, *Cato: A Tragedy, and Selected Essays*, eds. Christine Dunn Henderson and Mark E. Yellin (Indianapolis: Liberty Fund, 2004).

Adelman, Jeremy, "An Age of Imperial Revolutions," *American Historical Review*, vol. 113, no. 2 (2008), pp. 319–40.

———, *Sovereignty and Revolution in the Iberian Atlantic* (Princeton, NJ: Princeton University Press, 2006).

———, "What's in a Revolution?," *Latin American Research Review*, vol. 47, no. 1 (2012), pp. 187–95.

Ades, Dawn, *Art in Latin America: The Modern Era, 1820–1980* (New Haven, CT: Yale University Press, 1989).

Aguilar Rivera, José Antonio, "The Liberal Cloak: The Constant–De Pradt Controversy on Bolívar's Last Dictatorship," *Jahrbuch für Geschichte Lateinamerikas / Anuario de historia de América latina*, vol. 55 (2018), pp. 84–107.

Aikin, Anna, *Corsica: An Ode* (London: Ridley, 1769).

Aïqui, Francis, *Paoli, Boswell, Bonaparte: Trois hommes et des Révolutions* (Ajaccio: La Marge, 1989).

Albanese, Catherine L., *Sons of the Fathers: The Civil Religion of the American Revolution* (Philadelphia: Temple University Press, 1976).

Albertone, Manuela, and Antonino De Francesco, eds., *Rethinking the Atlantic World: Europe and America in the Age of Democratic Revolutions* (Basingstoke, U.K.; Palgrave Macmillan, 2009).

Alexander, John T., "Amazon Autocratrixes: Images of Female Rule in the Eighteenth Century," in *Gender and Sexuality in Russian Civilization*, ed. Peter I. Barta (London: Routledge, 2001), pp. 33–53.

Allen, W. B., ed., *George Washington: A Collection* (Indianapolis: Liberty Fund, 1988).

Almanach littéraire, ou Etrennes d'Apollon (Paris: Laurent Jeune, 1785).

Anderson, George P., "Pascal Paoli: An Inspiration to the Sons of Liberty," *Publications of the Colonial Society of Massachusetts: Transactions*, vol. 26 (1924), pp. 180–210.

Andress, David, "Living the Revolutionary Melodrama: Robespierre's Sensibility and the Construction of Political Commitment in the French Revolution," *Representations*, vol. 114, no. 1 (2011), pp. 103–28.

———, "The Sentimental Construction of Martyrdom as Motivation in the Thought of Maximilien Robespierre," in *Martyrdom and Terrorism: Pre-Modern to Contemporary Perspectives*, ed. Dominic Janes and Alex Houen (New York: Oxford University Press, 2014), pp. 131–51.

Andrews, Joseph, *Journey from Buenos Ayres Through the Provinces of Cordova, Tucuman, and Salta, to Potosi*, 2 vols. (London: John Murray, 1827).

The Annual Register; or, A View of the History, Politics and Literature for the Year 1798 (London: Burton, 1800).

The Annual Register; or, A View of the History, Politics and Literature for the Year 1802 (London: Wilks, 1803).

The Anti-Jacobin; or, Weekly Examiner. In Two Volumes, 4th ed., revised and corrected (London: J. Wright, 1799).

Arana, Marie, *Bolívar: American Liberator* (New York: Simon & Schuster, 2013).

Archives Parlementaires de 1787 à 1860. Recueil complet des débats législatifs et politiques des chambres françaises, ed. Jérôme Mavidal and M. E. Laurent (Paris: Libraire Adminstrative de Paul Dupont, 1879).

Archivo Santander, 24 vols. (Bogotá: Aguila Negra, 1913–24).

Ardouin, B. (Beaubrun), *Études sur l'histoire d'Haïti; suivies de la vie du général J.-M. Borgella*, 11 vols. (Paris: Dézobry et E. Magdeleine, 1853).

Arenas, Daniel, "Fuit Imperator: Towards a Critical Interpretation of the Malet Coup of October 23, 1812." Paper presented at the Western Society for French History, Bozeman, Montana, October 4, 2019.

Armitage, David, and Sanjay Subrahmanyam, eds., *The Age of Revolutions in Global Context, c. 1760–1840* (Basingstoke, U.K.: Palgrave Macmillan, 2010).

Arrêtés des différentes communes de la colonie de Saint-Domingue, adressées à l'agent particulier du directoire, au général en chef, et à l'administration municipale du Cap (Le Cap Français: P. Roux, 1799).

Atkins, Josiah, *The Diary of Josiah Atkins*, ed. Steven E. Kagle (New York: New York Times and Arno Press, 1975).

Atkinson, Rick, *The British Are Coming: The War for America, Lexington to Princeton, 1775–1777* (New York: Henry Holt, 2019).

Auguste, Claude Bonaparte, and Marcel Bonaparte Auguste, *L'expédition Leclerc, 1801–1803* (Port-au-Prince: H. Deschamps, 1985).

Aulard, Alphonse, *Les grands orateurs de la Révolution: Mirabeau, Vergniaud, Danton, Robespierre* (Paris: F. Rieder, 1914).

———, *Paris pendant la réaction thermidorienne et sous le Directoire*, 5 vols. (Paris: Léopold Cerf et al., 1898–1902).

———, *Paris sous le Consulat: Recueil de documents pour l'histoire de l'esprit public à Paris*, 4 vols. (Paris: Cerf, 1903).

Bache, Richard, *Notes on Colombia Taken in the Years 1822–3, with an Itinerary of the Route from Caracas to Bogotá* (Philadelphia: H. C. Carley and I. Lea, 1827).

Baczko, Bronislaw, *Comment sortir de la Terreur: Thermidor et la Révolution* (Paris: Gallimard, 1989).

———, *Politiques de la Révolution française* (Paris: Gallimard, 2008).

Baehr, Peter, *Caesarism, Charisma and Fate: Historical Sources and Modern Resonances in the Work of Max Weber* (New Brunswick, NJ: Transaction Publishers, 2008).

Baehr, Peter, and Melvin Richter, eds., *Dictatorship in History and Theory: Bonapartism, Caesarism, and Totalitarianism* (Cambridge: Cambridge University Press, 2004).

Baker, Keith Michael, *Inventing the French Revolution: Essays on French Political Culture in the Eighteenth Century* (Cambridge: Cambridge University Press, 1990).

———, ed., *The Old Regime and the French Revolution* (Chicago: University of Chicago Press, 1987).

Baker, William Spohn, ed., *Early Sketches of George Washington* (Philadelphia: Lippincott, 1894).

———, ed., *Character Portraits of Washington as Delineated by Historians, Orators and Divines: Selected and Arranged in Chronological Order with Biographical Notes and References* (Philadelphia: R. M. Lindsay, 1887).

Ballot, Charles, *Le coup d'état du 18 fructidor an V: Rapports de police et documents divers* (Paris: Au siège de la Société, 1906).

Barbauld, Anna Letitia, *Poems* (London: Joseph Johnson, 1773).

———, *Selected Poetry and Prose*, eds. William McCarthy and Elizabeth Kraft (Peterborough, Ontario: Broadview Press, 2002).

Barère, Bertrand, *Mémoires de Bertrand Barère, membre de la Constituante, de la Convention, du Comité de salut public, et de la Chambre des représentants*, eds. Hippolyte Carnot and Pierre-Jean David (d'Angers), 2 vols. (Paris: J. Labitte, 1842).

Barlow, Joel, *The Vision of Columbus* (Paris: English Press, 1793).

Barry, Étienne, *Discours sur les dangers de l'idolâtrie individuelle dans une république* (n.p., 1794).

Barskett, James, and Michel Placide-Justin, *Histoire politique et statistique de l'île d'Hayti, Saint-Domingue* (Paris: Brière, 1826).

Bartoloni-Tuazon, Kathleen, *For Fear of an Elective King: George Washington and the Presidential Title Controversy of 1789* (Ithaca, NY: Cornell University Press, 2014).

Batiffol, M. L., *Les journées des 5 et 6 octobre 1789 à Versailles* (Versailles: Aubert, 1891).

Baumgart, Max, *Literatur des in- und Auslandes über Friedrich den grossen, anlässlich des 100-jährigen todestages des grossen Königs* (Berlin: Decker, 1886).

Bayly, Christopher, *The Birth of the Modern World, 1780–1914* (Oxford: Blackwell, 2004).

———, "The 'Revolutionary Age' in the Wider World, c. 1790–1830," in *War, Empire and Slavery, 1770–1830*, eds. Richard Bessell et al. (London: Palgrave Macmillan, 2010), pp. 21–43.

Bell, David A., "Charismatic Authority in Revolutionary and Napoleonic France," in *Rethinking the Age of Revolutions: France and the Birth of the Modern World*, eds. David A. Bell and Yair Mintzker (New York: Oxford University Press, 2018), pp. 104–33.

————, *The Cult of the Nation in France: Inventing Nationalism, 1680–1800* (Cambridge, MA: Harvard University Press, 2001).

————, "Fake News Is Not the Real Media Threat We're Facing," *The Nation* magazine online, December 22, 2016.

————, *The First Total War: Napoleon's Europe and the Birth of Warfare as We Know It* (Boston: Houghton Mifflin, 2007).

————, "Haiti's Jacobin," *The Nation*, November 2, 2016.

————, *Napoleon: A Concise Biography* (New York: Oxford University Press, 2015).

————, "This Is What Happens When Historians Overuse the Idea of the Network," *The New Republic*, October 25, 2013.

————, "Total History and Microhistory," in *The Blackwell Companion to Historical Thought*, eds. Sarah Maza and Lloyd Kramer (Oxford: Blackwell, 2002), pp. 262–76.

————, "When the Farce Is Tragedy," *Dissent* magazine online, February 1, 2018.

Bell, Madison Smartt, *Toussaint Louverture: A Biography* (New York: Pantheon Books, 2007).

Bellos, David, *The Novel of the Century: The Extraordinary Adventure of "Les Misérables"* (New York: Farrar, Straus and Giroux, 2017).

Benoît, Jérémie, and Bernard Chevallier, *Marengo: Une victoire politique* (Paris: Editions de la Réunion des Musées Nationaux, 2000).

Bénot, Yves, *La démence coloniale sous Napoléon* (Paris: La Découverte, 1992).

Berenson, Edward, *Heroes of Empire: Five Charismatic Men and the Conquest of Africa* (Berkeley: University of California Press, 2010).

Berenson, Edward, and Eva Giloi, eds., *Constructing Charisma: Celebrity, Fame, and Power in Nineteenth-Century Europe* (New York: Berghahn Books, 2010).

Beretti, Francis, *Pascal Paoli et l'image de la Corse au dix-huitième siècle: Le témoignage des voyageurs britanniques* (Oxford: Voltaire Foundation, 1988).

Berghahn, Volker R., *Militarism: The History of an International Debate, 1861–1979* (New York: St. Martin's Press, 1982).

Bernadou, Vanessa, et al., eds., *Que faire du charisme?: Retours sur une notion de Max Weber* (Rennes: Presses Universitaires de Rennes, 2014).

Bernstein, Richard B., *The Founding Fathers Reconsidered* (New York: Oxford University Press, 2009).

Bertaud, Jean-Paul, *Guerre et société en France de Louis XIV à Napoléon 1er* (Paris: Armand Colin, 1998).

————, *La révolution armée: Les soldats-citoyens et la Révolution française* (Paris: Robert Laffont, 1979).

————, "Napoleon's Officers," *Past and Present*, no. 112 (1986), pp. 91–111.

Beyle, Marie Henri [Stendhal], *Vie de Napoléon, par Stendhal* (Paris: Calmann-Levy, 1877).

Biard, Michel, and Philippe Bourdin, eds., *Robespierre: Portraits croisés* (Paris: Armand Colin, 2012).

Bickham, Troy O., *Making Headlines: The American Revolution as Seen Through the British Press* (DeKalb: Northern Illinois University Press, 2009).

Bidwell, Barnabas, *The Mercenary Match: A Tragedy* (New Haven, CT: Meigs, Bowen and Dana, 1785).

Bienvenu, Richard T., ed., *The Ninth of Thermidor: The Fall of Robespierre* (New York: Oxford University Press, 1968).

Birzer, Bradley J., *American Cicero: The Life of Charles Carroll* (Wilmington, DE: Intercollegiate Studies Institute, 2010).

Biskup, Thomas, *Friedrichs Grösse: Inszenierungen des Preussenkönigs in Fest und Zeremoniell, 1740–1815* (Frankfurt: Campus Verlag, 2012).

Black, Jeremy, *The English Press in the Eighteenth Century* (London: Croom Helm, 1987).

Blackburn, Robin, *The Overthrow of Colonial Slavery, 1776–1848* (London: Verso, 1988).

Blanc, Félix, "L'organisation des pouvoirs de guerre et de paix aux origines du gouvernement représentatif: Essai sur l'invention du concours des pouvoirs en Angleterre, en France et aux Etats-Unis" (Paris: unpublished dissertation, École des Hautes Études en Sciences Sociales, 2014).

Blanchard, Claude, *Guerre d'Amérique, 1780–1783: Journal de campagne de Claude Blanchard, commissaire des guerres* (Paris: Librairie Militaire Dumaine, 1881).

Blanco, José Felix, et al., eds., *Documentos para la historia de la vida publica del Libertador*, 15 vols. (Caracas: Imprenta de "La Opinión Nacional," 1875–79).

Blanning, T. C. W., *The French Revolutionary Wars, 1787–1802* (London: Arnold, 1996).

Blaufarb, Rafe, *The French Army 1750–1820: Careers, Talents, Merit* (Manchester: Manchester University Press, 2002).

"Bolivar jugé par un officier de Napoléon," *Mercure de France*, vol. 115, no. 390 (1913), pp. 328–44.

Bólivar, Símon, *Doctrina del Libertador*, ed. Manuel Pérez Vila (Caracas: Biblioteca Ayacucho, 1976).

———, *El Libertador: Writings of Simón Bolívar*, ed. David Bushnell, trans. Frederick H. Fornhoff (New York: Oxford University Press, 2003).

Bolívar, Simón, and Francisco de Paula Santander, *Cartas Santander-Bolivar*, 6 vols. (Bogotá: Fundación para la Conmemoración del Bicentenario del Natalicio y el Sesquicentenario de la Muerte del General Francisco de Paula Santander, 1988).

Bollème, Geneviève, et al., *Livre et société dans la France du XVIIIe siècle*, 2 vols. (Paris: Mouton, 1965–70).

Bonaparte, Louis-Napoleon, *Des idées napoléoniennes* (Brussels: Jules Géruzet, 1839).

Bonaparte, Napoleon, *Correspondance de Napoléon 1er, publiée par ordre de l'empereur Napoléon III*, 20 vols. (Paris: Imprimerie Impériale, 1858–60).

———, *Discours de Napoléon sur les vérités et les sentiments qu'il importe le plus d'inculquer aux hommes pour leur bonheur* (Paris: Baudouin frères, 1826).

———, *Napoléon inconnu: Papiers inédits, 1786–1793*, eds. Frédéric Masson and Guido Biagi, 2 vols. (Paris: Ollendorff, 1895).

———, *Oeuvres littéraires et écrits militaires*, ed. Jean Tulard, 3 vols. (Paris: Claude Tchou, 2001).

Bonaparte, Napoleon, and Fondation Napoléon, *Correspondance générale de Napoléon Bonaparte*, 12 vols. (Paris: Fayard and Fondation Napoléon, 2004).

Bonet de Treyches, Joseph Balthazar, *Tableau politique de la France régénérée* (Paris: Pillardeau, 1800).

Bonnet, Jean-Claude, *Naissance du panthéon: Essai sur le culte des grands hommes* (Paris: Fayard, 1998).

Bossuet, Jacques-Bénigne, *Politique tirée des propres paroles de l'écriture sainte*, ed. Jacques Le Brun (Geneva: Droz, 1967).

Boswell, James, *An Account of Corsica, the Journal of a Tour to That Island, and Memoirs of Pascal Paoli* (Glasgow: Robert and Andrew Foulis, 1768).

———, *An Account of Corsica, the Journal of a Tour to That Island; and Memoirs of Pascal Paoli*, eds. James T. Boulton and T. O. McLoughlin (Oxford: Oxford University Press, 2006).

———, *Boswell on the Grand Tour: Italy, Corsica, and France, 1765–1766* (Melbourne: W. Heinemann, 1955).

———, *Boswell's "The Life of Samuel Johnson"* (New York: Scribner's Sons, 1917).

———, *Boswell's London Journal, 1762–1763* (New Haven, CT: Yale University Press, 2004).

———, ed., *British Essays in Favour of the Brave Corsicans* (London: Edward and Charles Dilly, 1769).

———, *Letters of James Boswell: Addressed to . . . W. J. Temple: Now First Published from the Original Mss.; with an Introduction and Notes* (London: Bentley, 1857).

Boucher, Geneviève, "Le héros robespierriste, entre l'incarnation du peuple et la victime sacrificielle," *Postscriptum.org*, vol. 10 (Autumn 2010).

Boudon, Jacques-Olivier, "Grand homme ou demidieu? La mise en place d'une religion napoléonienne," *Romantisme*, vol. 28, no. 100 (1998), pp. 131–41.

Boulton, Alfredo, *Iconografía del Libertador*, ed. Enrique Uribe White (Caracas: Ediciones Lerner, 1987).

Bourdais, S.-F., *Portrait de Frédéric le grand tiré des anecdotes les plus intéressantes et les plus certaines de sa vie militaire, philosophique et privée* (Berlin: De la Garde, 1788).

Bourne, H. E., "The Personality of Robespierre: Source Study for College Classes," *The Historical Outlook*, vol. 11 (1920), pp. 177–89.

Bourrienne, Louis-Antoine Fauevelet de, *Mémoires de M. de Bourrienne, Ministre d'état sur Napoléon: Le Directoire, le Consulat, l'Empire et la Restauration*, 10 vols. (Brussels: A. Wahlen and H. Tarlier, 1829).

Bowman, Frank, "Napoléon et Le Christ," *Europe*, vol. 480 (1969), pp. 82–104.

Brading, David, *Classical Republicanism and Creole Patriotism: Simon Bolivar (1783–1830) and the Spanish American Revolution* (Cambridge: Centre for Latin American Studies, 1983).

Branda, Pierre, and Thierry Lentz, *Napoléon, l'esclavage et les colonies* (Paris: Fayard, 2006).

Braudel, Fernand, *The Identity of France*, trans. Siân Reynolds, 2 vols. (New York: HarperCollins, 1989–91).

Breen, T. H., *The Marketplace of Revolution: How Consumer Politics Shaped American Independence* (New York: Oxford University Press, 2004).

———, *George Washington's Journey: The President Forges a New Nation* (New York: Simon & Schuster, 2016).

Breña, Roberto, "The Cádiz Liberal Revolution and Spanish American Independence," in *New Countries: Capitalism, Revolutions and Nations in the Americas, 1750–1870*, ed. John Tutino (Durham, NC: Duke University Press, 2016), pp. 71–104.

Breuer, Stefan, *Max Webers Herrschaftssoziologie* (Frankfurt: Campus Verlag, 1991).

Brewer, John, *Party Ideology and Popular Politics at the Accession of George III* (Cambridge: Cambridge University Press, 1976).

———, *The Pleasures of the Imagination: English Culture in the Eighteenth Century* (New York: Farrar, Straus and Giroux, 1997).

Briggs, Ronald, "A Napoleonic Bolívar: Historical Analogy, Desengaño, and the Spanish/Creole Consciousness," *Journal of Spanish Cultural Studies*, vol. 11, nos. 3–4 (2010), pp. 337–52.

Brissot de Warville, Jacques-Pierre, *Mémoires de Brissot*, ed. M. F. Montrol, 4 vols. (Paris: Ladvocat, 1832).

———, *Nouveau voyage dans les États-Unis de l'Amérique septentrionale, fait en 1788*, 3 vols. (Paris: Buisson, 1791).

Brodsky, Alyn, *Benjamin Rush: Patriot and Physician* (New York: Truman Talley Books, 2004).

Broers, Michael, *Napoleon: Soldier of Destiny* (New York: Pegasus, 2014).

Brooks, Jeffrey, *Thank You, Comrade Stalin! Soviet Public Culture from Revolution to Cold War* (Princeton, NJ: Princeton University Press, 2000).

Brooks, Peter, *The Melodramatic Imagination: Balzac, Henry James, Melodrama, and the Mode of Excess* (New Haven, CT: Yale University Press, 1976).

Brown, Howard G., *Ending the French Revolution: Violence, Justice, and Repression from the Terror to Napoleon* (Charlottesville: University of Virginia Press, 2006).

———, *Mass Violence and the Self: From the French Wars of Religion to the Paris Commune* (Ithaca, NY: Cornell University Press, 2019).

Brown, Jared, *The Theatre in America During the Revolution* (Cambridge: Cambridge University Press, 1995).

Brown, Matthew, "Richard Vowell's Not-So-Imperial Eyes: Travel Writing and Adventure in Nineteenth-Century Hispanic America," *Journal of Latin American Studies*, vol. 38, no. 1 (2006), pp. 95–122.

Brown, Thomas, "From Old Hickory to Sly Fox: The Routinization of Charisma in the Early Democratic Party," *Journal of the Early Republic*, vol. 11, no. 3 (1991), pp. 339–69.

Bruce, Michael, *Poems on Several Occasions by Michael Bruce* (Edinburgh: J. Robertson, 1770).

Bryan, William Alfred, *George Washington in American Literature, 1775–1865* (New York: Columbia University Press, 1952).

Buck-Morss, Susan, *Hegel, Haiti and Universal History* (Pittsburgh: University of Pittsburgh Press, 2009).

Burke, Peter, *The Fabrication of Louis XIV* (New Haven, CT: Yale University Press, 1992).

Burnard, Trevor, and John Garrigus, *The Plantation Machine: Atlantic Capitalism in French Saint-Domingue and British Jamaica* (Philadelphia: University of Pennsylvania Press, 2016).

Burney, Fanny, *The Early Journals and Letters of Fanny Burney*, eds. Lars E. Troide and Stewart J. Cooke, 5 vols. (Montreal: McGill University Press, 2012).

Burton, June K., *Napoleon and the Woman Question: Discourses of the Other Sex in French Education, Medicine, and Medical Law 1799–1815* (Lubbock: Texas Tech University Press, 2007).

Bushkovitch, Paul, *Peter the Great* (Lanham, MD: Rowman & Littlefield, 2001).

Bushnell, David, "The Last Dictatorship: Betrayal or Consummation?," *Hispanic American Historical Review*, vol. 63, no. 1 (1983), pp. 65–105.

Bushnell, David, and Lester D. Langley, eds., *Simón Bolívar: Essays on the Life and Legacy of the Liberator* (Lanham, MD: Rowman & Littlefield, 2008).

Businche, José Luis, *Bolívar visto por sus contemporáneos* (Mexico City: Fondo de Cultura Económica, 1960).

Byron, George Gordon, Lord, "Ode to Napoleon Buonaparte," www.bartleby.com/333/543.html.

Candela, Gilles, *L'armée d'Italie: Des missionnaires armés à la naissance de la guerre napoléonienne* (Rennes: Presses Universitaires de Rennes, 2011).

Carboni, Pierre, "Boswell et Paoli: Un Plutarque écossais et son Lycurge corse," in *Le culte des grands hommes au XVIIIe siècle*, eds. Jackie Pigeaud and Jean-Paul Barbé (Nantes: Institut Universitaire de France, 1996), pp. 109–18.

Carlyle, Thomas, *On Heroes, Hero-Worship and the Heroic in History: Six Lectures* (New York: John Wiley & Sons, 1866).

Carrera Damas, Germán, *El culto a Bolívar: Esbozo para un estudio de la historia de las ideas en Venezuela* (Caracas: Grijalbo, 1989).

———, "Mitología política e ideologías alternativas: El bolivarianismo-militarismo," in Germán Carrera Damas et al., *Mitos politicos en las sociedades andinas* (Caracas: Institut Français d'Études Andines, 2015), pp. 391–420.

———, "Simón Bolívar, el culto heroico y la nación," *Hispanic American Historical Review*, vol. 63, no. 1 (1983), pp. 107–45.

Casper, Gerhard, "Caesarism in Democratic Politics–Reflections on Max Weber," (2007), https://ssrn.com/abstract=1032647.

Castro Leiva, Luis, *De la patria boba a la teología bolivariana* (Madrid: Monte Avila, 1991).

Cauna, Jacques de, *Toussaint Louverture: Le grand précurseur* (Bordeaux: Sud-ouest, 2012).

Celius, Carlo, "Neoclassicism and the Haitian Revolution," in *The World of the Haitian Revolution*, eds. Norman Fiering and David Geggus (Bloomington: Indiana University Press, 2009), pp. 352–92.

Censer, Jack, *Debating Modern Revolution: The Evolution of Revolutionary Ideas* (London: Bloomsbury, 2015).

Cesarani, David, *Disraeli: The Novel Politician* (New Haven, CT: Yale University Press, 2016).

"Character of the Celebrated Black General Toussaint L'Ouverture," *American Intelligencer*, June 11, 1801, p. 1.

"Charisma," *Psychology Today: Basics* (2019). https://www.psychologytoday.com/us/basics/charisma.

Charron, Joseph, *Discours prononcé à Châlons le 10 prairial an V, fête de la reconnaissance* (Châlons-sur-Marne: Mercier, 1797).

Chartier, Roger, *The Cultural Origins of the French Revolution*, trans. Lydia G. Cochrane (Durham, NC: Duke University Press, 1991).

Chasteen, John Charles, *Americanos: Latin America's Struggle for Independence* (New York: Oxford University Press, 2008).

Chastellux, François-Jean de Beauvoir de, *Voyages de M. le marquis de Chastellux dans l'Amérique septentrionale dans les années 1780, 1781 & 1782*, 2 vols. (Paris: Prault, 1786).

Chateaubriand, François-René de, *Mémoires d'outre-tombe*, ed. Edmond Biré, 6 vols. (Paris: Garnier Frères, 1910).

———, *Œuvres complètes*, 38 vols. (Paris: Desrez, 1837–41).

Chernow, Ron, *Washington: A Life* (New York: Penguin Press, 2010).

Chesterton, George Laval, *A Narrative of Proceedings in Venezuela in South America in the Years 1819 and 1820* (London: John and Arthur Arch, 1820).

———, *Peace, War, and Adventure: An Autobiographical Memoir*, 2 vols. (London: Longman, 1853).

Chinard, Gilbert, and P. J. Conkwright, *George Washington as the French Knew Him* (Princeton, NJ: Princeton University Press, 1940).

Chinn, Sarah E., *Spectacular Men: Race, Gender and Nation on the Early American Stage* (New York: Oxford University Press, 2017).

Cini, Marco, and Francis Beretti, eds., *La nascita di un mito: Pasquale Paoli tra '700 e '800* (Pisa: BFS, 1998).

Clavin, Matthew J., *Toussaint Louverture and the American Civil War: The Promise and Peril of a Second Haitian Revolution* (Philadelphia: University of Pennsylvania Press, 2010).

Cloots, Anacharsis, *Appel au genre humain* (n.p., 1793).

Cockings, George, *The Paoliad* (London: n.p., 1769).

Cole, Juan, *Napoleon's Egypt: Invading the Middle East* (New York: Palgrave Macmillan, 2007).

Cole, Richard C., "James Oglethorpe as Revolutionary Propagandist: The Case of Corsica, 1768," *The Georgia Historical Quarterly*, vol. 74, no. 3 (1990), pp. 463–74.

Coleman, Charly, "Resacralizing the World: The Fate of Secularization in Enlightenment Historiography," *The Journal of Modern History*, vol. 82, no. 2 (2010), pp. 368–95.

———, *The Virtues of Abandon: An Anti-Individualist History of the French Enlightenment* (Stanford, CA: Stanford University Press, 2014).

Colonna, Dominique, *Le vrai visage de Pascal Paoli en Angleterre* (Nice: self-published, 1969).

Colvill, Robert, *The Cyrnean Hero: A Poem* (London: n.p., 1772).

The Conquest of Corsica by the French. A Tragedy. By a Lady. (London: n.p., 1771).

Constant, Benjamin, *De l'esprit de conquête et de l'usurpation dans leurs rapports avec la civilisation européenne* (Paris: Le Normant, 1814).

———, *Mémoires sur les cent-jours* (Paris: Pauvert, 1961).

Constitution of the Commonwealth of Massachusetts (1780).

Conway, Christopher B., *The Cult of Bolívar in Latin American Literature* (Gainesville: University Press of Florida, 2003).

Cooper, Samuel, "Diary of Samuel Cooper, 1775–1776," *American Historical Review*, vol. 6, no. 2 (1901), pp. 301–41.

Cope, Kevin Lee, ed., *George Washington in and as Culture* (New York: AMS Press, 2001).

Corbin, Alain, Jean-Jacques Courtine, and Georges Vigarello, eds., *A History of Virility*, trans. Keith Cohen (New York: Columbia University Press, 2016).

Corsica: A Poetical Address (London: n.p., 1769).

Courtois, Edme-Bonaventure, ed., *Papiers inédits trouvés chez Robespierre, Saint-Just, Payan, etc., supprimés ou omis par Courtois* (Paris: Baudouin Frères, 1828).

Covo, Manuel, "Baltimore and the French Atlantic: Empires, Commerce and Identity in a Revolutionary Age, 1783–1798," in A. B. Leonard and David Pretel, eds., *The Caribbean and the Atlantic World Economy: Circuits of Trade, Money and Knowledge, 1650–1914* (New York: Palgrave Macmillan, 2015), pp. 87–107.

Cowan, Brian, "News, Biography, and Eighteenth-Century Celebrity," *Oxford Handbooks Online* (2016), https://www.oxfordhandbooks.com/view/10.1093/oxfordhb.

———, ed., *The State Trial of Doctor Henry Sacheverell* (Oxford: Wiley-Blackwell, 2012).

Cox, Caroline, "The Continental Army," in *The Oxford Handbook of the American Revolution Online* (2013).

Craig, Gordon Alexander, *The Politics of the Prussian Army 1640–1945* (Oxford: Clarendon Press, 1955).

Crespo, María Victoria, *Del rey al presidente: Poder Ejecutivo, formación del Estado y soberanía en la Hispanoamérica revolucionaria, 1810–1826* (Mexico City: El Colegio de México, 2013).

Critical Memoirs of the Times: Containing a Summary View of the Popular Pursuits, Political Debates, and Literary Productions of the Present Age (London: n.p., 1769).

Cross, Anthony, "Catherine II Through Contemporary British Eyes," *Russica Romana*, vol. 4 (1997), pp. 55–65.

———, *Peter the Great Through British Eyes: Perceptions and Representations of the Tsar Since 1698* (Cambridge: Cambridge University Press, 2000).

Dallett, Francis James, Jr., "John Leacock and the Fall of British Tyranny," *The Pennsylvania Magazine of History and Biography*, vol. 78, no. 4 (1954), pp. 456–75.

Damrosch, Leo, *The Club: Johnson, Boswell, and the Friends Who Shaped an Age* (New Haven, CT: Yale University Press, 2019).

Danchet, Antoine, *Œuvres mêlées de M. Danchet*, 4 vols. (Paris: Grange, 1751).

Darnton, Robert, *The Great Cat Massacre and Other Episodes in French Cultural History* (New York: Basic Books, 1984).

Davies, Thomas, *Memoirs of the Life of David Garrick, Esq. Interspersed with Characters and Anecdotes of His Theatrical Contemporaries*, 2 vols. (Dublin: Joseph Hill, 1780).

Davis, David Brion, *The Problem of Slavery in the Age of Revolution, 1770–1823* (Ithaca, NY: Cornell University Press, 1975).

Day, Douglas, "Boswell, Corsica, and Paoli," *English Studies*, vol. 45, no. 1 (1964), pp. 1–20.

Dayan, Joan, *Haiti, History, and the Gods* (Berkeley: University of California Press, 1998).

De la Bruyère, Jean, "Discours prononcé le mesme jour 15. Juin 1693," in *Recueil des harangues prononcées par Messieurs de l'Académie française dans leurs réceptions*, 2 vols. (Amsterdam: Aux dépens de la Compagnie, 1709), vol. 2, pp. 262–88.

Decherf, Jean-Baptiste, *Le grand homme et son pouvoir: Histoire d'un imaginaire de Napoléon à de Gaulle* (La Tour d'Aigues: Éditions de l'Aube, 2017).

———, "Napoleon and the Poets: The Poetic Origins of the Concept of Charisma," *Studies in Ethnicity and Nationalism*, vol. 10, no. 3 (2010), pp. 362–76.

———, "Sociologie de l'extraordinaire: Une histoire du concept de charisme," *Revue d'histoire des sciences humaines*, vol. 23 (2010), pp. 203–29.

Decomberousse, Benoît-Michel, *Asgill, ou Le prisonnier anglais: Drame en 5 actes et en vers* (Paris: Hautbout-Dumoulin, 1793).

Delille, Jacques, *Œuvres complètes de Jacques Delille: Avec les notes et variantes, les imitations des poètes les plus estimés, et de nouvelles observations littéraires . . .* (Paris: Édouard Leroi, 1835).

Delprat, François, et al., *Miranda y Francia en la era de las luces et de las revoluciones* (Caracas: Embassy of France, 2016).

Démeunier, Jean-Nicolas, *L'Amérique indépendante, ou Les différentes constitutions des treize provinces qui se sont érigées en républiques sous le nom d'États-Unis de l'Amérique* (Ghent: P.-F. de Goesin, 1790).

Denby, David, *Sentimental Narrative and the Social Order in France, 1760–1820* (Cambridge: Cambridge University Press, 1994).

Derman, Joshua, *Max Weber in Politics and Social Thought: From Charisma to Canonization* (Cambridge: Cambridge University Press, 2012).

Desan, Suzanne, Lynn Hunt, and William Max Nelson, eds., *The French Revolution in Global Perspective* (Ithaca: Cornell University Press, 2013).

Descola, Jean, *Les messagers de l'indépendance: Les Français en Amérique latine de Bolivar à Castro* (Paris: Robert Laffont, 1973).

Descourtilz, Michel-Etienne, *Voyages d'un naturaliste, et ses observations faites sur les trois règnes de la nature, dans plusieurs ports de mer français*, 3 vols. (Paris: Dufart, 1809).

Diderot, Denis, "Éloge de Richardson" (1761); http://fr.wikisource.org/wiki/%C3%89loge_de _Richardson.

Diderot, Denis, and Jean Le Rond d'Alembert, eds., *Encyclopédie, ou Dictionnaire raisonné des sciences, des arts et des métiers*, 28 vols. (Paris: Briasson et al., 1751–72).

Dilworth, Thomas, *A New Guide to the English Tongue in Five Parts* (Philadelphia: Young, Stewart and McCullough, 1785).

Dilworth, W. H., *The Father of His Country; or, the History of the Life and Glorious Exploits of Peter the Great, Czar of Muscovy* (London: Woodgate and Brooks, 1760).

————, *The Life and Heroick Actions of Frederick III King of Prussia* (London: G. Wright, 1758).

Dollinger, Hans, *Friedrich II. von Preussen: Sein Bild im Wandel von Zwei Jahrhunderten* (Munich: List, 1986).

Donnadieu, Jean-Louis, *Toussaint Louverture: Le Napoléon noir* (Paris: Belin, 2014).

Dorat, Claude Joseph, *Poésies de Dorat* (Paris: n.p, 1777).

Dorigny, Marcel, *Léger-Félicité Sonthonax: La première abolition de l'esclavage. La Révolution française et la révolution de Saint-Domingue* (Paris: Société française d'histoire d'outre-mer, 1997).

Dow, Thomas, "The Theory of Charisma," *The Sociological Quarterly*, vol. 10, no. 3 (1969), pp. 306–18.

Dowling, William C., *The Boswellian Hero* (Athens: University of Georgia Press, 1979).

Drévillon, Hervé, *L'individu et la guerre: Du chevalier Bayard au soldat inconnu* (Paris: Belin, 2013).

Drexler, Michael J., and Ed White, "The Constitution of Toussaint: Another Origin of African-American Literature," in *A Companion to African-American Literature*, ed. Gene Andrew Jarrett (Chichester, U.K.: Wiley-Blackwell, 2010), pp. 59–74.

Duane, William, *A Visit to Colombia in the Years 1822 & 1823 by Laguayra and Caracas over the Cordillera to Bogota and Thence by the Magdalena to Cartagena* (Philadelphia: Thomas Palmer, 1826).

Dubois, Laurent, "An Enslaved Enlightenment: Rethinking the Intellectual History of the French Atlantic," *Social History*, vol. 31, no. 1 (2006), pp. 1–14.

————, *Avengers of the New World: The Story of the Haitian Revolution* (Cambridge, MA: Harvard University Press, 2004).

————, "Avenging America: The Politics of Violence in the Haitian Revolution," in *The World of the Haitian Revolution*, eds. Norman Fiering and David Geggus (Bloomington: University of Indiana Press, 2009), pp. 111–24.

————, "Dessalines Toro d'Haïti," *The William and Mary Quarterly*, vol. 69, no. 3 (2012), pp. 541–48.

————, *Haiti: The Aftershocks of History* (New York: Henry Holt, 2012).

Dubois-Crancé, Edmond-Louis-Alexis, *Le véritable portrait de nos législateurs, ou Galerie des tableaux exposés à la vue du public depuis le 5 Mai 1789, jusqu'au premier octobre 1791* (Paris: n.p., 1792).

Dubreton, Jean-Lucas, *Le culte de Napoléon, 1815–1848* (Paris: Albin Michel, 1960).

Dubroca, Jean-Louis, *La vie de Bonaparte, depuis sa naissance jusqu'au 18 brumaire an X* (Paris: Dubroca, 1802).

————, *Les quatre fondateurs des dynasties françaises* (Paris: Dubroca and Fantin, 1810).

————, *La vie de Toussaint-Louverture, chef des noirs insurgés de Saint-Domingue: Contenant son origine les particularités des plus remarquables de sa jeunesse . . .* (Paris: Dubroca, 1802).

Duffield, George, *A Sermon, Preached in the Third Presbyterian Church* (Philadelphia: F. Bailey, 1784).

Dun, James Alexander, *Dangerous Neighbors: Making the Haitian Revolution in Early America* (Philadelphia: University of Pennsylvania Press, 2016).

Dunbar, Erica Armstrong, *Never Caught: The Washingtons' Relentless Pursuit of Their Runaway Slave, Ona Judge* (New York: Simon & Schuster, 2017).

Dunbar, Louise Burnham, *A Study of "Monarchical" Tendencies in the United States, from 1776 to 1801* (Urbana: University of Illinois Studies in the Social Sciences, 1922).

Dupuy, Aimé, "Un inspirateur des juvenilia de Napoléon: L'Anglais James Boswell," *Bulletin de l'Association Guillaume Budé*, vol. 3 (1966), pp. 331–39.

Duquette, Elizabeth, "The Man of the World," *American Literary History*, vol. 27, no. 4 (2015), pp. 635–64.

Durkheim, Émile, *Suicide: A Study in Sociology* (New York: Free Press, 1951).

————, *The Elementary Forms of the Religious Life, a Study in Religious Sociology* (London: G. Allen & Unwin, 1915).

Dwight, Timothy, *The Conquest of Canaan* (Hartford: Elisha Babcock, 1785).

Dwyer, Philip, *Napoleon: Passion, Death and Resurrection, 1815–1840* (London: Bloomsbury, 2018).

———, *Napoleon: The Path to Power* (New Haven, CT: Yale University Press, 2008).

———, "Napoleon Bonaparte as Hero and Saviour: Image, Rhetoric and Behaviour in the Construction of a Legend," *French History*, vol. 18, no. 4 (2004), pp. 379–403.

Earle, Rebecca, "Information and Disinformation in Late Colonial New Granada," *The Americas*, vol. 54, no. 2 (1997), pp. 167–84.

Eatwell, Roger, "Charisma and the Radical Right," in *The Oxford Handbook of the Radical Right*, ed. Jens Rydgren (New York: Oxford University Press, 2018), pp. 251–68.

Echeverria, Durand, *Mirage in the West: A History of the French Image of American Society to 1815* (Princeton, NJ: Princeton University Press, 1957).

———, *The Maupeou Revolution: A Study in the History of Libertarianism: France, 1770–1774* (Baton Rouge: Lousiana State University Press, 1985).

Edelstein, Dan, "Do We Want a Revolution Without Revolution? Reflections on Political Authority," *French Historical Studies*, vol. 35, no. 2 (2012), pp. 269–89.

———, "Enlightenment Rights Talk," *The Journal of Modern History*, vol. 86, no. 3 (2014), pp. 530–65.

———, *The Terror of Natural Right: Republicanism, the Cult of Nature, and the French Revolution* (Chicago: University of Chicago Press, 2009).

Eisenstadt, Shmuel, ed., *Max Weber on Charisma and Institution Building* (Chicago: University of Chicago Press, 1968).

Ellis, Joseph J., *His Excellency: George Washington* (New York: Vintage Books, 2005).

Englund, Steven, *Napoleon: A Political Life* (New York: Scribner, 2004).

Ennker, Benno, *Die Anfänge des Leninkults in der Sowjetunion* (Cologne: Böhlau, 1997).

Épitre à Buonaparte (Paris: Le Normant, 1796).

Ettori, Fernand, "Pascal Paoli modèle du jeune Bonaparte," *Annales historiques de la Révolution française*, vol. 203 (1971), pp. 45–55.

Eustace, Nicole, *Passion Is the Gale: Emotion, Power, and the Coming of the American Revolution* (Chapel Hill: University of North Carolina Press, 2008).

Everett, Alexander Hill, *America; or, a General Survey of the Political Situation of the Several Powers of the Western Continent, with Conjectures on Their Future* (Philadelphia: H. C. Carey and I. Lea, 1827).

Everett, Edward, "South America," *North American Review*, vol. 3, no. 2 (1821), pp. 432–42.

Exposicion de los sentimientos de los funcionarios publicos, asi nacionales como departamentales y municipales, y demas habitantes de la ciudad de Bogotá (New York: n.p., 1827).

Fatton, Robert, Jr., *The Roots of Haitian Despotism* (Boulder, CO: Lynne Rienner Publishers, 2007).

Faulcon, Félix, *Mélanges législatifs, historiques et politiques*, 3 vols. (Paris: Henrichs, 1801).

Fe política de un Colombiano, o tres cuestiones importantes para la política del día (Bogota: Salazar, 1827).

Febvre, Lucien, and Henri-Jean Martin, *The Coming of the Book: The Impact of Printing 1450–1800*, trans. David Gerard (London: Verso, 1976).

Ferguson, J. A., "'Le Premier des Noirs': The Nineteenth-Century Image of Toussaint Louverture," *Nineteenth-Century French Studies*, vol. 15, no. 4 (1987), pp. 394–406.

Ferrer, Ada, *Freedom's Mirror: Cuba and Haiti in the Age of Revolution* (Cambridge: Cambridge University Press, 2014).

Feuillet de Conches, Félix-Sébastien, ed., *Louis XVI, Marie-Antoinette et Madame Elisabeth: Lettres et documents inédits*, 6 vols. (Paris: Plon, 1864–73).

Fick, Carolyn E., *The Making of Haiti: The Saint Domingue Revolution from Below* (Knoxville: University of Tennessee Press, 1990).

———, "The Saint-Domingue Slave Revolution and the Unfolding of Independence, 1791–1804," in *The World of the Haitian Revolution*, eds. David Geggus and Norman Fiering (Bloomington: Indiana University Press, 2009), pp. 177–98.

Fick, Heinz, *Der deutsche Militarismus der Vorkriegszeit; Ein Beitrag zur Soziologie des Militarismus* (Potsdam: Alfred Protte, 1932).

Filippi, Alberto, ed., *Bolívar y Europa en las crónicas, el pensamiento político y la historiografía*, 3 vols. (Caracas: Ediciones de la Presidencia de la República, 1986).

———, *El Libertador en la historia italiana: Ilustración, "risorgimento," fascismo* (Caracas: Biblioteca de la Academia Nacional de la Historia, 1987).

Finer, Samuel E., *The Man on Horseback: The Role of the Military in Politics* (New York: Praeger, 1962).

Fischer, David Hackett, *Washington's Crossing* (New York: Oxford University Press, 2004).

Fischer, Sybille, "Bolívar in Haiti: Republicanism in the Revolutionary Atlantic," in *Haiti and the Americas*, ed. Carla Calarge, Rafael Dalleo, Luis Duno-Gottberg, and Clevis Headley (Jackson: University Press of Mississippi, 2013), pp. 25–53.

———, *Modernity Disavowed: Haiti and the Cultures of Slavery in the Age of Revolution* (Durham, NC: Duke University Press, 2004).

Fisher, N., "Letter Describing Washington's Visit to Salem in 1789," *Historical Collections of the Essex Institute*, vol. 67 (1931), pp. 299–300.

Fishman, Ethan M., William D. Pederson, and Mark J. Rozell, *George Washington: Foundation of Presidential Leadership and Character* (Westport, CT: Greenwood Publishing Group, 2001).

Fitz, Caitlin, *Our Sister Republics: The United States in an Age of American Revolutions* (New York: W. W. Norton, 2016).

Fitzpatrick, John C., ed., *The Writings of George Washington from the Original Manuscript Sources, 1745–1799*, 39 vols. (Washington, DC: Government Printing Office, 1931).

Flexner, James Thomas, *George Washington in the American Revolution, 1775–1783* (Boston: Little, Brown, 1968).

Fliegelman, Jay, *Prodigals and Pilgrims: The American Revolution Against Patriarchal Authority, 1750–1800* (Cambridge: Cambridge University Press, 1982).

Foladare, Joseph, *Boswell's Paoli* (Hamden, CT: Archon Books, 1979).

Fontenelle, Bernard Le Bovier de, *Œuvres de Monsieur de Fontenelle* (Amsterdam: Au dépens de la Compagnie, 1754).

Ford, Worthington Chauncey, ed., *The Spurious Letters Attributed to Washington* (Brooklyn: Privately printed, 1889).

Forsdick, Charles, and Christian Høgsbjerg, *Toussaint Louverture: A Black Jacobin in the Age of Revolutions* (London: Pluto Press, 2017).

Fouchard, Jean, *Les marrons de la liberté* (Paris: Éditions de l'École, 1972).

Frank, Jason, "The People as Popular Manifestation," in Bas Leijssenaar and Neil Walker, eds., *Sovereignty in Action* (Cambridge: Cambridge University Press, 2019), pp. 65–90.

Frederick II, King of Prussia, *Examen du prince de Machiavel, avec des notes historiques & politiques*, 2 vols. (The Hague: Jean van Duren, 1741).

Freeman, Douglas Southall, John Alexander Carroll, and Mary Wells Ashworth, *George Washington, a Biography*, 7 vols. (New York: Scribner, 1948).

Freneau, Philip, *The Poems of Philip Freneau* (Philadelphia: Francis Bailey, 1786).

Freneau, Philip, and Fred Lewis Pattee, *The Poems of Philip Freneau, Poet of the American Revolution* (New York: Russell & Russell, 1963).

Freund, Amy, "The Legislative Body: Print Portraits of the National Assembly, 1789–1791," *Eighteenth-Century Studies*, vol. 41, no. 3 (2008), pp. 337–58.

Frevert, Ute, *Gefühlspolitik: Friedrich II. als Herr über die Herzen?* (Göttingen: Wallstein Verlag, 2012).

———, *A Nation in Barracks: Modern Germany, Military Conscription and Civil Society* (Oxford: Berg, 2004).

Friedland, Paul, *Political Actors: Representative Bodies and Theatricality in the Age of the French Revolution* (Ithaca: Cornell University Press, 2002).

Fuld, George, "Early Washington Medals," *American Journal of Numismatics*, vol. 14 (2002), pp. 105–63.

Furstenberg, François, *In the Name of the Father: Washington's Legacy, Slavery, and the Making of a Nation* (New York: Penguin Press, 2006).

Gaffield, Julia, *Haitian Connections in the Atlantic World: Recognition After Revolution* (Chapel Hill: University of North Carolina Press, 2015).

⸻, ed., *The Haitian Declaration of Independence: Creation, Context, and Legacy* (Charlottesville: University of Virginia Press, 2016).

Gainot, Bernard, "Le général Laveaux, gouverneur de Saint-Domingue, député néo-jacobin," *Annales historiques de la Révolution Française*, vol. 278 (1989), pp. 433–54.

⸻, "Persistance d'une culture de l'héroïsme républicain sous le directoire: *Le recueil des actions héroïques, ou Le livre du soldat français*, du général Championnet (1798–99)" in *Héros et héroïnes de la Révolution française*, ed. Serge Bianchi (Paris: Editions du Comité des travaux historiques et scientifiques, 2012).

⸻, "Rites et contexte dans les cérémonies funèbres en l'honneur des généraux de la république (1796–1800)" in *Représentation et pouvoir: La politique symbolique en France (1789–1830)*, eds. Natalie Scholz and Christina Schröer (Rennes: Presses Universitaires de Rennes, 2007), pp. 83–91.

García Márquez, Gabriel, *The General in His Labyrinth*, trans. Edith Grossman (New York: Vintage International, 1990).

Gardiner, John, *An Oration Delivered July 4, 1785, at the Request of the Inhabitants of the Town of Boston* (Boston: Peter Edes, 1785).

Garraway, Doris, "'Légitime Défense': Universalism and Nationalism in the Discourse of the Haitian Revolution," in *Tree of Liberty: Cultural Legacies of the Haitian Revolution in the Atlantic World*, ed. Doris Garraway (Charlottesville: University of Virginia Press, 2008), pp. 63–88.

Gates, Henry Louis, *The Trials of Phillis Wheatley: America's First Black Poet and Her Encounters with the Founding Fathers*, ACLS Humanities E-Book (2003). http://hdl.handle.net/2027/heb.07712.

Gattereau, Armand, *Quelques éclaircissements sur les troubles survenus dans le département du sud de Saint Domingue* (Hamburg: P. F. Fauche, 1797).

Gauchet, Marcel, *Robespierre: L'homme qui nous divise le plus* (Paris: Gallimard, 2018).

Geertz, Clifford, "Centers, Kings and Charisma: Reflections on the Symbolics of Power," in *Rites of Power: Symbolism, Ritual and Politics Since the Middle Ages*, ed. Sean Wilentz (Philadelphia: University of Pennsylvania Press, 1999), pp. 13–38.

Geggus, David, "British Opinion and the Emergence of Haiti, 1791–1805," in *Slavery and British Society, 1776–1846*, ed. James Walvin (Baton Rouge: Louisiana State University Press, 1982), pp. 123–50.

⸻, "The Caribbean in the Age of Revolution" in *The Age of Revolutions in Global Context, c. 1760–1840*, eds. David Armitage and Sanjay Subrahmanyam (Basingstoke, U.K.: Palgrave Macmillan, 2010), pp. 83–100.

⸻, "The Changing Faces of Toussaint Louverture: Literary and Pictorial Depictions," John Carter Brown Library online (2013). http://www.brown.edu/Facilities/John_Carter_Brown_Library/exhibitions/toussaint/pages/historiography.html#f39.

⸻, "The Haitian Revolution in Atlantic Perspective," in *The Oxford Handbook of the Atlantic World*, ed. Nicholas Canny (New York: Oxford University Press, 2011).

⸻, *The Haitian Revolution: A Documentary History* (Indianapolis: Hackett Publishing Company, Inc., 2014).

⸻, *Haitian Revolutionary Studies* (Bloomington: Indiana University Press, 2002).

⸻, ed., *The Impact of the Haitian Revolution in the Atlantic World* (Columbia: University of South Carolina Press, 2001).

⸻, "Toussaint Louverture and the Haitian Revolution," in *Profiles of Revolutionaries in Atlantic History, 1700–1850*, eds. R. William Weisberger, Dennis P. Hupchick, and David L. Anderson (Boulder: Social Science Monographs, 2007), pp. 115–35.

Gehred, Kathryn, "Did George Washington's False Teeth Come from His Slaves?: A Look at the Evidence, the Responses to That Evidence, and the Limitations of History." *The Washington Papers* (2016). http://gwpapers.virginia.edu/george-washingtons-false-teeth-come-slaves-look-evidence-responses-evidence-limitations-history/.

General Simón Bolívar en la campaña de la Nueva Granada en 1819 (Bogota: Imprenta del C.B.E., 1820).

"General Washington auf der Reise: Eine ganz neue Anecdote," *Literatur und Völkerkunde*, vol. 6 (1785).

Ghachem, Malick W., *The Old Regime and the Haitian Revolution* (Cambridge: Cambridge University Press, 2012).

Girard, Philippe R., "Jean-Jacques Dessalines and the Atlantic System: A Reappraisal," *The William and Mary Quarterly*, vol. 69, no. 3 (2012), pp. 549–82.

———, "Quelle langue parlait Toussaint Louverture?: Le *Mémoire* du Fort de Joux et les origines du kreyòl haïtien," *Annales: Histoire, Sciences Sociales*, vol. 68, no. 1 (2013), pp. 107–30.

———, *The Slaves Who Defeated Napoleon: Toussaint Louverture and the Haitian War of Independence, 1801–1804* (Tuscaloosa: University of Alabama Press, 2011).

———, *Toussaint Louverture: A Revolutionary Life* (New York: Basic Books, 2016).

Glassman, Ronald M., and William H. Swatos Jr., eds., *Charisma, History and Social Structure* (New York: Greenwood Press, 1986).

The Glory of America; or, Peace Triumphant Over War (Philadelphia: Oswald and Humphreys, 1783).

Goldstein, Jan, *The Post-Revolutionary Self: Politics and Psyche in France, 1750–1850* (Cambridge, MA: Harvard University Press, 2005).

Gómez Díaz, Marlo, and Hernan Rodriguez Hernández, *Importancia de Luis Perú de Lacroix en nuestra historia y su diario de Bucaramanga* (Bogota: Instituto de Estudios del Ministerio Público, 2016).

Gonzalez, Johnhenry, *Maroon Nation: A History of Revolutionary Haiti* (New Haven, CT: Yale University Press, 2019).

Goodman, Dena, *Becoming a Woman in the Age of Letters* (Ithaca, NY: Cornell University Press, 2009).

Görisch, Wilhelm, *Friedrich der Grosse in den Zeitungen: Beiträge zur Geschichte der Beurteilung Friedrichs durch die Zeitgenossen* (Berlin: Czarnikow & Hollstein, 1907).

Gosselman, Carl August, *Resa i Colombia: Åren 1825 och 1826*, 2 vols. (Nyköping: n.p., 1828).

Gotteri, Nicole, "L'esprit public à Paris avant le coup d'état de brumaire an VIII," in Jacques-Oliver Boudon, ed., *Brumaire: La prise de pouvoir de Bonaparte* (Paris: Éditions SPM, 2001), pp. 15–25.

Goulemot, Jean-Marie, *Ces livres qu'on ne lit que d'une main: Lectures et lecteurs de livres pornographiques au XVIIIe siècle* (Paris: Alinéa, 1991).

Grases, Pedro, ed., *Materiales para la historia del periodismo en Venezuela durante el siglo XIX* (Caracas: Escuela de Periodismo, 1950).

Gray, Edward G., and Jane Kamensky, eds., *The Oxford Handbook of the American Revolution* (New York: Oxford University Press, 2013).

Graziani, Antoine-Marie, *Pascal Paoli: Père de la patrie corse* (Paris: Tallandier, 2002).

Grégoire, Henri, *De la littérature des Nègres* (Paris: Maradan, 1808).

Grieder, Josephine, *Anglomania in France, 1740–1789: Fact, Fiction, and Political Discourse* (Geneva: Droz, 1985).

Grunwald, Lisa, and Stephen J. Adler, eds., *Women's Letters: America from the Revolutionary War to the Present* (New York: Dial Press, 2005).

Gueniffey, Patrice, *bonaparte, 1769–1802*, trans. Steven Rendell (Cambridge, MA: Harvard University Press, 2015).

———, *Le dix-huit brumaire. L'épilogue de la Révolution française (9–10 novembre 1799)* (Paris: Gallimard, 2008).

Guerra, François-Xavier, *Modernidad y independencias: Ensayos sobre las revoluciones hispánicas* (Madrid: MAPFRE, 1992).

Guibert, Jacques-Antoine-Hippolyte, "Éloge du Roi de Prusse," in *Œuvres militaires de Guibert*, 6 vols. (Paris: Magimel, 1803), vol. 5, pp. 321–484.

Guinier, Arnaud, *L'honneur du soldat: Éthique martiale et discipline guerrière dans la France des lumières* (Ceyzérieu: Champ Vallon, 2014).

Habermas, Jürgen, *The Structural Transformation of the Public Sphere: An Inquiry into a Category of Bourgeois Society*, trans. Thomas Burger and Frederick Lawrence (Cambridge, MA: MIT Press, 1989).

Haggard, Robert F., "The Nicola Affair: Lewis Nicola, George Washington, and American Military Discontent During the Revolutionary War," *Proceedings of the American Philosophical Society*, vol. 146, no. 2 (2002), pp. 139–69.

Haggerty, George, *Men in Love: Masculinity and Sexuality in the Eighteenth Century* (New York: Columbia University Press, 1999).

Haigh, Samuel, *Sketches of Buenos Ayres, Chile, and Peru* (London: Effingham Wilson, 1831).

"Half-Kilometre Long Kim Jong-un Propaganda Message Visible from Space," *National Post*, November 23, 2012.

Hamel, Ernest, *Histoire de Robespierre d'après des papiers de famille, les sources originales et des documents entièrement inédits* (Paris: A. Lacroix, 1865).

Hampson, Norman, *Saint-Just* (Oxford: Blackwell, 1991).

Hanley, Wayne, *The Genesis of Napoleonic Propaganda, 1796–1799* (New York: Columbia University Press, 2005).

Harari, Yuval Noah, *The Ultimate Experience: Battlefield Revelations and the Making of Modern War Culture, 1450–2000* (London: Palgrave Macmillan, 2008).

Harding, Nancy, Hugh Lee, Jackie Ford, and Mark Learmonth, "Leadership and Charisma: A Desire That Cannot Speak Its Name?" *Human Relations*, vol. 64, no. 7 (2011), pp. 927–49.

Hardman, John, *The Life of Louis XVI* (New Haven, CT: Yale University Press, 2016).

Harrington, James, *The Oceana of James Harrington and His Other Works* (Dublin: J. Smith and W. Bruce, 1737).

Harsanyi, Doina Pasca, "How to Make a Revolution Without Firing a Shot: Thoughts on the Brissot-Chastellux Polemic (1786–1788)," *French History*, vol. 22, no. 2 (2008), pp. 197–216.

Hart, Charles Henry, *Catalogue of the Engraved Portraits of Washington* (New York: Grolier Club, 1904).

Hart, Stephen M., "Blood, Ink and Pigment: Simón Bolívar as Proteus," *Bulletin of Spanish Studies*, vol. 82, nos. 3–4 (2005), pp. 335–52.

———, "Literary Print Culture in the Spanish Colonies," *Forum for Modern Language Studies*, vol. 36, no. 1 (2000), pp. 92–107.

Harwich, Nikita, "Un héroe para todas las causas: Bolívar en la historiografía," *Iberoamericana*, vol. 10, no. 3 (2003), pp. 7–20.

Hawke, David Freeman, *Benjamin Rush, Revolutionary Gadfly* (Philadelphia: Ardent Media, 1971).

Hay, Robert P., "George Washington: American Moses," *American Quarterly*, vol. 21 (1969), pp. 780–91.

Hazareesingh, Sudhir, *Black Spartacus: The Epic Life of Toussaint Louverture* (London: Allen Lane, 2020).

———, *The Legend of Napoleon* (Cambridge: Granta, 2005).

———, *The Saint-Napoleon: Celebrations of Sovereignty in Nineteenth-Century France* (Cambridge, MA: Harvard University Press, 2004).

Head, David, *A Crisis of Peace: George Washington, the Newburgh Conspiracy, and the Fate of the American Revolution* (New York: Pegasus Books, 2019).

Hébrard, Véronique, "El hombre en armas: De la heroización al mito (Venezuela, siglo XIX)," in *Mitos políticos en las sociedades andinas*, eds. Germán Carrera Damas et al. (Caracas: Travaux de IEA, 2006), pp. 281–300.

———, *Le Venezuela indépendant: Une nation par le discours, 1808–1830* (Paris: L'Harmattan, 1996).

———, "Opinión pública y representación en el Congreso Constituyente de Venezuela (1811–1812)," in *Los espacios públicos en Iberoamérica: Ambigüedades y problemas, siglos XVIII–XIX*, eds. François-Xavier Guerra et al. (Mexico City: Centro de Estudios Mexicanos y Centroamericanos, 2013), pp. 196–224.

Hegel, Georg Wilhelm Friedrich, *Briefe von und an Hegel*, ed. Johannes Hoffmeister, 4 vols. (Hamburg: Felix Meier, 1952).

———, *Reason in History: A General Introduction to the Philosophy of History* (New York: Bobbs-Merrill, 1953).

Heine, Heinrich, *Heinrich Heines sämmtliche Werke*, 12 vols. (Hamburg: Hoffman and Campe, 1876).

Hellmuth, Eckhart, "Die 'Wiedergeburt' Friedrichs des Grossen und der 'Tod fürs Vaterland': Zum patriotischen Selbstverständnis in Preussen in der zweiten Hälfte des 18. Jahrhunderts," *Aufklärung*, vol. 10, no. 2 (1998), pp. 23–54.

Henning, Herzeleide and Eckart, *Bibliographie Friedrich der Grosse 1786–1986* (Berlin: Walter de Gruyter, 1988).

Heredia, José María, *Niágara y otros textos* (Caracas: Bibliloteca Ayacucho, 1990).

———, *Poesía completa*, ed. Carmen Almany Bay (Madrid: Verbum, 2004).

Hicks, Peter, "Late 18th-Century and Very Early 19th-Century British Writings on Napoleon: Myth and History," *Napoleonica: La revue*, vol. 9 (2010), pp. 105–17.

Hill, Aaron, *The Northern Star, a Poem: On the Great and Glorious Actions of the Present Czar of Russia* (London: T. Payne, 1724).

The History of Jack Wilks, a Lover of Liberty. In Two Volumes . . . , 2 vols. (London: n.p., 1769).

Hitchcock, Tim, and Michele Cohen, eds., *English Masculinities, 1660–1800* (London: Longman, 1999).

Hoffmann, Léon-François, "Representations of the Haitian Revolution in French Literature," in *The World of the Haitian Revolution*, eds. Norman Fiering and David Geggus (Bloomington: Indiana University Press, 2009), pp. 339–51.

Holmes, Geoffrey, *The Trial of Doctor Sacheverell* (London: Methuen, 1973).

Hoock, Holger, *Scars of Independence: America's Violent Birth* (New York: Crown, 2017).

Hook, Sidney, *The Hero in History* (Boston: Beacon Press, 1943).

Hopkinson, Francis, *The Miscellaneous Essays and Occasional Writings of Francis Hopkinson, Esq.* (Philadelphia: Printed by T. Dobson, 1792).

Horace, *The Lyric Works of Horace, Translated into English Verse, to Which Are Added a Number of Original Poems* (Philadelphia: Eleazer Oswald, 1786).

Horn, Eva, "Introduction: Narrating Charisma," *New German Critique*, vol. 38, no. 3 (2011), pp. 1–16.

Hunt, Lynn, "The Many Bodies of Marie Antoinette: Political Pornography and the Problem of the Feminine in the French Revolution," in Lynn Hunt, ed., *Eroticism and the Body Politic* (Baltimore: Johns Hopkins University Press, 1990), pp. 108–30.

———, *Inventing Human Rights: A History* (New York: W. W. Norton, 2007).

———, ed., *The New Cultural History* (Berkeley: University of California Press, 1989).

Ibrahim, Vivian, and Margit Wunsch, eds., *Political Leadership, Nations and Charisma*, (Abingdon: Routledge, 2012).

Innes, Joanna, and Mark Philp, eds., *Re-imagining Democracy in the Age of Revolutions: America, France, Britain, Ireland, 1750–1850* (Oxford: Oxford University Press, 2013).

Isenberg, Nancy, and Andrew Burstein, *The Problem of Democracy: The Presidents Adams Confront the Cult of Personality* (New York: Random House, 2019).

Israel, Jonathan, *The Expanding Blaze: How the American Revolution Ignited the World, 1775–1848* (Princeton, NJ: Princeton University Press, 2017).

Jackson, Robert L., "Napoleon in Russian Literature," *Yale French Studies*, vol. 26 (1960), pp. 106–18.

Jacob, Louis, *Robespierre vu par ses contemporains* (Paris: Armand Colin, 1938).

James, C. L. R., *The Black Jacobins: Toussaint L'Ouverture and the San Domingo Revolution* (New York: Vintage Books, 1963).

Jameson, J. Franklin, *The American Revolution Considered as a Social Movement* (Princeton, NJ: Princeton University Press, 1926).

Jansen, Christian, *Der Bürger als Soldat: Die Militarisierung europäischer Gesellschaften im langen 19. Jahrhundert: Ein internationaler Vergleich* (Essen: Klartext, 2004).

Jarrett, Gene Andrew, *A Companion to African American Literature* (Hoboken, NJ: John Wiley & Sons, 2013).

Jenson, Deborah, *Beyond the Slave Narrative: Politics, Sex, and Manuscripts in the Haitian Revolution* (Liverpool: Liverpool University Press, 2011).

———, "Jean-Jacques Dessalines and the African Character of the Haitian Revolution," *The William and Mary Quarterly*, vol. 69, no. 3 (2012), pp. 615–38.

———, "Toussaint Louverture, Spin Doctor? Launching the Haitian Revolution in the French Media," in *Tree of Liberty: Cultural Legacies of the Haitian Revolution in the Atlantic World*, ed. Doris Garraway (Charlottesville: University of Virginia Press, 2008), pp. 41–62.

Johnson, Samuel, *The Rambler*, eds. W. J. Bate and A. B. Straus, 3 vols. (New Haven, CT: Yale University Press, 1969).

Jones, Calvin P., "The Images of Simón Bolívar as Reflected in Ten Leading British Periodicals, 1816–1830," *The Americas*, vol. 40, no. 3 (1984), pp. 377–97.

Jones, Trenton Cole, *Captives of Liberty: Prisoners of War and the Politics of Vengance in the American Revolution* (Philadelphia: University of Pennsylvania Press, 2019).

Jourdan, Annie, "L'éclipse d'un soleil: Louis XVI et les projets monumentaux de la Révolution," in *Symbols, Myths and Images of the French Revolution: Essays in Honor of James A. Leith*, eds. Ian Germani and Robin Swales (Regina: Canadian Plains Research Center, 1998).

———, *Mythes et légendes de Napoléon: Un destin d'exception, entre rêve et réalité* (Toulouse: Privat, 2004).

———, *Napoléon: Héros, imperator, mécène* (Paris: Aubier, 1998).

Jung, Theo, "Le silence du peuple: The Rhetoric of Silence During the French Revolution," *French History*, vol. 31, no. 4 (2017), pp. 440–69.

Junot, Laure, *Memoires de madame la duchesse d'Abrantes, ou Souvenirs historiques sur Napoléon, la Révolution, le Directoire, le Consulat, l'Empire et la Restauration* (Paris: Hauman Cattoir, 1837).

Kadish, Doris Y., and Deborah Jenson, eds.; Norman R. Shapiro, trans., *Poetry of Haitian Independence* (New Haven, CT: Yale University Press, 2015).

Kagan, Robert, "The Strongmen Strike Back," *The Washington Post*, March 14, 2019.

Kaiser, Thomas E., "Louis le Bien Aimé and the Rhetoric of the Royal Body," in *From the Royal to the Republican Body: Incorporating the Political in Seventeenth- and Eighteenth-Century France*, eds. Sara E. Melzer and Kathryn Norberg (Berkeley: University of California Press, 1998), pp. 131–61.

Kalyvas, Andreas, *Democracy and the Politics of the Extraordinary: Max Weber, Carl Schmitt, and Hannah Arendt* (Cambridge: Cambridge University Press, 2008).

Kaminski, John, ed., *George Washington: A Man of Action* (Madison: Wisconsin Historical Society Press, 2017).

Kaminski, John P., and Jill Adair McCaughan, eds., *A Great and Good Man: George Washington in the Eyes of His Contemporaries* (Madison: Madison House, 1989).

Kant, Immanuel, *Kritik der Urteilskraft*, trans. and ed. Karl Vorlaender (Leipzig: Felix Meiner, 1922).

———, "On the Common Saying, That May Be Correct in Theory, But It Is of No Use in Practice," in *Practical Philosophy*, ed. Mary J. Gregor (Cambridge: Cambridge University Press, 1996), pp. 275–309.

Karp, Matthew, *This Vast Southern Empire: Slaveholders at the Helm of American Foreign Policy* (Cambridge, MA: Harvard University Press, 2016).

Kenrick, William, *An Epistle to James Boswell, Esq. Occasioned by His Having Transmitted the Moral Writings of Dr. Samuel Johnson, to Pascal Paoli, . . . With a Postscript, Containing Thoughts on Liberty* (London: Fletcher and Anderson, 1768).

Kermes, Stephanie, *Creating an American Identity: New England, 1789–1825* (New York: Palgrave Macmillan, 2008).

Kershaw, Ian, *Hitler: A Biography* (New York: W. W. Norton, 2008).

———, "Hitler and the Uniqueness of Nazism," *Journal of Contemporary History*, vol. 39, no. 2 (2004), pp. 239–54.

———, " 'Working Towards the Führer': Reflections on the Nature of the Hitler Dictatorship," *Contemporary European History*, vol. 2, no. 2 (1993), pp. 103–18.

Ketcham, Ralph, *Presidents Above Party: The First American Presidency, 1789–1829* (Chapel Hill: University of North Carolina Press, 1984).

Kete, Kathleen, *Making Way for Genius: The Aspiring Self in France from the Old Regime to the New* (New Haven, CT: Yale University Press, 2012).

Klapthor, Margaret Brown, *G. Washington: A Figure Upon the Stage* (Washington: Smithsonian Institution Press, 1982).

Klooster, Wim, *Revolutions in the Atlantic World: A Comparative History* (New York: New York University Press, 2009).

Kloppenberg, James, *Toward Democracy: The Struggle for Self-Rule in European and American Thought* (New York: Oxford University Press, 2016).

Knott, Sarah, *Sensibility and the American Revolution* (Chapel Hill: University of North Carolina Press, 2009).

Koekkoek, René, *The Citizenship Experiment: Contesting the Limits of Civic Equality and Participation in the Age of Revolutions* (Leiden: Brill, 2020).

Kotkin, Stephen, *Stalin: Paradoxes of Power, 1878–1928* (New York: Penguin Press, 2014).

———, *Stalin: Waiting for Hitler, 1929–1941* (New York: Penguin Press, 2017).

Kraus, Michael, "America and the Utopian Ideal in the Eighteenth Century," *The Mississippi Valley Historical Review*, vol. 22, no. 4 (1936), pp. 487–504.

Kreiser, B. Robert, *Miracles, Convulsions, and Ecclesiastical Politics in Early Eighteenth-Century Paris* (Princeton, NJ: Princeton University Press, 1978).

Kruse, Wolfgang, *Die Erfindung des modernen Militarismus: Krieg, Militär und Bürgerliche Gesellschaft im politischen Diskurs der Französischen Revolution 1789–1799* (Munich: R. Oldenbourg, 2003).

———, "La formation du discours militariste sous le directoire," *Annales historiques de la Révolution française*, vol. 360 (2010), pp. 77–102.

Kuethe, Allan James, "The Military Reform in the Viceroyalty of New Granada, 1773–1796" (Gainesville, FL: unpublished dissertation, University of Florida, 1967).

Lacroix, Sigismond, ed., *Actes de La Commune de Paris pendant la Révolution*, 8 vols. (Paris: L. Cerf, 1894).

Lamb, Jonathan, "Recent Studies in the Restoration and Eighteenth Century," *Studies in English Literature 1500–1900*, vol. 41, no. 3 (2001), pp. 623–65.

Lambalot, Roland, *Toussaint Louverture au château de Joux* (Pontarlier: Office du Tourisme, 1989).

Lammel, Isabell, *Der Toussaint-Louverture-Mythos: Transformationen in der französischen Literatur, 1791–2012* (Bielefeld: Transcript Verlag, 2015).

Langley, Lester D., *The Americas in the Age of Revolution, 1750–1850* (New Haven, CT: Yale University Press, 1996).

Langlois, Claude, "Le plebiscite de l'an VIII, ou Le coup d'état du 18 pluviôse an VIII," *Annales historiques de la Révolution française*, vol. 207 (1972), pp. 43–65.

Las Cases, Emmanuel de, *Le mémorial de Sainte-Hélène, par le comte de Las Cases*. 4 vols. (Paris: Garnier Frères, 1823).

Lasch, Christopher, *The Culture of Narcissism: American Life in an Age of Diminishing Expectations* (New York: W. W. Norton, 1978).

Lasky, Melvin Jonah, *Utopia & Revolution: On the Origins of a Metaphor* (New Brunswick, NJ: Transaction Publishers, 1976).

Lattre, Philippe-Albert de, *Campagnes des Français à Saint-Domingue, et réfutation des reproches faits au capitaine-général Rochambeau* (Paris: Locard, 1805).

Lavant, A., *Éloge de Bonaparte* (Nîmes: B. Farge, 1800).

Laveaux, Étienne, *Compte rendu par le général Laveaux à ses concitoyens, à l'opinion publique, aux autorités constituées* (Paris: Imprimerie du Bureau Central d'Abonnement à tous les Journaux, 1797).

———, *Discours prononcé par C. Lavaux, député de Saint-Domingue* (Paris: Imprimerie Nationale, 1797).

———, *Réponse d'Étienne Laveaux, général de division, ex-gouverneur de St.-Domingue, aux calomnies que le citoyen Viénot Vaublanc, colon de St. Domingue et membre du Conseil des Cinq Cents s'est permis de mettre dans son discours prononcé dans la séance du 10 prairial dernier* (Paris: J. F. Sobry, 1797).

Laveaux, Marie-Jacobie-Sophie de, *Réponse aux calomnies coloniales de Saint-Domingue: L'épouse du républicain Lavaux, gouverneur-général (par intérim) des isles françaises sous le vent, à ses concitoyens* (Paris: Imprimerie de Pain, 1797).

La Vicomterie, Louis de, *Les crimes des rois de France* (Paris: Adolphe Havard, 1834).

Le Barbier, J.-L. (le jeune), *Asgill, Drame, en cinq actes, en prose* (Paris: n.p.,1785).

Le Gros, Gabriel, *An Historick Recital, of the Different Occurrences in the Camps of Grande-Riviere, Dondon, Sainte-Suzanne, and Others, from the 26th of October 1791, to the 24th of December, of the Same Year* (Baltimore: John and Samuel Adams, 1792).

Leacock, John, *The Fall of British Tyranny; or, American Liberty Triumphant, a Tragi-Comedy* (Philadelphia: Styner and Cist, 1776).

Leclerc, Charles, ed., *Lettres du général Leclerc: Commandant en chef de l'armée de Saint-Domingue en 1802* (Paris: Leroux, 1937).

Lecomte, L.-Henry, *Napoléon et l'empire racontés par le théâtre, 1797–1899* (Paris: Jules Raux, 1900).

Lee, Charles, and Edward Langworthy, *The Life and Memoirs of the Late Major General Lee: Second in Command to General Washington During the American Revolution, to Which Are Added His Political and Military Essays. Also, Letters to and from Many Distinguished Characters Both in Europe and America* (New York: Richard Scott, 1813).

Lengel, Edward G., *Inventing George Washington: America's Founder, in Myth and Memory* (New York: HarperCollins, 2011).

Lentz, Thierry, "Vers le pouvoir héréditaire: Le 'parallèle entre César, Cromwell, Monck et Bonaparte' de Lucien Bonaparte," *Revue du souvenir napoléonien*, vol. 431 (2000), pp. 3–6.

Leonard, Daniel, *Massachusettensis; or, A Series of Letters, Containing a Faithful State of Many Important and Striking Facts, Which Laid the Foundation of the Present Troubles in the Province of Massachusetts-Bay* (Boston: J. Matthews, 1776).

Lepsius, Rainer, "Charismatic Leadership: Max Weber's Model and Its Applicability to the Rule of Hitler," in *Changing Conceptions of Leadership*, eds. Carl F. Graumann and Serge Moscovici (Berlin: Springer, 1986), pp. 53–66.

Les époques, ou Précis des actions mémorables du général Bonaparte, par le C*** M*** (Paris: Batilliot, 1799).

Lescouflair, Arthur, *Thomas Madiou* (Port-au-Prince: Pan-American Institute of Geography and History, 1950).

"Letters of Toussaint Louverture and of Edward Stevens," *American Historical Review*, vol. 16, no. 1 (1910), pp. 64–101.

Leveau, *Chanson nouvelle sur la paix* (Paris: Daniel, 1797).

Lilti, Antoine, *Figures publiques: L'invention de la célébrité, 1750–1850* (Paris: Fayard, 2014).

———, *Le monde des salons: Sociabilité et mondanité à Paris au XVIIIe siècle* (Paris: Fayard, 2005).

Lindholm, Charles, *Charisma* (Oxford: Blackwell, 1990).

Lipset, Seymour Martin, "George Washington and the Founding of Democracy," *Journal of Democracy*, vol. 9, no. 4 (1998), pp. 24–38.

Lloyd, Vincent, *In Defense of Charisma* (New York: Columbia University Press, 2018).

Lofft, Capel, *The Praises of Poetry. A Poem* (London: W. Owen, 1775).

Loiselle, Kenneth, *Brotherly Love: Freemasonry and Male Friendship in Enlightenment France* (Ithaca, NY: Cornell University Press, 2014).

Lomonosov, Mikhail Vasilyevich, *L'Apothéose de Pierre le Grand, etc. Trois écrits historiques inconnus, présumés de M. V. Lomonosov, destinés à Voltaire* (Prague: Académie Tchécoslovaque des Sciences, 1964).

Lomonosov, Mikhail Vasilyevich, and Tschoudy, *Panégirique de Pierre le Grand prononcé dans la séance publique de l'Académie impériale des sciences, le 26. avril 1755* (Saint Petersburg: n.p., 1755).

Long, Luke Paul, "Britain and Corsica 1729–1796: Political Intervention and the Myth of Liberty" (unpublished Ph.D. dissertation, University of Saint Andrews, 2018).

Longmore, Paul K., *The Invention of George Washington* (Berkeley: University of California Press, 1988).

Lortholary, Albert, *Le mirage russe en France au XVIIIe siècle* (Paris: Boivin, 1951).

Loughran, Trish, *The Republic in Print: Print Culture in the Age of U.S. Nation Building, 1770–1870* (New York: Columbia University Press, 2007).

Louverture, Toussaint, *Extrait du rapport adressé au Directoire exécutif par le citoyen Toussaint Louverture, général en chef des forces de la République française à Saint-Domingue* (Le Cap Français: P. Roux, 1797).

———, *Réfutation de quelques assertions d'un discours prononcé au corps législatif le 10 prairial, an cinq, par Viénot Vaubalnc* (Le Cap Français: n.p., 1797).

———, *Lettres à la France, 1794–1798: Idées pour la libération du peuple noir d'Haïti*, eds. Antonio Maria Baggio and Ricardo Augustin (Bruyères-le-Châtel: Nouvelle cité, 2011).

———, *Mémoires du général Toussaint Louverture*, ed. Daniel Desormeaux (Paris: Classiques Garnier, 2011).

———, *The Memoir of General Toussaint Louverture*, ed. Philippe R. Girard (New York: Oxford University Press, 2014).

———, *Toussaint Louverture à travers sa correspondance, 1794 1798*, ed. Gérard M. Laurent (Madrid: Industrías graficas, 1953).

Louvet, Jean-Baptiste, *Accusation contre Maximilien Robespierre, à la Convention nationale, à la séance du 29 Octobre, 1792* (Paris: Imprimerie Nationale, 1792).

Lucena Salmoral, Manuel, *Visperas de la independencia americana: Caracas* (Madrid: Alhambra, 1986).

Lynch, John, *Latin America Between Colony and Nation: Selected Essays* (Houndmills, UK · Palgrave Macmillan, 2001).

———, *Simón Bolívar: A Life* (New Haven, CT: Yale University Press, 2006).

———, *The Spanish American Revolutions, 1808–1826* (New York: W. W. Norton, 1973).

Macaulay, Catherine, *Loose Remarks on Certain Positions to Be Found in Mr. Hobbes' Philosophical Rudiments of Government and Society with a Short Sketch of a Democratical Form of Government in a Letter to Signior Paoli* (London: T. Davies, 1769).

Macpherson, C. B., *The Political Theory of Possessive Individualism: Hobbes to Locke* (Oxford: Oxford University Press, 2011).

Macron, Emmanuel, *Révolution: C'est notre combat pour la France* (Paris: XO Éditions, 2016).

Madiou, Thomas, *Histoire d'Haiti*, 3 vols. (Port-au-Prince: J. Courtois, 1847).

Madsen, Douglas, and Peter G. Snow, *The Charismatic Bond: Political Behavior in a Time of Crisis* (Cambridge, MA: Harvard University Press, 1991).

Maier, Pauline, *From Resistance to Revolution: Colonial Radicals and the Development of American Opposition to Britain, 1765–1776* (London: W. W. Norton, 1991).

———, *Ratification: The People Debate the Constitution, 1787–1788* (New York: Simon & Schuster, 2010).

Maire, Catherine-Laurence, *Les convulsionnaires de Saint-Médard: Miracles, convulsions et prophéties à Paris au XVIIIe siècle* (Paris: Gallimard, 1985).

Malesherbes, Chrétien-Guillaume de Lamoignon de, *Œuvres inédites de Chrétien-Guillaume Lamoignon Malesherbes*, ed. Noël Pissot (Paris: Hénée et al., 1808).

Mann, Erika, *School for Barbarians: Education Under the Nazis* (New York: Dover, 2014).

Marat, Jean-Paul, *Œuvres*, ed. A. Velmorel (Paris: Décembre-Alonnier, 1869).

Marcus, Hans, *Friedrich der Grosse in der englischen Literatur* (Leipzig: Mayer & Mueller, 1930).

Marshall, Christopher, *Extracts from the Diary of Christopher Marshall*, ed. William Duane (Albany: Joel Munsell, 1877).

Marsollier de Vivetières, Benoît-Joseph, *Asgill, ou Le prisonnier de guerre. Drame lyrique en un acte et en prose* (Paris: Brunet, 1793).

Martin, Andy, *Napoleon the Novelist* (London: Polity, 2001).

Martin, Brian Joseph, *Napoleonic Friendship: Military Fraternity, Intimacy, and Sexuality in Nineteenth-Century France* (Lebanon, NH: University Press of New England, 2011).

Martin, Jean-Clément, *Nouvelle histoire de la Révolution française* (Paris: Perrin, 2012).

———, *Robespierre: La fabrication d'un monstre* (Paris: Perrin, 2016).

Martin, Marc, "Journaux d'armées au temps de la Convention," *Annales historiques de la Révolution française*, vol. 44, no. 1 (1972).

Martin, Peter, *A Life of James Boswell* (New Haven, CT: Yale University Press, 2000).

Marx, Karl, *The Eighteenth Brumaire of Louis Bonaparte* (New York: International Publishers, 1963).

Mathiez, Albert, *La théophilanthropie et le culte décadaire, 1796–1801* (Paris: Félix Alcan, 1903).

May, Henry Farnham, *The Enlightenment in America* (New York: Oxford University Press, 1976).

Mayer, Charles-Joseph de, *Asgill, ou Les désordres des guerres civiles: Anecdote anglais* (Amsterdam: Rue Serpente, 1784).

Mazeau, Guillaume, "Émotions politiques: La Révolution française," in *Histoire des émotions*, ed. Alain Corbin et al., 3 vols. (Paris: Seuil, 2016–17), vol. 2, pp. 98–141.

Mazzini, Giuseppe, *Life and Writings of Joseph Mazzini*, 6 vols. (London: Smith, Elder, 1864–70).

McConville, Brendan, *The King's Three Faces: The Rise and Fall of Royal America, 1688–1776* (Chapel Hill: University of North Carolina Press, 2006).

McCullough, David, *John Adams* (New York: Simon & Schuster, 2001).

McFarlane, Anthony, *War and Independence in Spanish America* (London: Routledge, 2013).

McKinley, P. Michael, *Pre-Revolutionary Caracas: Politics, Economy, and Society 1777–1811* (Cambridge: Cambridge University Press, 1985).

McLaren, Moray, *Corsica Boswell: Paoli, Johnson and Freedom* (London: Secker & Warburg, 1966).

McMahon, Darrin M., *Divine Fury: A History of Genius* (New York: Basic Books, 2013).

———, "The Fate of Nations Is the Work of Genius: The French Revolution and the Great Man Theory of History," in *Rethinking the Age of Revolutions: France and the Birth of the Modern World*, eds. David A. Bell and Yair Mintzker (New York: Oxford University Press, 2018), pp. 134–53.

McPhee, Peter, *Robespierre: A Revolutionary Life* (New Haven, CT: Yale University Press, 2012).

Meehan-Waters, Brenda, "Catherine the Great and the Problem of Female Rule," *The Russian Review*, vol. 34, no. 3 (1975), pp. 293–307.

Meigs, Josiah, *An Oration Pronounced Before a Public Assembly in New-Haven, On the 5th Day of November 1781, At the Celebration of the Glorious Victory over Lieutenant-General Earl Cornwallis* (New Haven, CT: Thomas and Samuel Green, 1782).

Mémoires littéraires de la Grande Bretagne pour l'an 1768 (London: Chez T. Becket & P. A. De Hondt, 1768).

Menant, Sylvain, and Robert Morrissey, eds., *Héroïsme et lumières* (Paris: Honoré Champion, 2010).

Mercier, Louis-Sébastien, *Paris pendant la Révolution (1789–1798), ou Le nouveau Paris* (Paris: Poulet-Malassis, 1862).

Mervaud, Christiane, and Michel Mervaud, "Le *Pierre le Grand et la Russie* de Voltaire: Histoire ou mirage?," in *Le mirage russe au XVIIIe siècle*, eds. Serguei Karp and Larry Wolff (Ferney-Voltaire: Centre International d'Étude du XVIIIe siècle, 2001), pp. 11–35.

Mestrovic, Stjepan Gabriel, *Durkheim and Postmodern Culture* (New York: A. de Gruyter, 1992).

Michaud, Stéphane, and Hugo Neira, "Los 'Libertadores' entre la herencia de la revolución y la sombra de Napoleón," *Cuadernos Americanos*, vol. 1, no. 1, pp. 74–88.

Michelena, Carmen, *Luces revolucionarias: De la rebelión de Madrid (1795) a la rebelión de La Guaira (1797)* (Caracas: Fundación Centro de Estudios Latinoamericanos Rómulo Gallegos, 2010).

Michelet, Jules, *Histoire de la Révolution française*, 2 vols. (Paris: Gallimard, 1952).

Middlekauff, Robert, *The Glorious Cause: The American Revolution, 1763–1789* (New York: Oxford University Press, 2005).

Mieszkowski, Jan, *Watching War* (Stanford, CA: Stanford University Press, 2012).

Miller, James, *Can Democracy Work? A Short History of a Radical Idea from Ancient Athens to Our World* (New York: Farrar, Straus and Giroux, 2018).

Miller, John, *Memoirs of General Miller in the Service of the Republic of Peru*, 2 vols. (London: Longman et al., 1829).

Minzloff, Rudolf, *Catalogue raisonné des Russica de la Bibliothèque impériale publique de Saint-Pétersbourg: Pierre le grand dans la littérature étrangère* (Saint Petersburg: Glasounow, 1872).

Miot de Melito, André-François, *Mémoires du comte Miot de Melito*, 2 vols. (Paris: Calmann-Levy, 1873–74).

Mirabeau, Honoré-Gabriel de Riqueti, comte de, *Considérations sur l'ordre de Cincinnatus, ou Imitation d'un pamphlet anglo-américain par le comte de Mirabeau* (London: J. Johnson, 1786).

———, *Reflections on the Observations on the Importance of the American Revolution, and the Means of Making It a Benefit to the World*, trans. Richard Price (Philadelphia: T. Seddon, 1786).

Miranda, Francisco de, *Colombeia*, 20 vols. (Caracas: Ediciones de la Presidencia de la Republica, 1978).

———, *The New Democracy in America: Travels of Francisco de Miranda in the United States, 1783–84*, ed. John S. Ezell, trans. Judson P. Wood (Norman: University of Oklahoma Press, 1963).

Misencik, Paul R., *The Original American Spies: Seven Covert Agents of the Revolutionary War* (Jefferson, NC: McFarland, 2014).

Miss Melmoth; or, The New Clarissa, 3 vols. (London: T. Lowndes, 1771).

Mitnick, Barbara J., ed., *George Washington: American Symbol* (New York: Hudson Hills Press, 1999).

———, *The Changing Image of George Washington* (New York: Fraunces Tavern Museum, 1989).

Mitre, Bartolomé, *The Emancipation of South America*, trans. William Pilling (London: Chapman and Hall, 1893).

Moïse, Claude, *Le projet national de Toussaint Louverture et la Constitution de 1801* (Port-au-Prince: Editions Mémoire, 2001).

Mollien, Gaspard Théodore, *Travels in the Republic of Colombia: In the Years 1822 and 1823* (London: C. Knight, 1824).

Monglond, André, *Le préromantisme français* (Paris: J. Corti, 1965).

Monod, Jean-Claude, *Qu'est-ce qu'un chef en démocratie?: Politiques du charisme* (Paris: Seuil, 2012).

A Monody in Honor of the Chiefs Who Have Fallen in the Cause of American Liberty, Spoken at the Theatre in Philadelphia, December 7, 1784 (Philadelphia: Thomas Bradford, 1784).

Montaigne, Michel de, *The Complete Works: Essays, Travel Journal, Letters* (New York: Alfred A. Knopf, 2003).

Montarlot, Paul, "Mayneaud de Laveaux," in *Mémoires de la Société éduenne*, vol. 39 (Autun: Dejussieu and Demasy, 1911), pp. 73–86.

Montecuccoli, Raimondo, *Opere* (Milan: Per Luigi Mussi, 1807).

Moore, Dafydd, "The Toast of Heroes and Fair Albion's Son: Jonathan Mitchell Sewall's Ossianic Versifications," in *Transatlantic Traffic and (Mis)Translations*, eds. Robin Peel and Daniel Maudlin (Durham, NH: University of New Hampshire Press, 2013), pp. 113–32.

Moore, Frank, ed., *Diary of the American Revolution from Newspapers and Original Documents*, 2 vols. (New York: Charles Scribner, 1860).

More, Thomas, *Poor Thomas Improved: Being More's Country Almanack for the Year of Christian Account 1770* (New York: Alexander and James Robertson, 1770).

Morrissey, Robert, *The Economy of Glory: From Ancien Régime France to the Fall of Napoleon* (Chicago: University of Chicago Press, 2014).

Morse, Jedidiah, *A True and Authentic History of His Excellency George Washington* (Philadelphia: n.p., 1790).

Mossé, Claude, *L'antiquité dans la Révolution française* (Paris: Albin Michel, 1989).

Mosse, George L., *The Image of Man: The Creation of Modern Masculinity* (New York: Oxford University Press, 1998).

Motadel, David, ed., *Waves of Revolutions* (Cambridge: Cambridge University Press, forthcoming 2020).

Mottley, John, *The Life of Peter the Great, Emperor of All Russia*, 3 vols. (London: M. Cooper, 1725).

Moyn, Samuel, "On the Intellectual Origins of François Furet's Masterpiece," *The Tocqueville Review*, vol. 29, no. 2 (2008), pp. 1–20.

Murray, John, *Jerubbaal; or, Tyranny's Grove Destroyed and the Altar of Liberty Finished* (Newburyport: John Mycall, 1784).

The Museum: A Miscellaneous Repository of Instruction and Amusement in Prose and Verse (Hartford: n.p., 1825).

Nelson, Eric, *The Royalist Revolution: Monarchy and the American Founding* (Cambridge, MA: Belknap Press of Harvard University Press, 2014).

Nesbitt, Nick, *Universal Emancipation: The Haitian Revolution and the Radical Enlightenment* (Charlottesville: University of Virginia Press, 2008).

Newman, Simon P., "Principles or Men? George Washington and the Political Culture of National Leadership, 1776–1801," *Journal of the Early Republic*, vol. 12, no. 4 (1992), 477–507.

Nicholls, Angus, *Goethe's Concept of the Daemonic After the Ancients* (London: Boydell and Brewer, 2006).

Nietzsche, Friedrich Wilhelm, *Zur Genealogie der Moral* (Berlin: Hofenberg, 2016).

Norris, Joseph Parker, *An Eulogium on General Washington Being Appointed Commander in Chief of the Federal Army in America* (Philadelphia: B. Towne, 1781).

Nougaret, Pierre-Jean-Baptiste, *Anecdotes du règne de Louis XVI*, 6 vols. (Paris: n.p., 1791).

O'Leary, Daniel Florence, *Bolívar y la emancipación de Sur-América: Memorias del general O'Leary*, 32 vols. (Madrid: Sociedad Española de Librería, 1915).

———, *The "Detached Recollections" of General D. F. O'Leary*, ed. R. A. Humphreys (London: Athlone Press, 1969).

Olmedo, José Joaquín, *La victoria de Junín: Canto a Bolívar* (Guayaquil: Imprenta Municipal, 1917).

Orations Delivered at the Request of the Inhabitants of the Town of Boston, to Commemorate the Evening of the Fifth of March, 1770 (Boston: Peter Edes, 1785).

Oriol, Michèle, *Images de la Révolution à Saint-Domingue* (Paris: Henri Deschamps, 1992).

Osman, Julia, "Ancient Warriors on Modern Soil: French Military Reform and American Military Images in Eighteenth-Century France," *French History*, vol. 22, no. 2 (2008), pp. 175–96.

———, "Cincinnatus Reborn: The George Washington Myth and French Renewal During the Old Regime," *French Historical Studies*, vol. 38, no. 3 (2015), pp. 421–46.

Ozouf, Mona, *La fête révolutionnaire, 1789–1799* (Paris: Gallimard, 1976).

Pagès de Vixouse, François-Xavier, *Histoire secrète de la Révolution française*, 3 vols. (Paris: Dentu, 1800).

Paine, Thomas, *The Crisis*, December 23, 1776, http://www.ushistory.org/paine/crisis/c-01.htm.

———, *Common Sense; Addressed to the Inhabitants of America* (Philadelphia: W. and T. Bradford, 1776).

———, *Letter to George Washington, on Paine's Service to America* (1796); http://www.thomas-paine-friends.org/paine-thomas_letter-to-george-washington-1796-01.html.

———, *The Writings of Thomas Paine*, ed. Moncure Daniel Conway, 4 vols. (New York: G. P. Putnam's Sons, 1894–1908).

Palmer, R. R., *The Age of the Democratic Revolution: A Political History of Europe and America, 1760–1800* (Princeton, NJ: Princeton University Press, 2014).

———, *Twelve Who Ruled: The Year of the Terror in the French Revolution* (Princeton, NJ: Princeton University Press, 1989).

Pamphile de Lacroix, François-Joseph, *Mémoires pour servir à l'histoire de la Révolution de Saint-Domingue*, 2 vols. (Paris: Pillet aîné, 1819).

Paoli, Pascal, *Lettres de Pascal Paoli*, ed. Pietro Perelli, 5 vols. (Bastia: Ollagnier, 1884–89).

Parallèle entre César, Cromwel, Monck et Bonaparte—fragment traduit de l'anglais (Paris: n.p., 1800).

Paris pendant l'année 1802 (Paris: J. Deboffe, 1803).

Parker, Harold T., *The Cult of Antiquity and the French Revolutionaries: A Study in the Development of the Revolutionary Spirit* (New York: Octagon Books, 1965).

Parkinson, Robert G., "Print, the Press, and the American Revolution," in *Oxford Research Encyclopedias: American History* (2015); http://americanhistory.oxfordre.com/view/10.1093/acrefore /9780199329175.001.0001/acrefore-9780199329175-e-9.

Parsons, Lynn Hudson, *The Birth of Modern Politics: Andrew Jackson, John Quincy Adams, and the Election of 1828* (New York: Oxford University Press, 2009).

Pasley, Jeffrey L., Andrew W. Robertson, and David Waldstreicher, eds., *Beyond the Founders: New Approaches to the Political History of the Early American Republic* (Chapel Hill: University of North Carolina Press, 2004).

Paulding, Hiram, "Bolivar in His Camp," in Rebecca Paulding Meade, *Life of Hiram Paulding* (New York: Baker & Taylor, 1910), pp. 19–84.

Pérez Vila, Manuel, "Entusiasmo y desencanto: Un joven criollo ante Napoleon," in *Bolívar en Francia*, eds. Alfredo Boulton et al. (Caracas: Comité Ejecutivo del Bicentenario de Simón Bolívar, 1984), pp. 109–44.

———, *La formación intelectual del Libertador* (Caracas: Ediciones de la Presidencia de la República, 1979).

———, *Simón Bolívar 1783–1830: Bibliografía básica* (Caracas: Ceilal, 1983).

———, and Horacio Jorge Becco, *Bibliografía directa de Simón Bolívar* (Caracas: Universidad Simón Bolívar, 1986).

Périn, René, *L'incendie du Cap, ou Le règne de Toussaint-Louverture* (Paris: Chez les Marchands de Nouveautés, 1802).

Perl-Rosenthal, Nathan, "Atlantic Cultures and the Age of Revolution," *The William and Mary Quarterly*, vol. 74, no. 4 (2017), pp. 667–96.

———, "The 'Divine Right of Republics': Hebraic Republicanism and the Debate over Kingless Government in Revolutionary America," *The William and Mary Quarterly*, vol. 66, no. 3 (2009), pp. 535–64.

Perroud, Henry, *Précis des derniers troubles qui ont eu lieu dans la partie du nord de Saint-Domingue* (Le Cap Français: P. Roux, 1796).

Persat, Maurice, *Mémoires du commandant Persat, 1806 à 1844*, ed. Gustave Schlumberger (Paris: Plon, 1910).

Person, Leland S., *The Cambridge Introduction to Nathaniel Hawthorne* (Cambridge: Cambridge University Press, 2012).

Perú de Lacroix, Luis, *El diario de Bucaramanga*, ed. Nicolás E. Navarro, 2 vols. (Caracas: Bohemia, 1949).

Petiteau, Natalie, *Napoléon Bonaparte: La nation incarnée* (Paris: Armand Colin, 2015).

———, *Napoléon: De la mythologie à l'histoire* (Paris: Seuil, 1999).

Pettegree, Andrew, *The Invention of News: How the World Came to Know About Itself* (London: Yale University Press, 2014).

Pierrot, Gregory, "'Our Hero': Toussaint Louverture in British Representations," *Criticism*, vol. 50, no. 4 (2008), pp. 581–607.

Pino Iturrieta, Elías, *El divino Bolívar: Ensayo sobre una religión republicana* (Caracas: Alfadil, 1988).

———, *Las ideas de los primeros Venezolanos* (Caracas: Monte Avila, 1992).

Plamper, Jan, *The Stalin Cult: A Study in the Alchemy of Power* (New Haven, CT: Yale University Press, 2012).

Pluchon, Pierre, "Toussaint Louverture d'après le général de Kerversau," in *Toussaint Louverture et l'indépendance de Haïti*, ed. Jacques de Cauna (Paris: Karthala, 2004), pp. 157–71.

———, "Toussaint Louverture défie Bonaparte: L'adresse inédite du 20 Décembre 1801," *Revue française d'outre-mer*, vol. 79, no. 296 (1992), pp. 383–89.

————, *Toussaint Louverture: Un révolutionnaire noir d'Ancien Régime* (Paris: Fayard, 1989).

Pocock, J. G. A., *The Machiavellian Moment: Florentine Political Thought and the Atlantic Republican Tradition* (Princeton, NJ: Princeton University Press, 1975).

A Poem Composed July 4, 1783, Being a Day of General Rejoicing, for the Happy Restoration of Peace and Independence to the United States of America (n.p., 1783).

A Poem, Spoken Extempore, by a YOUNG LADY, on Hearing the Guns Firing and Bells Chiming on Account of the Great and Glorious Acquisition of Their Excellencies Gen. Washington and the C. de Grasse, by the Surrender of York-Town (Boston: F. Russell, 1781).

Polansky, Janet, *Revolutions Without Borders: The Call to Liberty in the Atlantic World* (New Haven, CT: Yale University Press, 2016).

Popkin, Jeremy D., *You Are All Free: The Haitian Revolution and the Abolition of Slavery* (Cambridge: Cambridge University Press, 2010).

Porter, Robert Ker, *Sir Robert Ker Porter's Caracas Diary: 1825–1842*, ed. Walter Dupouy (Caracas: Walter Dupouy, 1966).

Post, Lydia Minturn, *Personal Recollections of the American Revolution: A Private Journal*, ed. Sidney Barclay (New York: Rudd and Carleton, 1859).

Pottle, Frederick A., *James Boswell: The Earlier Years, 1740–1769*, 1st ed. (New York: McGraw-Hill, 1966).

Potts, John, *A History of Charisma* (London: Palgrave Macmillan, 2009).

Poultier d'Elmotte, François-Martin, "Sur l'illustre Washington," *Almanach littéraire, ou Étrennes d'Apollon* (Paris: n.p., 1789), pp. 69–70.

Pradt, Dominique-Georges-Frédéric Dufour de, *Congrès de Panama* (Paris: Béchet, 1825).

————, *Les trois âges des colonies, ou De leur état passé, présent et à venir*, 2 vols. (Paris: Giguet, 1801).

Prasad, Pratima, *Colonialism, Race, and the French Romantic Imagination* (New York: Routledge, 2009).

Prendergast, Christopher, *Napoleon and History Painting: Antoine-Jean Gros's La Bataille d'Eylau* (Oxford: Oxford University Press, 1997).

Pride: A Poem. Inscribed to John Wilkes, Esquire. By an Englishman (London: J. Almon, 1766).

Prince, Joseph Allen, *Toussaint Louverture: Anthologie poétique*, 2 vols. (Paris: Publibook, 2013).

Proctor, Robert, *Narrative of a Journey Across the Cordillera of the Andes, and of a Residence in Lima, and Other Parts of Peru, in the Years 1823 and 1824* (London: Constable, 1825).

Purcell, Sarah J., *Sealed with Blood: War, Sacrifice, and Memory in Revolutionary America* (Philadelphia: University of Pennsylvania Press, 2002).

Quincy, Josiah, *Observations on the Act of Parliament, Commonly Called the Boston Port-Bill with Thoughts on Civil Society and Standing Armies. By Josiah Quincy, Junior* (London: Edward and Charles Dilly, 1774).

Quintero, Inès, "Historiografía e independencia en Venezuela," in *Debates sobre las independencias iberoamericanas*, eds. Manuel Chust and José Antonio Serrano (Madrid: AHILA, 2007).

Racine, Karen, *Francisco de Miranda: A Transatlantic Life in the Age of Revolution* (Wilmington, DE: Scholarly Resources, 2003).

————, "'This England and This Now': British Cultural and Intellectual Influence in the Spanish American Independence Era," *Hispanic American Historical Review*, vol. 90, no. 3 (2010), pp. 423–54.

Rainsford, Marcus, *A Memoir of Transactions That Took Place in St. Domingo in the Spring of 1799; Affording an Idea of the Present State of That Country, the Real Character of Its Black Governor, Toussaint Louverture, and the Safety of Our West-India Islands from Attack or Revolt* (London: R. B. Scott, 1802).

————, *An Historical Account of the Black Empire of Hayti*, eds. Paul Youngquist and Grégory Pierrot (Durham, NC: Duke University Press, 2013).

————, *St. Domingo; or, An Historical, Political and Military Sketch of the Black Republic, with a View of the Life and Character of Toussaint L'Ouverture* (London: R. B. Scott, 1802).

Rakove, Jack, *Revolutionaries: A New History of the Invention of America* (Boston: Houghton Mifflin Harcourt, 2010).

Ratto Ciarlo, José, *El correo del Orinoco: Expresión periodística de ecumenismo bolivariano* (Caracas: Oficina Central de Información, 1968).

Raynal, Guillaume-Thomas-François, et al., *Histoire philosophique et politique des établissements et du commerce des Européens dans les deux Indes*, 10 vols. (Paris: Chez les Libraires Associés, 1783).

Recueil de plusieurs pièces d'éloquence et de poésie présentées à l'Académie des jeux floraux (Toulouse: G.-L. Colomyez, 1696).

Reddy, William M., *The Navigation of Feeling: A Framework for the History of Emotions* (Cambridge: Cambridge University Press, 2001).

Regan, Patrick M., *Organizing Societies for War: The Process and Consequences of Societal Militarization* (Westport, CT: Praeger, 1994).

Régent, Frédéric, *La France et ses esclaves: De la colonisation aux abolitions (1620–1848)* (Paris: Grasset, 2007).

Regourd, François, "Lumières coloniales: Les Antilles françaises dans la république des lettres," *Dix-huitième siècle*, vol. 33 (2001), pp. 183–99.

The Repository; or, Half-Yearly Register. Containing Whatever Is Remarkable in the History, Politics, Literature and Amusements, of the Year 1/68. (London: n.p., 1769).

Restrepo, José Manuel, *Historia de la revolución de la república de Colombia*, 10 vols. (Paris: Libreria Americana, 1827).

A Review of the Conduct of Pascal Paoli. Addressed to the Rt. Hon. William Beckford, Esq., Lord Mayor of the City of London (London: n.p., 1770).

Restuccia, Andrew, "The Sanctification of Donald Trump," *Politico*, April 30, 2019.

Rhodehamel, John, ed., *The American Revolution: Writings from the War of Independence* (New York: Library of America, 2001).

Riall, Lucy, *Garibaldi: Invention of a Hero* (New Haven, CT: Yale University Press, 2007).

Riasanovsky, Nicholas V., *The Image of Peter the Great in Russian History and Thought* (New York: Oxford University Press, 1985).

Rice, Geoffrey W., "Deceit and Distraction: Britain, France and the Corsican Crisis of 1768," *International History Review*, vol. 28, no. 2 (2010), pp. 277–315.

Richard, C., *Briefe aus Columbien an seine Freunde von einem hannoverischen Officier* (Leipzig: Brockhaus, 1822).

Richard, Carl J., *The Founders and the Classics: Greece, Rome, and the American Enlightenment* (Cambridge, MA: Harvard University Press, 1994).

Richards, Jeffrey H., *Drama, Theatre, and Identity in the American New Republic* (Cambridge: Cambridge University Press, 2005).

Rieff, Philip, *Charisma: The Gift of Grace, and How It Has Been Taken Away from Us* (New York: Pantheon, 2007).

Riskin, Jessica, *Science in the Age of Sensibility: The Sentimental Empiricists of the French Enlightenment* (Chicago: University of Chicago Press, 2002).

Robb, Graham, *Victor Hugo: A Biography* (New York: W. W. Norton, 1997).

Roberts, Andrew, *Napoleon: A Life* (New York: Viking, 2014).

Robertson, J., *Poems, Consisting of Tales, Fables, Epigrams, &c. &c. By Nobody.* (London: Robinson and Roberts, 1770).

Robespierre, Maximilien, *Discours de Maximilien Robespierre sur la guerre, prononcé à la société des amis de la constitution, le 2 janvier 1792* (Paris: Imprimerie Nationale, 1792).

———, *Discours et rapports par Robespierre*, ed. Charles Vellay (Paris: Charpentier et Fasquelle, 1908).

———, *Discours prononcé par Robespierre à la Convention nationale dans la séance du 8 thermidor* (Paris: Imprimerie Nationale, 1794).

———, *Œuvres complètes de Maximilien Robespierre*, 11 vols. (Paris: various publishers, 1910–2007).

———, *Plan d'éducation nationale de Michel Lepelletier* (Paris: Imprimerie Nationale, 1793).

———, *Rapport sur les principes du gouvernement révolutionnaire* (Paris: Imprimerie des Administrations Nationales, 1793).

Robin, Charles-César, *New Travels Through North America, in a Series of Letters* (Philadelphia: Robert Bell, 1783).

———, *Nouveau voyage dans l'Amérique septentrionale, en l'année 1781; et campagne de l'armée de M. le comte de Rochambeau* (Paris: Moutard, 1782).

Rocafuerte, Vicente, *Bosquejo ligerísimo de la revolución de Mégico: Desde el grito de Iguala hasta la proclamación imperial de Iturbide* (Philadelphia: "Teracrouef and Naroajeb," 1822).

———, *Ideas necesarias a todo pueblo americano independiente que quiera ser libre* (Philadelphia: "Teracrouef and Naroajeb," 1821).

Rodríguez Demorizi, Emilio, *Poetas contra Bolívar: El Libertador a través de la calumnia* (Madrid: Gráficas Reunidas, 1966).

Rodriguez O., Jaime E., *The Independence of Spanish America* (Cambridge: Cambridge University Press, 1998).

Roger, Philippe, "Mars au Parnasse," in Jean-Claude Bonnet, ed., *L'Empire des muses: Napoléon, les Arts et les Lettres* (Paris: Belin, 2004), pp. 369–87.

Rojas, José María, *Tiempo perdido* (Paris: Garnier, 1905).

Rojas, Rafael, *Las repúblicas de aire: Utopía y desencanto en la revolución de Hispanoamérica* (Madrid: Taurus, 2009).

Romieu, Auguste, *L'ère des Césars* (Paris: Ledoyen, 1850).

Ronzeaud, Pierre, *Peuple et représentations sous le règne de Louis XIV: Les représentations du peuple dans la littérature politique en France sous le règne de Louis XIV* (Aix-en-Provence: Publications-Diffusion, 1988).

Rosanvallon, Pierre, *Good Government: Democracy Beyond Elections*, trans. Malcolm DeBevoise (Cambridge, MA: Harvard University Press, 2018).

Rosenberg, Emily S., ed., *A World Connecting: 1870–1945* (Cambridge, MA: Harvard University Press, 2012).

Rosenberg, Hans, *Bureaucracy, Aristocracy, and Autocracy: The Prussian Experience, 1660–1815* (Cambridge, MA: Harvard University Press, 1958).

Rosenfeld, Sophia A., *Common Sense: A Political History* (Cambridge, MA: Harvard University Press, 2011).

———, *Democracy and Truth: A Short History* (Philadelphia: University of Pennsylvania Press, 2019).

Rotundo, E. Anthony, *American Manhood: Transformations in Masculinity from the Revolution to the Modern Era* (New York: Basic Books, 1994).

Rouquié, Alain, *The Military and the State in Latin America* (Berkeley: University of California Press, 1987).

Rousseau, Jean-Jacques, *Collection complète des œuvres de J. J. Rousseau*, 24 vols. (Geneva: n.p., 1782).

———, *The Social Contract*, ed. Maurice Cranston (London: Penguin, 1968).

Roussier, Michel, "L'éducation des enfants de Toussaint Louverture et l'institution nationale des colonies," *Revue française d'outre-mer*, vol. 64, no. 236 (1977), pp. 308–49.

Rush, Benjamin, *A Memorial Containing Travels Through Life; or Sundry Incidents in the Life of Dr. Benjamin Rush* (Lanoraie, QC: Louis Alexander Biddle, 1905).

Sainson, Katia, "'Le Régénérateur de La France': Literary Accounts of Napoleonic Regeneration, 1799–1805," *Nineteenth-Century French Studies*, vol. 30, nos. 1–2 (Fall–Winter 2001–2002), pp. 9–25.

Saint-Just, Louis-Antoine de, *Fragments sur les institutions républicaines*, ed. Charles Nodier (Paris: Techener, 1831).

———, *Œuvres complètes de Saint-Just, avec une introduction et des notes* (Paris: Charpentier et Fasquelle, 1908).

———, *Œuvres de Saint-Just, représentant du peuple à la Convention nationale* (Paris: Prévot, 1834).

Saint-Lambert, Jean-François de, "Genius," *Encyclopedia of Diderot & d'Alembert—Collaborative Translation Project* (2007); http://hdl.handle.net/2027/spo.did2222.0000.819.

Saladin, Charles-Antoine, *Coup d'oeil politique sur le continent* (Paris: Honnert, 1800).

Salvador, José María, *Efímeras efemérides: Fiestas cívicas y arte efímero en la Venezuela de los siglos XVII XIX* (Caracas: Universidad Católica Andrés Bello, 2001).

Sandoz, Ellis, ed., *Political Sermons of the American Founding Era*, 2 vols. (Indianapolis: Liberty Fund, 1991).

Sang-Hun, Choe, and Norimitsu Onishi, "North Korea's Tears: A Blend of Cult, Culture and Coercion," *The New York Times*, December 20, 2011.

Sauvigny, Louis-Edme Billardon de, *Vashington, ou La liberté du Nouveau Monde* (Paris: Maillard d'Orivelle, 1791).

Savage, Kirk, "The Self-Made Monument: George Washington and the Fight to Erect a National Memorial," *Winterthur Portfolio*, vol. 22, no. 4 (1987), pp. 225–42.

Sawyer, Stephen W., *Demos Assembled: Democracy and the International Origins of the Modern State* (Chicago: University of Chicago Press, 2018).

Schama, Simon, *Citizens: A Chronicle of the French Revolution* (New York: Alfred A. Knopf, 1989).

Schechter, Ronald, *A Genealogy of Terror in Eighteenth-Century France* (Chicago: University of Chicago Press, 2018).

Scheer, Monique, "Are Emotions a Kind of Practice (and Is That What Makes Them Have a History?): A Bourdieuian Approach to Understanding Emotion," *History and Theory*, vol. 51, no. 2 (2012), pp. 193–220.

Scheltema, Jacobus, *Peter de groote, Keizer van Rusland in Holland en te Zaandam, in 1697 en 1717.* (Amsterdam: n.p., 1814).

Schiffer, Irvine, *Charisma: A Psychoanalytical Look at Mass Society* (Toronto: University of Toronto Press, 1973).

Schlenke, Manfred, *England und das Friderizianische Preussen, 1740–1763: Ein Beitrag zum Verhältnis von Politik und Öffentliche Meinung im England des 18. Jahrhunderts* (Freiburg: Verlag Karl Alber, 1963).

Schlesinger, Arthur M., Jr., *The Politics of Hope* (Boston: Houghton Mifflin, 1963).

Schmitt, Carl, *Constitutional Theory*, trans. Jeffrey Seitzer (Durham, NC: Duke University Press, 2008).

Schneider, Christian, "Le colonel Vincent, officier du génie à Saint-Domingue," *Annales historiques de la Révolution française*, vol. 329 (2002), pp. 101–22.

Schoelcher, Victor, *Vie de Toussaint Louverture* (Paris: Karthala, 1982).

Schwartz, Barry, "The Character of Washington. A Study in Republican Culture," *American Quarterly*, vol. 38, no. 2 (1986), pp. 202–22.

———, "George Washington and the Whig Conception of Heroic Leadership," *American Sociological Review*, vol. 48, no. 1 (1983), pp. 18–33.

———, *George Washington: The Making of an American Symbol* (New York: Free Press, 1987).

———, "Social Change and Collective Memory: The Democratization of George Washington," *American Sociological Review*, vol. 56, no. 2 (1991), pp. 221–36.

Schwartzberg, Melissa, "Shouts, Murmurs and Votes: Acclamation and Aggregation in Ancient Greece," *The Journal of Political Philosophy*, vol. 18, no. 4 (2010), pp. 448–68.

Scott, David, *Conscripts of Modernity: The Tragedy of Colonial Enlightenment* (Durham, NC: Duke University Press, 2004).

Scott, Julius S., *The Common Wind: Afro-American Currents in the Age of the Haitian Revolution* (London: Verso, 2018).

Scribble, Timothy, *The Weeds of Parnassus, a Collection of Original Poems* (Rochester: T. Fisher, 1774).

Sedgwick, Eve Kosofsky, *Between Men: English Literature and Male Homosocial Desire* (New York: Columbia University Press, 2016).

Seigel, Jerrold E., *The Idea of the Self: Thought and Experience in Western Europe Since the Seventeenth Century* (Cambridge: Cambridge University Press, 2005).

Semley, Lorelle, "To Live and Die, Free and French: Toussaint Louverture's 1801 Constitution and the Original Challenge of Black Citizenship," *Radical History Review*, vol. 115 (2013), pp. 65–90.

Semmel, Stuart, *Napoleon and the British* (New Haven, CT: Yale University Press, 2004).

Sepinwall, Alyssa Goldstein, ed., *Haitian History: New Perspectives* (New York: Routledge, 2012).

Serna, Pierre, Antonino De Francesco, and Judith A. Miller, eds., *Republics at War, 1776–1840: Revolutions, Conflicts, and Geopolitics in Europe and the Atlantic World* (Houndmills, U.K.: Palgrave Macmillan, 2013).

Sewall, Jonathan Mitchell, Gen. *Washington, a New Favorite Song, at the American Camp: To the Tune of the British Grenadiers* (n.p., 1776).

Sewell, William Hamilton, *A Rhetoric of Bourgeois Revolution: The Abbé Sieyes and What Is the Third Estate?* (Durham, NC: Duke University Press, 1994).

Shakespeare, William, *Julius Caesar*, http://shakespeare.mit.edu/julius_caesar/index.html.

———, *Richard II*, http://shakespeare.mit.edu/richardii/index.html.

Shalev, Eran, *American Zion: The Old Testament as a Political Text from the Revolution to the Civil War* (New Haven, CT: Yale University Press, 2013).

———, *Rome Reborn on Western Shores: Historical Imagination and the Creation of the American Republic* (Charlottesville: University of Virginia Press, 2009).

Sharp, Anthony, *Der gantz neue verbesserte Nord-Americanische Calendar auf das 1779ste Jahr Christi* (Lancaster: Francis Bailey, 1778).

Sharpe, Kevin M., *Rebranding Rule: The Restoration and Revolution Monarchy, 1660–1714* (New Haven, CT: Yale University Press, 2013).

Shaw, Peter, *American Patriots and the Rituals of Revolution* (Cambridge, MA: Harvard University Press, 1981).

Shils, Edward, *Center and Periphery: Essays in Macrosociology* (Chicago: University of Chicago Press, 1975).

———, "Charisma, Order, and Status," *American Sociological Review*, vol. 30, no. 2 (1965), pp. 199–213.

Shovlin, John, "Selling American Empire on the Eve of the Seven Years' War: The French Propaganda Campaign of 1755–56," *Past and Present*, no. 206 (2010), pp. 121–49.

Shultz, Doug, director, *The French Revolution* (The History Channel, 2005).

Sieyès, Emmanuel, *Qu'est-ce que le tiers état?* (Paris: n.p., 1789).

Silverman, Kenneth, *A Cultural History of the American Revolution: Painting, Music, Literature, and the Theatre in the Colonies and the United States from the Treaty of Paris to the Inauguration of George Washington, 1763–1789* (New York: T. Y. Crowell, 1976).

Simon, Joshua, *The Ideology of Creole Revolution: Imperialism and Independence in American and Latin American Political Thought* (Cambridge: Cambridge University Press, 2017).

Six, Georges, *Dictionnaire biographique des généraux et amiraux français de la Révolution et de l'empire (1792–1814)*, 2 vols. (Paris: Georges Saffroy, 1934).

Skalweit, Stephan, *Frankreich und Friedrich der Grosse: Der Aufstieg Preussens in der öffentliche Meinung des "Ancien Régime"* (Bonn: Ludwig Röhrscheid Verlag, 1952).

Skeen, C. Edward, and Richard H. Kohn, "The Newburgh Conspiracy Reconsidered," *The William and Mary Quarterly*, vol. 31, no. 2 (1974), pp. 273–98.

Sluhovsky, Moshe, *Patroness of Paris: Rituals of Devotion in Early Modern France* (Leiden: Brill, 1998).

Smith, Elihu Hubbard, *The Diary of Elihu Hubbard Smith*, ed. James E. Cronin (Philadelphia: American Philosophical Society, 1973).

Smith, Page, *John Adams*, 2 vols. (New York: Doubleday, 1962).

Smith, Philip, "Culture and Charisma: Outline of a Theory," *Acta Sociologica*, vol. 43, no. 2 (2000), pp. 101–11.

Smylie, James H., "'The President as Republican Prophet and King: Clerical Reflections on the Death of Washington," *Journal of Church and State*, vol. 18, no. 2 (1976), pp. 232–52.

Snyder, Timothy, *The Road to Unfreedom: Russia, Europe, America* (New York: Tim Duggan Books, 2018).

Society of Artists of Great Britain, *A Catalogue of the Pictures, Sculptures, Models, Designs in Architecture, Drawings, Prints, &c. Exhibited at the Great Room, in Spring-Garden, Charing-Cross, April the*

Sixteenth, 1770, by the Royal Incorporated Society of Artists of Great-Britain. The Eleventh Year of Exhibiting (n.p., 1770).

Some Account of the Early Years of Buonaparte, at the Military School of Brienne; and of His Conduct at the Commencement of the French Revolution (London: Hookham and Carpenter, 1797).

Song of Washington (n.p., 1778).

Soriano, Cristina, *Tides of Revolution: Information, Insurgencies, and the Crisis of Colonial Rule in Venezuela* (Albuquerque: University of New Mexico Press, 2018).

Sowell, David, "The Mirror of Public Opinion: Bolívar, Republicanism and the United States Press, 1821–1831," *Revista de historia de América*, no. 134 (2004), pp. 165–83.

Spalding, Phinzy, "James Oglethorpe and the American Revolution," *The Journal of Imperial and Commonwealth History*, vol. 3, no. 3 (1975), pp. 396–407.

Staël, Germaine de, *Considérations sur la Révolution française*, 2 vols. (Paris: Charpentier, 1862).

———, *Œuvres complètes de madame la baronne de Staël-Holstein*, 3 vols. (Paris: Firmin-Didot, 1871).

Staples, William R., and Reuben Aldridge Guild, eds., *Rhode Island in the Continental Congress* (Providence: Providence Press Company, 1870).

Stauffer, Donald A., *The Art of Biography in Eighteenth-Century England*, 2 vols. (Princeton, NJ: Princeton University Press, 1941).

Stefansky, Emma, "Trump Says Clinton's Beyoncé and Jay Z Concert Is 'Almost Like Cheating,'" *Vanity Fair* magazine online, November 6, 2016.

Stein, Robert Louis, *Léger Félicité Sonthonax: The Lost Sentinel of the Republic* (Rutherford, NJ: Fairleigh Dickinson University Press, 1985).

Stephen, James, *Buonaparte in the West Indies; or, The History of Toussaint Louverture, the African Hero*, 3 vols. (London: J. Hatchard, 1803).

Stiavelli, Giacinto, *Garibaldi nella letteratura italiana* (Rome: Enrico Voghera, 1901).

Stiles, Ezra, *The United States Elevated to Glory and Honor: A Sermon Preached Before His Excellency Jonathan Trumbull, Esq. L.L.D., Governor and Commander in Chief, May 8th, 1783* (New Haven, CT: Thomas & Samuel Green, 1783).

Stockton, Richard, "Oration upon the Character of a True Hero," *The Pennsylvania Packet or General Advertiser* (Philadelphia, October 23, 1779), p. 1.

Stout, Harry S., *The Divine Dramatist: George Whitefield and the Rise of Modern Evangelicalism* (Grand Rapids: William D. Eerdmans, 1991).

Suard, J. B. A., *Lettres* (Berkeley: University of California Press, 1932).

Tackett, Timothy, *The Coming of the Terror in the French Revolution* (Cambridge, MA: Harvard University Press, 2015).

Tarle, Eugene, *Napoleon's Invasion of Russia* (Oxford: Oxford University Press, 1942).

Taylor, Alan, *American Revolutions: A Continental History, 1750–1804* (New York: W. W. Norton, 2016).

Telesko, Werner, *Napoleon Bonaparte: Der "moderne Held" und die bildende Kunst 1799–1815* (Vienna: Bohlau, 1998).

Teow, Jeremy, "Black Revolt in the White Mind: Violence, Race, and Slave Agency in the British Reception of the Haitian Revolution, 1791–1805," *Australasian Journal of American Studies*, vol. 37, no. 1 (2018), pp. 87–102.

Teute, Fredrika J., and David S. Shields, "The Confederation Court," *Journal of the Early Republic*, vol. 35, no. 2 (2015), pp. 215–26.

Thacher, James, *A Military Journal During the American Revolutionary War* (Boston: Cottons and Barnard, 1827).

Thibaud, Clément, "Des républiques en armes à la République armée: Guerre révolutionnaire, fédéralisme et centralisme au Venezuela et en Nouvelle-Grenade, 1808–1830," *Annales historiques de la Révolution française*, no. 348 (2007), pp. 57–86.

———, "Entre les cités et l'état: Caudillos et pronunciamientos en Grande-Colombie," *Genèses*, vol. 62, no. 1 (2006), pp. 5–26.

————, *Républiques en armes: Les armées de Bolivar dans les guerres d'indépendance du Venezuela et de la Colombie* (Rennes: Presses Universitaires de Rennes, 2006).

Thibaudeau, Antoine-Claire, *Mémoires sur le Consulat par un ancien conseiller d'état* (Paris: Ponthieu, 1827).

Thiry, Paul-Henry (baron d'Holbach), *Système de la nature, ou Des loix du monde physique et du monde moral*, 2 vols. (London: n.p., 1781).

Thomas, Antoine-Léonard, *Œuvres complètes de Thomas, de l'Académie française; précédées d'une notice sur la vie et les ouvrages de l'auteur* (Paris: Verdière, 1825).

Thompson, E. P., *The Making of the English Working Class* (London: Victor Gollancz, 1964).

Thompson, J. M., *English Witnesses of the French Revolution* (Oxford: Blackwell, 1938).

————, *Napoleon Bonaparte* (Oxford: Blackwell, 1988).

————, *Robespierre*, 2 vols. (Oxford: Blackwell, 1988).

Thomson, James, *The Seasons* (Philadelphia, n.p., 1764).

Thomson, Sinclair, "Sovereignty Disavowed: The Tupac Amaru Revolution in the Atlantic World," *Atlantic Studies*, vol. 13, no. 3 (2016), pp. 407–31.

————, *We Alone Will Rule: Native Andean Politics in the Age of Insurgency* (Madison: University of Wisconsin Press, 2002).

Timothy, Ann, *The Travels of Fancy: Being a Political, Historical and Moral Account of Her Adventures During the Late War* (New Brunswick, NJ: Collock and Arnett, 1784).

Tinker, Chauncey Brewster, *Nature's Simple Plan: A Phase of Radical Thought in the Mid-Eighteenth Century* (Princeton, NJ: Princeton University Press, 1922).

Tissot, Samuel, *An Essay on Diseases Incidental to Literary and Sedentary Persons. With Proper Rules for Preventing Their Fatal Consequences. And Instructions for Their Cure. By S. A. Tissot, M. D. Professor of Physick at Berne. Now First Translated into English.* (London: Edward and Charles Dilley, 1769).

Tocqueville, Alexis de, *De la démocratie en Amérique*, 4 vols. (Paris: Charles Gosselin, 1835).

Tolstoy, Leo, *Voina i Mir (War and Peace)*, 2 vols. (Moscow: The Planet, 2015).

Tournay, Thomas, *Ambition. An Epistle to Paoli* (London: Edward and Charles Dilly, 1769).

Toussaint-Louverture's frühere Geschichte nach englischen Nachrichten bearbeitet (Fürth: Im bureau für litteratur, 1802).

Townsend, Isaiah, ed., *Eloges funèbres de Washington* (Paris: Casimir, 1835).

Trahard, Pierre, *La sensibilité révolutionnaire (1789–1794)* (Paris: Boivin, 1936).

Triomphe de la nation, ou Louis XVI au milieu de son peuple (Paris: n.p., 1789).

Trouillot, Michel-Rolph, *Silencing the Past: Power and the Production of History* (Boston: Beacon Press, 2015).

Trumbull, Benjamin, *God Is to Be Praised for the Glory of His Majesty, and for His Mighty Works: A Sermon* (New Haven, CT: Thomas and Samuel Green, 1784).

Tulard, Jean, *Napoléon, ou Le mythe du sauveur* (Paris: Fayard, 1983).

Turner, Stephen, "Charisma Reconsidered," *Journal of Classical Sociology*, vol. 3, no. 1 (2003), pp. 5–26.

Tyson, George F., Jr., *Toussaint L'Ouverture* (Englewood Cliffs, NJ: Prentice-Hall, 1973).

Uglow, Jennifer S., *In These Times: Living in Britain Through Napoleon's Wars, 1793–1815* (London: Faber & Faber, 2014).

Uribe Uran, Victor M., "The Birth of a Public Sphere in Latin America During the Age of Revolution," *Comparative Studies in Society and History*, vol. 42, no. 2 (2000), pp. 425–57.

Vagts, Alfred, *A History of Militarism* (Westport, CT: Greenwood Press, 1981).

Vanegas Carrasco, Carolina, "Iconografía de Bolívar: Revisión historiográfica," in *Ensayos: Historia y teoría del arte*, vol. 22 (2012), pp. 112–34.

Varnum, Fanny, *Un philosophe cosmopolite du XVIIIe siècle: Le chevalier de Chastellux* (Paris: Rodstein, 1936).

Venturi, Franco, *The End of the Old Regime in Europe, 1776–1789*, 2 vols. (Princeton, NJ: Princeton University Press, 1991).

Vergé-Franceschi, Michel, *Paoli: Un Corse des Lumières* (Paris: Fayard, 2005).

Verna, Paul, *Pétion y Bolívar: Cuarenta años (1790–1830) de relaciones haitano-venezolanas y su aporte a la emancipación de Hispanoamérica* (Caracas: Oficina Central de Información, 1969).

Vetter, Cesare, "Dictature: Les vicissitudes d'un mot. France et Italie (XVIII et XIX siècles)," Révolution-Française.Net, 2008, http://revolution-francaise.net/2008/03/01/212-dictature-vicis situdes-mot-france-italie-xviii-xix-siecles.

Viarz, Maurice de, *L'aide de camp, ou L'auteur inconnu: Souvenirs des deux-mondes* (Paris: Dufey et Vezard, 1832).

Vie privée, politique et militaire de Toussaint-Louverture; par un homme de sa couleur (n.p., 1801).

Viénot-Vaublanc, Vincent-Marie, *Discours sur l'état de Saint-Domingue et sur la conduite des agens du Directoire* (Paris: Imprimerie Nationale, 1797).

Vigny, Alfred de, and John Cruickshank, *Servitude et grandeur militaires* (Paris: F. Bonnaire and V. Magen, 1835).

Vila, Anne C., *Enlightenment and Pathology: Sensibility in the Literature and Medicine of Eighteenth-Century France* (Baltimore: Johns Hopkins University Press, 1998).

Vincent, Charles-Humbert, *Du seul parti à prendre à l'égard de Saint-Domingue* (Paris: Delaunay and Peliscier, 1819).

————, "Précis sur l'état actuel de la colonie de Saint-Domingue" (November 1799), manuscript report in Archives Nationales d'Outre-Mer (Aix-en-Provence, France), CC9A22, "Rapports de divers sur Saint Domingue."

Vinot, Bernard, *Saint-Just* (Paris: Fayard, 1985).

Vivian, Frances, "General Paoli in England," *Italian Studies*, vol. 4, no. 1 (1949), pp. 37–56.

The Vocal Standard; or, Star Spangled Banner: Being the Latest and Best Selection Ever Offered to the Public (Richmond: John Nash, 1824).

Voltaire, *Histoire de l'empire de Russie sous Pierre-le-Grand (Œuvres complètes de Voltaire)*, 25 vols. (Paris: Antoine-Augustin Renouard, 1817), vol. 22.

El voto de Venezuela (Caracas: G. F. Devisme, 1828).

Vowell, Richard Longeville, *Campaigns and Cruises in Venezuela and New Granada and in the Pacific Ocean*, 3 vols. (London: Longman, 1831).

Wackerbarth, A. I. L. von, *Parallele zwischen Peter dem Grossen und Karl dem Grossen* (Göttingen: J. G. Rosenbuch, 1792).

Waegemans, Emmanuel, *Peter de Grote in de Oostenrijkse Nederlanden* (Antwerp: Koninklijke Bibliotheek Albert I, 1998).

Wahrman, Dror, *The Making of the Modern Self: Identity and Culture in Eighteenth-Century England* (New Haven, CT: Yale University Press, 2007).

Waldstreicher, David, *In the Midst of Perpetual Fetes: The Making of American Nationalism, 1776–1820* (Chapel Hill: University of North Carolina Press, 1997).

————, "Rites of Rebellion, Rites of Assent: Celebrations, Print Culture, and the Origins of American Nationalism," *Journal of American History*, vol. 82, no. 1 (1995), pp. 37–61.

Walker, Charles F., *The Tupac Amaru Rebellion* (Cambridge, MA: Harvard University Press, 2014).

Walsh, John Patrick, *Free and French in the Caribbean: Toussaint Louverture, Aimé Césaire and Narratives of Loyal Opposition* (Bloomington: Indiana University Press, 2013).

Walter, Gérard, *Robespierre* (Paris: Gallimard, 1961).

Ward, John William, *Andrew Jackson: Symbol for an Age* (New York: Oxford University Press, 1955).

Warner, Michael, *The Letters of the Republic: Publication and the Public Sphere in Eighteenth-Century America* (Cambridge, MA: Harvard University Press, 1990).

Washington en Necker (Amsterdam: n.p., 1790).

Washington Eulogies: A Checklist of Eulogies and Funeral Orations on the Death of George Washington (New York: New York Public Library, 1916).

Washington, George, *Recollections and Private Memoirs of Washington by His Adopted Son George Washington with a Memoir of the Author by His Daughter; and Illustrative and Explanatory Notes by Benson J. Loosing: With Illustrations* (New York: Derby & Jackson, 1860).

————, *The Writings of George Washington*, ed. Jared Sparks, 12 vols. (Boston: Russell, Odiorne, and Metcalf, 1833).

Watson, Elkanah, *Men and Times of the Revolution; or, Memoirs of Elkanah Watson* (New York: Dana and Company, 1856).

Watters, Mary, "Bolivar and the Church," *Catholic Historical Review*, vol. 21, no. 3 (1935), pp. 299–313.

Weber, Max, *Economy and Society: An Outline of Interpretive Sociology*, eds. Guenther Roth and Claus Wittich, trans. Ephraim Fischoff et al., 2 vols. (Berkeley: University of California Press, 1978).

————, "Politics as a Vocation," in *From Max Weber: Essays in Sociology*, trans. and eds. H. H. Gerth and C. Wright Mills (New York: Oxford University Press, 1946), pp. 77–128.

————, *The Protestant Ethic and the Spirit of Capitalism*, trans. Talcott Parsons (London: Allen Unwin, 1930).

Webster, Noah, *An American Selection of Lessons in Reading and Speaking, Calculated to Improve the Minds and Refine the Taste of Youth, and Also to Instruct Them in the Geography, History, and Politics of the United States* (Philadelphia: Young and McCullough, 1787).

————, *Collection of Essays and Fugitive Writings* (Boston: I. Thomas and E. T. Andrews, 1790).

Weems, Mason Locke, *The Life of George Washington: With Curious Anecdotes, Equally Honourable to Himself, and Exemplary to His Young Countrymen* (Philadelphia: Joseph Allen, 1837).

Wette, Wolfram, *Militarismus in Deutschland: Geschichte einer kriegerischen Kultur* (Darmstadt: Primus, 2008).

Wharton, Charles Henry, *A Poetical Epistle to His Excellency George Washington, Esquire, Commander in Chief of the Armies of the United States of America* (London: C. Dilly and J. Almon, 1780).

Wheatley, Phillis, *Complete Writings*, ed. Vincent Carretta (New York: Penguin, 2001).

White, Ashli, *Encountering Revolution: Haiti and the Making of the Early Republic* (Baltimore: Johns Hopkins University Press, 2010).

————, "The Materiality of the Haitian Revolution in the Atlantic World," in *Proceedings of the American Philosophical Society*, forthcoming.

Wick, Wendy C., *George Washington, an American Icon: The Eighteenth-Century Graphic Portraits* (Washington, DC: Smithsonian Institution, 1982).

Wilkes, John, *The North Briton* (London: n.p., 1772).

Wilkinson, Eliza, *Letters of Eliza Wilkinson: During the Invasion and Possession of Charleston, S.C. by the British in the Revolutionary War* (New York: S. Colman, 1839).

Willems, Emílio, *A Way of Life and Death: Three Centuries of Prussian-German Militarism: An Anthropological Approach* (Nashville, TN: Vanderbilt University Press, 1986).

Williams, Hannah, "Saint Genevieve's Miracles: Art and Religion in Eighteenth-Century Paris," *French History*, vol. 30, no. 2 (2016), pp. 322–53.

Willner, Ann Ruth, *The Spellbinders: Charismatic Political Leadership* (New Haven, CT: Yale University Press, 1984).

Wills, Garry, *Cincinnatus: George Washington and the Enlightenment* (Garden City, NY: Doubleday, 1984).

————, *The Kennedy Imprisonment: A Meditation on Power* (Boston: Mariner Books, 2002).

Wilson, Bryan R., *The Noble Savages: The Primitive Origins of Charisma and Its Contemporary Survival* (Berkeley: Quantum Books, 1975).

Wilson, Kathleen, "Empire, Trade and Popular Politics in Mid-Hanoverian Britain: The Case of Admiral Vernon," *Past and Present*, vol. 121 (1988), pp. 74–109.

Wilson, Peter, "Social Militarization in Eighteenth-Century Germany," *German History*, vol. 18, no. 1 (2000), pp. 1–39.

Winiarski, Douglas L., *Darkness Falls on the Land of Light: Experiencing Religious Awakenings in Eighteenth-Century New England* (Chapel Hill: University of North Carolina Press, 2017).

Winter, Lucretia Wilhelmina van, "Poem for George Washington," ed. H. A. Höweler, *Tijdschrift voor Nederlandse Taal-en Letterkunde*, vol. 52 (1933), pp. 70–77.

Wolff, Larry, *Inventing Eastern Europe: The Map of Civilization on the Mind of the Enlightenment* (Stanford, CA: Stanford University Press, 1994).

Wood, Gordon S., "The Greatness of George Washington," *Virginia Quarterly Review*, vol. 68, no. 2 (1992), pp. 189–207.

———, *The Radicalism of the American Revolution* (New York: Vintage Books, 1993).

Worden, Blair, "Providence and Politics in Cromwellian England," *Past and Present*, vol. 109, no. 1 (1985), pp. 55–99.

Wortman, Richard S., *Scenarios of Power: Myth and Ceremony in Russian Monarchy: From Peter the Great to the Death of Nicholas II*, 2 vols. (Princeton, NJ: Princeton University Press, 1995–2000).

Yanes, Francisco Javier, and Cristóbal Mendoza, eds., *Colección de documentos relativos a la vida pública del Libertador de Colombia y del Perú, Simón Bolívar*, 22 vols. (Caracas: Imprenta de Devisme hermanos, 1826–33).

Yorke, Henry Redhead, *France in Eighteen Hundred and Two*, ed. J. A. C. Sykes (London: Heineman, 1906).

Zaretsky, Eli, "Trump's Charisma," *London Review of Books LRB Blog*, June 27, 2019.

Zaretsky, Robert, *Boswell's Enlightenment* (Cambridge, MA: Belknap Press of Harvard University Press, 2015).

———, *The Philosophers' Quarrel: Rousseau, Hume, and the Limits of Human Understanding* (New Haven: Yale University Press, 2009).

Zelinsky, Wilbur, *Nation into State: The Shifting Symbolic Foundations of American Nationalism* (Chapel Hill: University of North Carolina Press, 1988).

Zeuske, Michael, "The French Revolution in Spanish America," in *The Routledge Companion to the French Revolution in World History*, eds. Alan Forrest and Matthias Middell (London: Routledge, 2015), pp. 77–96.

———, *Simón Bolívar: History and Myth*, trans. Steven Rendall and Lisa Neal (Princeton, NJ: Markus Wiener, 2013).

ACKNOWLEDGMENTS

O ver the course of my career, I have only grown more aware of how much a book owes to many different communities of friends and colleagues, as well as to supportive institutions. This book has been long in the making, and my list of debts is correspondingly long.

In the early stages of the project, I was fortunate to receive an Old Dominion professorship from Princeton's Council of the Humanities, which provided a yearlong sabbatical leave and the chance to serve as a senior fellow in Princeton's Society of Fellows. I can't say enough good things about the wonderful atmosphere of the society. My deepest thanks to Susan Stewart and Mary Harper, its former director and associate director, and to all the fellows for their warm welcome and stimulating discussions (the formal ones introduced by Susan's request to "please put away or destroy your electronic devices"). As I was completing my research, I had the chance to try out my ideas and receive invaluable feedback as a visiting professor at the École des Hautes Études en Sciences Sociales in Paris. And then I had the great good fortune to spend the 2018–19 academic year at the Dorothy and Lewis B. Cullman Center for Scholars and Writers at the New York Public Library, where I held the John and Constance Birkelund Fellowship, allowing me to complete my research and actually to draft the book. I could not imagine a more perfect venue for research and writing than the Cullman Center. My deepest thanks to Salvatore Scibona, the director, to Paul

Delaverdac and Lauren Goldenberg, and to the fourteen wonderful "fellow fellows" who made my year at the center so rewarding: Jennifer Croft, Mary Dearborn, Ada Ferrer, Vona Groarke, francine j. harris, Faith Hillis, Martha Hodes, Brooke Holmes, Karan Majahan, Corey Robin, Marisa Silver, Kirmen Uribe, Amanda Vaill, and Frances Wilson.

In addition to these people and institutions, I am also deeply grateful to the Princeton University Department of History, which provided me with resources for research, helped support my stay at the Cullman Center, and has been such an amazingly dynamic intellectual community. I want especially to thank my colleagues in early modern European history and French history—Linda Colley, Yaacob Dweck, Anthony Grafton, Yair Mintzker, and Philip Nord—and my terrific graduate advisees during the period I worked on this book—David Moak, Katlyn Carter, Benjamin Sacks, Paris Spies-Gans, Benjamin Bernard, Matthew McDonald, Netta Green, Jeremy Teow, Jinwoo Choi, and Stephanie Zgouridi. Outside Princeton, I am deeply thankful to many fellow scholars for long-standing friendship, support, and advice—especially Dan Edelstein, Antoine Lilti, Darrin McMahon, and Sophia Rosenfeld.

Several friends, colleagues, and students read parts or all of the manuscript and provided invaluable feedback—all the more important because in several chapters I was venturing into new territory. My deep thanks to Jeremy Adelman, Jinwoo Choi, Jon Cooper, Alec Dun, Dan Edelstein, Ada Ferrer, François Furstenberg, Sudhir Hazareesingh, Jeff Horn, Antoine Lilti, Eran Shalev, and Jeremy Teow. Nathan Perl-Rosenthal and Sophia Rosenfeld gave extensive and hugely helpful comments on the full manuscript. I am also indebted to Sudhir Hazareesingh for sharing the manuscript of his biography of Toussaint Louverture, to Keith Michael Baker for sharing manuscript chapters of his biography of Jean-Paul Marat, to Nathan Perl-Rosenthal and Julia Gaffield for sharing research materials, to Ashli White for sharing her manuscript article "The Materiality of the Haitian Revolution in the Atlantic World," and to Gabriela Goldin, Claire Khe, and Benjamin Bernard for excellent research assistance. I owe a particularly great debt to Hannah Stamler for her extensive and scrupulous assistance as I prepared the manuscript for publication.

As I developed my ideas, I had the chance to try out my material and ideas in many venues: Princeton, New York University, Harvard, the University of Michigan, the University of Warwick, the Israel Academy of Sciences, the University of Haifa, the University of Montana, Dartmouth College, the New York City Eighteenth-Century French Group, Loyola University (Baltimore), Ohio State, the University of Tokyo, Yale, Cambridge, the University of Glasgow, the École des Hautes Études, the European University Institute, the "Le Monde Festival" in Paris, Wellesley, Columbia, Stanford, the Cullman Center, the University of New South Wales, the University of Melbourne, the University of Newcastle (Australia), the New York French History Group, and conferences at the Université de Paris-I Sorbonne, Boston College, Berkeley, King's College London, the John Carter Brown Library, and (again) the École des Hautes Études. My thanks to my hosts and audiences in all these places for their comments, questions, and criticisms. Together, all these readers and audiences improved the book immensely. The flaws and errors that remain are, of course, mine alone.

I had long wanted to publish with Farrar, Straus and Giroux, and to have Alex Star as an editor, and my experience with both has been everything I hoped for and much more. My thanks to Alex for his steadfast support and brilliant editing, and to all the FSG staff who worked on this project, including especially Ian Van Wye and Scott Auerbach for expertly guiding the book through publication.

And then there is, above all, my family. My father, Daniel Bell, was one of the writers who helped introduce the word "charisma" into common usage. I hope he would have appreciated this book, which I started to think about soon after he passed away in 2011 and which I completed in 2019, when he would have turned one hundred. I owe just as much to my mother, Pearl Kazin Bell, whose beautiful and gracious writing has always been a model and inspiration. I miss them both every day. I see much of them in Elana Kathleen Bell and Joseph Nathaniel

Bell, two young adults of whom I am enormously proud. *L'dor va'dor*. And as for Donna Lynn Farber, words fail me. She has been there every step of the way for more than a quarter century, a loving and supportive partner even as she has pursued her own brilliantly successful career. I can't begin to express how thankful I am to her, but I hope she knows.

This book is dedicated to three friends and mentors: John Merriman, Richard Kagan, and Gabrielle Spiegel. They were astonishingly kind, generous, and supportive to me in the early stages of my career at Yale and Johns Hopkins, and they have remained my friends ever since. They each offer a terrific example of how to combine great scholarship with a great zest for life, and I owe far more to them than I can ever repay.

INDEX

ILLUSTRATION CREDITS

FIGURE 1: Photograph by Bill Beebe / Copyright © 1962. Los Angeles Times. Used with permission

FIGURE 2: Photograph by Manuel Jesús Serrano / Instituto Nacional de Patrimonio Cultural, Ecuador

FIGURE 3: Wikimedia Commons

FIGURE 4: Saint Louis Art Museum / funds given by Mr. and Mrs. R. Crosby Kemper through the Crosby Kemper Foundations / accession number 74:1989 / oil on canvas

FIGURE 5: Collection Bosque García, Caracas

FIGURE 6: (*left and right*) © The Trustees of the British Museum. All rights reserved

FIGURE 9: New York Public Library

FIGURE 10: Yale University Library Numismatic Collection

FIGURE 11: Private collection / © Christie's Images / Bridgeman Images

FIGURE 12: Yale University Art Gallery

FIGURE 13: Bibliothèque Nationale de France

FIGURE 14: Wikimedia Commons

FIGURE 15: Bibliothèque Nationale de France

FIGURE 16: Wikimedia Commons

FIGURE 17: (*left*) Courtesy John Carter Brown Library / Brown University, (*right*) Clark Art Institute Library, Williamstown, Massachusetts

FIGURE 18: © RMN-Grand Palais / Art Resource, NY

FIGURE 19: © 2020 Jeffrey L. Ward

FIGURE 20: © Casa Museo Quinta de Bolívar / Jairo Gómez

FIGURE 21: Gill La Rosa Family Collection

David A. Bell is the Sidney and Ruth Lapidus Professor in the Era of North Atlantic Revolutions at Princeton University and the author of six previous books, among them *The First Total War* and *Shadows of Revolution*.